Lyndon Johnson Confronts the World

This book is the most comprehensive, perceptive, and nuanced review to date of the foreign policy of the Lyndon Johnson era. It demonstrates not only U.S. concern with the Soviet Union, Europe, and nuclear weapons issues but also the overwhelming preoccupation with Vietnam that shaped policy throughout the world. During this period, Johnson also faced a series of emergencies ranging from turmoil in the Congo, to war in the Middle East, to a perceived communist challenge in the Caribbean, to a lingering hostage crisis in Asia. Using the most recently declassified documents, it explains in thoroughly readable prose the intricacies of the foreign policy dilemmas that forced Johnson's Great Society domestic agenda into retreat.

Lyndon Johnson
Confronts the World
American Foreign Policy, 1963–1968

Editors

WARREN I. COHEN
University of Maryland,
Baltimore County

NANCY BERNKOPF TUCKER
Department of History and
School of Foreign Service,
Georgetown University

CAMBRIDGE
UNIVERSITY PRESS

CAMBRIDGE UNIVERSITY PRESS
Cambridge, New York, Melbourne, Madrid, Cape Town, Singapore,
São Paulo, Delhi, Dubai, Tokyo

Cambridge University Press
The Edinburgh Building, Cambridge CB2 8RU, UK

Published in the United States of America by Cambridge University Press, New York

www.cambridge.org
Information on this title: www.cambridge.org/9780521424790

First published 1994

A catalogue record for this publication is available from the British Library

Library of Congress Cataloguing in Publication data

Lyndon Johnson confronts the world: American foreign policy, 1963–1968
/ editors, Warren I. Cohen, Nancy Bernkopf Tucker.
p. cm.
Includes index.
ISBN 0-521-41428-8 (hardback). – ISBN 0-521-42479-8 (pbk.)
1. United States – Foreign relations – 1963–1969. 2. Johnson,
Lyndon B. (Lyndon Baines), 1908–1973. I. Cohen, Warren I.
II. Tucker, Nancy Bernkopf.
E846.L95   1994   94-17951
327.73 – dc20   CIP

ISBN 978-0-521-41428-9 Hardback
ISBN 978-0-521-42479-0 Paperback

Transferred to digital printing 2010

Contents

In memory of
BENNO BERNKOPF
(1909–1991)
and
FAY COHEN
(1910–1991)

Acknowledgments

The man who made this all possible was David C. Humphrey, senior archivist of the LBJ Library, University of Texas, Austin. David and his staff went well beyond the call of duty to process documents with alacrity, call our attention to files of value, recommend restaurants, and facilitate our research generally. Most of us also received financial assistance from the Library in the form of Moody travel grants. The Johnson Library is everything a presidential library should be, everything LBJ would have insisted it be – and it was a pleasure to work there.

The editors are grateful to Georgetown and Michigan State universities for continual support of their research and writing. They are especially grateful to John Eadie, dean of the College of Arts and Letters, Michigan State University, for all he did to ameliorate the complications of their commute between Washington and East Lansing from 1988 to 1993. Eileen Scully of Georgetown University provided research assistance, limousine service, and the kind of bagels only the Irish could eat.

Sam Wells of the Wilson Center called our attention to an important document assessing the Soviet–American strategic relationship, and Bill Burr of the National Security Archives (an important national treasure) obtained a copy for us.

The editors are also grateful to the contributors, all of whom turned in their manuscripts within seven months of the deadline we established. LBJ would have snorted in contempt at our failure to strong-arm the tardiest. We shudder to think of what he might have said.

Contributors

WARREN I. COHEN served as editor of the four-volume *Cambridge History of American Foreign Relations*. He is Distinguished University Professor of History at the University of Maryland, Baltimore County.

WALDO HEINRICHS is Dwight Stanford Professor of History at San Diego State University. His most recent book was *Threshold of War*.

WALTER LAFEBER is Marie Underhill Noll Professor of History at Cornell University. The author of many books, he is best known for his *America, Russia, and the Cold War*, now in its eighth edition.

RICHARD H. IMMERMAN is a professor of history at Temple University. He has written widely on issues relating to Vietnam, the foreign policies of the Eisenhower administration, and the uses of political psychology in the study of world affairs.

NANCY BERNKOPF TUCKER is a professor of history and member of the faculty of the School of Foreign Service, Georgetown University. Her most recent book is *Taiwan, Hong Kong, and the United States, 1945–1992: Uncertain Friendships*.

ROBERT J. MCMAHON has written several books and articles on American policy toward South and Southeast Asia, most recently *The Cold War on the Periphery: The United States, India, and Pakistan*. He is a professor of history at the University of Florida.

FRANK COSTIGLIOLA is a professor of history at Rhode Island University. His most recent book is *France and the United States: The Cold Alliance Since World War II*.

JOSEPH S. TULCHIN is director of Latin American Programs at the Woodrow Wilson International Center for Scholars, Smithsonian Institution. He has written many books and articles on Latin American relations with the United States.

TERRENCE LYONS is a senior research analyst specializing on the Horn of Africa at the Brookings Institution. He is the author of *Models of Multilateral Intervention: The Case of Somalia.*

Introduction

WARREN I. COHEN

In 1968, shortly after Lyndon Johnson announced his decision to retire, a member of his staff prepared an assessment of Soviet–American relations during the Johnson presidency and called the president's tenure "the most productive period in the history of our relations, despite Vietnam."[1] A few months later, the Department of State in its internal history of the era described it as one of Soviet–American "coolness," of conflict and cooperation, with conflict dominant.[2] Of course, during the intervening months the Soviets had led their Warsaw pact allies in an invasion of Czechoslovakia, precluding the agreement on strategic arms control with which Johnson had intended to cap his career. But the conflicting estimates of the central relationship of the Cold War provide a useful framework for studying Lyndon Johnson's foreign policy – and its frustrations. It is against the background of the strategic competition between Moscow and Washington that the events analyzed in this book – in Asia, Europe, Latin America, Africa, and the Middle East – come into focus.

John F. Kennedy's legacy to Lyndon Johnson was a world, including America's NATO allies, increasingly less responsive to American leadership. Kennedy left Johnson a people who were losing interest in foreign aid, which seemed to be accomplishing little, and in the United Nations, which had become a forum for newly emergent states not sympathetic to American values or con-

1. "Box Score of Soviet and Eastern European Developments, 1963–1968" [dated June 4, 1968], Subject File, Box 18, "Progress – Foreign Policy Since 1964," National Security File, Lyndon B. Johnson Library, Austin, Texas (hereafter / LBJ Library).
2. "The Soviet Union and the United States," Administrative History of the Department of State, vol. 1, chapter 3, LBJ Library.

cerns. And he left Johnson a war that was going poorly in Vietnam. But the world seemed less dangerous as Kennedy and Nikita Khrushchev groped toward détente after the Cuban missile crisis. The limited test ban treaty of 1963 constituted enormous progress over the confrontation of October 1962, when the world was closer to nuclear war than anyone had imagined.[3]

Retreating from the brink, Khrushchev and his advisers reached two not altogether compatible conclusions about the nuclear age. First, war was unthinkable, and finding a way to compete peacefully with the United States was imperative. Second, the Soviet Union could never again confront the United States from a position of strategic inferiority. It would have to accelerate the deployment of its intercontinental missile force.[4] In other words: pray for peace, prepare for war.

On December 5, 1963, the National Security Council met in Washington to discuss Soviet military capabilities. Secretary of Defense Robert McNamara detailed the enormous advantage the United States had in first-strike capability, the result of the buildup of strategic forces over which he and Kennedy had presided from 1961 to 1963. He warned, nonetheless, that there would be no winner in a nuclear exchange. Secretary of State Dean Rusk stressed the enormous effort the Soviets were making to overcome both their economic problems and American nuclear superiority. He insisted that the United States could not relax its efforts to contain Soviet influence. At the beginning and again at the end of the meeting, the president read from a prepared statement: "The greatest single requirement is that we find a way to ensure the survival of civilization in the nuclear age. A nuclear war will be the death of all our hopes and it is our task to see that it does not happen."[5]

Johnson, no less sincere in his concern than Khrushchev, immediately proposed a freeze on strategic missiles and cutbacks in plu-

3. See recent revelations about Soviet tactical nuclear weapons in Cuba and indications that the decision to use them had been vested in the local commander. Raymond L. Garthoff, "The Havana Conference on the Cuban Missile Crisis," in Woodrow Wilson International Center for Scholars, *Cold War International History Project Bulletin* 1 (Spring 1992): 2–4.

4. R. Craig Nation, *Black Earth, Red Star: A History of Soviet Security Policy, 1917–1991* (Ithaca, N.Y.: Cornell University Press, 1992), 243.

5. Summary Record of NSC Meeting, December 5, 1963, NSC Meetings File, Box 1, National Security File, LBJ Library.

tonium production. Given the tremendous American advantage of the moment, the Soviet response was tepid, and the effort collapsed when agreement on verification procedures could not be reached. The Soviets were not willing to reveal the full extent of their vulnerability. In fact, in the mid-1960s, Soviet and American strategic policies were asynchronous. The United States, having invested heavily in a massive strategic buildup in the early 1960s, was facing budgetary pressures that could be alleviated only by capping its forces. The Soviets, having been left behind in the early 1960s and humiliated during the missile crisis, were gathering all available resources in an attempt to match or surpass American strategic power. It was not an ideal climate for agreement on arms limitation. Moreover, the removal of Khrushchev in October 1964 brought to power a group of men, especially Leonid Brezhnev, more responsive to the Soviet military-industrial complex than Khrushchev had been.[6]

Another major obstacle to improvement of Soviet–American relations was the intensification of the war in Vietnam early in 1965. Soviet support for the Democratic Republic of Vietnam in its long struggle against the United States was necessitated by Moscow's claim to be the champion of all peoples fighting wars of national liberation. Moreover, there were obvious gains for the Soviets as America's blood, treasure, and honor were squandered in southeast Asia. But the U.S. bombing of Hanoi in February 1965, while Soviet Premier Alexei Kosygin was visiting there, embarrassed Kosygin, allegedly the politburo's strongest opponent of increased military spending, and resulted in an increase in mistrust and hostility in Moscow.[7] On the other hand, the extraordinary concentration of America's efforts on Vietnam, as evidenced in the essays in this volume, was possible only because Johnson and his advisers never feared a Soviet attack, because of the lack of strategic concern in Washington. Despite the Soviet military buildup, despite enormous Soviet support for Hanoi, the president's men were confident of American superiority and of the potential for détente with the Soviets.

6. Harry Gelman. *The Brezhnev Politburo and the Decline of Detente* (Ithaca, N.Y.: Cornell University Press, 1984), 80–3, 92–5.
7. Georgi Arbatov, *The System: An Insider's Life in Soviet Politics* (New York: Times Books, 1992), 117.

One important reason for Washington's confidence in the long-run promise of improved relations with the Soviet Union was the series of bilateral and multilateral agreements the two countries reached in the 1960s – examples of what Dean Rusk called "the little threads that bind."[8] Gradually the one-time allies were re-learning the value of cooperation, finding areas of mutual benefit, building trust. They signed their first bilateral agreement, a con-sular convention, in 1964; overcame a series of obstacles, includ-ing the opposition of J. Edgar Hoover; and ratified it in 1967. There were agreements on fishing in the Pacific and Atlantic, on the rescue and return of astronauts, and on civil air transport. They agreed to prohibit the stationing of weapons of mass destruction in outer space, and, most important, they finally agreed in July 1968 on a treaty to prevent the proliferation of nuclear weapons. Slowly, in the end too slowly for the Johnson administration to sign, they edged toward agreement on strategic arms limitation.[9]

Johnson and supporters of his vision for a Great Society were dis-inclined to spend more on missiles after the surge of deployments of the early 1960s. As the Soviet buildup proceeded in the mid-1960s, the administration, specifically McNamara, sought a cost-effective way to respond. By 1964, McNamara had been persuaded that there was no way to defend the United States against a nuclear exchange, that deterrence was the only answer. He also concluded that an anti-ballistic missile (ABM) system, such as the Soviets were beginning to deploy around Moscow, was unworkable, that it would merely stimulate production of offensive weapons and be overwhelmed by them.[10] Understanding that the Soviets, too, would have to be assured of their security, McNamara concluded that a balance of terror – mutually assured destruction – was the appro-priate formula. When the Soviets had deployed weapons sufficient to assure them of a second-strike capability, to assure them of their ability to retaliate against an American nuclear attack, when they

8. See Warren I. Cohen, *Dean Rusk* (Totowa, N.J.: Cooper Square, 1980), 37, 84, 284.
9. "U.S. Soviet Relations" April 1, 1968, Subject File, Box 19, "Foreign Affairs Data Sheets," National Security File, LBJ Library.
10. Ernest R. May, John D. Steinbruner, and Thomas W. Wolfe, "History of the Strategic Arms Competition 1945–1972," II OSD Historical Office (March 1981), 800–2, Na-tional Security Archive; Deborah Shapley, *Promise and Power: The Life and Times of Robert McNamara* (Boston: Little, Brown, 1993), 197–9.

had reached a rough parity in strategic missiles with the United States, the arms race might end and the danger begin to recede.

McNamara ultimately won conditional approval from Johnson for negotiations with the Soviets to limit ABM deployments. He had six months in which to win an agreement. An approach in January 1967 failed, however, and Kosygin evinced little interest in limiting defensive weapons when he met with McNamara and Johnson at Glassboro, New Jersey, in June of that year.[11] Given the fact that the Soviets had an operational ABM system in 1967 and the president was disinclined to be held responsible for an "ABM gap," McNamara was forced in September to announce plans for the United States to build twelve ABM sites.[12] Soviet interest was whetted immediately, and the course toward what eventually became SALT I, the first strategic arms limitation agreement, was set. The agreement likely would have been signed in late 1968 had it not been for the Soviet repression of Czechoslovakia in August of that year and the election of Richard Nixon.

The June 1967 Glassboro meeting between Johnson and Kosygin was itself a modest indicator of the relative stability Soviet–American relations had achieved, despite the war in Vietnam. The "hot line" had been used for the first time a few days earlier to avert confrontation in the Middle East and, face to face, the two leaders continued their discussion of that region and discussed Vietnam and arms control issues as well. But National Security Adviser Walt Rostow's hope for further movement on extricating the United States from Vietnam received no more encouragement than McNamara's for strategic arms limits.[13]

However much the dark shadow of America's war in Vietnam hung over all other activities, it did not prevent the Soviets from seeking a major strategic arms limitation agreement once they had made the internal political decision to put a ceiling on their own deployments. After their huge SS-9s were in place, they could feel

11. For an interesting report on Soviet impressions of McNamara's presentation, indicating that he told Kosygin and Johnson far more than they wanted to know, see memorandum of conversation between Boris N. Sedov (a known KGB officer) and Raymond Garthoff, June 28, 1967, "Soviet Impressions of Hollybush," National Security Archive.
12. May et al., "Strategic Arms Competition," 803; Shapley, *McNamara*, 199–200.
13. For Rostow's hopes, see Rostow memorandum for Johnson, June 21, 1967, Country File, USSR, Hollybush (II), Box 230, National Security File, LBJ Library.

a little more secure about their deterrent capability. The threat of
an ABM race when the Americans were perceived as retaining technological superiority was an excellent incentive to arms control –
before the Americans could come up with a defensive system that
could minimize Soviet second-strike potential. In June 1968, Soviet
Foreign Minister Andrei Gromyko informed the Supreme Soviet
that the time had come for strategic missile talks.[14]

On August 19, 1968, the Soviet Union agreed to begin negotiations toward limiting the deployment of strategic arms. On August 20, Warsaw Pact forces invaded Czechoslovakia. Johnson's
planned announcement of a summit meeting had to be canceled.
Brezhnev, Kosygin, and their colleagues apparently believed that
their willingness to go ahead with the talks despite American
atrocities in Vietnam would be reciprocated by American tolerance of their aberrant behavior in Czechoslovakia. If so, they had
misread the American political climate. Momentum toward détente was lost. Much as Johnson would have liked to proceed
with the summit, he recognized that the new repression in
Czechoslovakia – the crushing of the Prague Spring – precluded
public and congressional acceptance of a meeting with Soviet
leaders. As late as November and December 1968, after the election of Richard Nixon, Johnson and Rostow cast about for a way
to hold the talks, which they perceived as being in the interest of
the Czechs as well as of all humanity – and of Lyndon Johnson –
but the bell had tolled for the administration.[15]

Although the documentary record for the foreign relations of the
United States in the Johnson era is only beginning to be published,
an enormous amount of material has been declassified and is available at the LBJ Library. Scholars studying the 1960s continue to be
amazed by the contrast between the Johnson and Kennedy presidential libraries. Declassification at the Kennedy Library has been

14. David Holloway, *The Soviet Union and the Arms Race*, 2nd ed. (New Haven, Conn.:
Yale University Press, 1987), 45; Nation, *Black Earth, Red Star*, 257.
15. Memoranda, Rostow for Johnson, November 20, 1968, and December 11, 1968,
Files of Walt W. Rostow, "Strategic Missile Talks," Box 11, National Security File,
LBJ Library.

notoriously dilatory, and the staff has been almost as uncooperative as the old regime at the Hoover Institute at Stanford. The atmosphere in Austin is strikingly different. The archivists have
earned a reputation for responsiveness, and David Humphrey in
particular has demonstrated again and again just how critical
archival support is to the advancement of scholarship. In brief, we
concluded that a scholarly examination of the record of Lyndon
Johnson's foreign policy was not only needed, but practicable.

In the pages that follow, several of America's leading diplomatic
historians analyze the events of 1963–1968 and look closely at
Lyndon Johnson's role. Two chapters focus on the American domestic context. The first, by Waldo Heinrichs, is an elegantly written sketch of the president: his personality, his work habits, and his
view of the world. Walter LaFeber follows with a provocative discussion of the role of public opinion and foreign policy in the Johnson era, especially as related to the conflict in Vietnam.

The succeeding essays center on various regions of the world with
particular attention to how the men and women in Washington devised responses. Richard H. Immerman, using the most recently declassified materials, offers fresh insights into Lyndon Johnson's war
in Vietnam. Excepting only avoidance of nuclear catastrophe, no
other foreign policy issue was of greater saliency to the public. None
consumed more of the time and energy of the president and his advisers. Nancy Bernkopf Tucker writes of the Johnson administration's policies toward China, Japan, and Korea, as East Asia came
to loom larger and larger in American concerns. Fear of a nuclear-
armed China, writhing in the throes of the Cultural Revolution, and
concern for Japan's markets in Southeast Asia, were sometimes put
forward as explanations for the involvement of the United States in
Vietnam. Robert J. McMahon completes the examination of Asian
affairs with a perceptive look at relations with South Asia, especially the unending tension between India and Pakistan.

Despite the machinations of Charles de Gaulle and the "special
relationship" with Great Britain, Germany loomed largest in alliance politics in the mid-1960s. Frank Costigliola writes incisively
about NATO, about the concept of a multilateral nuclear force
(MLF) to finesse the issue of who controlled the use of NATO's nu-

clear weapons, and especially about Germany. Closer to home – and perhaps closer to Lyndon Johnson's heart and interests – were the affairs of Latin America. Joseph S. Tulchin explains the complexities of American policy from the southern cone to the intervention in the Dominican Republic.

More remote were the affairs of Africa and the Middle East, but intense public interest in the threat to Israel's survival, growing Afro-American interest in African affairs, and the fear of Soviet influence in both regions denied Johnson and his aides any respite. Terrence Lyons illuminates the dark continent, casting light as well on the responses in Washington. My own contribution is an essay on the Middle East, in which I share my new-found understanding of Gamal Abdul Nasser and American behavior during and immediately after the Six Day War.

Together the chapters in this volume provide the most comprehensive and revealing study of Lyndon Johnson's foreign policy that we have thus far – or are likely to get in the 1990s. What is still lacking is the documentation from "the other side." With the collapse of the Soviet Union, Soviet archives have suddenly become accessible to us, and in the next decade there is every reason to hope that we will see a reasonably complete record of Soviet activities through the 1960s. Chinese documents on a more selective basis have begun to be released, but their reliability will – and should – continue to be questioned until the Chinese government is more forthcoming. We may even live to see the relevant Vietnamese archival materials. But for the American side, thanks to David Humphrey and his colleagues, we are pleased to offer the following reflections.

1

Lyndon B. Johnson:
Change and Continuity

WALDO HEINRICHS

The eight years of the Lyndon Baines Johnson vice presidency and presidency were the culmination of his life and career, but they were not simply the consequences of what went before. To some extent we are the sum of what we have been, prefigured by genetics, shaped by home, environment, and early adulthood; the past explains us. Yet we change, too: needs, expectations, and capabilities shift; personalities alter and psyches realign to meet new demands; we learn and often grow. The stages and current circumstances of our life also define us.

Johnson's election as vice president in 1960 marked the most radical departure in his life and career since he entered the national government in 1931. The executive branch was fundamentally different from the legislative, as America in the 1960s was from America in the 1950s. Biographies of Johnson naturally dwell on his antecedents, early childhood, and Texas background, and the value of these dimensions for understanding his presidency is undeniable. Conclusions about the younger Johnson cannot be indiscriminately carried forward to the presidential years, however. He faced wholly new challenges when he arrived in the executive branch, and it seems reasonable to suppose that these elicited novel as well as familiar responses. Vice President and President Johnson were not necessarily the same as Senate Majority Leader Johnson. Whether this was particularly the case in foreign affairs, which occupied much less of his time and interest in Congress than in the White House, is a question: was he less innovative and adaptable in this unfamiliar terrain than in dealing with domestic problems?

The Dynamics of Personality

No one who knew or has studied Lyndon Johnson can deny the primal force of his personality, nor its complexity, contradictions, ambiguities, and, for most, ultimately its mystery. Richard Goodwin notes his "immense vitality – intense . . . direct." "When LBJ entered a room," writes George Reedy, "everyone knew it immediately. . . . He was . . . the focal point of action."[1] Johnson was a charming host and a hilarious mimic. He managed the transition after the death of President Kennedy with consummate skill, tact, and grace. He was a magical persuader. Yet seen by those close to him Johnson was also boorish and overbearing and could be sulky, tempestuous, and vindictive. Even so, he was sentimental and corny, and people found in some of his faults a naïve, childlike appeal. Johnson was both attractive and repellent.

Central to the dynamics of Johnson's personality was ambition. This demanding, pushing, restless, storming man wanted not only to win but also to outstrip all previous winners: a legislative record that outshone the New Deal, a State of the Union speech interrupted more times by applause than Kennedy's. His outsized ego must have yearned, beyond highest office, for a place on Mt. Rushmore. Johnson no doubt acquired a will to succeed at an early age, and his winning way with people nourished it. But his ambition was fed by insecurity as well.

Explorations of this dark side of Johnson's personality have been speculative and contradictory. Doris Kearns Goodwin takes a psychoanalytic approach: "From the world of work and the conquest of ever-widening circles of men, Johnson hoped to obtain the steady love he had lacked as a child." Robert Dallek acknowledges the young LBJ's emotional deprivation, arising from a mother who conditioned love on performance and an overbearing father, but he balances this against the strengths that Johnson gained from his parents. Paul Conkin, shunning psychological explanation and debunking LBJ legends, argues persuasively that Lyndon had a "quite ordinary childhood." Family and kin provided warmth, encour-

---

1. Richard N. Goodwin, *Remembering America: A Voice from the Sixties* (New York: Little, Brown, 1988), 270; George Reedy, *Lyndon B. Johnson: A Memoir* (New York: Andrews and McMeel, 1982), 158.

agement, and support he sorely missed when he left the hill country of Texas.[2] For Conkin, the deprivation that stoked Johnson's ambition was of a different sort.

What Johnson lacked, according to this theory, was status. Along the Pedernales he was "special" but, as he came to recognize, a duck in a very small pond. He was not favored with the affluence, social background, and Ivy League education of so many who trooped through Washington to run the New Deal and national security affairs. He felt the difference keenly, reflecting almost in caricature the antagonism of "po' boy," southern-western Populist America toward the eastern establishment. He wanted to believe that having "brushed up against the grindstone of life" a man gained more "polish," but, he confessed in retirement, somehow he never could.[3] All the more need, then, for hard work and achievement. Spurring him on was fear of failure. His father and two grandfathers had "gone bust." Fleeing the Pedernales into political life, he strove for success but risked failure with every election.[4]

Much of Johnson's behavior can be explained by his twin demons, the need for self-advancement and self-protection. His life was work, and his work seemed exclusively defined by the prism of the self. In that light one can better understand his tendency to personalize issues, his hypersensitivity to criticism, his intimidation of staff, his infuriation at news leaks, his bridling at pressure, his obsession with his public image, and his need to know everything that was happening and to know it first.

Important as these dynamics were in Johnson's personality, he was not entirely their prisoner. For Johnson, politics was a profession, a term loosely used but meaningful in his case. He was an avid student of politics from the age of ten, when he ran errands for his

2. Doris Kearns Goodwin, *Lyndon Johnson and the American Dream* (New York: Harper & Row, 1976), 45; Robert Dallek, *Lone Star Rising: Lyndon Johnson and His Times, 1908–1960* (New York: Oxford University Press, 1991), 37–45; Paul K. Conkin, *Big Daddy from the Pedernales: Lyndon Baines Johnson* (Boston: Twayne, 1986), 16–20. Also see Ronnie Dugger, *The Politician: The Life and Times of Lyndon Johnson: The Drive for Power, from the Frontier to Master of the Senate* (New York: Norton, 1982); Robert A. Caro, *The Years of Lyndon Johnson: The Path to Power* (New York: Knopf, 1983); Merle Miller, *Lyndon: An Oral Biography* (New York: Putnam, 1980); Rowland Evans and Robert Novak, *Lyndon B. Johnson: The Exercise of Power, A Political Biography* (London: Allen and Unwin, 1967).
3. As quoted in D. K. Goodwin, *Johnson*, 42.
4. Dallek, *Lone Star*, 53; Conkin, *Big Daddy*, 12–15, 24.

father in the Texas state legislature. Nearly three decades of congressional committees and constituent needs gave him an exceptional grasp of the American government as a whole and how it worked. He became one of the most successful legislative tacticians and craftsmen in American history. He revered American institutions of government and loved and was endlessly fascinated by American politics. He would have liked to sample every booth and try every ride in the grand Washington carnival of power.

This overarching professional sensibility permitted him to disengage from the immediate play of forces and self-interest and take an appraising look at where he fitted into the larger picture. He could weigh his interests and prospects in the larger balances of politics and institutions. He was an expert on his situation, and this served as a monitor and corrective to his self-centered dynamics.

Presidential Circumstances

A good illustration of these forces at work was Johnson's bid for the presidency and acceptance of the vice presidential nomination in 1960. It would be difficult to prove that any particular period in Johnson's life was more turbulent than the rest, but his behavior in the years after his heart attack in 1955 seemed unusual. Reedy describes him as restless, moody, and irascible, more given to bouts of heavy drinking and less sure-handed in managing the Senate. He may have been grappling with the fear of early death, as Conkin suggests: his heart attack had been nearly fatal, and his mother died in 1958.[5]

At the same time his "golden years" of dominating the Senate and cooperating with President Eisenhower faded. The Democratic victories in the 1958 midterm elections brought an unwieldy majority, including a band of liberals who resisted his rule. The minority was more recalcitrant, the president more partisan and conservative. The future was unpromising: the majority leader would be overshadowed by a Democratic president or engaged in combat rather than consensus building with the likely Republican,

5. Reedy, *Memoir*, 51–4, 127; Conkin, *Big Daddy*, 146.

Richard Nixon. In moments of wrath Johnson spoke of quitting politics to make money or retiring to his beloved ranch on the Pedernales, which he had acquired in 1951 and was remodeling and expanding with swimming pool and landing strip.

Johnson wanted the presidency "so much his tongue was hanging out."[6] He believed he was the most experienced candidate and the one most capable of unifying the party and nation. Yet he was reluctant to enter the ring because that would require slugging it out with Senator John F. Kennedy in the new terrain of successive state primaries lit up by national television. The value of his Senate role was hard to convey to crowds; his conservative positions and southern drawl would not play well before northern liberal–labor audiences. A shift to the left would imperil his concurrent Senate race in Texas, he could be trounced North and South and have to limp back to the ranch a failure. Realistic considerations of this sort lay behind his determination to stay above the fray, hoping that a deadlocked convention would turn to him as a moderate and consensus builder. This passivity, enforced by his insecurity as well as his political sense, was intensely frustrating, yet he held to it almost until the end.[7]

Failing to win the presidential nomination, he was well positioned for the second spot. The vice presidency traditionally has been an office of so little substance that Johnson's acceptance of the nomination has been hard to explain. If we carry forward the foregoing interpretation of Johnson's presidential bid, however, Kennedy's offer of the vice presidency must have seemed a welcome release. It gave him the opportunity of escaping the confines of Senate and South and achieving national status. By running he strengthened the national ticket in the South, improving prospects against Nixon, whom Johnson's mentor, Sam Rayburn, detested and was determined to defeat. By not running, Johnson could be blamed for a Democratic defeat. He hoped to make something of the vice presidency, perhaps as manager of the administration's legislative program. In any case the vice presidency would give him a

6. James Rowe as quoted in Dallek, *Lone Star*, 544.
7. On the decisions of 1960: ibid., 538–51, 576–8; Conkin, *Big Daddy*, 151–5; Evans and Novak, *Lyndon B. Johnson*, 206–7, 226, 231, 247; D. K. Goodwin, *Johnson*, 160–2; William S. White, Arthur Krock Oral History Transcripts (hereafter cited as OHT), Oral History Collection, Lyndon Baines Johnson Library, Austin, Texas.

new field of endeavor and a chance to reconstitute himself for national executive power. At fifty-two he was young enough to try again in 1968. In understanding his choice one should balance the disappointment he experienced as vice president against the diminishing power and confined ambition he expected to suffer if he continued as majority leader.

As the vice-presidential nominee, Johnson campaigned with gusto to rousing receptions that must have encouraged belief in his viability as a national candidate. In Boston he mounted a policeman's horse and waved a cowboy hat. The crowd, said Thomas P. "Tip" O'Neill (later Speaker of the House), went wild. In a Dallas hotel, surrounded by a screaming crowd of right-wingers, he lingered long enough to ensure that TV cameras captured their abusive attack on a vice-presidential candidate and his wife.[8] It is impossible to know whether Johnson made the difference in a close election, but no one can say for sure that he did not.

After an exhilarating campaign, Johnson found the vice presidency an exercise in boredom. He sought to retain influence in the Senate as chair of the Democratic caucus but was opposed by a minority of seventeen of his former colleagues who resented his domineering ways and feared the intrusion of executive power. Johnson was offered the position but, feeling snubbed, declined. From the new president he sought important executive responsibilities but was denied; presidential power as always was indivisible. Kennedy gave him important, though more limited, assignments, but an ordinary mortal's workload barely tapped Johnson's "furious" energy, and his political impotence was almost unbearable.[9] The vice president struck observers variously as uninterested, gloomy, resentful, withdrawn, and subdued. His was a "spectral" presence at meetings.[10]

It was not simply a case of frustration and pique. Arthur Schlesinger Jr., then a member of the Kennedy staff, was impressed with Johnson's reticence. In accepting a marginal role, he "submitted himself to exacting self-discipline," in Schlesinger's view,

8. Thomas P. O'Neill OHT: Dallek, *Lone Star*, 587–8.
9. White OHT.
10. Arthur S. Schlesinger Jr. OHT; Evans and Novak, *Lyndon B. Johnson*, Ch. 15; Reedy, *Memoir*, Ch. 13; Conkin, *Big Daddy*, 156–70.

"at great psychic cost for a man of his overpowering temperament." According to William S. White, a close friend of Johnson's, these years were confining but not "terribly frustrating." Johnson remained a loyal subordinate; he and the president acted with "remarkable magnanimity toward each other." The vice president was unhappy, Drew Pearson observed, but not vastly so.[11]

His reticence can be more fully understood by considering what result he believed a more active role would produce. According to Rowland Evans and Robert Novak, Kennedy wanted to harness Johnson's skills to his legislative program, but the vice president proved mostly uncooperative. The Kennedy legislative program was carefully developed but slow starting. Knowing how Johnson operated as majority leader and president, one can imagine his impatience with it. He would want a more forceful strategy with more powerful inducements and pressures and the president mobilizing public support and leading the charge. Johnson may well have reasoned that this sort of advice was not likely to fit the Kennedy scheme and if pressed would lead to a division with the president, which not only would damage the administration – *his* administration as well – but might lead to his being dropped from the ticket in 1964 or being denied the Kennedy blessing in 1968. His situation called for caution. He was not an assistant president but a successor president.[12]

Johnson participated only perfunctorily in National Security Council deliberations even when asked for his views by the president. He hung back because he had a deeply ingrained respect for the president's preeminence in foreign affairs and was loath to establish a differing position in this large (and leaky) forum. He undoubtedly understood as well that his most important task was to listen so that he knew what policy was and learned how a president made policy. He apparently advised the president privately, however, for, according to Schlesinger, Kennedy was aware that they disagreed regarding the overthrow of Ngo Dinh Diem, that Johnson was dubious about the policy adopted in the Cuban mis-

11. Schlesinger, White, Pearson OHT.
12. For an example of the way the Johnson and Kennedy approaches differed, see Johnson's advice on a civil rights bill in 1963: Conkin, *Big Daddy*, 166. O'Neill OHT; Evans and Novak, *Lyndon B. Johnson*, 305–20, 360–5.

sile crisis, and that he was unhappy about the sale of wheat to the Soviet Union.[13]

Another source of discontent in the vice-presidential years, of little consequence then but poisonous later, was antagonism between Johnson and the president's brother Robert. The feud began as a personality clash between Bobby Kennedy and Johnson, a problem of gut dislike. It quickened with Bobby's unfortunate visit to Johnson at the Democratic convention conveying the suggestion, already overtaken by events, that the offer of the vice presidency needed to be reconsidered. During the vice-presidential years the two disagreed on the pace of civil rights reform but mostly stayed at arm's length. However, jokes circulated about the silent vice president ("Whatever happened to Lyndon?"). Johnson felt isolated in a sea of Kennedy loyalists, a self-assured, tightly knit band with more than its share of Harvards and intellectuals. This was a White House bound to arouse Johnson's deepest insecurities.[14]

The feud became pernicious after the president's assassination. The circumstances lent themselves to dark, symbolic meanings that in turn intensified antagonism. The killing occurred in Johnson's home state on a mission to heal its "malignant" politics.[15] To grief-stricken Kennedyites Johnson appeared as an interloper, even a usurper, a Macbeth. The new president paid full tribute to his fallen predecessor, went to great lengths to meet the needs of his mourning family, and pleaded with the Kennedy staff to stay on and fulfill New Frontier programs and promises. Nevertheless, Robert Kennedy, as "custodian of the Kennedy dream," remained an obstacle to Johnson's heartfelt wish to command his own presidency.[16] He told Bobby that regional considerations ruled him out as the vice-presidential candidate in 1964. The Johnson ego could not let well enough alone, however; soon he was mimicking what he took to be Bobby's shocked reaction, and the story spread. In this fashion two camps formed, one at the Kennedy residence at Hickory Hill, the other at the White House, each with

13. Schlesinger, White OHT.
14. Schlesinger in his oral history transcript states that there was no intent to drop Johnson in 1964 and that Kennedy staff ignored Johnson but were not disdainful. Evans and Novak, *Lyndon B. Johnson,* 314, and James Rowe OHT disagree.
15. Krock OHT.
16. Evans and Novak, *Lyndon B. Johnson,* 435.

its media camp followers, each with its jokes and mimes; and as the Vietnam conflict lengthened, Hickory Hill gravitated to the antiwar movement.[17]

The Senate was a world away from the White House, but Johnson made the transition successfully. He moved from the enclosed personal influence of the one to the open-ended institutional power of the other, from the "roaring . . . farting . . . scratching" domesticity of the Senate to the decorum of the executive offices.[18] He managed to translate his huge political skills into the presidential idiom. Fate had moved Johnson to the presidency but he had positioned himself carefully. With his decisive election victory in 1964 he became president in his own right. He had reached the top, and he loved it.

The familiar swashbuckling figure did not disappear, though it was more in evidence at the ranch than at the White House. He was much the same but different. With his election in 1964 he had an untrammeled exercise of power and no immediate challenger. He was more confident, focused, and disciplined. All his energies were bent on realizing his legislative program and fulfilling his presidential duties. His ego for the time being was appeased; his demons were less troubling. Judging the Johnson presidency as of, say, January 1965, one could reasonably predict that it would indeed be a successful and perhaps a great one.

Conduct of Foreign Affairs

White House life was more routine and less frenetic than the Senate because Johnson and not the legislative system set the agenda and because of the "royal" services provided a president. His workday, however, was longer. Indeed, *workday* is a misnomer, for he erased any useful distinction between day and night. He arose at 6:30 A.M. and, before dressing, worked into the morning instructing staff and soaking up news and briefings. Oval Office

---

17. D. K. Goodwin, *Johnson,* 201; Stewart Alsop OHT; Evans and Novak, *Lyndon B. Johnson,* Ch. 20; Schlesinger, White, Clark Clifford, Hugh Sidey, Krock, Rowe OHT.
18. Sidey OHT.

appointments (as many as twenty a day) began at 10:30 or 11:00 A.M. and were followed by a working lunch, a nap, and a return to the office until a late dinner. After the 11:00 P.M. news he retired to several hours of "night reading," a pile of reports and memos waiting on his bedside table, and then slept three or four hours. He relaxed by lapsing into reminiscence or taking a paddle in the nude about the White House pool, "the massive presidential flesh . . . a sun-bleached atoll breaching a placid sea."[19]

During 1964 and 1965 Johnson committed his personal and institutional resources almost exclusively to enactment of his Great Society program. Facing a shocked and pliant Congress in the wake of the Kennedy tragedy, he saw what he described as a "once-in-a-lifetime opportunity" to achieve economic and social justice. "I never thought I'd have the power," he mused. "I wanted power to use it. And I'm going to use it."[20]

World affairs in the Johnson years were relatively stable. Vietnam was a worsening hemorrhage but not an acute international crisis or war involving a great power. The Dominican intervention, the Panama flag crisis, the Cyprus conflict, and the *Pueblo* incident paled beside the Berlin blockade, the Korean War, the offshore islands crises, and the Cuban missile crisis. The Six Day War was not as severe internationally as Suez. In 1964–5, before Vietnam drained his influence and infested his outlook, Johnson could concentrate on his domestic program and adopt a posture of avoidance internationally.

President Johnson's Great Society was one of the most extensive reform programs in American history, rivaling the New Deal, if not, as Johnson intended, outdoing it. To secure the legislation – more than 200 major bills – Johnson was determined to mastermind the campaign personally. This meant employing not only the political skills he had used in forging Senate coalitions but unfamiliar techniques as well. In the Senate Johnson, working from a moderate position, aimed at the best available consensus. In 1964–5 as president he operated from the left for radical change and needed constant

---

19. Goodwin, *Remembering*, 268. Also: Notes of Meeting, 15 Nov. 1967, with Lyle Denniston et al. of *Washington Star*, Box 1, Meetings with Correspondents, July 1967–May 1968, Tom Johnson's Notes of Meetings, Lyndon B. Johnson Library.
20. Goodwin, *Remembering*, 257, 270.

public pressure to sustain momentum. Furthermore, in the Senate he worked among peers so that his influence was individually exerted, whereas now he operated on Congress from the outside and needed to maintain an image of power. These conditions required the mobilization of public opinion.

Johnson was a surprisingly effective communicator – on his chosen ground – in spite of diction where "value" came out "valya" and "think" verged on "thank." A "highly articulate man," according to Ben Wattenberg, one of his speechwriters, Johnson sought neither literary nor Pedernales idiom but clear and simple language laced with a little poetry, humor, and newsworthiness. His best speeches scored on account of their substance and the passion that animated his words, like his Great Society commencement address at the University of Michigan, which roused the audience from gothic decorum to "unrestrained, accepting delight."[21] Adlibbing to small groups he could he mesmerizing. His responses at press conferences had a detached, nonprovocative tone lightened here and there with mordant humor. He almost never made regrettable statements.[22]

"Pungent" and lucid in person, he was a bore on television.[23] The camera seemed alien and spurious to him, according to William White; he approached it nervously, his hands clenched. He did not regard himself as photogenic (as a congressman he practiced speech poses for the camera), and so he came across as studied and wooden with a "fixed periodic smile."[24]

With the press Johnson had an unsatisfactory and ultimately disastrous relationship. He understood the importance of correspondents, columnists, and publishers in gathering attention and favor for his programs, and he wooed them ardently. Yet he failed to win them – was bound to fail – for his expectations and methods were wrong.[25]

21. Ibid., 280.
22. Ben J. Wattenberg, Douglas Cater OHT; George W. Johnson, series ed., Doris Kearns Goodwin, introd., *The Johnson Presidential Press Conferences* (2 vols.; New York: E. M. Coleman Enterprise, 1978); Conkin, *Big Daddy*, 183–4.
23. Wattenberg OHT.   24. Krock OHT.
25. On press relations: Schlesinger, White, Thomas G. Wicker, Sidey, Pearson, Chalmers Roberts, Robert Kintner, Krock OHT; Harry McPherson, *A Political Education* (Boston: Little, Brown, 1972), 263–7; Reedy, *Memoir*, Ch. 7; Conkin, *Big Daddy*, 184–6; Evans and Novak, *Lyndon B. Johnson*, 501–9.

Part of his problem lay in trying to replicate in the White House his media experience in the Senate. As Douglas Cater says, he saw the necessity for "total mastery of the communications system in [the] confined environment of Congress." To Senator Henry Jackson of Washington, the Johnson intelligence network seemed to cover the Senate "like the morning dew."[26] Reporters were part of that network; information was exchanged and favorable treatment in the press expected. Criticism left a reporter frozen out.

The Oval Office was not a place where the president could put his feet on the desk and jaw with a reporter over a drink. It was lonely. One can imagine that in surrounding himself with ticker tape machines and triple-set television arrays and by reaching every spare moment for the phone Johnson was trying to re-create the flow, immediacy, and intimacy of his former political arena. As a senator he prized secrecy, dealing individually while keeping overall strategy shrouded. It was said of him that he considered the shortest distance between two points to be a tunnel. Now he dealt with reporters as a body, in a formal setting that tended to be adversarial. An effort to come across more informally by inviting a group to the ranch ended with published reports of his exuberant, high-speed driving, cooling relations further.

Press management is an established part of the Washington political culture. In the Senate Johnson practiced it inconspicuously, as president blatantly and crudely. The difference was personal as well as situational. Johnson's triumphs of 1964–5 deeply engaged his ego. This was the high point of his life; he was euphoric. His legislative achievements should be making his mark in history, and he wanted them reflected in the record. Thus it was not just as instruments of public policy that he dealt with the press but as draftsmen of his historical stature. This placed an intolerable burden on his relations with the press.

Johnson insisted on absolute control of the news, centralizing distribution at the White House, manipulating information to maintain his flexibility and enhance the drama of his choices, and rampaging at leaks. He had no compunction about coloring, shading, evading, and denying the truth, nor deceiving, misleading, punishing, and rewarding reporters. He undoubtedly regarded the truth as malleable

26. Cater, Henry M. Jackson OHT.

during the political process and ethics relevant only to the outcome. Reporters tended to respond by pressing their criticism and asserting their objectivity. Some had regarded him as a riverboat gambler to begin with; a growing number found him untrustworthy.

Johnson in turn was the more inclined to see reporters as minions of Kennedy and the eastern establishment, to withdraw from the press corps as a whole and to deal only with a select few. In 1964–5 this estrangement was of little significance because, as Harry McPherson says, the news was mostly favorable and wrote itself.[27] With Vietnam the standoff became destructive.

In gaining control of the executive branch Johnson wanted Johnson men about him, loyal subordinates who owed their appointments to him. At the same time he needed continuity, appropriate skills, and experience in running the government. The result was a mixture of Kennedy holdovers, Johnson veterans, and Johnson newcomers. Personnel change occurred most frequently among those closest to the president, the White House staff. Most Kennedy staff left, a few very soon, but many staying until after the election, some to the end or near the end. Staff left regardless of affiliation, too, because they found Johnson outrageously demanding, or had worked themselves to exhaustion, or dissented on Vietnam. Thus turnover of personnel was extensive but, except in the moribund final year, spread over time and was therefore less disruptive than if there had been a mass exodus at the beginning.

For staff, the White House was a cross between a palace and a plantation. It was prebureaucratic in the sense that assignments were loosely defined and overlapping. Like an early medieval monarchy, power depended on access, even to the bedchamber. Those with unrestricted access – Bill Moyers, Jack Valenti, and Walter Jenkins in their day – stood in the first rank.[28] Alternatively, Johnson was like a southern patriarch, the Big Daddy of Conkin's biography, dominating, protective, providing. Some saw his habit of continuing conversations into the bathroom as another way of subduing subordinates to his will, but it is just as likely that he accepted them as part of his household and hated to waste time sitting in solitary confinement.[29]

27. McPherson, *Political Education*, 264.   28. Schlesinger, Michael V. Forrestal OHT.
29. Conkin, *Big Daddy*, 180–2; Kearns, *Johnson*, 237–49.

In contrast, Johnson treated government departments in the accepted bureaucratic manner, allowing Dean Rusk at State and Robert McNamara at Defense broad latitude. Undersecretaries, assistant secretaries, and ambassadors remained presidential appointments, but unlike Kennedy, Johnson did not deal directly with Rusk's subordinates without the secretary's knowledge. As Warren Cohen has shown, Rusk and Johnson had a warm relationship based on similar humble southern roots and foreign policy values. Rusk gave absolute loyalty to the president. The McNamara case was somewhat different. Johnson, never close to the Defense Secretary, was greatly impressed by his forceful intellect. McNamara worked closely with Rusk and always deferred to him on foreign relations questions. Unlike the rest of the White House, the National Security Council staff had a defined and stable position. McGeorge Bundy as National Security Adviser played a vital role in keeping track of problems, defining issues, and shaping options. The epitome of Ivy – Groton, Yale, Harvard Fellow – Bundy stayed until 1966, as long as Johnson could keep him, and McNamara stayed until he faltered on Vietnam in 1967. Johnson prized loyalty and retained his suspicions of the eastern elite, but he would not willingly dispense with the skills and teamwork of these three key players in external affairs.[30]

Outside the White House Johnson was by no means a busybody chief executive. He avoided becoming "swamped in details," according to Cater, but he encouraged good administration, pressing departments, for example, to convert to the new programmed planning budgeting system introduced in Defense. He used his formidable persuasive talents to recruit outstanding chiefs of mission. John J. McCloy, under siege to become ambassador to Vietnam, was flattered to be called "the greatest proconsul the Republic ever had" and with visions of toga and laurel almost succumbed. Johnson, said McCloy, "was *very* courteous [and] much more exacting and penetrating in his questions" than Kennedy. According to subordinates, Johnson carefully defined the borders of their authority, made clear what he wanted, and otherwise gave them a free hand.

---

30. Benjamin H. Read OHT; Evans and Novak, *Lyndon B. Johnson,* 501–9; Philip Geyelin, *Lyndon B. Johnson and the World* (New York: Praeger, 1966), 96; Warren I. Cohen, *Dean Rusk* (Totowa, N.J.: Cooper Square, 1980), 218–21.

Richard Helms, who served as his director of Central Intelligence, found him a "first class boss."[31]

Johnson's decision making would also be regarded as first class if it were evaluated in terms of procedure. He kept himself informed assiduously. CIA and State Department reports, briefs, analyses, and estimates formed a substantial portion of his night reading. He had a capacity for intense concentration and an extraordinarily retentive memory, especially for facts and figures. Helms could tell the next day that he had "hoisted aboard what he read." Johnson preferred written rather than oral briefings because he could quickly grasp what he needed from a page but was at the mercy of a briefer's speaking pace. According to Helms, Johnson never asked him for advice at policy meetings, reserving him as a guardian of facts to "keep the game honest."[32]

In consultation and decision making every president has had his own style and Johnson was no exception. President Eisenhower placed great importance on the National Security Council (NSC) meeting, which provided him an airing of differing views, briefings, and a consolidated, orderly, informed process. Johnson, on the contrary, found the Council too large, and therefore vulnerable to leaks. He resisted a bureaucratic decision system that tended to restrict his flexibility. Besides, NSC procedure was tedious, discussion often, according to William Bundy, a mere recital of positions. Like other predecessors, most recently Kennedy, this president preferred individual or small-group discussion.[33]

The alternative for Johnson was the Tuesday luncheon, a regular meeting of the secretaries of State and Defense, the director of Central Intelligence, the National Security Adviser, the chair of the Joint Chiefs, and one or two White House aides. As the historian and archivist David Humphrey has shown, meetings of the NSC still took place irregularly but with different purposes: to ratify decisions already made, to give the government and the public a sense that decisions were being made with due consultation, and to provide a forum, as one NSC member said, for "reflective and educational discussions." The Tuesday luncheons provided the small, tight circle Johnson wanted for frank discussion. The disadvan-

31. Richard Helms, John J. McCloy, Sol Linowitz, Cater OHT.
32. Helms OHT.   33. William P. Bundy OHT.

tages were the unstructured nature of discussion in this informal setting and the lack of "read-out" informing relevant officials what had been decided.[34]

It could be argued that Johnson's deliberative system was fundamentally at fault in not providing room for dissent. None of the principal advisers he met with regularly in the Tuesday luncheons (Rusk, McNamara, and Bundy, later Walt Rostow) offered the kind of dissent on Vietnam that Undersecretary of State George Ball did in the National Security Council meetings. It could also be argued that opposing Johnson was a daunting task. He had a "very, very big and tough mind," according to one official, and he did not like being opposed, said another.[35]

Nevertheless, the argument for procedural inadequacy falls short. Johnson deliberations were not restricted to White House meetings. He also brought in for consultation as a group such foreign policy elder statesmen as Dean Acheson, General Omar Bradley, and Robert Lovett. He frequently called in two old friends, Abe Fortas and Clark Clifford, and made a point of keeping in touch with former presidents Truman and Eisenhower, especially the latter. With the "scores and scores of people" he used as a sounding board, as well as his constant attention to newspapers, television, and polls, he was if anything excessively preoccupied with consultation and testing opinion.[36] He listened closely to George Ball's dissents, given orally and in writing, and absorbed the contents. One memoirist after another emphasizes his caution and carefulness in decision making.[37]

The problem was not consultation, nor in a broader sense Johnson's management of foreign affairs. The fact was that only a handful in the American governing elite opposed the Vietnam intervention in the initial stages. The failure was cognitive, not procedural.[38] President Johnson believed correctly that he had a massive official consensus for his Vietnam policy in 1965.

34. Quotation respectively from David Humphrey, "NSC Meetings During the Johnson Presidency," *Diplomatic History* (forthcoming); Bundy OHT.
35. Respectively, Bundy, Helms OHT.   36. Helms OHT.
37. George Ball, Anna Rosenberg Hoffman, James H. Rowe Jr., Helms OHT.
38. See Larry Berman, *Planning a Tragedy: The Americanization of the War in Vietnam* (New York: Norton, 1982).

World View and Mindset

It seems that the mind and personality of Lyndon Johnson were well endowed for diplomacy. Political and diplomatic talents are similar. Both operate in realms of power. Both need intuitive understanding and interpersonal skills – sensitivity, tact, charm – and require the ability to achieve compromise. One might think that Johnson's proven strengths in these capacities domestically, together with his intelligence, memory, and energy, would serve him well in foreign affairs.

In many respects they did. He wisely avoided challenging France's withdrawal from NATO, determined not to engage in a "pissing match" with Charles de Gaulle. "We got out of France with dispatch and dignity," commented Charles Bohlen.[39] American diplomats gave Johnson high marks for his performance at regional conferences. At the Manila Pacific Summit in 1966 he took the lead but adjusted to the needs of the conferees; he followed a complex script except where he departed from it brilliantly.[40] The Hemisphere Summit Conference at Punta del Este, Uruguay, in 1967 was a "triumph of personal contact." The president displayed a sharp sense of the aptness of things.[41] At the funeral of Konrad Adenauer he drove out of his way to the chancellor's Rhine hillside home to console the family.

Less fitting was the state dinner at which he popped ten-gallon hats on the members of the Japanese cabinet. Finding the Scandinavians stuffy and unreceptive, he left a trail of insults across northern Europe.[42] Usually, though his style may have been "ranch," he acted "with good will and with a real desire to be courteous."[43] During the Berlin Wall crisis, he gave a speech of "triumphant reassurance" to worried West Berliners.[44]

Public and representational diplomacy was only the most visible side of foreign affairs. More fundamental was Johnson's conception of the nature of world affairs and the United States' role

39. Ball, Charles E. Bohlen OHT.   40. Bundy OHT
41. Linowitz OHT.
42. Edwin O. Reischauer OHT; Reedy, *Memoir*, 25–6; Conkin, *Big Daddy*, 169.
43. McCloy OHT.
44. Evans and Novak, *Lyndon B. Johnson*, 325; Conkin, *Big Daddy*, 168.

therein. Johnson "always felt a little limited in the field of foreign policy," said Walter Jenkins, who observed him closely for many years. Philip Geyelin put it best: "King of the river," he was "stranger to the open sea."[45] He had scarcely been abroad at all before the vice presidency and never learned a foreign language. As a young man, Johnson aimed at becoming a school teacher, and although he took a broad array of social science courses his B-average grades fell short of the intellectual capacity he demonstrated in maturity. In fact, earning his way through college, he spent little time on his studies, few of which dealt with the world beyond the United States.[46]

Beyond politics, his mind was not speculative, inquisitive, or acquisitive. It was practical and problem solving, not theoretical. He liked numbers and relied too heavily on box-score answers.[47] Beyond government business and news he read almost nothing. As a result, his appreciation of foreign nations was shallow, circumstantial, and dominated by the personalities of heads of state he had met. Lacking a detached critical perspective, he was culture-bound and vulnerable to clichés and stereotypes about world affairs.

Strangely, this master of domestic politics seemed to lack a sense of power in world politics. International relations in the Cold War had been dichotomous, a simple confrontation between the Soviet and American alliance systems. By the 1960s, however, they were becoming more complex, and power was becoming more diffuse. The Johnson administration was aware of change but slow to discard early Cold War assumptions and unsure of how to deal with new realities.[48] Johnson had no "independent instinct" in foreign affairs.[49]

On this score, Johnson's idol Franklin D. Roosevelt was different. Roosevelt understood power among nations as well as at home; but he came to maturity at the turn of the century when great power politics could still be seen as a fascinating game, whereas Johnson in his generation had never seen a world of fluctuating alignments except at the onset of World War II. Otherwise

45. Walter Jenkins OHT; Geyelin, *Lyndon B. Johnson and the World*, 15.
46. Dugger, *The Politician*, 121.   47. Sidey OHT; Reedy, *Memoir*, 52, 77.
48. Gordon H. Chang, *Friends and Enemies: The United States, China, and the Soviet Union, 1948–1972* (Stanford, Calif.: Stanford University Press, 1990); Ch. 9.
49. Schlesinger OHT.

he knew only the hardened confrontations of the First and Second World Wars and the Cold War as well as the relative absence of world politics in the 1920s. Roosevelt, of course, was more attuned to international affairs by family and travel, but the generational difference is significant too.

If Johnson had a limited understanding of social forces and politics abroad, he had sensitivity for the common people. He had an uncanny ability to shape himself to the particular situation he was addressing. Like an actor, he fashioned a set of roles he could play: now a southern "po' boy," now a western rancher. No role was more authentically and passionately played, however, than champion of the underprivileged.[50]

In 1928 Johnson took a year out of his college studies to serve as principal and teacher of the fifth, sixth, and seventh grades in Cotulla, "one of the crummiest little towns in Texas." His pupils were impoverished Mexican-Americans, "whose little brown bodies had so little and needed so much."[51] He worked furiously to provide not only good teaching but also sports, debate, and even toothpaste. Cotulla was thereafter a metaphor for his commitment by way of the New Deal and the Great Society to social justice in America.

Cotulla was also his gateway to empathy for the poor countries of the world. His Mexican-American experience led to an interest in Mexico, and that to a special claim on Latin American policy and advocacy of an American mission to the Third World.[52] America offered not charity, he insisted, but practical assistance to those prepared to help themselves. According to William Bundy, Assistant Secretary of State for East Asia, he "*cared*" about Asians; he was more at home with them than with Europeans. Reedy noted the rapt attention of Indian peasants at Johnson's graphic description of his boyhood experience drawing water from the well, showing how the rope occasionally slipped and burned the palms of his hands. They rubbed their palms too.[53] In the Third World, Johnson could establish cultural beachheads. Asia made more demands on his time than Europe but undoubtedly seemed more relevant to his own experience and open to change and American accomplishment.

50. White OHT; Geyelin, *Lyndon B. Johnson and the World*, 23–6.
51. Johnson quoted in Dallek, *Lone Star*, 77, 78.
52. Ball OHT; Reedy, *Memoir*, 26; Geyelin, *Lyndon B. Johnson and the World*, 38–9.
53. Bundy OHT; Reedy, *Memoir*, 24–5.

Johnson's view of world politics was heavily affected by the years between Munich and Pearl Harbor, when he was thirty to thirty-three years old. He was a down-the-line New Dealer and supporter of the president's preparedness measures and aid to Britain, though he stopped short of advocating direct involvement in the European war. He condemned appeasement and facilitated entry into the United States of hundreds of Jews seeking escape from Hitler's Europe. The lessons he and his generation drew from these years were graven on their minds: (1) that the United States had erred in retreating into isolationism after World War I and must hereafter play a leading role in world affairs, (2) that appeasement of aggressors was folly, that they must be met from the beginning with firmness and force if necessary, and (3) that the United States had been imperiled by military weakness and must always have sufficiency and readiness in the future.

When World War II ended, these articles of faith moved over to undergird policy in the Cold War: (1) the United States must fulfill its commitments and maintain its reliability as world leader and ally; (2) until "situations of strength" had been created and the fundamental purposes of communist powers had changed, the function of diplomacy was registering situations created by force or threat of force and keeping allies in line; (3) adequate defense depended on projection overseas of American power, on the credibility of its deterrence, and therefore on its willingness if necessary to use force.[54]

At the heart of these lessons of the World War II era was Johnson's belief – indeed, according to an old friend, obsession – that this nation's difficulties in the world stemmed from foreign miscalculation that the United States was easygoing and self-indulgent and not prepared to defend its interests. Thus the two World Wars and Korea. To overcome that misapprehension and prevent war and the risk of nuclear war, Johnson believed, the United States must convey its interest and intent "loud and clear and over and over, and by deeds rather than words."[55]

Skeptical of the uses of diplomacy, Johnson was a powerful advocate of strong defense. His principal committee assignments in

54. Dallek, *Lone Star*, 169–70 (assistance to Jews), 177, 197, 257, 292; Dugger, *The Politician*, 236; Kintner OHT.
55. As quoted in Geyelin, *Lyndon B. Johnson and the World*, 44–5.

Congress were in military affairs. He pushed especially hard for the buildup of air power and then missiles. Armed might accorded with his style; the cowboy was one of his roles; "don't tread on me" was his banner; "tall in the saddle" was how he liked to be seen. He was keenly aware of the value to his political fortune of military contracts he funneled to Texas.[56]

At the same time, he was by no means infatuated with the military. During World War II, during his brief stint as a naval officer, he displayed a refreshingly free spirit toward military formalities in securing the greatest possible political mileage from his one trip to a combat theater. He went to the southwest Pacific as a naval observer, conferred with the army's hero of Bataan, General Douglas MacArthur, and flew an air corps combat mission. According to Anna Rosenberg Hoffman, who was Assistant Secretary of Defense in the Truman administration, Senator Johnson would "ride the military terribly hard" at congressional hearings. "He was very suspicious. . . ." When he became president, however, he "listened to them completely," Hoffman said, because they now had "become part of him." Johnson explained it somewhat differently to her: he was now responsible for the lives of Americans fighting in Vietnam, and the military leaders were, after all, those "who know how to fight a war."[57]

Johnson fully and uncritically shared the assumptions, axioms, dogmas, and doctrines that composed the American Cold War mindset. He first saw Soviet expansion in Europe as a threat as early as May 1945. He shied away from dangerous Cold War scripts put forward by MacArthur and right-wing Republicans, but he consistently supported the containment initiatives of Truman and, with some reservations, those of Eisenhower as well.[58] He subscribed with most others to the Eisenhower domino theory and shared the Kennedy view that the People's Republic of China currently represented the most powerful and dangerous manifestation of communist expansion. He had lived through the Joseph McCarthy years in the Senate and played a key role in forming the committee that finally brought him down. Thus he was intimately aware of the political consequences of a foreign reverse like the so-called "loss" of China.

56. Ibid., 154; Dallek, *Lone Star*, 294–5, 383; Kintner OHT.
57. Hoffman OHT.   58. Dallek, *Lone Star*, 272, 291–3, 383–4, 396–400, 443–5.

Johnson tried to escape predetermined decisions. He proceeded cautiously, read carefully, questioned intently, consulted widely, and sought options. Yet he had no independent way of thinking about the world, no framework of analysis, that could offer him more satisfactory answers than those provided by the close-fitting elements of the powerful Cold War paradigm.

The Final Balance

The Vietnam war was an agonizing and devastating experience for Lyndon Johnson. He became melancholy; one could "actually see him getting older by the month."[59] A web of anxieties plagued him: the dangers, uncertainties, and human costs of the war, the threat it posed to the Great Society, and the rise of opposition to the war, tied into his suspicions of the Kennedy camp and the press. He faced not simply failure but monumental failure yet felt obliged stubbornly to persevere.

He became a psychologically afflicted president. Richard Goodwin believes that in 1965 Johnson experienced certain episodes of paranoid behavior, as he illustrates by selections from his diary of that time. Paul Conkin described Johnson's condition as "near paranoia."[60] Nevertheless, after the Tet offensive in 1968, instead of sinking further into despondency, Johnson rallied to make a rational and statesmanlike decision not to seek a second term in office. In doing so he consulted a number of close advisers, asking Eisenhower, for example, if he would be doing less than his duty by not running again.[61] One final time his ability to take a detached and politically professional view of his situation helped him counterbalance and contain his inner demons.

59. Earle G. Wheeler OHT.
60. Goodwin, *Remembering*, 394; Conkin, *Big Daddy*, 289.
61. General Andrew J. Goodpaster OHT.

2

Johnson, Vietnam, and Tocqueville

WALTER LaFEBER

Conducting a successful foreign policy for the United States requires a dual approach: constructing a strategy that is workable abroad, and developing a political explanation that creates and maintains sufficient consensus at home. The Founders believed that the two approaches were two sides of the same coin. Nearly fifty years later, however, a French visitor, Alexis de Tocqueville, noted a change: during the Jacksonian era Americans enjoyed considerable security in foreign affairs, so they were engrossed in their favorite public activity of making money for themselves. Tocqueville wondered how Americans would deal with foreign policy crises when their nation became a great power. He was not sanguine, but he did define the problem that 130 years later helped destroy Lyndon Johnson's policies in Vietnam: "[A] democracy," Tocqueville wrote, "can only with great difficulty regulate the details of an important [foreign policy] undertaking, persevere in a fixed design, and work out its execution in spite of serious obstacles. It cannot combine its measures with secrecy or await their consequences with patience." He believed democracy of the American variety to be singularly ill suited for conducting a successful diplomacy.[1]

Several presidents, notably Woodrow Wilson in 1919–20 and Franklin D. Roosevelt between 1934 and 1939, dramatically failed to solve Tocqueville's problem. No chief executive solved it more successfully than did Harry Truman when, on March 23, 1947, he issued his Truman Doctrine, which, by defining the world as di-

1. Gaillard Hunt, ed., *The Writings of James Madison*, 9 vols. (New York: Putnam's 1901), V, 146; Alexis de Tocqueville, *Democracy in America*, 2 vols. (New York: Knopf, 1948), II, 234–5.

vided between free and enslaved and shrewdly demanding that Americans decide which side they were on, created an anticommunist consensus that stretched across the next four decades.[2] This consensus was significantly breached only twice – in 1951–2, when Truman himself could not resolve the stalemate in the Korean War, and after 1965 when Lyndon Johnson's political support collapsed as he escalated the U.S. commitment in South Vietnam.

In retrospect, that collapse appears to resemble a row of dominoes falling: important intellectuals went first, along with key newspaper correspondents and columnists, then congressional leaders, the print media, the television pundits, and, finally, the business community. Without these necessary pillars (to change the metaphor), by early 1968 Johnson's policies had crumbled, and the president announced that he would not seek reelection. Underneath those pillars, moreover, the social foundation itself was shifting. James Madison and Tocqueville, among many others, had argued that a pivotal feature of American society was its pluralism, the many nearly self-sufficient "factions" (as Madison termed them in Federalist #10) that were based on religion, ideology, and property. The Truman Doctrine and the reality of fighting the Cold War had quieted these pluralisms in the 1950s, but by 1963–4, as Johnson assumed the presidency, they again erupted. Art, as usual, anticipated and reflected this eruption. Given the way art has been "blasted wide open, ripped, patched, and shattered, cut, split, rent, lacerated, and thrown around generally," *New York Times* critic John Canaday wrote in 1965, it less deserves the name "Modern art" than it does the term "Fragmented Mannerism." The "present generation," Canaday continued, is "a more restive lot" that "seems to accept no responsibility of seeing things whole or even to care much that this capacity has been denied them."[3]

The new pluralism took many forms. The most explosive turned out to be a civil rights movement whose national impact became apparent with the 1963 March on Washington and then, after

2. Richard Freeland, *The Truman Doctrine and the Origins of McCarthyism* (New York: Knopf, 1972), is important for this interpretation.
3. *New York Times*, October 24, 1965, 33. *Pluralism* is used here in a general sense, not in the sense of the "pluralist theory" in the 1950s and 1960s as dissected by Allen J. Matusow, *The Unraveling of America: A History of Liberalism in the 1960s* (New York: Harper & Row, 1964), 6–8.

1964, in a series of deadly urban riots that climaxed in 1967 with twenty-six fatalities in Newark and forty killed in Detroit. Immediately after those cities burst into flames, polls showed that Johnson's overall job rating had dropped from 47 percent to 39 percent in a single month; his disapproval rating on Vietnam policies simultaneously reached an all-time high of 54 percent – even though U.S. forces finally seemed to be gaining ground in South Vietnam. White House aide Jack Valenti had defined the problem a year earlier when he warned the president: "Vietnam bugs the people right now – particularly those who have sons nearing draft age. . . . The riots upset the people. The administration is caught in a whipsaw, like a shuttlecock in a badminton game – the Negroes on the one hand and the fearful whites on the other." There was also another danger: "The cost of living worries the people. They are afraid of the unknown. They don't know what lies ahead and they fret."[4]

Johnson had shown he could create consensus, but it had been on the U.S. Senate floor in the 1950s. Perhaps the most successful majority leader in American history, the Texan had followed a general policy of bipartisanship with the Eisenhower foreign policies and had dealt with disagreements privately, through both bullying and patronage, to create consensus. Open debate had been reduced along with principled, public dissent. In 1964, Johnson gladly yielded the far right position, the demand for total victory in Vietnam and liberation of the communist bloc, to the Republican presidential nominee, Barry Goldwater. Johnson and the Democratic Party platform took a more moderate position that lay squarely in the middle of U.S. foreign policy as it had evolved from Truman through John F. Kennedy.[5] The president covered himself by using alleged North Vietnamese torpedo boat attacks on U.S. warships in

4. Larry Berman, "From Intervention to Disengagement," in Ariel Levite, Bruce W. Jentleson, and Larry Berman, *Foreign Military Intervention* (New York: Columbia University Press, 1992), 44; "Memorandum for the President," from Jack Valenti, September 18, 1966, Valenti 1965–1966 file, Office of the President File, Lyndon B. Johnson Library, Austin, Texas (hereafter LBJ Library). Other examples of how important the new pluralism was becoming are in Thomas L. Hughes, "Policy-Making in a World Turned Upside Down," *Foreign Affairs* XLV (January 1967), 202–14; and Walt Whitman Rostow, "Domestic Determinants of U.S. Foreign Policy: The Tocqueville Oscillation," *Armed Forces Journal*, June 27, 1970, 16G–16H.
5. Doris Kearns Goodwin, "Lyndon Johnson's Political Personality," *Political Science Quarterly* XCI (Fall 1976), 396; Louis Heren, *No Hail, No Farewell* (New York: Harper & Row, 1970), 60–1.

the Gulf of Tonkin to obtain Congress's authorization to use retaliatory force and then by bombing North Vietnam in August 1964. This reaction, however, seemed to be the exception that dramatized the rule: dedicated to passing his Great Society domestic legislation and staking out a traditional – and consensual – foreign policy position, Johnson seemed to understand (and was determined to transcend) the dangers lurking in the Tocqueville problem.

Less visible dimensions of his foreign policy were nonetheless present and ominous. With 18,000 "fellow citizens" in Vietnam, Johnson declared in December 1963, "we should, all of us, not go to bed any night without asking whether we have done everything that we could do that day to win the struggle here and bring victory to our group." To "win" in Vietnam already seemed difficult, yet the president vividly recalled how Truman's consensus threatened to collapse into political (or at least Democratic Party) chaos after the earlier president had not "won" in China in 1949 or in Korea during 1950–2. Another dimension also became more visible, as LBJ recalled in his memoirs: "When we made mistakes, I believe we erred because we tried to do too much too soon. . . . If the Presidency can be said to have been employed and to have been enjoyed, I had employed it to the utmost, and I had enjoyed it to the limit."[6]

This imperial presidency began to be used systematically for an imperial policy in February 1965, when Johnson ordered expanded bombing attacks on North Vietnam. In March, he began to send in 75,000 combat troops. On July 28 he committed 125,000 more. The deteriorating military and political situation in South Vietnam, as well as intense pressure from his closest advisers, forced these decisions. By October, Americans were suffering more than a thousand casualties each week. Johnson had never explained to the public the process of and reasons for the escalation. Not only had Vice President Hubert Humphrey directly urged him to present "a cogent, convincing case if we are to enjoy sustained public support," but (contrary to one important later study), so had other advisers, including Horace Busby, a White House staff member

6. National Archives and Records Service, *Public Papers of the Presidents . . . Lyndon B. Johnson . . . 1963* (Washington: U.S. Government Printing Office, 1964), 28 (hereafter cited as *Public Papers of the Presidents,* followed by year, publication year, and page numbers); Lyndon B. Johnson, *The Vantage Point: Perspectives of the Presidency, 1963–1969* (New York: Holt, Rinehart & Winston, 1971), 566.

especially close personally to the president. In February 1965 Busby begged Johnson to give a full explanation to a joint session of Congress before the "pro-negotiation, pro-withdrawal" forces took the country back into isolationism, or "the elements defeated on November 3 . . . revive with new strength."[7] LBJ rejected the advice. He had discovered virtue in secret foreign policymaking. In 1964, for example, Johnson had covertly cooperated with Brazilian army leaders who successfully overthrew an elected civilian government that LBJ deeply mistrusted. In terms of Vietnam policy, it was clear that as many as one-quarter to one-third of the American electorate knew and cared nothing about the U.S. involvement. As long as casualties and other costs remained low, the president was not overly concerned. "For most Americans this is an easy war," he noted publicly in May 1965. "Men fight and men suffer and men die," but for "most of us" the times "are untroubled. Prosperity rises, abundance increases, the Nation flourishes."[8]

A relatively small group of students and intellectuals, many from elite colleges where this prosperity seemed notably abundant, forced the first crack in Johnson's foreign policy consensus. Higher education was undergoing incredible change. The Baby Boomers born in the late 1940s were nearly doubling the college population of 1950. They found some faculty who were action-intellectuals, that is, persons who had worked closely with government officials (especially in Secretary of Defense Robert McNamara's Pentagon, where technologically proficient "whiz kids" quantified and streamlined a supposedly ever more efficient military strategy). These intellectuals' skills often made them popular in Washington, but suspect to many on their home campuses. Other faculty and students had used funding from the postwar foundations (such as Ford and Rockefeller) to develop expertise on specific areas, such as southeast Asia, that gave them a unique perspective and access to information that, in turn, allowed them to question, legitimately

7. Richard Neustadt and Ernest R. May, *Thinking in Time: The Uses of History for Decision-Makers* (New York: Free Press, 1986), 87; "Memorandum" from Busby to Johnson, February 27, 1965, Aides' Memos on Vietnam, Reference File, Vietnam, LBJ Library.
8. Especially important here is George Herring's essay in Robert Divine, ed., *Exploring the Johnson Years* (Austin: University of Texas Press, 1981), 38; Berman, "From Intervention to Disengagement," 32–3, 42–3; Barry Hughes, *Domestic Context of American Foreign Policy* (San Francisco: W. H. Freeman, 1978), 91; *Public Papers of the Presidents . . . 1965* (Washington, 1966), 525–6.

and knowledgeably, Johnson's policies. Professor George Kahin and Cornell University's pioneering Southeast Asia Program exemplified these highly informed scholars.[9]

Often apart from these critics appeared a New Left movement. Differing from the 1930s left generationally, culturally, and in its belief that prosperity rather than economic depression was to be the long-term norm, the New Left was shaped by the civil rights movement as well as by the Vietnam involvement, and – especially – by a growing disbelief in the government's credibility. That credibility, unfortunately for Johnson, was savaged between 1963 and 1966 by revelations of "dirty tricks" by the Central Intelligence Agency. Former CIA director Allen Dulles's memoirs of 1963 actually bragged about such operations. Haynes Johnson's *Bay of Pigs* revealed the sordid truths about that 1961 covert activity. *The Invisible Government* by David Wise and Thomas B. Ross stunningly informed readers about the agency's formerly secret past. As Erik Barnouw observes, Americans once used to the squeaky-clean cowboy as the national symbol suddenly confronted on their television a new symbol: the spies of "Mission: Impossible," whose tasks were so politically (and sometimes morally) delicate that their instructions self-destructed in seconds.[10]

In 1965, then, conditions were ripe for the revolt of some intellectuals. The revolt could draw energy not only from the experts who knew southeast Asia well but also from a broader ideological critique of postwar America by C. Wright Mills, Michael Harrington, William Appleman Williams, and others. In 1965, just as

9. This interpretation of the intellectuals' importance differs in some particulars from the provocative argument in Russell Jacoby's *The Last Intellectuals: American Culture in the Age of Academe* (New York: Basic Books, 1987), esp. 153–7. Kahin's perspective is in his and John Wilson Lewis's *The United States in Vietnam* (New York: Dell, 1967) and Kahin's *Intervention: How America Became Involved in Vietnam* (New York: Knopf, 1986); important on the New Left is a contemporary account, Jack Newfield, *A Prophetic Minority* (New York: New American Library, 1966), 21–31. The critics who were expert on southeast Asia became influential but were few in number in 1964–5. As Kahin recalled, "That's one of the real tragedies of that situation. We needed Vietnam specialists in this country, but the very few who existed were working with government – and they weren't all that good; we hadn't trained people who were really knowledgeable about Vietnam." ("Interview of Professor George McT. Kahin, October 2, 1990" by Professor James W. Clinton; transcript in Kahin's possession.)

10. Eric Barnouw, *Tube of Plenty* (London: Oxford University Press, 1975), 367; Lewis A. Coser, *Men of Ideas: A Sociologist's View* (New York: Free Press, 1965), 248, 323.

Johnson ordered two divisions to Vietnam, the first of many "teach-ins" on the war was held at the University of Michigan on March 24. The next day the president tried to head off the growing dissent by grandly announcing that "the United States will never be second in seeking a settlement in Vietnam that is based on an end of Communist aggression." White House aide and Vietnam expert Chester Cooper correctly assessed the announcement as "merely rhetoric, a public relations holding action." Serious-minded observers shared that interpretation, as did many college students who faced military induction. Within seven weeks, fifty more colleges across the country held teach-ins. (At teach-ins, faculty led informal discussions of the war with usually large audiences of students.) As one reporter phrased it, the schools ranged "from the predictable (Berkeley) to the unexpected (Texas)." With leading academics as speakers, and large student bodies as potentials for protest, the teach-ins formed the first significant mass debate – and, in most cases, condemnation – of LBJ's foreign policy.[11]

On May 17 and 18, 1965, George Kahin and others condemned that policy in a national teach-in at Washington, D.C. Several hundred colleges dispatched student–faculty delegations, and most of these institutions dismissed classes so that students could follow the debate on television or radio. Arthur Schlesinger Jr., historian and former member of John F. Kennedy's White House staff, was a chief apologist for the U.S. commitment; he urged that more U.S. troops be sent to give "much clearer evidence of our determination to stay" until a political settlement could be reached. National Security Adviser McGeorge Bundy, once a dean at Harvard, was to debate Kahin, but Johnson, frowning on such a public spectacle that would give his opponents a nationwide audience, suddenly sent Bundy on a diplomatic mission to the Dominican Republic. A month later, however, Bundy did debate Professor Hans Morgenthau on national television. The best-known scholar of international relations in the country, Morgenthau had been ardently anticommunist, but he condemned U.S. policy toward Vietnam as so misplaced and confused that, he believed, Johnson's ignorance could find solace

11. Kahin, *Intervention*, 324; Charles DeBenedetti, *An American Ordeal; The Antiwar Movement of the Vietnam Era*, Charles Chatfield, Assisting Author (Syracuse, N.Y.: Syracuse University Press, 1990), 107–9; Matusow, *Unraveling of America*, 377–8.

only in public opinion polls that "perform for the President the same psychological function as . . . the constellation of the stars did for the statesmen of old. They put his doubts to temporary rest." Bundy tried to discredit Morgenthau by publicly reading a few earlier Morgenthau judgments that in Bundy's view had been proven wrong; to some viewers the attack was reminiscent of McCarthyite techniques of the early 1950s.[12] Morgenthau was joined in his protest by such prominent liberal intellectuals as Reinhold Niebuhr, John Kenneth Galbraith of Harvard, and Mary Wright of Yale. Johnson was understandably confused; he believed he was only applying the kind of military, anticommunist containment policy that these same intellectuals had urged since the 1940s.[13]

Chester Cooper and Jack Valenti believed, correctly, that the critics were a minority in the universities. These two White House officials urged that the administration organize and encourage the prowar majority through the American Friends of Vietnam, an organization formed by academic intellectuals that included Schlesinger and other Cold War liberals on its national committee. The support was to be given quietly, of course, so there would be, in Cooper's words, no "impression that the Government is sponsoring its own pressure group." Cooper, with major support from Colonel Trevor Dupuy's Pentagon-financed Historical Evaluation Research Organization, targeted college faculties for help. Valenti told Johnson that the State Department was sending "bright young men" to speak at colleges and considering "regional seminars" where professors could be educated about the war. In June 1965, LBJ agreed to a frontal attack, proposed by his aides and led by Richard Goodwin, to invite leading intellectuals to the White House for a day with the president. Just before the occasion, nov-

12. Melvin Small, *Johnson, Nixon, and the Doves* (New Brunswick, N.J.: Rutgers University Press, 1988), 50–1; Kahin, *Intervention*, 322; U.S. Senate, Committee on the Judiciary, Staff, 89th Cong., 1st Sess., *The Anti-Vietnam Agitation and the Teach-in Movement. The Problem of Communist Infiltration and Exploitation* (Washington: Government Printing Office, 1965), 17–19, 36, 154, 156, 188, 233–4; a notably succinct statement of Morgenthau's thoughts may be found in his review of Philip Geyelin's *Lyndon B. Johnson and the World*, *The New York Review of Books*, August 18, 1966, 4–5.

13. "Paradoxically," James Reston writes, Johnson "failed in Vietnam in large part because he followed the advice of the intellectuals he inherited from Kennedy." James Reston, *Deadline: A Memoir* (New York: Random House, 1991), 305.

elist Saul Bellow told Goodwin that poet Robert Lowell was going to reject the invitation, then call a press conference to condemn policies in Vietnam and in the Dominican Republic (where, in early May, the president had dispatched 22,000 troops to stop a supposed procommunist revolt). The president was livid. "I've been very dubious about this from the beginning," he told Goodwin. "When you get in a pen with pigs you get more of it on you."[14]

A number of visible (or hoping-to-be-visible) academics tried to counter Lowell's public protest. Harvard's Henry Kissinger, a best-selling analyst of possible nuclear war who had even bigger things in mind, flattered Bundy and Johnson in the spring of 1965 by announcing his support of their Vietnam policies. In December, after returning from Vietnam as an administration consultant, Kissinger defended U.S. policy in a debate on CBS-TV against British Labour Party leader Michael Foot. Two Harvard students (Robert Shrum, later, ironically, a speechwriter for Senator George McGovern; and Laurence Tribe, later a liberal legal expert) supported Kissinger in the debate. That same month, Kissinger was among the 190 academics, including Samuel Beer and Morton Halperin of Harvard, who signed a petition supporting Johnson's conduct of the war.[15]

Nevertheless, by 1966, ever-larger segments of the academic, democratic left were more outspokenly critical. Johnson needed this group to pass his Great Society domestic programs, to which he had given a much greater personal commitment in the previous two years than he had given Vietnam. Some 477,000 students in 322 universities and colleges pledged support for the war effort, but many represented conservative groups more interested in anticommunist crusades than in the Great Society. Bundy and Secretary of State Dean Rusk frontally attacked the liberal intellectual

14. Cooper to Valenti, April 24, 1965, in Valenti to Johnson, April 24, 1965, Aides' memos on Vietnam, Reference File, Vietnam, LBJ Library; Kahin, *Intervention,* 80; Cooper spelled out the arrangements on May 6, 1965, to Valenti: Professor Wesley Fishel of Michigan State, National Chairman of the American Friends of Vietnam (AFV), believed he could conduct an effective educational campaign if he had enough funds. "In my talk with him last Saturday he confirmed that Mr. Sidney Weinberg, at your [*sic*] initiative, had contacted him on fund raising requirements, and he had given Mr. Weinberg the figure of $55,000 as the desired goal." ("Memorandum for Mr. Valenti," May 6, 1965, LBJ Library, in possession of Professor George Kahin.)
15. Walter Isaacson, *Kissinger: A Biography* (New York: Simon and Schuster, 1992), 117–19.

critics. "They are a prejudiced lot," Bundy declared, who "never learned internationalism with respect to Asia." Rusk condemned a "jaded and cynical" liberalism that wanted to turn 14 million Vietnamese over "to a totalitarian regime." Allegedly he complained privately about "a minority of Communist agitators among the peace movement." As the protests gathered momentum in early 1965, Horace Busby advised the president to beware the intellectuals' teeth, then suggested dulling those teeth with talks to Americans that would note "a rising acceptance of the pro-isolationist, pro-negotiation, pro-withdrawal position as 'the' intellectual position to the detriment of you and the country. What is so widely forgotten is that before World War II, many intellectuals were in the vanguard of that era's isolationists."[16] In other words, the ghost of Munich was to be released again to bedevil those who dissented from Johnson's policy.

Eric Goldman of Princeton had joined Johnson's staff to act as a conduit to the intellectual community (or, as the president once candidly phrased it, "to keep the intellectuals happy"). Goldman urged Johnson to win back dissenters by stressing postwar reconstruction of Vietnam and the Great Society, while downplaying the war. Other key staffers also bombarded the president with memos on how to court intellectuals. Valenti proposed that James Perkins, president of Cornell University, and Barbara Ward (a British author whose upbeat accounts of how the West should help develop the non-industrialized world ranked among Johnson's favorite reading) "be commissioned to bring to the White House ... groups of four or five" intellectuals "who would feel flattered that the President would seek them out." LBJ responded that "I just can't do anymore," but he in fact did meet sporadically with small groups of professors to enlist their support, and the White House staff remained in touch with Perkins and Ward. In one talk, the president expressed gratification that "the intellectual today is an

16. Melvin Small, "The Impact of the Antiwar Movement on Lyndon Johnson, 1965–8: A Preliminary Report," *Peace and Change* X (Spring 1984), 1–22; Small, *Johnson, Nixon and the Doves,* esp. 117–19; *New York Times,* January 7, 1966, 1; *New York Times Magazine,* March 20, 1966, 130; Rusk quoted indirectly on communist influence in the *New York Times,* November 26, 1967, E2; crucial on Rusk is the evaluation in Warren I. Cohen, *Dean Rusk* (Totowa, N.J.: Cooper Square, 1980), 310–30; "For: the President, From: Horace Busby, About: Leadership on Vietnam," February 27, 1965, Memos to the President, Office Files of Horace Busby, LBJ Library.

inside man," but he added that "the responsible intellectual who moves between his campus and Washington knows above all that his task is, in the language of the current generation, 'to cool it.' "[17]

The president could appeal colorfully: "I regard it as wise for the flame of learning to be applied occasionally to the seats of power." But he disliked and mistrusted intellectuals, especially from the North and East, even if at times they supported him. After the Dominican Republic invasion of early 1965, he said privately that turning the small country over to a politician he considered weak "would be like turning it over to Arthur Schlesinger Jr." The president's press secretary, George Reedy, later observed that LBJ had little capacity for reflection or "real interest in 'academic subjects' " but valued a " 'practical education,' " a view that "led him to equate beauty school with a university." Senator J. William Fulbright, the Arkansas Democrat, had been a Johnson intimate but began to break with him not only over policy in Vietnam and the Dominican Republic but also over the intellectuals' role. Fulbright, formerly a Rhodes Scholar and president of the University of Arkansas, warned "that when a university becomes very closely oriented to the current needs of government it takes on some of the atmosphere of a place of business while losing that of a place of learning."[18] He emphatically rejected LBJ's hope that the intellectual become "an inside man." The senator was much closer to Morgenthau's belief that an intellectual's proper role was to speak truth to power. In Johnson's White House, that was not always the way to remain an "inside man."

The administration's leading critic of Vietnam policy, Undersecretary of State George Ball, carefully distanced himself from the university protests. Unlike Kahin and Morgenthau, Ball said little about the historic origins and the complexities of the conflict but

17. "Memorandum for the President" from Goldman, July 9, 1966, in Kintner to Johnson, July 11, 1966, Aides' Memos on Vietnam, Reference File, Vietnam, LBJ Library; Philip Geyelin, *Lyndon Johnson and the World* (New York: Praeger, 1966), 131–2; "Memorandum for the President," from W. W. Rostow, May 11, 1966, Rostow Files, Box 14, National Security File, LBJ Library; "Memorandum" for Johnson from Valenti, May 22, 1967, Valenti File, Office of the President File, LBJ Library; text of Johnson speech in the *New York Times* May 12, 1966, 14, on intellectuals.
18. *Public Papers of the Presidents . . . 1964* (Washington, 1965), 1176; Geyelin, *Lyndon Johnson and the World*, 131–3; George Reedy, *Lyndon Johnson: A Memoir* (New York: Andrews and McMeel, 1982), 22–3; Fulbright's view of intellectuals' roles is in the *New York Times*, May 11, 1966, 36.

stressed its unpredictability and political costs. Busby heard Ball's criticisms (kept private within Johnson's circle) and told the president that the undersecretary "is conscientious, not a critic. . . . Significantly his argument is not the argument of the academic intellectuals – it is much more sane and sound, and merits respect as such." Ball himself later wrote that the ever-louder public protests did not slow Johnson's escalation of the war in 1965–6 but instead "dug us in ever more deeply" and led the administration "to new extremes of overstatement to justify the mounting investment. . . . It was a classical reaction to frustration, recalling the tourist in a foreign land who compensates for his linguistic deficiencies by shouting English words loudly." Political scientist Bernard Cohen reinforced Ball's case when he interviewed fifty State Department officials in early 1966. Cohen noted that "the tendency to dismiss the protests as the work of a small fringe group on the radical left . . . is exemplified by a Deputy Assistant Secretary who in January 1966 referred to the National Teach-in of the year before as "the high-water mark of the Vietnam protest."[19]

The protest movement, of course, had barely begun in 1965–6. Intellectual leaders had accurately pinpointed how Johnson's policy was shaped by historical ignorance (such as believing Vietnam's nationalist revolution was comparable to dealing with the Red Army's threat to Western Europe), political illusions (that Americans would indeed "bear any burden"), and false military assumptions (such as the belief that escalating U.S. power would discover a so-called "break-point" that would force the Vietnamese to give up their thousand-year-old effort to drive out all foreign powers).[20] The intellectuals' dissent of 1965–6 was the small hole in the dike that had been thrown up by Johnson and his advisers to protect them as they searched for a workable Vietnam policy. By 1968 that hole had been rapidly enlarged by the print media, congressional

19. "Memorandum for the President," from Busby, July 21, 1965, Aides' Memos on Vietnam, Reference File, Vietnam, LBJ Library; *New York Times Magazine*, April 1, 1973, 43, for Ball's opinion; Bernard Cohen, *The Public's Impact on Foreign Policy* (Boston: Little, Brown, 1971), 124. In his important book, Melvin Small concludes that "a careful analysis" of Bundy's, Rostow's, Rusk's, Johnson's, and other top officials' "formal memoranda and policy papers suggests that [public] opinion was a negligible factor in most cases" of decision-making. *Johnson, Nixon and the Doves*, 3, 7.
20. Neustadt and May, *Thinking in Time*, 81–3.

critics, and finally television and the business community until the onrush swept away not only the president's policy but Johnson himself. In 1965–6 (and, indeed, earlier), the newspaper reporting from southeast Asia proved to be of special importance. Not only did many of the intellectual critics rely heavily upon such reporting (unless they were those such as Kahin and Wright, who had years of personal involvement in Asia to draw on), but some reporters themselves became of particular importance to the protest movement when they went to Vietnam as supporters of U.S. policy and then, after witnessing the war, grew skeptical.

The press had generally been uncritical of John F. Kennedy's foreign policies, including those that escalated the conflict in southeast Asia. Certainly the majority of newspapers in the United States supported Johnson's policies. Exceptions existed, most notably the *New York Times,* whose young correspondent David Halberstam dispatched reports from South Vietnam so contradicting the good news coming out of Washington that Kennedy suggested to the *Times'* owners that Halberstam needed a vacation. The newspaper conspicuously kept Halberstam in South Vietnam. After 1964, as U.S. troop strength climbed, casualties rose, and results remained murky, others also questioned the effort, most notably Neil Sheehan of the *New York Times;* Charles Mohr, who quit *Time* magazine after it rewrote his pessimistic reports and joined the *New York Times;* Peter Arnett of the Associated Press; and the respected *New Yorker* author Robert Shaplen.

These correspondents again did not represent a consensus by 1966. One study of six leading newspapers' coverage of crucial battles in 1965, 1967, and 1971 concludes that in all three years the government controlled information about these battles rather successfully, and the journals' interpretations of the conflicts varied depending on each newspaper's general assessment of the overall war. In May 1966, Bill Moyers (in charge of the White House's public affairs effort) warned Johnson that "considerable Senatorial and other criticism of U.S. policy on Vietnam has appeared in the press during the past week." One critic urged greater force to win immediately. The others opposed "escalating military action" and instead wanted "prompt negotiations." These were exemplified by Fulbright, "former Ambassador Kenneth Galbraith, . . . Americans for Democratic Action, and the American pacifists in Saigon." But Moyers then noted a list of newspapers ranging from the *Baltimore Sun* and the *Christian Science Monitor* to the Hearst and Scripps-Howard chains that supported Johnson's policies.[21]

Concerned about the news accounts (less so the editorials), the president and his military command considered imposing but decided not to impose censorship on daily reports coming out of Vietnam. When they considered such a policy, they invariably concluded that censorship would further reduce the administration's already declining credibility, and that it would be nearly impossible to enforce given the huge number of foreign and American journalists who swarmed over southeast Asia. The president and his commanders greatly regretted this decision not to censor. When later chief executives imposed tough censorship in military operations in Grenada, Panama, and the Persian Gulf, Americans and the press protested little. In the 1960s, on the other hand, their protests had gone far to make such government control of information impossible. Not only were some mainstream national newspapers therefore publishing critical reports, but some 440 underground papers appeared between 1965 and 1969. Many had the lifetime of a moth, but the underground press did reach an estimated 3 million readers, and it offered alternative views. One, *Ramparts*, became nationally famous for its exposure of university–Pentagon links and the war's brutality.[22]

The critical press was drawing several conclusions about U.S. policy: it was not succeeding as the administration announced it was, and U.S. officials were trying to cover their growing problems by misleading journalists. *Aviation Week,* not known for being unduly critical of Washington's containment policies, declared that the Pentagon's – and especially Defense Department press spokesman

21. Clarence R. Wyatt, " 'At the Cannon's Mouth': The American Press and the Vietnam War," *Journalism History* XIII (Autumn–Winter 1986), 111; Peter Stoler, *The War Against the Press* (New York: Dodd, Mead, 1986), 7–8; "Memorandum for the President," from Moyers, May 3, 1966, Office Files of Bill Moyers, "BDM Memos," LBJ Library.
22. William M. Hammond, *United States Army in Vietnam. Public Affairs: The Military and the Media, 1962–1968* (Washington: Center of Military History, 1988), 234–6; James Aronson, *The Press and the Cold War* (Indianapolis: Bobbs-Merrill, 1970), esp. 284–6.

Arthur Sylvester's – credibility had "sunk so low" that reporters refused to believe a story "until it had been officially denied." In Saigon, the daily military briefing became known as "the Five-O'clock Follies." Journalist Michael Herr recalled listening to a U.S. colonel explain that Americans would win the war because they were "high protein, meat-eating hunters, while the other guy just ate rice and a few grungy fish heads. We were going to club him to death with our meat; what could you say except, 'Colonel, you're insane'?"[23]

Johnson and his top advisers tried to reverse such impressions with a full-court press on journalists. "We will never eliminate altogether the irresponsible and prejudiced coverage of men like Peter Arnett and Morris [*sic*] Safer [of CBS], men who are not Americans and do not have the basic American interest at heart," Bill Moyers wrote Johnson in August 1965, "but we will try to tigthen [*sic*] things up." (LBJ scrawled "good!" at the bottom of the memo.) Administration officials targeted those they considered the opinion makers, that is, leading syndicated columnists (such as James Reston of the *New York Times,* Walter Lippmann of *Newsweek,* and Joseph Kraft of the *Washington Post*), and other leading reporters on national journals. The president, according to documents in the Lyndon Baines Johnson Library at the University of Texas, could never have spent as much time with the correspondents as his staff pleaded with him to do, but he was nevertheless nearly superhuman in his efforts. "He was not only available to reporters," Reston recalled, "but unavoidable. He devoured newspapers every morning in the sure conviction that the entire press corps was conspiring with his enemies to defeat his policies, mock his character, and even vilify his family." Selected journalists were given supposed inside information that discredited the critics, especially those in the intellectual and newspaper communities. An eighty-six-minute "strictly off the record" briefing of John Pomfret of the *New York Times* on June 24, 1965, revealed the Johnson treatment. The president began by bragging about the breadth and intelligence of his advisers; tried (unsuccessfully, in Pomfret's opinion) to justify the war's escalation; intimated that he (LBJ) was taking the careful, middle-of-the-road position, and if he

23. Hammond, *The Military and the Media,* 89–91, 184; Michael Herr, *Dispatches* (New York: Knopf, 1977), 60.

failed the wild right wing would grow dangerously in power; alleged that Lippmann actually supported him privately "but won't in his columns"; declared that "I may never run [for the presidency] again," a remark Pomfret interpreted as an attempt to gain his sympathy; and then showed off his instant phone communications while recounting in vivid language anecdotes about foreign policy and politics. Pomfret came away with an "overall impression: the man is desperately worried about Vietnam and sees no way out."[24]

McGeorge Bundy also spent large chunks of time with close journalist friends, but with much the same result. Bundy, like the rest of the White House staff, had been instructed to inform the president whenever he talked with a journalist and to relay the conversation's content. Bundy lunched often with Lippmann and listened patiently to proposals that the NSC adviser later described to Johnson as "foolish," or indicating that the distinguished columnist may "gradually line himself up on the pro-Communist side" of a proposed peace settlement. Bundy tried to make Lippmann think that the columnist was directly influencing White House speeches and policy. The meetings did not produce the desired results. Two days after one such talk, Lippmann blasted Johnson's South Vietnamese allies, warned that the war was becoming Americanized, and concluded, "There must be negotiations to end it. . . . [O]nly fools will go to the brink and over it."[25]

Bundy had better luck with others, and also with his encouragement to reporters whose stories pleased the administration. He worked on his contacts at *U.S. News and World Report* "to do a long interview on Vietnam with Professor Lucien Pye of M.I.T. . . . who would be both helpful and influential if we can get his views where other reporters will read them." Bundy later deemed the interview, published in October 1965, a success. He worked hard, as did other Johnson aides, on columnist Joseph Kraft, through whom

24. "Mr. President," from Moyers, Handwriting File, August 1–15, 1965, LBJ Library; Reston, *Deadline,* 300; "Strictly off the Record," Pomfret interview with Johnson, June 24, 1965, in Arthur Krock Papers, Princeton University, Princeton, New Jersey; Small, *Johnson, Nixon, and the Doves,* 18.
25. "Memorandum for the President," from McGeorge Bundy, March 20, 1965, National Security File, Subject File, Press Appointments, LBJ Library; "Memorandum to the President," from McGeorge Bundy, April 10, 1965, ibid.; *Newsweek,* April 12, 1965, 25.

the administration made calculated leaks. Bundy nevertheless expressed skepticism in a memorandum to the president:

Kraft . . . is highly impressionable and easily persuaded, if people want to take the time to do it. Ted Sorensen [John Kennedy's closest aide] used to use him as a straight Administration mouthpiece, which took Ted a lot of time. We can do the same if we want to. . . . The question we always face, therefore, is whether to take the time to turn around such rudderless types as Kraft. . . . [26]

Bundy later ripped into Kraft privately when the columnist suggested that the keys to a settlement were the communists in the South rather than Ho Chi Minh's government in the North. Columnist Robert Novak, however, received the full blast of Bundy's temper when at a June 3, 1965, dinner hosted by Katharine Graham, owner of the *Washington Post,* the next day's *Post* was brought in "and Novak foolishly directed our attention to the Evans–Novak column on Dean Rusk. . . . I read it and then tore into him. I pointed out that most of the facts were wrong. . . . I told him that this was as bad a piece of reporting as I had seen in the column, and I was so rough on Rowlie [Evans] that Mary [Bundy's spouse] told me afterwards that I had overdone it."[27]

In reporting such episodes, Bundy perhaps increased his credibility with Johnson, but he and other administration officials did not reverse the growing tide of criticism. On the other hand, although critics influenced the attentive and more knowledgeable audience in the universities and Washington, they did not turn mass public opinion against Johnson's policies in 1965–6. James Reston lamented that the president continually carried public opinion polls in his pocket to show at the slightest opportunity. "Popular support and sound policy," Reston wrote in the November 21, 1965, *New York Times,* "are obviously not the same thing. Nothing was more popular or more disastrous than the isolationist policy of the United States before the two World Wars. . . . The President is still confusing popularity with policy, and this could

26."Memorandum for the President," from McGeorge Bundy, September 23, 1965, National Security File, Subject File, Press Appointments, LBJ Library; "Memorandum for the President, from McGeorge Bundy, September 13, 1965, ibid.
27. "Memorandum for the President," from McGeorge Bundy, June 3, 1965, ibid.

easily lead us deeper into the bog." A year later, *Times* correspondent R. W. Apple Jr. caused a commotion in the White House
when he wrote, "Victory is not close at hand. It may be beyond
reach." Bill Moyers told Johnson on June 6, 1966, that the press
corps believed its relations with the White House "are 'worse than
ever before.' " Three days later, Moyers noted that talks with professional pollsters led to one conclusion: "[O]ur standing is down
and likely to drop further. . . . What is the cause? Unanimously
they agree: Vietnam is the major issue, inflation . . . is next." Moyers quoted pollster Lou Harris as warning that "You will continue
to go down until there is some movement – either toward a military victory or toward a negotiated settlement."[28]

Johnson could find the strategy neither for a victory nor for a settlement. Polls showed that more Americans wanted a victory and
then the troops brought home than wanted a simple pullout. The
president, however, could please neither hawk nor dove, and because he prided himself on bending to neither extreme, his domestic support splintered. White House aides such as Francis Bator
urged him to win back key intellectuals and other critics in 1967
precisely by warning that the president was protecting the nation
against "wild men" in American politics. After a May luncheon in
the White House that failed to sway critical academic guests,
Bator played to Johnson's own prejudices by writing that Zbigniew
Brzezinski of the State Department's Policy Planning Staff "has a
grip on part of the truth when he says that 'the intellectuals' will
never come to like Lyndon Johnson. The people Brzezinski has in
mind don't like politicians to begin with, and have a particularly
hard time trusting Texans." But Bator (who had taught at MIT)
thought "it is dead *wrong* to conclude that the best academics are
hopelessly lost to you – that they are so prejudiced, so bigoted, and
so hostile that their minds are closed to any evidence that conflicts
with the stereotype. A lot of these people were solid for you, not
only in the autumn of 1964 – when it was easy – but before that

28. *New York Times,* November 21, 1965, E1O; Edwin Emery and Michael Emery, *The
    Press and America: An Interpretive History of the Mass Media,* 5th ed., (Englewood
    Cliffs N.J.: Prentice-Hall, 1984), 566; Moyers to the President, June 6, 1966, Moyers
    Folder, 1966–67, Office of the President File, LBJ Library; "Memorandum for the Pres-
    ident," from Moyers, June 9, 1966, Aides' memos on Vietnam, Reference File, Vietnam,
    LBJ Library.

and well into 1965." Bator argued that "they can be convinced that you are dead committed to holding off the wild men and to waging and limiting this painful war with restraint, control, and without the crutch of a simple-minded notion of victory."[29]

In the eyes of many informed Americans, however, Johnson appeared to be joining, not countering, the "wild men." The time seemed ripe for a congressional rebellion, especially after evidence appeared in late 1967 and early 1968 that the Tonkin Gulf crises of 1964 (which the administration had used to trigger the near-unanimous congressional support for LBJ's military response against Vietnam) had, especially in the second attack, not occurred at all, or at least not as Johnson and McNamara had reported the incidents.

Extensive congressional criticism, stretching across parties and geographical sections, nonetheless did not appear between 1965 and 1968. Charles DeBenedetti observes in his superb study of the antiwar movement that "antiwar liberals" and other critics "made little headway . . . in the absence of strong congressional opposition." Johnson's ability to deal with the legislators was famous. "I doubt there has ever been a period in American history," Johnson declared in June 1965, "when the Court and the Congress and the Executive were working more harmoniously." That harmony suffered little discord when Johnson was unable to explain satisfactorily to many why he sent troops into the Dominican Republic and South Vietnam in early 1965, but those actions did raise questions in the mind of Senator Fulbright, chair of the Foreign Relations Committee. The worried Arkansas senator constantly asked Johnson for reassurance. As early as February 1965, LBJ responded to an aide's request that the Johnson and Fulbright families have a "get together" with a scribbled: "He [Fulbright] is a crybaby – and I can't continue to kiss him every morning before breakfast."[30]

Through early 1965 the senator softened his public criticisms after private meetings with the president. The Dominican interven-

29. "Memorandum for the President," from Bator, May 19, 1967, Box 5, Francis Bator personal papers, LBJ Library. I am indebted to Professor Frank Costigliola for a copy of this document.
30. DeBenedetti, *An American Ordeal*, 106–7; John Rourke, *Congress and the Presidency in U.S. Foreign Policymaking* (Boulder, Colo.: Westview Press, 1983), 111; *Public Papers of the Presidents . . . 1965*, 665; Cater to the President, not dated, but probably February 1965, Cater Memos on Vietnam, Reference File, Vietnam, LBJ Library.

tion and his growing sense that Johnson had deceived him about Vietnam in 1964–5 moved Fulbright to the forefront of the opposition. In early 1966, he held extensive televised committee hearings to create a forum for debate about the war. By 1967, Fulbright, known as a conservative on issues of race and presidential power, had expanded his criticism to the larger crisis. "If, as Mr. Rusk tells us," the senator declared at the American Bar Association in August, "only the rain of bombs can bring Ho Chi Minh to reason, why should not the same principle apply at home? Why should not riots and snipers' bullets bring the white man to an awareness of the Negro's plight when peaceful programs for housing and jobs and training have been more rhetoric than reality?"[31]

Fewer than a dozen Democratic senators joined Fulbright in public opposition, and, with the exception of Albert Gore Sr. of Tennessee and John Sherman Cooper of Kentucky, nearly all were from northern states. The Republicans, led by Senate Minority Leader Everett Dirksen of Illinois, attacked from the right. A later study confirmed that bipartisanship on the war measures held up well in the 1960s. It began to decline only in the early 1970s as a result of war-related crises (such as the Watergate scandal and economic problems), but not in the first instance because of the war itself.[32]

Johnson, as Joseph Kraft observed, followed John Kennedy's policy of trying to have "no enemies on the right." The president feared the American right wing more than he did the left of the nation's political spectrum. "I don't give a damn about those little pinkos on the campuses," he told George Ball; "they're just waving their diapers and bellyaching because they don't want to fight. The great black beast for us is the right wing. If we don't get this war over soon they'll put enormous heat on us to turn it into an Armageddon and wreck all our other programs." Johnson nevertheless moved to try to counter the liberal-left critics who were becoming familiar on the multiple television screens in Johnson's

31. Especially interesting is I. F. Stone's review of Tristram Coffin, *Senator Fulbright: Portrait of a Public Philosopher*, in *The New York Review of Books*, December 29, 1966, 5–6; Senator J. William Fulbright, "The Great Society Is a Sick Society," *New York Times Magazine*, August 20, 1967, 90–6.
32. James McCormick and Eugene R. Wittkopf, "Bipartisanship, Partisanship, and Ideology in Congressional–Executive Foreign Policy Relations, 1947–1988," *Journal of Politics* LII (November 1990), 1086, 1097; *New York Times*, December 14, 1965, 6; *New York Times*, February 8, 1966, 10.

office. For example, he dispatched top officials to deal quietly with congressional critics. Ball engaged in a series of lunches to try to neutralize such liberal antiwar critics as Senate Democrats George McGovern of South Dakota and Joseph Tydings of Maryland. Knowing what worked in congressional lobbying, Johnson allowed so many uniformed officers to appear on Capital Hill and television to sell the administration's argument that the *New York Times* warned of a dangerous military influence on decisions that should be made by "civilian branches of government."[33]

The president especially used his top Vietnam commander, General William Westmoreland, at the end of 1967 to assure a joint session of Congress and many media interviewers that the war was finally being won. Then, at the end of January 1968, the Viet Minh launched a Tet offensive that, though it was incredibly costly (some 30,000 Viet Minh died in the fighting), proved to many Americans that Westmoreland and Johnson had deceived them. One of the most widely watched and respected television newscasters, Walter Cronkite of CBS, had not previously questioned the war effort. After Tet, however, he declared that the United States was bogged down in a stalemated war that had to be ended by negotiations from which Americans would not be able to emerge as victors.

Vietnam, as Valenti told Johnson in August 1966, was "the first war totally covered by TV." One U.S. soldier had observed a year earlier: "Cameras. That's all I see wherever I look. Sometimes I'm not sure whether I'm a soldier or an extra in a bad movie." Until 1968, however, television reporting was "strongly supportive" of U.S. actions, according to Daniel Hallin's scholarly analysis. Johnson himself had used television with great effectiveness during the week of the Gulf of Tonkin crises in 1964 to mobilize public and congressional support for his resolutions. In one year he appeared on the medium more than Kennedy had in three or Eisenhower in eight. He demanded, and received, instant access to the networks, with virtually no notice – until, at least, late 1967, when his con-

33. Joseph Kraft, *Profiles in Power* (New York: New American Library, 1965), 16–17; LBJ's fear of the right wing is a theme in Kathleen J. Turner, *Lyndon Johnson's Dual War: Vietnam and the Press* (Chicago: University of Chicago Press, 1985); Hammond, *The Military and the Media*, 249, and also 287–90 for the U.S. military's reluctance to act as propagandists for the war effort; *New York Times*, August 16, 1967, 36; George Ball, "The Rationalist in Power," *New York Review of Books*, April 22, 1993, 34.

stant demands and speeches with little new in them led the networks to begin to refuse his demands and, for the first time, offer Republican leaders the opportunity to respond to Johnson's speeches.[34]

The problem was not antiwar bias on the part of the television networks. Morley Safer's famous 1965 segment showing U.S. Marines torching Vietnamese huts with Zippo lighters led Johnson to order an investigation of Safer's past. The private investigation revealed, in the words of one observer, "possibly to [LBJ's] surprise, that the reporter was not a Communist, merely a Canadian" – or a "cheap Canadian," as the Pentagon's press secretary called Safer. But Johnson's willingness to strong-arm friends like Frank Stanton, head of CBS, and Robert Kittner of NBC – who later worked for the president in the White House and directly interceded in 1966 to assure that the "Today" show would have the proper "balance" – won the support for administration policy from television that it had not been able to get from key print journalists. Leaving little to chance, the president personally briefed (and overwhelmed) reporters like Harry Reasoner of CBS before they went to Vietnam. Bill Moyers meanwhile led a massive White House effort to justify the administration's views to the networks.[35] Then too, as Erik Barnouw has noted, of the hundred largest suppliers for the war effort, "over half were companies heavily involved in broadcasting. . . . There was no conspiracy – there were merely innumerable parallel incentives. They tended to make television entertainment an integral part of the escalation machine." When Fulbright held his dramatic 1966 Senate hearings, CBS decided to air the fifth rerun of an "I Love Lucy" episode (although NBC did carry the proceedings). Television reporting changed markedly after Tet, as Cronkite's turn symbolized, but the turn was late, the White House worked overtime to get its interpretation of the offensive on the airwaves, and – in any case – the public reaction to Tet appears not to have had a decisive impact on

34. "Memorandum for the President," from Valenti, August 23, 1966, Valenti 1965–1966 Folder, Office of the President File, LBJ Library; Stoler, *The War Against the Press,* 57, 60–1; Daniel C. Hallin, *The "Uncensored War": The Media and Vietnam* (New York: Oxford University Press, 1986); Joe S. Foote, *Television Access and Political Power* (New York: Praeger, 1990), 34–6, 38.
35. Stoler, *The War Against the Press,* 66; "Memorandum for the President," from Robert E. Kintner, June 24, 1966, Confidential File, PR 18 (1966), Box 83, LBJ Library.

Johnson's decision to turn down Westmoreland's demand for 206,000 more troops.[36]

As the prowar consensus was finally shattering by early 1968, the Tocqueville problem sharpened to a dangerous edge for Johnson, but not primarily because of television coverage or congressional critics. The breakdown was due more to the intellectuals and university protesters, key members of the print media, and, finally, a series of economic problems in 1967–8 that combined with the Tet offensive's ripping of illusions to convince some of the president's most important advisers, and leading members of the business community for whom many of these advisers spoke, that – as Johnson scribbled in a March 26, 1968, meeting – we "can no longer do the job we set."[37]

The business community, of course, was never monolithic. Crucial reactions of the stock markets and New York City leaders nevertheless told an important story to the White House. When the president announced a peace approach in late 1965, the stock exchanges were hit hard, and one New York broker observed that "a genuine peace offer" could "knock the market out of bed" because of the $60 billion of military spending scheduled for the coming year. The downturn was repeated for similar reasons in February 1966; Wall Street analysts were quoted as believing that peace in Vietnam could cause several months of turmoil in the market.[38] By late 1967, however, the combination of continued violence in the cities and on campuses and a sudden, disastrous inflation that was seen to be war-generated began to haunt New York and Washington. In a post-Tet briefing for Johnson, NSC adviser Walt Whitman Rostow began with an upbeat assessment of the war's progress, then shifted to warn that "the world monetary system has come under heavy pressure" because of British problems, but also because the U.S. balance of payments was deteriorating to the point that gold supplies were becoming "inadequate." The dollar, "the only remaining world currency," was weakening. When

---

36. Barnouw, *Tube of Plenty*, 376–7, 381–4; "Memorandum for Walt Rostow," from William J. Jorden, February 8, 1968, National Security File, Subject File, Press Appointments, LBJ Library; Divine, ed., *Exploring the Johnson Years*, 52.
37. March 26, 1968, personal notes, Handwriting File, LBJ Library.
38. *New York Times*, December 28, 1965, 39; New York *Herald-Tribune*, December 23, 1965, 22; *New York Times*, February 13, 1966, F2.

Washington insider and Johnson intimate Clark Clifford became
Secretary of Defense in 1968, he worked successfully to turn Johnson away from more rapid escalation – not only because Clifford
discovered, to his surprise, that the Pentagon had no idea of how
to end the war successfully but also because after long conversations with the nation's business and legal elite, Clifford reported (in
the words of top White House staff member Harry McPherson)
that "These guys who have been with us and who have sustained
us are no longer with us."[39]

Given the growing economic problems, rising urban demands
and unrest, the dissenting intellectuals' ruthless identification of
the administration's false assumptions and deceits, and Johnson's
inability to devise a strategy to win either the war or a peace, it is
astonishing that the president maintained the consensus and
avoided the Tocqueville problem as long as he did. Rostow correctly concluded, "If the war goes well, the American people are
with us. If the war goes badly they are against us." The dissenting
intellectuals and a relative few reporters and columnists understood at least by 1965 that given the nature of the conflict and the
restraints on U.S. resources, little chance existed for the war to go
well. These dissenters understood also that the United States had
become mired in a thousand-year-old antiforeign war, not another
conventional conflict such as the one a generation earlier in Korea;
they understood, as McNamara understood by 1966, that U.S.
bombing could destroy all of the North Vietnamese oil, power,
port, and water systems, "and they could still carry on;"[40] they understood that U.S. interests in Vietnam were not worth the blood-
letting and treasure that would be the costs in a wider war; and –
above all – they understood, the fragility and possible disasters inherent in a policy of taking democracies into war. As the best U.S.
military analysis of the Tocqueville problem and Vietnam concludes, Americans turned against the war not because of television
or slanted news coverage, but because "Public support for . . . war

39. "Mr. President," from Walt Whitman Rostow, March 15, 1968, National Security File,
    Subject File, Press Contacts – Memos to the President, LBJ Library; Oral History of
    Harry McPherson, tape #5, 16–17, LBJ Library.
40. "Notes of the President's Meeting with Senior Foreign Policy Advisers," February 6, 1968,
    President's Appointment File, LBJ Library; *New York Times,* February 16, 1966, 1.

dropped inexorably by 15 percentage points whenever total U.S. casualties increased by a factor of ten."[41]

On March 12, 1967, Johnson issued three statements that commemorated the twentieth anniversary of the Truman Doctrine. He linked the 1947 pronouncement to his efforts to rebuild a faltering consensus on Vietnam policy: "Today America is again engaged in helping to turn back armed terrorists. As in your day," he told the aged Truman in a public letter, "there are those who believe that effort is too costly. . . . But our people have learned that freedom is not divisible."[42] Johnson, however, would have been better advised to have read not Truman but Tocqueville and to have listened not to the policymakers of 1947 but to the dissenting intellectuals and journalists of 1965.

———————————

I am especially indebted to David Humphrey of the Lyndon Baines Johnson Library and Lizann Rogovoy of Cornell University for their help in researching this essay.

41. Hammond, *The Military and the Media*, 387; this important analysis is published by the Center of Military History, U.S. Army, Washington, D.C.
42. *Public Papers of the Presidents . . . 1967* (Washington, 1968), II, 316–18.

3

"A Time in the Tide of Men's Affairs": Lyndon Johnson and Vietnam

RICHARD H. IMMERMAN

Lyndon B. Johnson transformed the security blanket for South Vietnam he inherited from his predecessors into an armored shield. By 1967 some half-million U.S. troops were engaged in combat, American deaths were approaching 15,000, the Air Force was dropping more bombs than in all the World War II theaters, and the price of the effort exceeded $2 billion per month.[1] Unable nevertheless to achieve a military victory or coerce Hanoi to negotiate on America's terms, Johnson the next year abandoned his quest for reelection. Running in his stead, Hubert H. Humphrey lost to Richard M. Nixon. Johnson's war polarized Americans to an extent unparalleled since the Civil War, shattered the Cold War consensus on foreign policy, crippled the Great Society, and eroded the public's faith and confidence in its government.

Johnson's responsibility for both the Americanization of the war and the peace talks that eventually brought U.S. involvement to a close has skewed the historiography. A disproportionate percentage of the immense scholarship on America in Vietnam focuses on the years from 1964, when the president engineered the Gulf of Tonkin Resolution, which provided the legal mechanism for direct military intervention, to 1968, Johnson's final full year in office.[2]

1. George C. Herring, *America's Longest War: The United States and Vietnam, 1950–1975*, 2nd ed. (New York: Knopf, 1986), 145–7, 174. *The Vietnam War: An Almanac*, general ed. John S. Bowman (New York: World Almanac Publications, 1985), is a convenient chronology and compendium of statistics on the war.
2. On the Gulf of Tonkin Resolution see Joseph C. Goulden, *Truth Is the First Casualty: The Gulf of Tonkin Affair – Illusion and Reality* (New York: Rand McNally, 1969); John Galloway, *The Gulf of Tonkin Resolution* (Rutherford, N.J.: Farleigh Dickinson University Press, 1970); Eugene C. Windchy, *Tonkin Gulf* (Garden City, N.Y.: Doubleday 1971); and Anthony Austin, *The President's War: The Story of the Tonkin Gulf Resolution and How the Nation Was Trapped in Vietnam* (Philadelphia: Lippincott, 1971).

This literature especially highlights the escalation of America's intervention from the February 1965 launching of Rolling Thunder, the sustained (in contrast to retaliatory) bombing campaign of North Vietnam, to July of that year, when Johnson announced what was tantamount to an open-ended commitment to employ American military force to preserve an independent, noncommunist South Vietnam.[3] It likewise concentrates on the prosecution of the air war and strategy of attrition, the communists' 1968 Tet Offensive, and Johnson's subsequent decision to initiate a partial halt to the bombing of North Vietnam and seek a diplomatic settlement.[4]

Because Johnson's quest for an honorable peace proved futile, it has received less scholarly attention.[5] This lacuna is also due to the

3. The excellent literature on Johnson's escalation in 1965 is represented by James Clay Thompson, *Rolling Thunder: Understanding Policy and Program Failure* (Chapel Hill: University of North Carolina Press, 1980); Larry Berman, *Planning a Tragedy: The Americanization of the War in Vietnam* (New York: Norton, 1982); George McT. Kahin, *Intervention: How America Became Involved in Vietnam* (New York: Knopf, 1986); William Conrad Gibbons, *The U.S. Government and the Vietnam War: Executive and Legislative Roles and Relationships, Part III: 1965–1966* (Princeton, N.J.: Princeton University Press, 1988); John P. Burke and Fred Greenstein in collaboration with Larry Berman and Richard H. Immerman, *How Presidents Test Reality: Decisions on Vietnam, 1954 and 1965* (New York: Russell Sage, 1989); Brian Vandemark, *Into the Quagmire: Lyndon Johnson and the Escalation of the Vietnam War* (New York: Oxford University Press, 1990).

4. Illustrative works include Raphael Littauer and Normal Uphoff, eds., *The Air War in Indochina* (Boston: Beacon, 1972); Robert L. Gallucci, *Neither Peace Nor Honor: The Politics of American Military Policy in Vietnam* (Baltimore: Johns Hopkins University Press, 1975); Gunter Lewy, *America in Vietnam* (New York: Oxford University Press, 1978); Harry Summers, *On Strategy: A Critical Analysis of the Vietnam War* (Novato, Calif.: Presidio Press, 1982); Bruce Palmer, *The 25-Year War: America's Military Role in Vietnam* (Lexington: University of Kentucky Press, 1984); Andrew Krepinevich, *The Army and Vietnam* (Baltimore: Johns Hopkins University Press, 1986); Larry Cable, *Unholy Grail: The US and the Wars in Vietnam, 1965–8* (New York: Routledge, 1991); Don Oberdorfer, *Tet!* Garden City, N.Y.: Doubleday, 1971); Peter Braestrup, *Big Story: How the American Press and Television Reported and Interpreted the Crisis of Tet 1968 in Vietnam and Washington*, 2 vols. (Boulder, Colo.: Westview Press, 1977); James J. Wirtz, *The Tet Offensive: Intelligence Failure in War* (Ithaca, N.Y.: Cornell University Press, 1991); Herbert Y. Schandler, *Lyndon Johnson and Vietnam: The Unmaking of a President* (Princeton, N.J.: Princeton University Press, 1983); and Larry Berman, *Lyndon Johnson's War: The Road to Stalemate in Vietnam* (New York: Norton, 1989).

5. The two most meticulous examinations of Johnson's efforts to disengage following Tet – Schandler, *Johnson and Vietnam*, and Berman, *Johnson's War* – conclude with his March 31, 1968, speech. General studies of efforts to negotiate a settlement include Gareth Porter, *A Peace Denied: The United States, Vietnam, and the Paris Agreements* (Bloomington: Indiana University Press, 1975), and Allan E. Goodman, *The Lost Peace: America's Search for a Negotiated Settlement of the Vietnam War* (Stanford, Calif.: Hoover Institution, 1978). Subsequent to their publication the Pentagon Papers docu-

chronological parameters of the so-called "Pentagon Papers" and concomitant archival limitations.[6] The publication of memoirs by former Secretary of State Dean Rusk and former Secretary of Defense Clark Clifford,[7] however, and more significantly the light shed on the administration's last months by the declassification of thousands of pages of documents, demonstrate that the president's inability to get out of Vietnam reflected the dynamics of his policy and the advisory system that produced it throughout his tenure. What emerges from these materials is a president determined not to "lose" Vietnam, to call into question existing international treaty obligations, or otherwise to undermine American credibility. At the same time, Johnson was driven by his perception of the domestic environment, his devotion to the Great Society, and his personality and ambition. Johnson came to grief in Vietnam because of an enemy he could not understand, a client he could not manage, and political forces he could not control.

Notwithstanding the diversity of opinion among students of Johnson and Vietnam, they agree that only reluctantly did he escalate U.S. military involvement. As Senate majority leader in 1954 Johnson had opposed American intervention to relieve the besieged French at Dien Bien Phu, and as vice president he had shared President John F. Kennedy's ambivalence about fighting a war in an inhospitable theater that, like Korea, bordered China. Yet profoundly influenced by the lessons of Munich and the fallout from Mao Zedong's triumph, his resolve to contain North Vietnam was unshakable. To allow the party of Ho Chi Minh and its National Liberation Front (NLF, or Vietcong to Americans) ally to encroach south of the seventeenth parallel, let alone to overthrow the gov-

ments concerned with negotiations were made available. See George C. Herring, ed., *The Secret Diplomacy of the Vietnam War: The Negotiating Volumes of the Pentagon Papers* (Austin: University of Texas Press, 1983). Ronald H. Spector, *After Tet: The Bloodiest Year in Vietnam* (New York: Free Press, 1993), concentrates on military operations and dynamics.

6. The strengths and weaknesses of the various editions of the Pentagon Papers are discussed in George McT. Kahin, "The Pentagon Papers: A Critical Evaluation," *American Political Science Review* 64 (June 1975): 675–84.

7. Dean Rusk as told to Richard Rusk, *As I Saw It*, ed. Daniel S. Papp (New York: Norton, 1990); Clark Clifford with Richard Holbrooke, *Counsel to the President: A Memoir* (New York: Random House, 1991).

ernment of South Vietnam (GVN), would make a mockery of the Southeast Asian Treaty Organization (SEATO) and dangerously tilt the balance of power in Asia and the Pacific, and by extension worldwide, in the communists' favor. Also at risk was Johnson's presidential power and his legislative program. Neither, he believed, could survive the conservative tidal wave he predicted a defeat in Vietnam would generate.

Encroaching on South Vietnam was precisely what the communists were doing when Johnson took office. In the aftermath of the November 1963 assassination of South Vietnamese President Ngo Dinh Diem, the party leadership in Hanoi instructed the NLF to accelerate its political and military operations. The infiltration of North Vietnamese materiel and regular troops into the South increased commensurately. This became a recurrent scenario over the succeeding months as the communists sought to exploit the chronic weakness of the GVN and the constraints inherent in America's political process to bring about a rapid disintegration of South Vietnam, thereby forcing the United States to disengage. They miscalculated. Like his forebearers at the Alamo, Lyndon Johnson would stand and fight. He had pledged to fulfill the Kennedy legacy, and in his mind America's defense of South Vietnam was integral to it. His chief foreign policy aides, Rusk, Secretary of Defense Robert McNamara, and National Security Adviser McGeorge Bundy, all holdovers from the Kennedy era, agreed.[8]

Consequently, albeit incrementally and after anguished deliberation, the administration expanded the American role in Vietnam. Initially Johnson rejected the advice of the Joint Chiefs of Staff (JCS) to initiate an air and ground offensive against North Viet-

8. David Halberstam, *The Best and the Brightest* (New York: Random House, 1969), 401–59; Robert J. Donovan, *Nemesis: Truman and Johnson in the Coils of War in Asia* (New York: St. Martin's Press, 1984), 38–45. Had he lived Johnson would have summarily dismissed the argument, most recently advanced in Oliver Stone's film *JFK* and John M. Newman's monograph *JFK and Vietnam: Deception, Intrigue, and the Struggle for Power* (New York: Warner Books, 1992), that Kennedy intended to withdraw U.S. forces from Vietnam. He looked on "his task as a partnership with President Kennedy," Johnson told Robert Kennedy in April 1968, and "felt President Kennedy was looking down on what he had done and would approve." Notwithstanding Johnson's political motives, his sentiments appear genuine. Walt Rostow, Memorandum of Conversation, April 3, 1968, Box 5, "Kennedy, Robert F.," Files of Walt W. Rostow, Box 5, National Security File, Papers of Lyndon B. Johnson, Lyndon Baines Johnson Library, Austin, Texas (unless otherwise indicated, hereafter all archival references are from the Papers of Lyndon B. Johnson).

nam. He hoped that it would suffice for America's military to "do more of the same" but to "do it more efficiently."[9] The continued deterioration of the situation in South Vietnam extinguished this hope. Henceforth, Johnson concluded, the United States would have to do more. But even then he sought to do enough but not too much. Johnson carefully calibrated America's response to North Vietnam in order to prevent its conquest of the South without alienating international opinion, overextending America's global strategic posture, precipitating direct Chinese or Soviet intervention, or disrupting the economic and political bases of his domestic program.[10]

Beginning shortly after the 1964 election, Johnson cast the die for his presidency's conduct in Vietnam. Already he had on hand the August Tonkin Gulf Resolution, by which Congress authorized Johnson to take whatever measures he deemed necessary to protect U.S. forces and to deter further aggression.[11] Also on hand was a strategy formulated in the Pentagon gradually to intensify American military pressure north of the seventeenth parallel. A compromise between continuing the existing policy indefinitely and escalating rapidly and comprehensively, and designed to induce Hanoi to cease supporting the southern insurgency, curtail the traffic along the Ho Chi Minh Trail, and boost South Vietnam's morale, the strategy had as its linchpin sustained bombing attacks against select North Vietnamese targets. In February 1965 Johnson implemented Rolling Thunder.[12]

Soon thereafter, regular U.S. ground troops arrived in Vietnam. To safeguard the primary air base, in March two battalions of Marines splashed ashore near Danang. The line against their introduction had been breached, with predictable consequences. The next month Johnson approved the deployment of 40,000 additional troops in order to secure additional bases. Then in June Gen-

9. Doris Kearns, *Lyndon Johnson and the American Dream* (New York: Harper & Row, 1976), 196.
10. Alain C. Enthoven and K. Wayne Smith, *How Much Is Enough? Shaping the Defense Program, 1961–1969* (New York: Harper & Row, 1971).
11. The verbatim Gulf of Tonkin Resolution is published in U.S. Congress, Senate, Subcommittee on Public Buildings and Grounds, *The Pentagon Papers* [*The Senator Gravel Edition*], 4 vols. (Boston: Beacon, 1971) 3:722.
12. The most recent examinations of the strategy's origins are Burke and Greenstein, *How Presidents Test Reality*, 121–49; Vandemark, *Into the Quagmire*, 23–38.

eral William Westmoreland, appointed the previous year to head the United States Military Assistance Command, Vietnam (MACV), requested 150,000 more. His request triggered within the administration an intense debate that has been scrutinized elsewhere.[13] Johnson recognized that if he acceded to Westmoreland he would be opening a new chapter in the conflict, one that would dramatically increase its cost and be very difficult to close. To refuse, however, would risk domestic turmoil reminiscent of the Joseph McCarthy era, turmoil inimical to Johnson's legislative agenda. Johnson also feared that saying no to Westmoreland would be equivalent to saying yes to communist aggression everywhere. Hence, although the president listened attentively to dissenters, most notably Undersecretary of State George Ball, and peppered the JCS and other advocates of escalation with probing questions, he sought confirmation of his predispositions rather than challenges to them.[14] Westmoreland would get his troops. But before making his final decision, Johnson used his trademark political skills to forge a consensus within his administration and Congress. And when he publicly announced his intentions on July 28, 1965, he artfully concealed their extent – and his own reservations.[15]

Neither Johnson nor any of his advisers were under the illusion that with these additional troops MACV could accomplish anything more than prevent South Vietnam's collapse. Westmoreland had conceded that to turn the tide against the Communists in order to force a settlement on American terms (he never estimated the requirements for a military victory) more troops would be needed in the future – many more.[16] Johnson was prepared to give them to him, and he was also prepared to intensify the bombing of the North. What he was not prepared to do was place the United States on a war footing by raising taxes or calling up the reserves, nor

13. See especially Berman, *Planning a Tragedy*, 68–129; Burke and Greenstein, *How Presidents Test Reality*, 195–254; Vandemark, *Into the Quagmire*, 153–214.
14. Burke and Greenstein, *How Presidents Test Reality*, 144–5, 343–4. For an opposing argument, see David M. Barrett, "Secrecy and Openness in Lyndon Johnson's White House: Political Style, Pluralism, and the Presidency," *Review of Politics* 54 (1992): 72–111.
15. "The President's News Conference of July 28, 1965," *Public Papers of the Presidents of the United States: Lyndon B. Johnson, 1965* (Washington: Government Printing Office, 1966), 794–803.
16. Westmoreland's estimate is analyzed in *Pentagon Papers [Gravel ed.]* 3:481.

would he allow the military to bomb Hanoi, mine Haiphong harbor, or take any other action that might provoke Chinese or Soviet intervention. He paid obsessive attention to the conduct of the war, rising in the middle of the night to read situation and casualty reports and devoting endless hours to monitoring operations in order to assure that the United States steered prudently between withdrawal and total commitment.[17] Johnson would follow the path of controlled escalation that Kennedy had applied to the Cuban Missile Crisis.[18] To proceed differently, he was convinced, would unleash America's right wing, demand unacceptable sacrifices from the public, undermine the free world's system of collective security, or increase the risk of World War III. From Johnson's perspective, moreover, these possibilities were not mutually exclusive.

There were two essential requisites for the success of what Johnson insisted remain a limited war.[19] On the one hand, the United States had to inflict so much pain on the communists and so diminish their capacity to wage war that they would abandon their aggression and concede to American terms. On the other hand, the GVN and Army of the Republic of Vietnam (ARVN) had to develop sufficient support from the indigenous population and military capability for South Vietnam to stand on their own. Neither happened. The alienation of the GVN from the people, especially in the countryside, progressively worsened, exacerbated by endemic corruption and incessant feuding between such rivals as Nguyen Van Thieu and Nguyen Cao Ky. What is more, the greater the burden assumed by America's military, the less inclined the ARVN was to shoulder any of it. As for North Vietnam's pain threshold, it appeared nonexistent, and the losses to its military equipment and supplies caused by the bombing were compensated by aid from the Soviet Union and China.[20]

Citing body counts, kill ratios, and similar indices, the administration nevertheless claimed that it was winning. A growing num-

17. Rusk, *As I Saw It,* 338; Burke and Greenstein, *How Presidents Test Reality,* 239.
18. Vandemark, *Into the Quagmire,* 114–15.
19. George C. Herring, " 'Cold Blood': LBJ's Conduct of Limited War in Vietnam," *The [U.S. Air Force Academy] Harmon Memorial Lectures in Military History* 33 (1990): 1–34.
20. On North Vietnam's behavior during the war, see Jon M. Van Dyke, *North Vietnam's Strategy for Survival* (Palo Alto, Calif.: Pacific Books, 1972), and Gabriel Kolko, *Anatomy of a War: Vietnam, the United States, and the Modern Historical Experience*

ber of antiwar protesters and critics in Congress felt otherwise. So, too, did key architects of the Vietnam strategy. By 1967 Robert McNamara, the official most closely associated with the escalation, was advising Johnson that neither the bombing campaign nor ground operations had produced the desired effect on Hanoi or Saigon, but they had cost the United States dearly in the hearts and minds of America and the world. He also doubted whether the domestic and international economies could sustain Johnson's program of guns and butter. McNamara recommended placing a ceiling on U.S. force levels, reassessing Westmoreland's search-and-destroy tactics, completely or at least partially halting the bombing of North Vietnam, and launching a new American peace initiative. Johnson would have nothing to do with such defeatism. If anything his secretary of defense's defection stiffened his resolve to persevere. When the top position at the World Bank became vacant at the end of the year, Johnson appointed McNamara to it.[21]

Then came the Tet Offensive. In the early morning hours of January 30, 1968, a team of Vietcong sappers assaulted the U.S. embassy in Saigon. Practically every South Vietnamese city simultaneously came under attack. Apparently the manifest weaknesses of the GVN had persuaded the communists that they would be greeted by the South Vietnamese with open arms, and they expected America's upcoming election and the increased domestic disaffection with the war to constrain Johnson's response. Probably Hanoi did envision a military victory. Failing that, it sought at the very least to pressure Washington to stop the bombing and to

(New York: Pantheon, 1985). Examinations of the GVN and ARVN include Joseph Buttinger, *Vietnam: A Political History* (New York: Praeger, 1968); Francis Fitzgerald, *Fire in the Lake: The Vietnamese and Americans in Vietnam* (Boston: Little, Brown, 1972); and Kahin, *Intervention*. For the roles of the Soviet Union and the People's Republic of China, see Donald Zagoria, *Vietnam Triangle: Moscow, Peking, Hanoi* (New York: Pegasus, 1967); W. R. Smyser, *Independent Vietnamese: Vietnamese Communism Between Russia and China, 1956–1969* (Athens: Ohio University Press, 1980); Daniel S. Sapp, *Vietnam: The View from Moscow, Peking, Washington* (Jefferson, N.C.: McFarland, 1981); William J. Duiker, *China and Vietnam: The Roots of Conflict* (Berkeley: University of California Press, 1986); and Douglas Pike, *Vietnam and the Soviet Union: Anatomy of an Alliance* (Boulder, Colo.: Westview Press, 1987).

21. Lyndon Baines Johnson, *The Vantage Point: Perspectives of the Presidency, 1963–1969* (New York: Holt, Rinehart & Winston, 1971), 372–8; 600–1; Berman, *Johnson's War,* 93–113. For the shift in McNamara's views, see Deborah Shapley, *Promise and Power: The Life and Times of Robert McNamara* (Boston: Little, Brown, 1993), 405–37.

agree to a settlement that called for the withdrawal of U.S. forces and the establishment of a coalition government.[22]

To a degree less than it had hoped for but more than Johnson would admit, Hanoi succeeded. The South Vietnamese did not embrace their liberators, with American encouragement and assistance both the GVN and ARVN performed credibly, and after horrific destruction and loss of life on all sides the communists were everywhere repulsed. That they could have launched such a massive and coordinated offensive and managed if only temporarily to take control of putatively secure urban centers, nevertheless, suggested to many Americans that the light at the end of the tunnel was much dimmer than they had been led to believe. "I thought we were winning the war," sputtered an aghast Walter Cronkite.[23] Further, in order to defeat the offensive, shore up his defenses, and regain the initiative, General Westmoreland once again requested additional troops. As in 1965, his request ignited an administration debate that would set Johnson's future policy in Vietnam.

By the time of the Tet Offensive Johnson had developed the mentality of a man surrounded by enemies. Agents in the pay of the Soviets, he remarked, were operating throughout the United States to undermine his efforts. Their goal was to "discredit this government and its military establishment," and abetted by the press, academics, and politicians they were making progress. Johnson felt let down even by his own advisers. You have "counseled, advised, consulted, and then – as usual – placed the monkey on my back," he complained to his senior officials. This is not to say that Johnson was uncertain what to do with it. First he demanded improved public relations. Second, he ruled out any talk of surrender. "We are going to stand up out there," he vowed. "If it takes more men to avoid defeat let's get them. . . . If we have to move quickly I want to be ready. If we have to call up more troops let's make the preparations now."[24]

22. Wirtz, *The Tet Offensive*, 51–83.   23. Quoted in Oberdorfer, *Tet*, 158.
24. Notes of the President's Meeting with the Democratic Leadership, January 23, 1968, "January 23, 1968, Democratic Congressional Leadership," Box 2, Tom Johnson Notes; Notes of the President's Meeting with Senior Foreign Policy Advisers, February

Johnson was right to suspect that his advisers, and not just Mc-Namara, no longer shared his resolve. Except for Rusk, National Security Adviser Walt Rostow, and Ambassador to Saigon Ellsworth Bunker, hardly any civilians in the administration were keen on increasing America's force levels. In the aftermath of Tet, Westmoreland galvanized an incipient opposition. Pessimistic about the prospects for the war of attrition, for the past year MACV in consultation with the JCS had been planning to initiate an "alternate," more aggressive strategy. It would require an "optimum force" increment of about 200,000 U.S. troops.[25] Invited by JCS chairman Earle C. Wheeler on February 8 to request reinforcements, Westmoreland then jumped at the opportunity to implement the plans. He asked for the 82nd Airborne and 69th Marine divisions. Predictably, Wheeler immediately endorsed the request. He warned, however, that in order to avoid depleting America's strategic reserve Johnson would have to authorize extending the present terms of service and calling up additional reserves. "I want to point out, Mr. President," Wheeler added, "that . . . I know this will be a serious problem for you politically."[26]

Indeed, politics weighed as heavily on policymaking as did the military exigencies. Fearing "the possibility of civil disturbances here in the U.S.," McNamara advised against further deployments, especially if it meant calling up reserves.[27] General Maxwell Taylor favored the deployments, but for reasons similar to McNamara's opposed a reserve call-up. Clark Clifford, whose long relationship with Johnson, reputation for loyalty, and political acumen drove

6, 1968, "February 6, Senior Foreign Policy Advisers," ibid.; Notes of President's Tuesday Luncheon Meeting, February 6, 1968, "February 6, 1968, Tuesday Luncheon," ibid.; Notes of the President's Meeting with Senior Foreign Policy Advisers, February 9, 1968, "February 9, 1968, Senior Foreign Policy Advisers," ibid.

25. Charles F. Brower IV, "Strategic Reassessment in Vietnam: The Westmoreland 'Alternate Strategy' of 1967–1968," *Naval War College Review* 44 (Spring 1991): 20–51; William C. Westmoreland [Paul L. Miles], "The Origins of the Post-Tet 1968 Plans for Additional American Forces in RVN," November 9, 1968, Papers of William C. Westmoreland (currently in Box 3, Declassified and Sanitized Documents and Unprocessed Files [hereafter, DSDUF]).

26. JCS 01529, Wheeler to Westmoreland, February 8, 1968, "Westmoreland Papers, 'Eyes Only' Message File: February 1–29, 1968," currently in Box 3, DSDUF; Westmoreland to Wheeler, February 8, 1968, ibid.; Notes of the President's Meeting with the Joint Chiefs of Staff, February 9, 1968, "February 9, 1968, Joint Chiefs of Staff," Box 2, Tom Johnson Notes.

27. McNamara remained in the cabinet through the end of February in order to complete work on the budget.

his selection as McNamara's successor, pinpointed the problem. How could the administration justify a request for additional reservists, he asked, after it had publicly claimed that Tet represented a desperate attempt by the communists to stave off defeat, and they had failed?[28]

Confronted with a seemingly irreconcilable dilemma, decision makers may avoid making a choice by reevaluating the risk of inaction.[29] The administration's deliberations exhibited this dynamic. At a meeting the day after the debate over calling up reservists, Wheeler and Rusk argued that Westmoreland had not asked for additional troops. Taylor responded that he had read Westmoreland's cables, and he could not understand how anyone could deny that the general had made the request. He advised the president to send Wheeler to Saigon to clear up the confusion. Johnson agreed that the reports of Wheeler and Rusk did not square with the intelligence he had received. He understood that Tet's climax remained ahead. Therefore it did not make sense that " 'Just before the battle Mother' the JCS is now recommending against deploying emergency troop units. . . . In my mind I think he [Westmoreland] really wants more troops." Sending Wheeler to speak with Westmoreland would attract too much publicity. He would send Deputy Secretary of Defense Cyrus Vance, already in South Korea in connection with the *Pueblo* affair, instead. The meeting, then, provided Johnson with a rationale to reserve judgment and a hope that, by doing so, his problem would go away.[30]

It did not. Westmoreland's cable the next day clarified matters but injected another and most critical variable into the equation: was the administration willing to turn its tactical defeat of the communists into a strategic victory that could win the war? Indeed, MACV's commander portrayed Tet as the catalyst necessary for

28. Notes of the President's Meeting with the Senior Foreign Affairs Advisory Council, February 10, 1968, "February 10, 1968, Senior Foreign Affairs Advisory Council," Box 2, Tom Johnson Notes; Maxwell T. Taylor Memorandum for the President, February 10, 1968, "March 31st Speech, vol. 8, Excerpts and Taylor's Memos," Box 49, March 31st Speech, National Security Council History, National Security File (hereafter NSCH, NSF).
29. Irving L. Janis and Leon Mann, *Decisionmaking: A Psychological Analysis of Conflict, Choice, and Commitment* (New York: Free Press, 1977), 91–5.
30. Notes of the President's Meeting with Senior Foreign Policy Advisers, February 11, 1968, "February 11, 1968, Senior Foreign Policy Advisers," Box 2, Tom Johnson Notes. On the *Pueblo* affair see Trevor Ambrister, *A Matter of Accountability: The Study of the Pueblo Affair* (New York: Coward-McCann, 1970).

him to launch his planned offensive campaign. Because he had them on the ropes, Westmoreland maintained, Hanoi's leaders had abandoned their strategy of protracted warfare in favor of scoring a knockout punch during America's election year. Their failure notwithstanding, the military balance left them no alternative but to continue. For this reason, Westmoreland explained, he needed immediate reinforcements to hold the line. The additional manpower, moreover, would allow him to "capitalize" on the enemy's losses. Johnson and his advisers, working as usual without an agenda or strategic plan that related means to goals, had concentrated exclusively on the present. Westmoreland addressed the future. "We are now in a new ball game" that presented a "situation of great opportunity," he wrote. "Exploiting this opportunity could materially shorten the war."[31]

Westmoreland's perspective and assessment electrified the administration's hawks – and provided the answer to Clifford's question. "Herewith Westy's message: loud and clear and, in my judgment, correct," read Rostow's cover memorandum to Johnson. Westmoreland "wants to shorten the war," said Rusk, and that "has a certain attractiveness to all of us." Taylor concurred and advised Johnson to approve "the dispatch without delay of additional forces." But McNamara remained reluctant, and Clifford expressed misgivings over the imprecision of Westmoreland's analysis. Johnson, too, was worried. He would feel more comfortable, he averred, if Vance had already spoken with Westmoreland. The president explained, "I have a mighty big stake in this. I am more unsure every day." Still, after polling his senior advisers, and hearing no objections, Johnson said, "Let's do it." He authorized sending Westmoreland 10,500 reinforcements.[32]

Before Johnson would send more, he wanted to know how large the reserve call-up would have to be, how much it would cost, and what were the political implications. Answers required

31. MAC 0197, Westmoreland to Wheeler, February 12, 1968, "March 31st Speech, vol. 2, Tabs a–z," Box 47, March 31st Speech, NSCH, NSF.
32. Rostow memorandum to the President, February 12, 1968, ibid.; Taylor memorandum for the President, February 12, 1968, "March 31st Speech, vol. 8, Excerpts and Taylor's memos," Box 49, ibid.; Notes of President's Meeting with Senior Foreign Policy Advisers, February 12, 1968, "February 12, 1968, Senior Foreign Policy Advisers," Box 2, Tom Johnson Notes.

Westmoreland's providing specific data as to his needs, both for securing the South and initiating a counter-offensive. To get them, Johnson decided to send Wheeler to Saigon after all. The JCS chairman left on February 21. For three days he held talks with Westmoreland; his deputy, General Creighton Abrams; Bunker; South Vietnamese President Thieu; and other military and political officials. The consensus was that "1968 will be the pivotal year," Wheeler wrote Johnson in a memorandum dated February 27, the day he departed from Saigon. One side will gain the "decisive advantage." Americans needed 205,000 additional troops to ensure it was not the communists.[33]

That same day Johnson's national security managers met in the president's absence to discuss Wheeler's memorandum. The assessment was much more grim than Westmoreland had led them to expect. Hardly in a position to seize the initiative, MACV's margin was "paper thin . . . and we can expect some cliff-hangers." Westmoreland lacked a theater reserve, and with the ARVN having withdrawn from the countryside to protect the cities, he was overextended. To defend against continued communist pressure, he wanted 105,000 more troops by May 1, and the remaining 100,000 in two installments by the end of the year. Even with an increased draft, these numbers would require a minimum reserve call-up of 150,000 men. It would also add at least another $10 billion appropriation for fiscal year 1969 and add an automatic $5 billion to the fiscal year 1970 military budget. Johnson's advisers were horrified by the request, with only Rostow unequivocally in favor. But the only alternatives seemed to be withdrawal or sending in another 500,000 troops. No one advocated leaving force levels where they were; the status quo was patently insufficient. The question of revising strategy arose, but none could be agreed on. Nor was there agreement on how any of MACV's plight could be explained to the public and to Congress. "This is unbelievable and

33. Notes of the President's Luncheon Meeting with Rusk, McNamara et al., February 13, 1968, "February 13, 1968, Tuesday Luncheon Group," ibid.; Notes of the President's Luncheon Meeting with Foreign Policy Advisers, February 20, 1968, "February 20, 1968, Tuesday Luncheon Group," ibid.; Wheeler memorandum for the President, "Military Situation and Requirements in South Vietnam," February 27, 1968, "Vietnam (March 19, 1970, Memo to the President [III])," Box 127, Country File, Vietnam, National Security File (hereafter CF, V, NSF). See also Clifford. *Counsel to the President,* 479–83.

futile, commented White House special assistant and speechwriter Harry McPherson. He wondered whether Johnson's advisers would present their doubts to the president.[34]

To an extent atypical for the Johnson administration, they did. Following the meeting Rostow wrote the president at the LBJ Ranch. After reviewing the debate, he recommended that Johnson decide nothing until he had heard from Wheeler personally. It might be wise, in fact, to put together a "team" to consider the options, perhaps with Clifford serving as chair. Johnson returned to Washington on February 28 and that morning convened his senior advisers. Wheeler summarized his memorandum. In his judgment, if Westmoreland did not receive the additional troops he would have to retreat from vital areas. What about taking the initiative, Johnson asked? Did Westmoreland have any "surprise moves of his own"? No, replied Wheeler, notwithstanding his participation in MACV's planning for an alternate strategy. Johnson adopted Rostow's suggestion. He established a task force under Clark Clifford to assess the military, diplomatic, political, and budgetary implications of Westmoreland's request and to examine available options. In the words of the "Pentagon Papers" authors, a "fork in the road had been reached."[35]

The administration never unambiguously decided which fork to take. Clifford played a pivotal role, however, in influencing the direction toward which it veered. In his memoir Clifford claims that by this time, "deep in the privacy of" his mind, his "disillusionment with the war was already well advanced."[36] If so, Johnson and Rostow were unaware of it when they selected him to chair the task force. Clifford had opposed the escalation of America's military commitment in 1965, but after the decision he had supported the

34. Wheeler memorandum for the President, February 27, 1968; Harry McPherson Notes of Meeting, February 27, 1968, "February 27, 1968, Meeting of Advisers on Vietnam," Box 2, Meeting Notes File.
35. Rostow memorandum for the President, February 27, 1968, "Vietnam: January – February 1968," Box 6, Files of Walt W. Rostow, NSF; Notes of the President's Meeting to Discuss General Wheeler's Trip to Vietnam, February 28, 1968, "February 28, 1968, Senior Advisers on Vietnam," Box 2, Tom Johnson Notes; Johnson memorandum to the Secretaries of State and Defense, February 28, 1968, "Vietnam, March 12 and 13, 1970, Memos to the President re: Townsend Hoopes," Box 127, CF, V, NSF; Rostow memorandum for the President, February 28, 1968, ibid.; Rostow memorandum for President Johnson, March 12, 1970, ibid.; *Pentagon Papers [Gravel ed.]*, 4:549.
36. Clifford, *Counsel to the President*, 492–3.

war effort unreservedly. Indeed, when McNamara had proposed de-escalation and negotiations in late 1967, Clifford had encouraged Johnson to stay the course. Now the president and his hawkish national security adviser no doubt expected him to behave similarly and use his considerable political skill to build a consensus in the administration in favor of committing the additional forces.[37] Clifford might have tried had he not recognized that he could not build a consensus within the nation. The evidence suggests that he was not so disillusioned with the war as he was with the political fallout from it. "I hope we do not have to ask for a completely new program," he said shortly after Tet. "This is a bad time for it." How do we avoid "creating the feeling that we are pounding troops down a rathole?" he had asked at the meeting on February 27. At no time subsequently did Clifford receive a satisfactory answer.[38]

What he received was a rude awakening. As a Democratic stalwart, Johnson confidant, and periodic consultant, Clifford had been frequently briefed on developments in Vietnam. He had, moreover, participated in White House meetings prior to taking office on March 1. In the context of the task force, however, he was bombarded by the views of subordinate officials, especially those in the Pentagon whose views paralleled, or were even more extreme than, McNamara's – in particular, Deputy Secretary of Defense Paul Nitze and Paul Warnke, the assistant secretary of defense for international affairs. Warnke had never been enthusiastic about the war, and his reservations had grown with the lack of progress. Nitze had converted from a hawk to a dove when he concluded that the effort undermined America's strategic relationship with the Soviet Union. Traveling different paths, each was convinced by 1968 that the war in Vietnam was unwinnable.[39]

They convinced Clifford as well.[40] The task force was composed of representatives from State, Defense, the JCS, Treasury, and the

---

37. Vandemark, *Into the Quagmire*, 202–7; Berman, *Johnson's War*, 93–109; Schandler, *Johnson and Vietnam*, 121–2.
38. Notes of Meeting of Senior Foreign Affairs Advisory Council, February 10, 1968; McPherson Notes of Meeting, February 27, 1968; Clifford, *Counsel to the President*, 473–5.
39. Schandler, *Johnson and Vietnam*, 124–8; Clifford, *Counsel to the President*, 491.
40. Clark M. Clifford, "A Vietnam Appraisal: The Personal History of One Man's View and How It Evolved," *Foreign Affairs* 47 (July 1969): 609–13.

CIA. Of the many papers written, nevertheless, those generated by the Pentagon's civilians were the most influential, and the most pessimistic. Warnke supervised their drafting, and among those who participated were Townsend Hoopes, Alain Enthoven, and Morton Halperin. The fundamental argument was that an increase in force levels could not bring about a successful conclusion to the war because the communists could compensate. The best that could be expected would be indefinite stalemate, which the American economy and its political complexion could not sustain without disastrous effects. Further, the introduction of additional U.S. forces would signal both the GVN and ARVN that they could rely that much more on their patrons, making them less disposed to adopt the recommended reforms that everyone in Washington agreed were essential. "There is a valid strategic principle that cautions against reinforcing weakness," read one draft, and "there is a point at which the price can become so high as to impair our ability to achieve other, and equally important, foreign policy objectives." MACV should redefine its mission, Warnke's shop proposed. Rather than attempt to search out and destroy communists, America's military should concentrate on denying the enemy access to a "demographic frontier" by providing security to the population centers of South Vietnam. This posture would allow time for – and force – the South Vietnamese themselves to develop the capability to govern and defend effectively.[41]

The State Department, under the direction of William Bundy, assistant secretary of state for Far Eastern Affairs, submitted a paper on negotiations. The United States, it held, had four options. The first was to stand pat on the San Antonio formula, named for the city where Johnson had announced it in a September 1967 speech. The formula stipulated that the United States would cease

41. "The Case Against Further Significant Increases in U.S. Forces in Vietnam," March 3, 1968, "March 31st Speech, vol. 7, Meeting with the President and Draft Memos," March 31st Speech, NSCH, NSF; "Memorandum on Strategic Guidance," March 3, 1968, ibid.; "Further Memorandum on Strategic Guidance, March 3, 1968, ibid.; "Necessity for In-Depth Study of Vietnam Policy and Strategic Guidance," n.d., ibid. "Increasing the Effectiveness of Vietnamese Efforts in Conjunction with U.S. Troop Increase," n.d., ibid.; *Pentagon Papers [Gravel ed.]*, 4:546–84. For a dated but still instructive discussion of the Clifford Task Force, see Schandler, *Johnson and Vietnam*. 133–80.

bombing the North if Hanoi agreed not to take military advantage and to enter into prompt discussions of a settlement.[42] Alternatively, advised the State Department, Johnson could advance a new initiative, in public or privately, that involved a change in the formula. Or, as a third option, the administration could do nothing for the present but make a "strong move for negotiations when and if we have countered Hanoi's offensive." Finally, the United States could cease bombing unconditionally and wait for the communists to respond. None of the options looked good to State, which held that the communists were unlikely to accept a peace on any terms other than their own, that they would undoubtedly take advantage of a bombing halt, and that Saigon would oppose any talks at this time. The task force, accordingly, excluded negotiations from further consideration.[43]

The Central Intelligence Agency (CIA) agreed with Defense. The JCS did not. Wheeler was "appalled" by the civilians' diagnosis and described their prescription as "fatally flawed." Faced with this implacable opposition, and probably the president's as well, Clifford refused to endorse his subordinates' proposals. He instructed the task force to arrive at a compromise. The memorandum Clifford sent to Johnson recommended that as close to May as possible Westmoreland receive an estimated 22,000 more troops to meet his immediate needs. It also recommended a reserve call-up sufficient to fulfill the entire 205,000 request should Johnson decide to do so. But that decision should be delayed pending an in-depth study of "possible new political and strategic guidance for the conduct of U.S. operations in South Vietnam, and of our Vietnamese policy in the context of our world-wide politico-military [sic] strategy." Regardless of the result of this review, Clifford added, future increases in America's force levels in Vietnam should be made contingent on the improved performance of both the

42. On the San Antonio formula, see Herring, ed., *The Secret Diplomacy of the Vietnam War,* 522, 537–44, 726–71.
43. "Negotiating Posture Options, and Possible Diplomatic Actions," n.d., "March 31st Speech, vol. 7, Meeting with President and Draft Memos," Box 49, March 31st Speech, NSCH, NSC; "Option A Delayed: Stop Bombing and Naval Bombardment of North Viet-Nam," n.d., "March 31st Speech, vol. 7, Advisory Group Papers," Box 49, ibid.; W. P. Bundy First Draft, "Options on Our Negotiating Posture," February 29, 1968, "March 31st Speech, vol. 3, Tabs RR–ZZ and a–d," Box 47, ibid.

GVN and ARVN. The United States should begin at once to apply maximum pressure on Saigon to induce this improvement.[44]

On March 4 Rostow wrote Johnson that Clifford's memorandum would be ready for discussion at 5:30 that afternoon.[45] Although neither he nor anyone else had had time to read it, the president met with his senior aides at 5:33. "There is a deep-seated concern by your advisers," Clifford said by way of introduction. "There is a concern that if we say yes [to Westmoreland and Wheeler] and step up with the addition of 205,000 more men that we might continue down the road as we have been without accomplishing our purpose." There was no reason to expect the enemy not to match American increases, the new secretary of defense continued. Consequently, there was reason to expect Westmoreland to request "another 200,000 to 300,000 men with no end in sight."

To Clifford and the task force, the war's toll on America's economy, strategic posture, and political stability demanded an end. Therefore, recommending that Westmoreland receive the reinforcements required by the present emergency was "*as far as we are willing to go.*" The task force might be willing to go farther in the future, Clifford asserted, but only after Westmoreland's strategy was reexamined, the South Vietnamese demonstrated the willingness to take on greater responsibility for their defense, and America's strategic reserve was replenished by a call-up of units and individuals, an increase in the draft, and an extension of terms of service. This last condition, moreover, required a new fiscal program, including tax increases and cuts in domestic spending.[46]

Because Clifford provided robust evidence that it was beyond America's present capabilities to meet Westmoreland's full request under any circumstances yet did not rule out fulfilling it at a later date, made no mention of the bombing campaign, and sidestepped the issue of negotiations, he forfeited the opportunity to advocate

44. Central Intelligence Agency memorandum, "Questions Concerning the Situation in Vietnam," March 1, 1968, "March 31st Speech, vol. 8, Draft Memos for the President," Box 49, ibid.; *Pentagon Papers [Gravel ed.]*, 4:550–3, 575–6; Clifford memorandum for the President, March 4, 1968, "March 31st Speech, vol. 7, Meeting with the President and Draft Memos," Box 49, March 31st Speech, NSCH, NSC.
45. Rostow Memorandum for the President, "The Clifford Committee," March 4, 1968, "Memos to the President/Walt Rostow, vol. 65," Box 30, NSF.
46. Notes of the President's Meeting with Senior Foreign Policy Advisers, March 4, 1968, "March 4, 1968, Senior Foreign Policy Advisers," Box 2, Tom Johnson Notes.

a fundamental change in policy, critics have charged. He acknowledged that the United States had reached a fork but "seemed to recommend that we continue rather haltingly down the same road, meanwhile consulting the map more frequently and in greater detail to insure that we were still on the right road."[47] This criticism is not without foundation; Clifford himself pleads guilty to it.[48] It underestimates, however, the most profound impact of Clifford's task force. Up until now Johnson, his reservations notwithstanding, had assumed that he would grant Westmoreland's request just as he had all previous ones.[49] As before, he used his advisory process to reinforce and generate support for his predispositions. The task force proved less susceptible to such manipulation than any of its predecessors. That someone like Clark Clifford, whose political instincts and loyalty Johnson trusted, would sign onto its conclusions and candidly present them deeply troubled the president. In terms of Johnson's decision making on Vietnam, what happened at the March 4 meeting was unprecedented; policy would never be the same.[50]

Johnson never formally approved – or disapproved – Clifford's memorandum. He instructed Wheeler to inform Westmoreland that for the time being 22,000 more troops was the maximum the United States could afford to send him but *"no decision has yet been made"* on the request.[51] Yet by deferring judgment on Clifford's recommendations, Johnson propelled the administration down a track that went beyond them. Almost all the president's senior advisers, including Clifford, held that the current environment in Vietnam was inappropriate for a new peace initiative. Rusk

47. *Pentagon Papers* [*Gravel ed.*], 4: 583–4. See also Schandler, *Johnson and Vietnam,* 173–6.
48. Clifford, *Counsel to the President,* 494–5.   49. Johnson, *Vantage Point,* 406–7.
50. Burke and Greenstein, *How Presidents Test Reality,* 243–4. On the manipulation of advisory processes, see Zeev Maoz, "Framing the National Interest: The Manipulation of Foreign Policy Decisions in Group Settings," *World Politics* 42 (October 1990): 77–110.
51. Tom Johnson memorandum for the President on March 5 meeting with Senior Foreign Policy Advisers, March 6, 1968, "March 5, 1968, Senior Foreign Policy Advisers," Box 2, Tom Johnson Notes. See also draft message from the President for General Westmoreland, n.d., attached to Rostow memorandum for the President, March 7, 1968, "March 31st Speech, vol. 4, Tabs N–Z and AA–KK," Box 48, March 31st Speech, NSCH, NSF; JCS 2766 and 2767, Wheeler to Westmoreland, March 9, 1968, "Westmoreland Papers, 'Eyes Only' Message File: March 1–31, 1968," currently in Box 3, DSDUF.

nonetheless raised the possibility of launching one. "Really 'get on your horses' on that," Johnson quickly replied.[52] Rusk did. The secretary of state recognized that Tet had sapped much of the remaining grassroots support for continuing the war. Unless the administration seemed genuinely interested in a political settlement, the option of deploying additional troops would be foreclosed regardless of what transpired over the next months. If, however, the United States offered a plan for peace, which Rusk was certain the communists would reject, Hanoi would be saddled with the onus for its failure. Its perceived culpability would strengthen the case for a military solution.[53]

Within hours Rusk had formulated a proposal. During the rainy season, when the risk was minimal, Johnson would announce his intention unconditionally to stop bombing North Vietnam except in support of American troops already in place or engaged in battle. On the one hand, this halt could lead immediately to talks if Hanoi responded by ceasing its military activities in the Demilitarized Zone (DMZ) and South Vietnam. On the other hand, the United States would interpret any subsequent aggression as evidence of communist intractability and the futility of negotiations. Rusk conceived of the proposal as a win–win proposition. In the unlikely event that Hanoi responded positively, the offer had a better chance than the existing San Antonio formula to promote negotiations. In the likely event that Hanoi rejected the offer or responded by not responding, the administration could claim it had "walked 'the last mile' for peace" and was left with no alternative other than to continue, indeed to expand, the war. As usual, Rusk's thinking paralleled Johnson's precisely.[54]

That Rusk's proposal led not only to Johnson's speech of March 31 but also his decision seven months later to cease bombing North Vietnam altogether and enter into negotiations with Hanoi and the NLF testifies to the extent to which the president had lost control of developments in Vietnam, the United States, and even his own administration. While aides examined Rusk's idea behind closed doors, the incentive for taking some kind of peace initiative took a quantum leap. With Johnson's approval rating at 36 percent, on

52. Notes of Meeting with Senior Foreign Policy Advisers, March 4, 1968.
53. Rusk, *As I Saw It*, 480–1.   54. Clifford, *Counsel to the President*, 497.

March 13 Eugene McCarthy captured 20 of the 26 convention delegates in the New Hampshire Democratic primary. On March 16 Robert Kennedy announced his candidacy for president. That same day, the speculative fever touched off by international uncertainty as to how the administration would respond to Tet forced the London gold market to close, threatening to precipitate the most serious crisis yet in America's balance of payments.[55]

Against this backdrop, at a March 19 Tuesday Luncheon with his senior advisers Johnson tabled another proposal he had just received from Arthur Goldberg. The ambassador to the United Nations suggested that the United States indefinitely cease all bombing north of the DMZ without stipulating any criteria for beginning peace talks. At the meeting Johnson made clear his opposition to Goldberg's plan. He made equally clear, however, that dramatic action was mandatory to reverse the tide of domestic and global opinion about Vietnam and restore confidence in his leadership. Johnson instructed his speechwriters to begin work on an address to be broadcast over television to the nation. Shortly thereafter, he announced that he was replacing Westmoreland.[56]

Like Johnson, Clifford "was not impressed by the merits of the Goldberg proposition." Over the preceding days, nevertheless, he had been barraged by memoranda from his Pentagon civilian subordinates arguing that negotiations were the only solution to the war but that Rusk's disingenuous proposal was unsatisfactory.[57] He may also have been influenced by former Secretary of State and Democratic icon Dean Acheson's suggestion of a study by the "brightest and ablest civilians and military in the Government" to

55. Specter, *After Tet,* 5; Berman, *Johnson's War,* 186–91; Schandler, *Johnson and Vietnam,* 225–9.
56. Johnson, *Vantage Point,* 408–9; Notes of the President's Meeting with his Foreign [Policy] Advisers at the Tuesday Luncheon, March 19, 1968, "March 19, 1968, Tuesday Luncheon," Box 2, Tom Johnson Notes.
57. Warnke memorandum for the Secretary of Defense, "Hanoi's Position on Settling the Conflict in Vietnam," March 11, 1968, enclosed with Warnke memorandum for the Secretary of Defense through the Deputy Secretary of Defense, March 14, 1968, "Vietnam (February 1–March 15, 1968) [1]," Box 26, Clark Clifford Papers, Lyndon B. Johnson Library; Townsend Hoopes memorandum for Clifford, "The Infeasibility of Military Victory in Vietnam," March 14, 1968, "Memos to Read (1)," Box 1, ibid.; Warnke to Mr. Clifford, March 18, 1968, "Memos to Read (2)," ibid.; Draft memorandum, "Vietnam Policy for the Next Six Months," March 18, 1968, attached to Warnke memorandum for the Secretary of Defense, "Draft Presidential Memorandum on Vietnam," n.d., ibid.

chart "a path looking towards progressive disengagement over whatever period of time we judge appropriate."[58] Clifford advised Johnson to reassemble the "Wise Men" to ascertain their current thinking.[59] Because these veteran national security managers had consistently supported the military effort in Vietnam, administration hawks jumped at the recommendation. They were confident the group would buttress their position. Further, public knowledge that the president had consulted these venerable statesmen and that they had advocated holding the line would go far toward puncturing sentiment for appeasement. "I think the committee would be a defensive public relations move," remarked longtime Johnson confidant Abe Fortas. "There is safety in reconvening this group," seconded Rusk.[60]

The Wise Men met for two days, beginning on March 25. The results were far different from what the hawks expected – or Johnson wanted. Following briefings by Deputy Assistant Secretary of State Philip Habib, the CIA's George Carver, and General William Depuy from the JCS staff, the distinguished gathering quickly arrived at the consensus, "summed up" by Acheson, that "we can no longer do the job we set out to do in the time we have left and we must begin to take steps to disengage." There was disagreement as to how to proceed toward negotiations, particularly regarding the timing of the requisite bombing halt. Still, the overwhelming majority favored a political settlement. "On troop reinforcements the dominant sentiment was [that] the burden of proof rests with those who are urging the increase," read McGeorge Bundy's notes. "We all felt there should not be an extension of the conflict. This would be against our national interest."[61]

58. Rostow memorandum for the record, March 14, 1968, "March 31st Speech, Vol. 4, Tabs N–Z and AA–KK," Box 48, March 31st Speech, NSCH, NSF.
59. The "Wise Men" was a bipartisan group of America's elder statesmen, many of them no longer serving in government, whom Johnson periodically consulted. Clifford had been one of them. Among the others were Acheson, George Ball, McGeorge Bundy, Douglas Dillon, Arthur Dean, Omar Bradley, Matthew Ridgway, Robert Murphy, and Henry Cabot Lodge.
60. Notes of the President's Tuesday Luncheon Meeting, March 19, 1968.
61. Clifford, *Counsel to the President*, 511–19; Notes of the President's Meeting with his Foreign Policy Advisers, March 26, 1968, "March 26, 1968, Foreign Policy Advisers Luncheon–regulars plus added group," Box 2, Tom Johnson Notes; Summary of Notes, March 26, 1968, "March 26, 1968, Meeting with Special Advisory Group," Box 2, Meeting Notes File.

Johnson was devastated – and infuriated. Someone "poisoned the well," he raged, and he accused unspecified "pessimists" of "lobbying" the Wise Men. He also demanded that the briefers repeat their presentations the next day in his presence. "Everybody is recommending surrender," he complained. That they were, nonetheless, that "the enemy's efforts produced such a dismal effect" on people "whom I had always regarded as staunch and unflappable," provided the president with the most compelling evidence yet that the military option was no longer viable. "We have no support for the war," he lamented to Wheeler and General Creighton Abrams, Westmoreland's successor. "This is caused by the 206,000 troop request, leaks, Ted and Bobby Kennedy."[62]

Precisely when Johnson decided to retire from politics remains unclear.[63] But there is no doubt that the defection of the Wise Men – Acheson above all – was a key catalyst to his announcement of March 31 that he would order a partial bombing halt in Vietnam and forgo the campaign for reelection in order to work full time on negotiating a settlement.[64] Until the Wise Men met, administration efforts to decide what if any peace initiative Johnson should include in his televised address were at an impasse. Rusk continued to advocate his proposal, but Clifford insisted that the president should offer something more – and more concrete. On March 22 Johnson commanded his advisers to "get together on their thinking."[65]

The next day speechwriter Harry McPherson came up with a compromise. Johnson would announce that he was halting all bombing north of the 20th parallel and sending negotiators to

62. Clifford, *Counsel to the President*, 518; "Some Questions & Answers (for CBS)," October 25, 1969, "CBS Television Interview: 'Why I Chose Not to Run,' " currently in Box 3, DSDUF; CIA–DOD Briefing by General Depuy and George Carver, March 27, 1968, "March 27, 1967 CIA Briefing," Box 2, Tom Johnson Notes; Johnson, *Vantage Point*, 383–4; Notes of the President's Meeting with Wheeler and Abrams, March 26, 1968, "March 26, 1968, Military Advisers," Box 2, Tom Johnson Notes.
63. Memorandum to Drew Pearson from George Christian, May 15, 1968, "March 31, 1968 (1)," Box 94, The President's Appointment File (Diary Back-up); Memorandum of conversation between Dorothy Territo and George Christian, March 19, 1969, ibid.
64. Rusk, *As I Saw It*, 480–1. For Acheson's continuing influence on Democratic presidents, see Douglas Brinkley, *Dean Acheson: The Cold War Years, 1953–1971* (New Haven, Conn.: Yale University Press, 1992).
65. Notes of Meeting of March 20, 1968, "March 20, 1968, Senior Foreign Policy Advisers," Box 2, Tom Johnson Notes; Notes of March 19 [*sic*] meeting, "March 20, 1968 meeting with Advisers on Vietnam," Box 2, Meeting Notes File; George Christian notes of Luncheon Meeting, March 22, 1968, "March 22, 1968, Luncheon Meeting with Advisers," ibid.

Geneva and Rangoon to await Hanoi's response. When the communists demanded more, as McPherson reckoned they would, Johnson would offer to stop bombing altogether in return for Hanoi's agreement to send representatives to meet with the United States' and pledge to refrain from all attacks on South Vietnamese cities, American bases, and the DMZ. At the very least, McPherson concluded, this "exercise" would "show the American people that we are willing to do every reasonable thing to bring about talks."[66]

The "sequence" McPherson proposed laid the foundation for the March 31 speech. Rusk wrote Johnson that "[m]y own mind is running very close to that of Harry McPherson." He enclosed his earlier proposal supplemented by a commentary that brought it more into line with McPherson's.[67] Clifford, however, was dissatisfied. What was essential, he argued, was to place more emphasis on the de-escalatory steps the United States was willing to take and its sincere interest in constructive negotiations. At Clifford's prompting and with the assistance of Warnke and like-minded Pentagon officials, McPherson drafted a new speech. Johnson would propose a unilateral, immediate, and unconditional bombing halt north of the 20th parallel. Even this limited bombing would cease if Hanoi matched America's restraint, and if Vietnam withdrew its forces from the South, the United States would follow suit. It would also meet with Hanoi anywhere and at anytime to negotiate a peaceful settlement. Johnson, albeit unenthusiastically and not until the Wise Men rendered their verdict, approved the draft. Other than replacing "north of the 20th parallel" with "the area north of the Demilitarized Zone, where the continuing enemy buildup directly threatened allied forward positions," all that remained to be written was the closing. For that Johnson took personal responsibility. Hours before he went on television, he inserted into the speech a statement removing himself as a candidate for president.[68]

66. Harry C. McPherson Jr., Memorandum for the President, March 23, 1968, "Vietnam (March 19, 1970, Memo to the President [II])," Box 127, CF, V, NSF.
67. Rusk memorandum for the President, March 25, 1968, ibid.; Rusk draft statement, March 25, 1968, ibid.; Rusk comments on the attached draft, March 25, 1968, ibid.
68. Johnson, *Vantage Point*, 418–24; Rusk, *As I Saw It*, 481–3, 519–26; President's Remarks, Alternative Draft, McPherson/28 March 1968, "Vietnam (March 19, 1970, Memo to the President [II])," Box 127, CF, V, NSF. The full text of the speech appears in *Public Papers of the Presidents of the Untied States: Lyndon B. Johnson, 1968–1969* (2 vols., Washington: Government Printing Office, 1970) 1:469–76.

Johnson was not sanguine about the prospects for his proposal's moving the combatants toward the conference table.[69] The last-minute revisions of the speech helped to turn his doubts into a self-fulfilling prophecy. Changing "north of the 20th parallel" to the more general "area north of the Demilitarized Zone, where the continuing enemy buildup directly threatened allied forward positions" proved ill advised. At issue was whether Johnson had proscribed bombing above the 20th parallel, the 19th, or somewhere in between. The demarcation line was sufficiently vague to allow Hanoi to charge the United States with violating its word and to generate additional discord within the administration and among Congress and the public as to the validity of the allegation.[70] Johnson's decision not to run, moreover, which he explained was motivated by his desire to insulate the peace process from partisan maneuvering, appeared if anything to increase the political stakes – both in the United States and South Vietnam – that inhered in a settlement.

The problems caused by the revised wording of the speech led McPherson to write Johnson that his decision-making and policy-planning procedure demanded reform. No meeting had been held to discuss the revisions. Even if one had been, the president's preference for conferring with his advisers in free-wheeling sessions without formal agendas or position papers was not conducive to informed debate. This shortcoming, McPherson opined, militated against the quality decisions Johnson would have to make in the critical period ahead. In order to assure that officials, especially in the State Department and Pentagon, carefully considered the implications of their recommendations, and to improve coordination among departments and agencies, McPherson suggested that Johnson appoint someone "to manage the peace talks – military scenario" during the forthcoming months. Because National Security Adviser Walt Rostow was a poor choice owing to his "rigidity" and "bellicosity," McPherson nominated McGeorge Bundy. "I

69. Notes of the President's Meeting with U Thant, April 4, 1968, "April 4, 1968, U Thant," Box 3, Tom Johnson Notes.
70. Untitled handwritten notes, April 2, 1968, "April 2, 1968, Tuesday Luncheon," ibid.; Handwritten notes, Cabinet Meeting, April 3, 1968, "April 3, 1968, Cabinet Meeting," ibid.; Untitled handwritten notes, April 3, 1968, "April 3, 1968, House and Senate Leaders," ibid.; Rostow memorandum to the President, April 2, 1968, "Memos to the President/Walt Rostow, vol. 70," Box 32, NSF.

can't think of anyone else," he wrote, "who combines the knowledge of the subject" with "the tenacity to ask the question everyone else is too tired to ask."[71]

Johnson apparently rejected McPherson's advice. There is no evidence he replied to it; he certainly did not appoint a process manager. The extent to which this contributed to his subsequent disappointment and frustration cannot be gauged. What is indisputable is that Johnson's advisory apparatus remained haphazard and ad hoc. Perhaps the president was unpersuaded by McPherson's arguments. Or perhaps in light of the rush of events, he was unwilling to commit the time and energy necessary to smooth the feathers such an appointment would surely ruffle. On April 3, the day before McPherson sent his memorandum, North Vietnam responded to Johnson's speech. After denouncing American imperialism and describing the March 31 offer as "a perfidious trick of the U.S. government to appease public opinion," Hanoi announced that it was nevertheless prepared "to contact U.S. representatives with a view to determining" the "unconditional cessation of the U.S. bombing raids and all other acts of war . . . so that talks may start."[72]

After a hastily called meeting with his advisers, Johnson issued a statement reiterating his pledge to meet with the North Vietnamese anywhere and anytime. But in confidence he warned, "Let's be awfully careful. . . . The time to keep your head is when everybody else loses theirs." Johnson wanted Ellsworth Bunker's assessment of the offer, and for America's ambassador to discuss it with Thieu and Ky. The next day Bunker reported that he had talked with both, and each considered it simply a propaganda move designed "to put us on [the] spot in [the] eyes of U.S. and world opinion." The communists, they felt, would not seriously negotiate until after the U.S. presidential election. In the meantime, Hanoi would keep on fighting while doing what it could to keep the bombing halt in effect. Bunker did not disagree. Further, he cautioned, the "cooperative" attitude of Thieu and Ky "is one of our most precious assets and must be preserved." The United States must recognize the domestic problems that any gesture toward accommodating the communists

71. McPherson memorandum for the President, April 4, 1968, "April 3–6, 1968," Box 95, The President's Appointment File (Diary Back-Up).
72. Text of Hanoi Offer to Discuss Bombing, *Washington Post*, April 4, 1968, "Vietnam 6 G(3), April 1–October 1968 Talks with Hanoi," Box 95, CF, V, NSF.

would cause the GVN. Tet represented a great victory for both the United States and South Vietnam, Bunker wrote at greater length a few days later, when he returned to Washington for consultations. The administration should be "tough, patient, and not too anxious in our negotiating stance."[73]

Johnson was sympathetic – to Bunker and the GVN. He had his own political problems, however. Not only did he lack domestic support for the war; the viability of his Great Society required a new tax bill, which Congress held hostage to progress toward peace in Vietnam.[74] Summoning his advisers to Camp David on April 9, the president confirmed his decision to pursue Hanoi's overture. Already instructions had been drafted at Foggy Bottom for Averell Harriman, who would represent the United States in any talks. Harriman was to make whatever arrangements were necessary for them to begin. To avoid complications, he was not to raise such a bone of contention as North Vietnam's continued infiltration into the South or Washington's expectation that in return for its bombing restraint all military activity in the DMZ, shelling of South Vietnamese cities, and the like would cease. Harriman would reserve these issues for the conference table.[75]

Not until May 3 did Washington and Hanoi agree on Paris as the site for the meeting. By this time, Johnson had decided to send Cyrus Vance to join Harriman in order to keep the Kennedy confederate's dovish instincts in check.[76] By this time, also, within the administration opposition to the talks had hardened. Those of the

73. Untitled handwritten notes, April 3, 1968, "April 3, 1968, Foreign Policy Advisers," Box 3, Tom Johnson Notes; Handwritten Notes, Cabinet Meeting, April 3, 1968; State 141536, Bunker from Acting Secretary of State [Katzenbach], April 4, 1969, "6G(3), Talks with Hanoi," Box 96, CF, V, NSF; Saigon 23912, Bunker to Secretary of State, April 4, 1968, ibid.; Bunker, "Viet-Nam Negotiations: Dangers and Opportunities," April 8, 1968, ibid.

74. Handwritten Notes, Cabinet Meeting, April 3, 1968; Handwritten Notes, House and Senate Leaders Meeting, April 3, 1968.

75. Notes of President's Meeting at Camp David, April 9, 1968, "April 9, 1968, Camp David Meeting with Rusk, Clifford, Wheeler, Bunker, Staff," Box 2, Meeting Notes File; Instructions for Governor Harriman, draft as reviewed at the White House, April 6, 1968, attached to Memorandum from Rusk to Clifford, April 15, 1968, "Second Set [Memos on Vietnam: April–May 1968]," Box 4, Vietnam Files, Clifford Papers; William P. Bundy memorandum for the Secretary of State, April 9, 1968, 6G (3), "Talks with Hanoi," Box 96, CF, V, NSF.

76. Johnson, *Vantage Point*, 496–505; Rusk, *As I Saw It*, 484–5; Rudy Abramson, *Spanning the Century: The Life of W. Averell Harriman*, (New York: Morrow, 1992), 658–9.

mindset of Rostow and Westmoreland argued that "North Vietnam is crying for peace because of battle wounds," and therefore to negotiate would play into its hands.[77] They found an ally in Bunker. If the communists appeared more tractable, he advised, it was because the "[t]rend in the South is running against" them, and they had learned from the failure of the Tet offensive that the "old political and military tactics have not been able to reverse it." Their offer to talk was a new tactic, a ruse designed to force the withdrawal of America's military presence, divide Washington and the GVN, and produce a coalition government "leading to eventual communist control of South Vietnam." In Bunker's judgment, then, Johnson's March 31 speech had been a mistake. Resigned to the inevitability of peace talks, he recommended that Johnson put Hanoi on notice by authorizing bombing up to the 20th parallel.[78]

Johnson felt much the same way. "I do not want to go to Paris," he said. "We need to find out what my March 31 speech has done to us."[79] Nonetheless, he, too, was resigned to the talks. What his speech had done was constrain his military options. Characteristically, the president sought relief from his anxiety by forging a consensus among his advisers. "I don't want to influence you with my pessimism," he told them at a May 6 meeting called to formulate a bargaining position. "Just think of the national interest – now and ten years from now." The lack of previous preparation and planning, however, and diversity of opinion on Johnson's intent – did he seek to end the war or revive support for it – was all too evident. At this meeting and those that followed, agreement could be reached on neither a negotiating nor a military strategy. The hardline faction advocated confronting Hanoi with an immediate ultimatum. The United States should demand that North Vietnam

77. Rostow memorandum for the President, April 2, 1968, "Vietnam: March–June 1968," Box 6, Files of Walt W. Rostow, NSF; Notes of Meeting in the Cabinet Room, April 8, 1968, "April 8 Meeting with the President, Rusk, Clifford, Rostow, Christian," Box 2, Meeting Notes File.
78. Saigon 24993, Bunker to Secretary of State, April 17, 1968, "6G (4)b, Talks with Hanoi," Box 96, CF, V, NSC; Saigon 26928, Bunker to Secretary of State, May 10, 1968, attached to Rostow memorandum to the President, May 10, 1968, "Memos to the President/Walt Rostow, vol. 76," Box 34, NSF.
79. Notes on the Tuesday Luncheon, April 30, 1968, "April 30, 1968, Tuesday Luncheon," Box 3, Tom Johnson Notes.

cease all forms of aggression; withdraw its forces from South Vietnam, the DMZ, and Laos and Cambodia; and accept a political settlement in the South that excluded the NLF. If Hanoi hesitated on conceding to any of the above, Johnson should order the resumption – and expansion – of the bombing campaign: "our primary persuader." Another faction, led by Clifford with the support of the diplomats in Paris, countered that for the talks to have any chance to succeed, from the start the United States had to express its willingness to negotiate everything. In addition, it should not place time restrictions on the partial bombing halt and should explicitly confine it to the 19th parallel. Johnson equivocated. "We must feel our way – every step of the way," he said on May 8, adding a week later, "I want to hear both sides." At the end of the month he was still asking each for a list of "pros and cons."[80]

In the eight weeks following Johnson's March 31 speech, 3,700 Americans died in Vietnam.[81] With progress in the negotiations at a standstill, the administration deadlocked, and communist attacks on South Vietnamese cities continuing, on June 4 Rusk recommended intensifying American bombing. "Let's hit them," he advised, "and not say anything about it."[82] The next day Johnson received a letter from Soviet Premier Alexei Kosygin indicating he had "grounds to believe" that a total bombing halt could break the impasse and enhance the prospects for a peaceful settlement. No one doubted that Kosygin's "grounds" were discussions he had held with Hanoi. No one doubted that how the United States responded would set policy until Johnson left office.[83]

80. Rostow memoranda for the President, 4:40 and 4:45 P.M., May 5, 1968, "Memos to the President/Walt Rostow, vol. 74," Box 33, NSF; Notes of the President's Meeting with Foreign Policy Advisers, May 6, 1968, "May 6, Foreign Policy Advisers," Box 3, Meeting Notes File; Notes on the President's Meeting with the Negotiating Team, May 8, 1968, "May 8, Negotiating Team," Box 3, Tom Johnson Notes; Maxwell Taylor memorandum to Johnson, May 13, 1968, "Vietnam (May 3–July 9, 1968) [3]," Box 26, Clifford Papers; Notes of the President's Meeting with the Cabinet, May 14, 1968, "May 14, Cabinet," Box 3, Tom Johnson Notes; Notes of the Tuesday Lunch Meeting with Foreign Policy Advisers, May 21, 1968, "May 21, Tuesday Luncheon," ibid.; Notes of the President's Meeting with Foreign Policy Advisers, May 28, 1968, "May 28, 1968, Foreign Policy Advisers," ibid.
81. Spector, *After Tet*, 25.
82. Notes of the President's Tuesday Luncheon, June 4, 1968, "June 4, 1968, Tuesday Luncheon," ibid.
83. Johnson briefing paper, October 28, 1968, "Paris Negotiations – 1968 File No. 2 (4)," Box 6, Vietnam Files, Clifford Papers; Clifford, *Counsel to the President*, 546–7.

Rusk and Clifford faced off once again. Kosygin's letter was "very significant," the secretary of state said, and "a complete bombing cessation could lead to a breakthrough." Yet once the United States stopped all bombing, he warned, it would be difficult to restart any. Rusk recommended that Johnson defer replying until he received guarantees of specific concessions from Hanoi in return for a total halt. Clifford objected. "We have a great opportunity here," he argued. "We should take advantage of it." Bombing the North was not going to end the war any more than would increasing troop levels in the South. What was needed was negotiations; Kosygin was offering to help arrange them. "The President should accept [the offer] in good faith." Clifford proposed that the United States cease all bombing for two weeks and make clear that it was doing so in response to the Soviet note. "Let's give it a test. . . . I am willing to try for a political settlement by taking this risk of stopping the bombing."[84]

Prior to the meeting Rusk had spoken with Johnson in an effort to "cut the ground out from under Clifford before he had a chance to present his position."[85] He succeeded. The president dismissed the secretary of defense's proposal as "unrealistic." "Why not try to get clarification before burning our bridges?" he asked. "If they have a serious interest in peace, they can let us know what certain specific things will happen" in the event he ordered a complete bombing halt. "I would take the chance," he explained, but only "if I had a reasonable supposition of results." The president instructed Harriman and Vance in Paris to probe the North Vietnamese's intentions. He also wanted estimates of the impact a Washington–Hanoi *quid pro quo* would have on the GVN and on America's forces in Vietnam.[86]

Left unaddressed was what assurances Johnson would need on any of these fronts in order for him to cease bombing North Vietnam. Whatever they were, over the next weeks he did not receive them. But he did continue to restrict bombing to the 19th parallel,

84. Notes of the President's Meeting with Foreign Policy Advisers, June 9, 1968, "June 9, 1968, Foreign Policy Advisers," Box 3, Tom Johnson Notes.
85. [Averell Harriman], "General Review of the Last Six Months," December 14, 1968, "Harriman Material," Box 32, Papers of Francis M. Bator, LBJ Library.
86. Notes of the President's Meeting with Foreign Policy Advisers, June 9, 1968.

which was sufficient to cause Rostow to worry about "this growing fever for a commitment to a unilateral bombing cessation."[87] Rostow had reason to fret. Through the remainder of June and into July, Clifford and his allies prepared for any development they could exploit. It was in the Department of Defense, not State, where officials formulated negotiating positions. They focused on such thorny issues as the communists' attitude toward the GVN; what type of representation Hanoi would want for the NLF; how "mutual withdrawal," "unconditional," and the like would be defined; and what would be the range between America's minimum and maximum demands. On each score they recommended that the United States be as flexible as possible. In mid-July Clifford visited the American commands in Saigon and Honolulu. He came back more convinced than ever that the United States could not win the war.[88]

Johnson's generals insisted otherwise. They likewise insisted that the antidote to the political stalemate in Paris was for the United States to break the military stalemate in Vietnam. In fact, whereas Clifford, along with Harriman and Vance, justified their pleas for a bombing halt by interpreting the July lull in communist fighting as Hanoi's signal that it was serious about negotiating, Wheeler and Taylor countered that it was evidence of the enemy's exhaustion. They counseled that the time was right to remove the restrictions on bombing and launch a new ground offensive as well. Johnson conceded he would "like to see us knock the hell out of them" but rejected both extremes.[89]

87. Rostow memorandum to Johnson, July 26, 1968, "Memos to the President/Walt Rostow, vol. 89," Box 38, NSF.
88. "Proposal for an analysis of alternative U.S. objectives at the Paris Talks," n.d., and "The Value of a Mutual Withdrawal Strategy," n.d., attached to Warnke memorandum for Mr. Nitze, July 26, 1968, "Vietnam (May 3 – July 9, 1968) [3]," Box 26, Clifford Papers; Warnke memorandum for Mr. Clifford, July 1, 1968, ibid.; George Christian notes, private, July 19, 1968, "Classified–George Christian [1 of 2]," Box 12, Office Files of George Christian, George Christian Papers, LBJ Library; U.S. Military Strategy in SVN, n.d., "South Vietnam Trip, July 13–19, 1968: Miscellaneous," Box 5, Vietnam Files, Clifford Papers.
89. Clifford memorandum for the President, "Trip to South Vietnam, July 13–18," July 18, 1968, "Memos on Vietnam: February–August 1968," Box 2, Clifford Papers; Maxwell Taylor memorandum for the President, July 30, 1958, "Vietnam (July 10–August 29, 1968) [4]," Box 26, ibid.; Wheeler memorandum for the President, "Alternative Bombing Proposals," August 1, 1968, "Memos to the President/Walt Rostow, vol. 90," Box 38, NSF; Notes of the President's Meeting with Foreign Policy Advisers," July 30, 1968, "July 30, 1968, Foreign Policy Advisers," Box 3, Tom Johnson Notes.

Johnson's frustration and despair increased over the summer. He was unused to irreconcilable differences among his advisers, and his wait-and-see middle course satisfied no one. His mood deteriorated further when during the same week in late August the Soviets invaded Czechoslovakia and the Democratic Convention erupted in violence. With time running out on his administration and Johnson sensitive to the war's cost to Humphrey's candidacy, he finally accepted the judgment of his envoys in Paris that talks with Hanoi would be stillborn unless he completely halted the bombing.[90] He finally also decided what he would demand in return. Hanoi would have to agree to discontinue all forms of infiltration across the DMZ, stop the shelling of South Vietnamese cities, and, most important, acknowledge formal GVN representation at the negotiations. At a rare official meeting of the NSC on September 25, the president polled his advisers on this formula. Although both he and Rusk voted with the minority who opposed it, Johnson accepted the majority's will.[91]

At lunch immediately following, Rostow predicted that the next two weeks would be critical.[92] They were. A convoluted game of diplomatic cat and mouse between Harriman and Vance and North Vietnam's negotiators Le Duc Tho and Xuan Thuy led to the communists' acquiescing to deal with the GVN. "I told you the chances were 1 in 3 or 1 in 4 that we would get the kind of exchange we did in Paris today. I was wrong," confessed Rostow to Johnson on October 11. "We must now face the possibility – even the likelihood – that they wish to wind up the war fast." But Hanoi wanted comparable status accorded the NLF and proposed that procedural talks exclusively between itself and Washington precede quadrangular substantive ones.[93]

90. Notes on Meeting with Tuesday Luncheon Group, September 12, 1968, "September 12, 1968, Tuesday Luncheon," Box 4, ibid.; Paul Warnke memorandum for Mr. Clifford, "Proposed October Meeting of Troop Contributing Countries," September 23, 1968, "Memoranda – Miscellaneous," Box 7, Clifford Papers.
91. Notes on the NSC Meeting, September 25, 1968, "September 25, 1968, NSC," Box 4, Tom Johnson Notes.
92. Notes of President's Weekly luncheon Meeting with Foreign Policy Advisers, September 25, 1968, "September 25, 1968, Weekly Luncheon," ibid.
93. Paris 22106, Harriman and Vance to Secretary of State, October 9, 1968, "Memos to the President/Bombing Halt Decision, vol. 1," Box 137, CF, V, NSC; Paris 22253, Harriman to Secretary of State, October 11, 1968, ibid.; Rostow memorandum for the president, October 11, 1968, ibid.; Paris 22466, Harriman to Secretary of State, October 15, 1968, ibid.

The spate of meetings that ensued confirms that Hanoi's concession caught the administration off guard. This surprise, coupled with the communists' additions to the formula, complicated formulating a response. "There comes a time in the tide of men's affairs that it is time to move," said Clifford on October 14 in arguing for an immediate bombing halt. Johnson was not so sure. Indeed, the imminent prospect of ceasing bombing North Vietnam appears to have exacerbated his already considerable doubts. He expressed concern over NLF representation and the difficulty of resuming the bombing should the communists stonewall or violate their word. He received assurances from his advisers, including Wheeler and Rusk, that all these potentialities could be managed. Even Thieu, they reported, had indicated that he favored going ahead. What about the political implications, Johnson then asked. He would be attacked by the Republicans for an eleventh-hour partisan ploy. "Mark Twain said, 'When in doubt, do right,' " replied Clifford. Once again Johnson polled his advisers. This time they unanimously agreed to proceed if an understanding could be reached in Paris. "We'll try it," announced Johnson. "We'll be scared, but let's try it." As Johnson left the October 15 Tuesday luncheon, CIA director Richard Helms "looked at the president, shook hands and said, 'good luck.' "[94]

Johnson was sure he would need it. With the details of a mutually acceptable protocol still to be worked out, moreover, he would not rule out changing his mind. Then, on October 27, Vance reported that Hanoi had consented to "*everything* we have asked for." In his view, "*We should accept.*"[95] "I still smell blitzing,"

94. Notes of the President's Meeting with Military Advisers, October 14, 1968, "October 14, 1968, Military Advisers on Vietnam," Box 4, Tom Johnson Notes; Notes on Meeting with Foreign Policy Advisory Group, October 14, 1968, "October 14, 1968, Foreign Policy Advisory Group," ibid.; Notes of Meeting with Rusk, Clifford, Wheeler, et al., October 14, 1968, "October 14, 1968, Senior Advisers on Vietnam," ibid.; Meeting with the President, October 14, 1968, "October 14, 1968, Foreign Policy Advisory Group," Box 3, Meeting Notes File; Summary Notes of President's Meeting with the Joint Chiefs on Vietnam, October 14, 1968, "October 14, 1968, President's Meeting with Joint Chiefs on Vietnam," ibid.; Notes on the President's Meeting with the Tuesday Lunch Group, October 15, 1968, "October 15, 1968, Tuesday Luncheon," Box 4, Tom Johnson Notes.

95. Rostow memorandum for the record, "Meeting with the President," October 23, 1968, "November 11, 1968," Box 15, The President's Appointment File (Diary Back-up); Notes on Meeting with Foreign Policy Group, Friday, October 25, 1968, "October 25, 1968, Foreign Policy Group," Box 4, Tom Johnson Notes; Benjamin H. Read memorandum of telephone conversation, October 27, 1968, "Paris Negotiations – File No. 2 (4)," Box 6, Vietnam Files, Clifford Papers.

Johnson reflexively reacted. "Let's not do anything that is fatal to us." Although Rusk joined Clifford in assuring him that the administration's eyes were wide open, Johnson sought more. "I want to know what kind of dress I have before I agree to go to the dance." More important than the view from either Washington or Paris, he said, was that from Vietnam. On October 29 he asked Abrams, back from Saigon for consultations, whether as president he would cease bombing in order to get the negotiations going. "I think it is [the] right thing to do," the general promptly responded. "It is [the] proper thing to do." For the second time in two weeks, Johnson approved a bombing halt.[96]

The administration was confident it was prepared for all contingencies. Despite Rusk's concern with Saigon's "theology," however, it had neglected to plan for the possibility that at the last minute the GVN would refuse to go to Paris.[97] Even as the president scheduled the bombing halt to begin on October 31, he learned that Thieu was balking. Saigon's leaders had gone back on their word, Johnson fumed. "This may mean that everything we have done is in vain." He suspected that the Republicans had convinced South Vietnam's leaders it was in their interest to prevent any talks from beginning until the presidential election because they could cut a better deal were Nixon elected. Bunker must "take Thieu up on the mountain and really let him know what the facts are," Johnson instructed. They were that Nixon would "doublecross" him after November 5; that Johnson would be president until January 20, 1969; that the GVN had agreed previously to negotiate; and that the United States would proceed unilaterally if necessary.[98]

Johnson recognized, nevertheless, the compelling reasons not to charge ahead. Thieu could support Republican accusations that the

96. Notes on President's Meeting with Group of Foreign Policy Advisers, October 27, 1968, "October 27, 1968, Foreign Policy Advisers," Box 4, Tom Johnson Notes; Rostow memorandum to Johnson, October 28, 1968, "Memos to the President/Bombing Halt Decision, vol. 2," Box 137, CF, V, NSF; Notes of the President's Meeting with Rusk, Clifford et al., October 29, 1968, "October 29, 1968, Senior Advisers on Vietnam," Box 4, Tom Johnson Notes.

97. State 258563, Rusk to Harriman and Bunker, October 19, 1968, "Memos to the President/Bombing Halt Decision, vol. 1," Box 137, CF, V, NSF.

98. Notes on Tuesday Luncheon, October 29, 1968, "October 29, 1968, Tuesday Luncheon," Box 4, Tom Johnson Notes; Notes on Foreign Policy Meeting, Cabinet Room, October 29, 1969, "October 29, 1968, Foreign Policy Advisers," ibid.; Additional Notes on Meeting in the Cabinet Room, October 29, 1968, "October 29, 1968, Addi-

administration was sacrificing America's longtime ally to benefit Humphrey's candidacy.[99] Further, a disunited front at the negotiating table was a recipe for disaster. Thieu, consequently, had to be persuaded to come on board. From Saigon, Bunker recommended that the United States extend the interval between the bombing halt and the beginning of the negotiations in order to give him more time to work on South Vietnam's president. Clifford said "horseshit"; Johnson consented.[100]

Arguing that he needed "materially more time," Thieu would not budge. Bunker characterized his talks as "a sterile exercise, with the GVN generally throwing up obstacles to agreement faster than we could remove them." Thieu averred that his national security council had not formulated a negotiating position, that he needed to receive authorization from "leaders of parliamentary groups" to enter into talks, and that under any circumstances all procedural questions had to be resolved before he would send a delegation to Paris. He predicted that Hanoi would orchestrate recognition for the NLF but avoid dealing directly with the GVN. Acting on instructions from Washington, Bunker sought to allay these concerns and warned that the United States had no alternative but to proceed. Thieu grew "testier." Speaking "emotionally and disjointedly," he complained, "You are powerful. You can say to small nations what you want. . . . But you cannot force us to do anything against our interest." When he left Independence Palace on October 31, Bunker wrote several days later, "we knew – and they knew – that our announcement of the bombing halt would have to be [a] unilateral one."[101]

tional Notes," ibid. In his memoir Johnson elaborates on his suspicion of Republican dirty tricks but exonerates Nixon himself. Rusk writes in the same vein. Clifford is less charitable. Johnson, *Vantage Point*, 517–18; Rusk, *As I Saw It*, 487–8; Clifford, *Counsel to the President*, 581–4. See also Rostow memorandum to Johnson, October 29, 1968, "Richard Nixon and Vietnam," Box 5, Walt Rostow Files, NSF.

99. Rostow memorandum to Johnson, October 28, 1968, "Memos to the President/Bombing Halt Decision, vol. 2," Box 137, CF, V, NSF; Rusk memorandum to Rostow, October 29, 1968, "Memos to the President/Bombing Halt Decision, vol. 3," ibid.

100. Saigon 41436 and 41491, Bunker to Secretary of State, October 29, 1969, ibid.; Notes of Foreign Policy Meeting, October 30, 1968, "October 30, 1968, Foreign Policy Advisers," Box 4, Tom Johnson Notes.

101. Saigon 41450, Bunker to Secretary of State, October 19, 1968, "Memos to the President/Bombing Halt Decision, vol. 6," Box 138, CF, V, NSF; Saigon 41521, Bunker to Secretary of State, October 30, 1968, "Paris Negotiations – 1968 File No. 2 (1)," Box 6, Vietnam Files, Clifford Papers; Secretary of State to Bunker, unnumbered cable

Johnson had already reached this conclusion. After what Rostow called "the most sustained day and night effort I've had since the Cuban missile crisis," the president met with his full NSC for a brief 10 minutes late in the afternoon on October 31. That evening he would announce that at 8:00 the next morning all bombing of North Vietnam would cease, said the president in a hoarse voice. He hoped that the GVN would alter its position afterward. If only for the historical record, but probably also for his own peace of mind, Johnson reviewed the steps leading up to his decision and polled his advisers one last time. They unanimously concurred. Still not through, Johnson turned to Wheeler. "We do recommend this, all [the] Joint Chiefs of Staff, don't we, Bus [Wheeler]?" he asked. "Yes, sir," replied the JCS chair. "We were cut in on this one – we were not on the Bay of Pigs." Johnson was satisfied.[102]

The bombing halt began on schedule; the negotiations did not. Washington and Hanoi continued to debate procedure, and Saigon refused to send a delegation to Paris and denounced Johnson's decision as evidence of "the true face" of American "duplicity."[103] Although Nixon was careful not to undercut the administration's effort, his election evidently strengthened the GVN's resolve.[104] Thieu, moreover, had an advocate in Bunker. The South Viet-

drafted by W. Bundy, October 30, 1968, "Paris Negotiations – 1968 File No. 2 (2)," ibid.; Saigon 41542, Bunker to Secretary of State, October 30, 1968, "Paris Negotiations – 1968 File No. 2 (3)," ibid.; Saigon 41688, Bunker to Secretary of State, November 1, 1968, "Memos to the President/Bombing Halt Decision, vol. 4," Box 137, CF, V, NSF; Saigon 41768, Bunker to Secretary of State, November 3, 1968, ibid.

102. Harry McPherson Notes of Meeting in the Cabinet Room, October 31, 1968, "October 31, 1968," Meeting Notes File; Bromley Smith Summary Notes of 593rd NSC Meeting, October 31, 1968, " NSC Meetings, Vol. 5, Tab 75, October 31, 1968," National Security Council File, NSF; Exchange of Comments between the President and General Wheeler, October 31, 1968, "November 7, 1968, Foreign Policy Meeting," Box 4, Tom Johnson Notes. For the text of Johnson's speech, see "The President's Address to the Nation Upon Announcing His Decision to Halt the Bombing of North Vietnam," *Public Papers of the Presidents: Johnson, 1968–1969*, 1099–103.

103. Unnumbered telegram from CIA to White House Situation Room, November 2, 1968, "Memos to the President/Bombing Halt Decision, vol. 4," Box 137, CF, V, NSF.

104. Statement dictated by Lucien Warren with the Nixon campaign in New York, October 25, 1968, "Correspondence: President (2)," Box 10, Clifford Papers; Notes of the President's Meeting with President-Elect Richard Nixon, November 11, 1968, "November 11, 1968, President-Elect Nixon," Box 4, Tom Johnson Notes; Saigon 42368, Bunker to Secretary of State, November 9, 1968, "Memos to the President/Bombing Halt Decision, vol. 5," Box 138, CF, V, NSF; Saigon 894, For the President from Ambassador Bunker, January 16, 1969, "HARVAN – Double Plus, Chron. Papers and Other Misc. Material," Box 260, ibid.

namese president, counseled the ambassador, was more disposed to negotiations than his seemingly obstructionist posture suggested. He would come around. First, however, he had to generate additional support among the public and within his political base. Once he had, his regime would be that much stronger and more stable, and Hanoi's efforts to portray the GVN as nothing more than an American puppet would be thoroughly discredited. In addition, Thieu's maneuvering worked to the alliance's advantage. Bunker reiterated that the communists' concessions had been forced by the defeat of the Tet offensive and by the improved performance of the GVN and ARVN. In a consequently weak bargaining position to begin with, they would have to concede further if confronted by a united front disinclined to compromise. The hard line taken by South Vietnam, then, sent Hanoi the right signals. America should be patient, exploit the delay, and avoid at all costs any appearance of feuding with Saigon.[105]

The perspective from Paris and Washington was very different. Intent to get on with the negotiations and reach a political settlement, Harriman and Vance considered the potential withdrawal of American forces from Vietnam their strongest card. They were also unsympathetic to Thieu's position or Bunker's defense of it.[106] So were Clifford and Rusk. Since late October the former had criticized Thieu's conduct as "sinister," "reprehensible," and "utterly without merit."[107] So irate had he become by the second week of November that he went public with his complaint. Washington had kept the GVN informed of every development leading to the bombing halt, Clifford explained at press conference. The "understanding was as clear as two partners can have." At the last minute Thieu had changed his mind, and subsequently he threw more and

105. Saigon 42368, Bunker to Secretary of State, November 9, 1968, "Memos to the President/Bombing Halt Decision, vol. 5," Box 138, CF, V, NSF; Saigon 4236 and 4237, Bunker to Secretary of State [and Harriman and Vance], November 10, 1968, ibid.; Saigon 42653, Bunker to Secretary of State, November 14, 1968, "Presentation on Peace Talks, November 18, 1968 (7)," Box 6, Vietnam Files, Clifford Papers; Saigon 43666, For the President from Bunker, November 30, 1968, "Memos to the President/Walt Rostow, vol. 108," Box 43, NSF. For a summary of Bunker's analyses, see Saigon 894, For the President from Ambassador Bunker, January 16, 1969.
106. Paris 24229, Harriman to Secretary of State, November 21, 1968, "Memos to the President/Bombing Halt, vol. 7," Box 138, CF, V, NSF.
107. Notes on Tuesday Luncheon, October 29, 1968; Notes on the President's Meeting with Rusk, Clifford et al., October 29, 1968.

more roadblocks in the way of the negotiators. Rather than allow "Saigon a veto," Johnson "owed it to the American people to proceed with the talks." Asked whether he would characterize Thieu's "operations" as "sabotaging" or a "doublecross," Clifford replied curtly, "Take your pick."[108]

Thieu was furious with what Rostow called "Sec. Clifford's arm twisting in public," and Bunker could not blame him.[109] Johnson ducked the controversy by instructing Rostow to prepare for the record a memorandum indicating that Clifford was expressing his personal views, not those of the president. Still, through a newly established backchannel Johnson had already expressed his displeasure with Thieu "without any ambiguity."[110] What is more, Rusk in this instance sided with the secretary of defense. In his opinion Bunker was putting a Panglossian spin on Thieu's behavior. Worse, he was repeating what the secretary of state had come to believe were America's two great mistakes regarding Vietnam: underestimating the "tenacity of the North Vietnamese" and overestimating the "patience of the American people."[111] Even before the press conference he had written the ambassador that by generating momentum in Congress and the press for a break with Saigon that the administration could not resist much longer, Thieu "has been unhelpful, to say the least." As November wore on, Rusk's own patience wore thin. He complained that the GVN's "primary purpose in dealing with us at this stage is to stall." There was "no excuse" for Saigon's boycott of the talks, he cabled on November 22. There was likewise no reason to expect Hanoi to buckle under more than it already had. The "underlying fact remains that we must not only get a GVN delegation to Paris but get visible talks

108. News Conference of Secretary of Defense Clark M. Clifford, November 12, 1968, "Press Conferences," Box 7, Clifford Papers.
109. Rostow memorandum to Johnson, November 12, 1968, "Memos to the President/Bombing Halt Decision, vol. 6," Box 138, CF, V, NSF; Saigon 42653, Bunker to Secretary of State, November 14, 1968; Bunker to Secretary of State, November 15, 1968, "Presentation on Talks, November 18, 1968 (6)," Box 6, Vietnam Files: Clifford Papers.
110. Rostow Memorandum for the Record, "Sec. Clifford's Press Conference of November 12, 1968," November 23, 1968, "Memos to the President/Bombing Halt Decision, Vol. 7," Box 138, CF, V, NSF; Rostow memorandum to Johnson, November 15, 1968, "Memos to the President/Bombing Halt Decision, vol. 6," ibid.; Rostow "Back Channel Draft" to Jim Jones for the President, November 5, 1968, "Memos to the President/Bombing Halt Decision, vol. 4," ibid.
111. Rusk, *As I Saw It*, 497.

started." If there was no movement on Thieu's part in a few days, Rusk concluded, "we will have to carry out in some way our repeated statements that we should go ahead on our own, bilaterally or with the NLF, privately or semi-publicly, or even on an announced basis." The United States, he advised Johnson, must "assert and take care of our own interest."[112]

Bunker – and Thieu – got the message. Meeting with a variety of GVN officials, the ambassador presented Rusk's ultimatum. "Washington has gone to the very limit in meeting the requirements of the local situation here," he said. The "orange is squeezed dry." He then conveyed the "sense of extreme urgency" with which the administration viewed the start of negotiations. On November 26 Thieu gave his reply. Although it would take time to decide on the right people and he "[did] not see how [they] could go into serious talks this week or even early next week," he would put together a delegation and send it to Paris. That day Johnson met with his most senior advisers. "The logjam has been broken," Rusk announced. "Now we will have Paris talks," commented Clifford.[113]

Their optimism was premature. Thieu continued to stall. "We have stood about all the delay from South Vietnam we can," exploded Johnson. In addition to Thieu's antics, what fueled the president's ire were reports that North Vietnam was resuming its infiltration of the DMZ. To Johnson, the only thing less tolerable than being played for a fool was appearing to be a coward. "I would like to leave office de-escalating," he said, but "I do not want to run." His hands would be tied, however, so long as Hanoi could attribute its conduct to the lack of progress toward a settlement. Rusk, Johnson ordered, "should turn the heat" on Thieu. He should give Saigon until December 11 to get a delegation to Paris, or the United States would begin negotiations without GVN rep-

112. State 269935, Rusk to Bunker, November 9, 1968, "Memos to the President/Bombing Halt Decision, vol. 5," Box 138, CF, V, NSF; State [unnumbered], Rusk to Bunker [drafted by BH Read], November 19, 1968, "Memos to the President/Bombing Halt Decision, Vol. 6," ibid.; State [unnumbered], Rusk to Bunker [drafted by WP Bundy], November 22, 1968, "Memos to the President/Bombing Halt Decision, vol. 7," ibid.; Rusk memorandum for the President, November 21, 1968, ibid.

113. Saigon 43269, Bunker to Secretary of State, November 22, 1968, ibid.; Saigon 43342 and 43345, Bunker to Secretary of State, November 23, 1968, ibid.; Saigon 43517, Bunker to Secretary of State, November 26, 1968, ibid.; Notes on Foreign Policy Meeting, November 26, 1968, "November 26, 1968, Foreign Policy Advisers," Box 4, Tom Johnson Notes.

resentation. If after they began Hanoi continued to violate the DMZ border, Johnson declared, he would be "justified in *resuming the bombing.*"[114]

Thieu did not allow Johnson the opportunity to make good on his threat. The South Vietnamese delegation, headed by Vice President Ky, arrived in Paris on December 8, in advance of the deadline. Washington was unable, however, to move the talks past procedural matters. Ky continued to insist that under the "our side/your side" formula that all parties had agreed to, the GVN receive recognition equal to that of the United States, and the NLF receive no recognition at all. Finally, on January 18, 1969, an accord was reached. The two sides would be "clearly separated" by two rectangular tables with a round one in the middle. There would be no nameplates, no flags, and no written minutes of the understanding. The United States proposed to hold the first plenary session immediately, but Thieu demanded an additional meeting on procedure. Not until January 25 – five days after Nixon's inauguration – did substantive talks begin. "I regretted more than anyone could possibly know that I was leaving the White House without having achieved a just, honorable, and a lasting peace in Vietnam," a frustrated, bitter Johnson later wrote.[115]

Blame for Johnson's failure falls on many shoulders. Undoubtedly the intransigence of Thieu and the GVN, influenced implicitly and probably explicitly by Nixon supporters, was the most salient last-minute factor.[116] There is no reason to believe, nevertheless,

114. Notes on the Tuesday Luncheon Meeting, December 3, 1968, "December 3, 1968, Tuesday Luncheon," ibid.; Notes on President's Foreign Policy Meeting, December 5, 1968, "December 5, 1968, Foreign Policy Advisers," ibid.

115. Paris 781, 788/1, and 790, Harriman to Secretary of State, January 18, 1969, "Peace Talk Material for Ginsburgh, Hold for Ginsburgh," Box 260, CF, V, NSF; Paris 797, Vance to Secretary of State, January 19, 1969, ibid.; State 9170, Rusk to Bunker, January 18, 1969, "Paris – Delto – Todel, Codeword, TDCS, & Memos & Misc. – Bamboo," ibid.; Bunker to Secretary of State, January 20, 1969, ibid.; Johnson, *Vantage Point*, 529.

116. For robust evidence that Nixon Republicans were culpable, see James H. Rowe Jr., Interview with Michael L. Gillette, Interview #4, November 10, 1968; Bui Diem with David Chanoff, *In the Jaws of Victory* (Boston: Houghton Mifflin, 1987), 235–46; Stephen E. Ambrose, *Nixon: The Triumph of a Politician, 1962–1972* (New York: Simon & Schuster, 1989), 207–35; Herbert Parmet, *Richard Nixon and His America* (Boston: Little, Brown, 1990), 519–23. Anna Chennault, the Nixon camp's alleged contact with Thieu, denies the charge. See Anna Chennault, *The Education of Anna* (New York: Times Books, 1980), 174–98.

that the North Vietnamese would have been more tractable on fundamental issues had negotiations begun on schedule. Also at fault was America's military, which to the end promised victory but never formulated a viable strategy for achieving it, and the frequently ill-informed, tension-ridden, and even opportunistic agendas pursued by diverse elements in Congress and the public at large.

Still, Johnson himself must bear primary responsibility. From start to finish he refused to acknowledge incompatibility between his domestic and international goals. He insisted on finding the middle ground between the two and always favored short-term solutions over long-term imperatives. He resisted systematic examinations of the consequences of his actions, and he ignored or distorted advice and information discordant with his beliefs. Instead, Johnson sought comfort in the consensus he demanded from those who surrounded him, the hubris produced by his interpretation of America's and his own history, and his values, which he considered universal ones. Only when his political antennae told him he had no alternative, and his advisers in his eyes betrayed him, did he deny the military its troop requests and cease bombing North Vietnam in an effort to reach a negotiated settlement. His effort, however, was too little and too late. That it was cost Lyndon Johnson dearly. But it cost the people of the United States and Vietnam much more.

I gratefully acknowledge the assistance and counsel of George C. Herring, Robert Jervis, and Colonel Paul L. Miles, U.S. Army, ret. I must also personally express my appreciation to David Humphrey, who continually frustrated my efforts to call an end to my research.

4

Threats, Opportunities, and Frustrations in East Asia

NANCY BERNKOPF TUCKER

Although we are making real progress in developing a distinctive approach of this Administration to Africa, Latin America, and Europe, it is clear that a good part of your Administration's place in history will consist in the reshaping of Asia and our relations in it.[1]

Walt Rostow's optimistic assessment of the impact that Lyndon Johnson's presidency would have upon Asia carries in retrospect more than its share of bitter irony. For the policies that the National Security Adviser celebrated actually entailed decisions that devastated the administration, winning Johnson no credit in the region. At the heart of Johnson's vision of Asia stood Vietnam. Beyond that commitment, to which LBJ sought to bind the United States' Asian allies and by which he judged the United States' Asian enemies, his ideas lacked energy and imagination. No new era dawned. Johnson made little progress toward normalization with China; inaugurated few departures in relations with Japan, South Korea, or Taiwan; and reached possibly the nadir, following the Korean War, in interaction with North Korea. Rostow, of course, proved correct in his estimate that Lyndon Johnson would be remembered for his involvement in Asia, but the weight of the Vietnam disaster precluded initiatives or accomplishments that would have made his place in history a positive rather than a negative chapter.

LBJ's preoccupation with Vietnam provided the framework for the president's approach toward and assessments of the nations of

1. Memo Walt W. Rostow to Lyndon Johnson, October 12, 1966, Memos to the President, Walt Rostow, Box 10, Folder: Vol. 14, October 1–31, 1966 [2 of 2], Lyndon Baines Johnson Library, Austin, Texas (hereafter LBJL). Rostow suggested to the president that they compile a book of LBJ's speeches on Asia.

Asia.[2] His determination to command multinational support in Indochina meant that the White House and State Department bargained aid and bartered military equipment to secure troops or logistic units from South Korea, Taiwan, and Japan, creating an international but also a mercenary fighting force. The obsession exposed Washington to manipulation by weak allies whose interests were not always compatible with American goals but whom Johnson often placated in the effort to attain victory in Vietnam. Seoul and Taipei in particular saw the entreaties to help the United States in Vietnam as hooks by which to link Washington to their distinct agendas and to discourage demands for internal reform that might otherwise have caused disharmony in relations. Although Washington tried assiduously to characterize the struggle against communism in southeast Asia as a battle protecting all of its allies in the area, the allies focused on more immediate threats to their individual commands of power, whether from North Korea to the south or from mainland China across the Taiwan Straits. Meanwhile, the Japanese absorbed themselves in economic development, providing minimal assistance to the Vietnam effort while generally disapproving of U.S. actions there.

Vietnam also shaped Johnson's picture of China. Here he saw evidence of the conviction, shared by his primary foreign policy adviser, Secretary of State Dean Rusk, that aggressive communism invariably sought ways to expand. Soviet communist pressures on Europe might have lessened, but the same could not be said of Chinese communist influence over the North Vietnamese, whose refusal to reach a compromise settlement owed much to Beijing's[3] support and encouragement.[4] So long as China appeared to Johnson to be expounding a "doctrine of violence" and advocating wars of national liberation, improvement in Sino–American rela-

2. James C. Thomson of the National Security Council staff lamented to McGeorge Bundy that the United States devoted inordinate energy to the Indochina problem, ignoring China in the process, even while assuming that Vietnam was the tail of the dog. "I am not even sure that this tail belongs to that particular dog; there is danger in pushing too far the thesis of Peking's responsibility for the South Vietnam crisis." Memo, October 28, 1964, NSF Country File China, Box 237–8, F: China memos, Vol. II, September 1964–February 1965, LBJL.
3. A note on romanization: Names of people and places associated with the People's Republic of China are rendered in *pinyin,* whereas those identified with the Nationalist Chinese on Taiwan follow older systems in which they are more commonly transcribed.
4. Dean Rusk, *As I Saw It* (New York: Penguin, 1990), 286.

tions would not claim his serious attention.[5] Thus, the president, although sensitive to the challenge to China's security that the war in Indochina posed, pushed to the limits of Beijing's tolerance for military action along its border and for use of Taiwan's assistance. The frequent and anxious discussions within the administration of the possibility of massive Chinese intervention in Vietnam acted as a serious but not absolute restraint.[6] And the Johnson administration learned to live with more modest, though hardly negligible, Chinese participation in the war effort as, between 1965 and 1968, some 50,000 People's Liberation Army (PLA) troops took up positions in North Vietnam from which they "engaged in combat, inflicted losses, and suffered casualties."[7]

Confirmation that Chinese communism posed a danger throughout Asia, moreover, appeared early in 1968 when North Korea reached out from behind its cloistered frontiers to seize the U.S.S. *Pueblo*. Washington almost immediately interpreted the move as more than a local gesture connected with increased northern harassment of South Korea. The United States believed that Pyongyang (spurred on by Beijing) wanted to aid Hanoi by distracting Washington and discouraging Seoul's involvement in Vietnam. When, shortly thereafter, the Tet Offensive erupted, linkage appeared undeniable.

China

Rostow's emphasis on the centrality of Asia to the Johnson administration might have been implied also by the speech delivered on

5. Lyndon B. Johnson, *The Vantage Point: Perspectives of the Presidency, 1963–1969* (New York: Holt, Rinehart & Winston, 1971), 53.
6. Countless conversations and memos raised the issue, but possibly the most impassioned was that of George Ball completed October 5, 1964, which warned of a "fair chance" of a Korean-style crisis. Ball believed that "Johnson was deeply preoccupied with the China menace and the more I emphasized it, the stronger was my case for cutting our losses." McNamara, on the other hand, concluded that a limited air war could be fought safely. Even he drew the line at sending ground troops north, which Walt Rostow considered acceptable. Deborah Shapley, *Promise and Power: The Life and Times of Robert McNamara* (Boston: Little, Brown, 1993), 302, 311, 341; George Ball, *The Past Has Another Pattern* (New York: Norton, 1982), 406 (quotation); Rusk, *As I Saw It*, 456–7; Allen S. Whiting, *The Chinese Calculus of Deterrence* (Ann Arbor: University of Michigan Press, 1975), 194.
7. These soldiers performed logistical support activities and acted as a deterrent to an American invasion. Whiting, *Chinese Calculus of Deterrence*, 170–95, quotation, 187.

December 13, 1963, by Roger Hilsman, assistant secretary of state, to the Commonwealth Club of San Francisco. One of the first foreign policy initiatives in the frantic days of the new Johnson presidency, the address proved sensational in its suggestion that there be an open door to a more pragmatic China. Taiwan would continue to be protected, but the possibility of a "two Chinas" policy ought not to be ignored, because the Chinese communist government clearly could no longer be considered a passing phenomenon.[8] Although the talk actually broke little new ground, it elicited comment throughout the nation and the world, congratulating Washington on adopting a more sensible and constructive attitude.[9]

To Lyndon Johnson the Chinese would, however, have to prove that they merited flexibility in U.S. policy. Jim Thomson, National Security Council analyst, had optimistically predicted, "now that we have talked dispassionately about China without having the roof fall in, we will have the courage to talk a good deal more about China."[10] In fact, few bold actions followed. The administration was stunned and distraught when in January 1964 Charles de Gaulle broke ranks with the United States to offer diplomatic recognition to the People's Republic. Whereas Rusk favored signals to Beijing that there would be room in the world community for a more cooperative, less dogmatic, peaceable China, he rejected the French move because it would mislead a still-belligerent Beijing as to what sort of behavior was internationally acceptable.[11] French laxity made it all the more imperative that Washington maintain a

8. James Thomson recorded a history of the genesis of the speech that made clear the somewhat cursory clearances it received and the dismay after it attracted so much attention. Memorandum, May 6, 1964, James C. Thomson Papers, Box 9, F: Hilsman December 13, 1963 San Francisco – Thomson Notes on Genesis and Reaction, John F. Kennedy Library, Boston, Massachusetts (hereafter JFKL).
9. Clipping files in the Thomson papers highlight the attention that the speech commanded and the care with which Thomson and Hilsman watched the responses. Thomson Papers, Box 10, 3 folders: Hilsman 12/13/63 San Francisco Correspondence and Press, December 9–31, 1963, JFKL. In retrospect Thomson noted that conservative and Republican journals joined the liberal press in favorable comment, and no one on Capitol Hill voiced any objections either. Memo for Bundy, n.d., Thomson Papers, Box 16, F: Far East: Communist China, January 1966–February 1966, JFKL.
10. Thomson Papers, Box 10, F: Hilsman December 13, 1963 San Francisco Correspondence and Press, December 26–31, 1963, JFKL.
11. Rusk's biographer Warren I. Cohen argues that the hard line against China in the early 1960s was more a result of Kennedy's obsessions than Rusk's intractability, whereas Kennedy insider James C. Thomson blames everything on Rusk. Warren I. Cohen, *Dean Rusk* (Totowa, N.J.: Cooper Square, 1980), 172, 281.

stern demeanor. Indeed, Johnson and Rusk's view of de Gaulle's decision as foolhardy seemed to them to have been validated later in the year when China exploded its own nuclear device, implicitly threatening its Asian neighbors if not yet the United States directly.

China's siren call for revolutionary action, moreover, echoed elsewhere in Asia in the mid-1960s. Early in 1965 President Sukarno led Indonesia out of the United Nations into Beijing's open arms and pursued an increasingly pro-communist, anti-American policy. The U.S. embassy became the target of repeated and sometimes violent demonstrations. To Johnson's chagrin, this appeared to be just the first step in a frightening transformation of southeast Asia. That September, Mao Zedong's heir apparent Lin Biao delivered a speech entitled "Long Live the Victory of People's War" in which he pledged the country's support for national liberation struggles everywhere. American analysts saw this as a Chinese *Mein Kampf,* committing Beijing to undermine vulnerable colonial and newly independent countries. For LBJ, who remembered vividly what the "loss of China" had done to the political fortunes of the Truman administration, the echo of falling dominoes seemed intolerably loud. Fortunately, however, the crisis in Indonesia broke the following month when a communist coup, involving a bloody purge of the national army (and accusations of a CIA plot against Sukarno), was thwarted by General Suharto, triggering a nationwide reaction against the communist party (PKI), ultimately toppling Sukarno and totally undermining China's influence.[12] The broader challenge of Chinese revolutionary nationalism, however, remained.

The worsening of the Sino–Soviet split further exacerbated the image of China as irresponsible and unpredictable. During the Kennedy years, Americans had been slow to accept the reality of the rift, fearing that the quarrel between Moscow and Beijing was either a sham or so insubstantial that it would soon pass. By the mid-1960s, however, oft-repeated public denunciations and secret

12. Marshall Green's account of his ambassadorship describes the problems Americans confronted along with a discussion of the coup that came to be known as the GESTAPU (September 30 movement) affair. *Indonesia: Crisis and Transformation, 1965–1968* (Washington: Compass Press, 1990), Chs. 1–6. Regarding earlier CIA involvement see Howard P. Jones, *Indonesia: The Possible Dream* (New York: Harcourt Brace Jovanovich, 1971).

U.S. intelligence assessments had convinced Washington that the dispute existed, would endure, and rested in part upon Chinese opposition to Soviet–American reconciliation. As the split intensified, so too did Beijing's promotion of anti-American movements and the volume of Beijing's anti-American rhetoric. The contrast with a newly sober and cautious Soviet Union worsened China's standing, particularly when Soviet diplomats confided in their American counterparts that Chinese competition had forced Soviet leaders reluctantly to adopt hardline policies. Whereas at one time American officials had anticipated a day when China could be aligned with the West against Moscow, in the Johnson years it appeared that the United States had a better chance of siding with a mature Soviet Union against the fanatic Chinese. In fact, in the Vietnam war theater rivalry between Moscow and Beijing over Hanoi's loyalties had sharpened their conflict and made plausible a Soviet willingness to try to end the fighting promptly, thereby providing one of the few bright spots in American analysis of the war's progress.[13]

China's own instability became apparent when the excesses of the Great Proletarian Cultural Revolution spilled over into foreign affairs.[14] Chinese demonstrated in capitals around the world, ambassadors were withdrawn, and, in a paroxysm of radical frenzy, Red Guards sacked and burned the British Embassy in Beijing during August 1967. Americans could only be grateful that their lack of formal relations with the Chinese spared them similar experiences with proletarian diplomacy.

Following a pattern in Sino–American relations that saw China and the United States always at incompatible points regarding accommodation, China's plunge into fanaticism came just at the moment that Americans moved to moderate their view of relations with China. Inside and outside, a search for new approaches to China began. This exploration appeared rooted in acceptance of the reality of a strong communist regime in China, its endurance,

13. George Herring, *America's Longest War* (New York: Knopf, 1986), 148.
14. Ironically in a CIA report prepared in the first half of 1966 the agency predicted that the radical turn in internal politics would not spread to foreign policy. The CIA also saw the internal situation as reducing chances for Chinese intervention in Vietnam. Memos to the President: Walt Rostow, Box 9, F: Vol. VIII July 1–15, 1966 [1 of 2], LBJL.

effectiveness, and even popularity. Concern with the spread of communism in Asia mandated continued containment, but various groups contemplated increased contact. Hearings conducted by the Senate Foreign Relations Committee in 1966 helped popularize the strategy as one of "containment without isolation," suggesting inclusion of China in the world community.[15] The Council on Foreign Relations and the newly formed National Committee on U.S.–China Relations stimulated public discussion through sponsorship of publications and discussions on Sino–American interaction. Organizations like the U.S. Chamber of Commerce passed resolutions advocating new channels of communication with mainland China.[16] At the same time, the tenaciously pro-Nationalist China Lobby appeared to be in decline as the public became more willing to contemplate coexistence with China.[17]

A comprehensive review of developments in and approaches toward communist China by a special group assembled from the State and Defense Departments made the case in mid-1966 that the United States "should try to induce present or future Communist leaders to reappraise U.S. intentions" and "increase Peking's interest in developing a more constructive relationship," because "a strategy of containment need not result in a frozen confrontation." Thus the group recommended public and private reassurance that Washington was not seeking to overthrow the Chinese Communist Party (CCP). Moreover, it called for changes in trade controls to permit humanitarian assistance, proposals of educa-

---

15. "Statement of A. Doak Barnett, Professor of Government and Acting Director of the East Asian Institute, Columbia University," in Hearings, Senate Committee on Foreign Relations, *U.S. Policy with Respect to Mainland China*, 89th Congress, 2nd sess. (Washington: Government Printing Office, 1966), 4.
16. Memo Thomson to Bundy, May 26, 1965, Thomson Papers, Box 11, JFKL.
17. The trend in public views appeared cautiously to be moving in favor of recognition and admission to the United Nations (although the totals continued to register majorities opposing these actions) until the chaos of the Cultural Revolution reversed it. Thomson Memo, August 21, 1964, NSF Country File China, Box 237–8, F: China Memos Vol. I, December 1963–September 1964, LBJL; Hayes Redmon to Bill Moyers, July 11, 1966, White House Confidential File (hereafter WHCF), Executive, Box 22, F: CO 50–2 May 17, 1966, LBJL; Gallup Survey, February 20, 1969, *The Gallup Poll: Public Opinion, 1935–1970*, 3 Vols. (New York: Random House, 1972), 2183. A somewhat more negative assessment can be found in Leonard A. Kusnitz, *Public Opinion and Foreign Policy: America's China Policy, 1949–1979* (Westport, Conn.: Greenwood Press, 1984), 105–20.

tional and cultural exchanges, and a generally nonprovocative stance on the part of the Johnson administration.[18] Hopes that the Cultural Revolution might eventually result in a change of leadership, allowing more pragmatic elements to assume control, encouraged analysts to consider policies more attuned to helping a needy and chastened China.[19]

Increasingly the thrust in Washington reflected interest around the nation in liberalizing China policy. The rhetorical excesses of the Eisenhower and Kennedy years gave way to conciliatory speeches by government officials at all levels, asserting not just the United States' lack of aggressive ambitions but also the need for dialogue. By the spring of 1966 even Secretary of Defense Robert S. McNamara and Secretary of State Dean Rusk were calling for building bridges to China, although Rusk was quick to emphasize that the Chinese would first have to stop seeking world revolution.[20] Lyndon Johnson on July 12, 1966, called for reconciliation and tried to reassure China that the United States intended neither to conquer North Vietnam nor to attack southern China.[21] Indeed, the tough stand being followed in Vietnam seemed useful protective coloration for a more constructive China policy to men such as Jim Thomson and Robert Komer of the National Security Council (NSC) and Edwin O. Reischauer, ambassador to Japan.[22] Former Vice President Richard Nixon, having no need for camouflage given his belligerently anticommunist credentials, explicitly remarked in a 1967 article in *Foreign Affairs* that the time to isolate China had passed, that China should be drawn into the world community.[23]

Greater flexibility in thinking about China produced gains, if rather small ones, in relaxing restrictions on relations with the Chinese. That changes remained minor stemmed in part from the justification for them, which amounted to shifting the blame for

18. Special State–Defense Study Group, "Communist China – Long Range Study," pp. 19–20, June 1966, NSF Country File China, Box 245, LBJL.
19. Department of State, Administrative History, Vol. I, Chapter VII (East Asia), sections A–D, November 1963–January 1969, pp. 26–7, LBJL.
20. Shapley, *Promise and Power,* 381–2; Rusk, *As I Saw It,* 288.
21. Murray Marder, "LBJ States U.S. Power Role in Asia," *Washington Post,* July 13, 1966.
22. Komer to the President, August 16, 1966, NSF Country File China, Box 239, F: China Memos Vol. VI, March 1966–September 1966, LBJL.
23. Richard M. Nixon, "Asia After Viet Nam," *Foreign Affairs* 46 (October 1967).

China's isolation to China. Whereas some policymakers genuinely wished to open new channels of contact, others wanted only to diminish criticism from America's allies regarding the hardline approach to Beijing.[24] In 1965 and 1966 travel prohibitions were removed for several categories of professionals such as doctors, journalists, scientists, and scholars. U.S. government officials abroad received authorization to pursue informal social contacts with the communist Chinese should occasions arise without "undue risk of conveying the public impression of a change in the US policy of non-recognition." During 1967 the U.S. government liberalized trade controls to permit sales of pharmaceuticals for several diseases reported in epidemic proportions in China. Certainly a humanitarian gesture, the move also sought to protect U.S. servicemen fighting in Vietnam.[25] And in 1968 the United States Information Agency issued an invitation for Chinese journalists to travel to the United States in order to report on the presidential election campaign and use Voice of America broadcasting to send uncensored reports home.[26] Washington also minimized its criticism of expanding contacts, including economic and financial transactions, between China and the nations of western Europe and Japan.

The Chinese did not welcome alterations in U.S. policy, insisting that improvements in relations must await movement on the problem of Taiwan. They denounced the lifting of trade bans on drugs as an effort to embarrass China and refused to issue visas for Americans holding newly validated passports.[27] Initiatives inviting Chinese journalists and scientists to the United States were ignored.

Nevertheless, the Sino–American ambassadorial talks held periodically at Warsaw since the offshore islands crisis of 1958 persisted during the Johnson administration. Although there were only twenty-one formal sessions, beginning in May 1966 informal conversations at the Chinese Embassy supplemented the stilted official exchanges. Not notable for concrete progress, the contacts

24. Memo for Bundy (not sent), n.d., Thomson Papers, Box 16, F: Far East: Communist China January 1966–February 1966, JFKL.
25. Administrative History, Chapter VII (East Asia), pp. 29–30, 34–8, 49 (quotation).
26. Roderick MacFarquhar, ed., *Sino–American Relations 1949–1971* (Newton Abbot, Great Britain: David & Charles, 1972), 236.
27. Administrative History, Chapter VII (East Asia), 31, 38.

did provide a degree of regular interaction that many embassies in Beijing lacked. Through Warsaw, moreover, the Americans found it possible to reassure the Chinese that military operations in Vietnam would not spill over the frontier.

Less successful were efforts to bring China into international disarmament agreements. Initially the United States did not, in fact, encourage invitations to the Chinese lest arms control prove an indirect route to UN admission, but soon the need to control nuclear weapons took precedence. China refused to adhere to the test ban treaty of 1963, denounced the nuclear nonproliferation treaty as an effort to perpetuate a Soviet–American monopoly, rejected or ignored opportunities to participate in conferences at Geneva, and, in 1966 after American press leaks, aborted discussions at Warsaw regarding linkage between a no-first-use pledge and suspension of nuclear testing.[28]

China's obduracy regarding nuclear issues alarmed Washington policymakers. Beijing had moved beyond Mao's early dismissal of the atomic bomb as "a paper tiger which the U.S. reactionaries use to scare people."[29] Clearly Beijing intended to join the nuclear club. As the moment of the first Chinese explosion neared, anxiety reached such heights that the president discussed with his secretaries of state and defense and CIA Director John McCone an approach to Moscow suggesting "preventive military action." Although entrusted with the responsibility, Dean Rusk never actually raised the issue with Soviet Ambassador Anatoly Dobrynin.[30] Instead the administration accepted the fact of the Chinese bomb and moved expeditiously to reassure China's neighbors that the nuclear device would be primitive, that it would not significantly change the power balance, and that the United States would stand by its commitments in the area.[31] In 1967 when the United States failed

28. Ibid., 51–5.
29. Mao Zedong, *Selected Works of Mao Tse-tung*, Vol. IV (Peking: Foreign Language Press, 1969), 100. On the other hand, the CIA reported a disturbing mid-1966 indoctrination film which purported to show that atomic bombs were not so very dangerous if one dug deep shelters. CIA, Intelligence Information Cable, January 14, 1967, NSF Country File China, Box 240, Vol. VIII, LBJL.
30. John L. Gaddis, *Strategies of Containment* (New York: Oxford University Press, 1982), 210; Shapley, *Promise and Power*, 288.
31. John Wilson Lewis and Xue Litai, *China Builds the Bomb* (Stanford, Calif.: Stanford University Press, 1988), 1–2; Lyndon Johnson made the guarantee explicit in a televised speech on October 18, 1964. Memo Thomson to Valenti, March 4, 1965, WHCF, Countries, Box 23, F: CO 50–2 China, People's Republic of, January 13, 1965–December 6, 1965, LBJL.

to get Soviet Premier Alexei Kosygin to agree not to construct an anti-ballistic missile defense system, agitation by the Joint Chiefs of Staff and Johnson's worries about political repercussions led to creation of a limited ABM (Sentinel) packaged as protection against a Chinese threat. A scientist, Richard Garwin, reflecting the fact that the Chinese had no delivery capability, remarked that it was not "an anti-Chinese ABM" but rather "an anti-Republican one."[32] Still it highlighted China's potential and its unwillingness to cooperate in limiting weapons development.

China's very resistance to arms-control agreements heightened the desire of many nations to bring Beijing into the United Nations and other international organizations that might have the effect of restraining Chinese behavior. Pressures had been increasing, in any case, as fourteen new African states recognized Beijing during 1964, cutting substantially into the majority in the United Nations that Washington had been able to preserve for Taiwan since 1949.[33] By 1965 analysts within the U.S. government recognized that Washington faced imminent defeat on the representation issue.[34] Recommendations to deal with this impending crisis ranged from finding new tactics to block Chinese admission to promoting

32. Shapley, *Promise and Power*, 390–4; Gregg Herken, *Counsels of War* (New York: Oxford University Press, 1987), 196–8 (quotation). At the end of 1966 U.S. analysts concluded that the Chinese had no "militarily useful nuclear capability," might be able to threaten their Asian neighbors "within a few years," and could conceivably have "a few ICBMs by the early 1970s." However, the State Department believed "we will for the foreseeable future have such a marked superiority that it would be suicidal for them to attempt a nuclear attack on the US." #CA 4864. "Recent Developments in Strategic Forces," pp. 9–10, December 31, 1966, NSF Country File USSR, Box 231, F: ABM Negotiations, January 1967–September 1968, LBJL. Nevertheless, as Walt Rostow warned the president, the report of the Congressional Joint Committee on Atomic Energy suggesting a Chinese capability by the early 1970s would make headlines. Memo Rostow to LBJ, August 1, 1967, Memos to the President, Walt Rostow, Box 20, F: Vol. XXXVII August 1–10, 1967 [2 of 2], LBJL.
33. Gordon H. Chang, *Friends and Enemies: The United States, China, and the Soviet Union, 1948–1972* (Stanford, Calif.: Stanford University Press, 1990), 261.
34. The vote in the UN in the autumn of 1965 proved extremely close. On the important-question resolution, which held that a change in representation would be an important question under Article 18 of the UN Charter requiring a two-thirds vote, fifty-six voted in favor, forty-nine against with eleven abstentions. On the substantive (Albanian) resolution, ejecting the ROC and seating the PRC, the vote was forty-seven in favor, forty-seven against, and twenty abstentions. State Department analysts noted that had Israel and the Congo stayed home, the United States would have lost. Telcon Sisco and Ball, November 17, 1965, Ball Papers, Box 1–3, F: China (Peking) January 27, 1964–July 22, 1966, LBJL. Moreover, there was the fear that if the proponents of admission could get a simple majority this might produce a major shift of undecided countries or those like Great Britain, which had recognized the PRC but had not supported it in the UN.

the idea of seating one China and one Taiwan. The bottom line became inclusion of the Republic of China (ROC) rather than exclusion of the People's Republic of China (PRC).[35] But miraculously in 1966 the tide turned, the margin once again widened, and the ROC's position was strengthened. This result, which endured beyond the end of the Johnson years, arose from a combination of the chaos of China's Cultural Revolution (particularly as it spilled into the international arena), the vituperativeness of the Sino–Soviet split, and the reluctance of a sufficient number of countries to expel Taiwan as the price for Chinese communist entry.

Ironically, the events that would permit a real breakthrough in Sino–American relations occurred in the waning days of the Johnson presidency but did not produce action until Richard Nixon took office. On March 31, 1968, when Lyndon Johnson announced that he would not seek reelection and would actively pursue peace in Vietnam, he also declared limits on the American bombing of North Vietnam. This reduction in the intensity of the U.S. effort produced, in turn, a decision by the Chinese communists gradually to withdraw their troops from Vietnam. Thus a major source of friction between Washington and Beijing diminished during 1968.[36] More important, the August Soviet invasion of Czechoslovakia and the accompanying Brezhnev Doctrine, which declared Moscow's right to intervene in bloc states to preserve socialism, frightened Beijing with the specter of a war against the Soviet Union. Suddenly it seemed imperative to reach an accommodation with the United States so as to deter aggression from Moscow. Zhou Enlai in November called for a resumption of the Warsaw talks, to which the Johnson administration replied favorably, but both sides recognized that action would have to wait until the new administration was in place.[37] Ultimately this Chinese initiative would progress haltingly, because of internal opposition, but culminate in Nixon's journey to Beijing and the 1972 Shanghai Com-

---

35. When the United States explained to the ROC that the important-question approach could no longer be sustained and that it (the United States) might have to vote in favor of an Italian proposal for a group to study the representation issue, Taipei threatened to walk out of the UN. Under intense U.S. pressure the Taiwan authorities finally agreed only to suspend active participation. Department of State, Administrative History, Vol. I, Chapter 10: The UN: sections A & B, LBJL.
36. Whiting, *Chinese Calculus of Deterrence,* 186.
37. Kusnitz, *Public Opinion and Foreign Policy,* 131.

muniqué, completely changing the complexion of U.S.–China relations forever.

Taiwan

In Taipei the modest changes in American rhetoric about and policies toward mainland China produced anxiety and despair. The *China News* questioned how Johnson and his China advisers could have "forgotten Hitler and Mussolini and Tojo so soon" in their eagerness to placate Mao.[38] Chiang Kai-shek became convinced that U.S. resistance to Beijing's ploys would quickly collapse. Taipei began to brace for a series of disasters, including the PRC's admission into the UN, its own ensuing walkout, and, ultimately, total abandonment as Washington recognized Beijing.[39]

The United States insisted that the improvement of relations with Beijing "detracts in no way from our support of the Republic of China." To strengthen that argument the Johnson administration agreed to speed delivery of aircraft, continue exchanges of intelligence information, and provide briefings on the Warsaw talks with Beijing.[40] Johnson even pledged that he would honor John Kennedy's secret commitment to use the United States' Security Council veto to keep Nationalist China in the United Nations if absolutely necessary, although his advisers feared that this would not be enough to save Taipei.[41]

As American ardor for the Nationalist Chinese visibly slackened Chiang Kai-shek devised a new strategy to try to keep Washington committed to Taiwan. Aware of the growing U.S. obsession with fighting communism in southeast Asia, Chiang aggressively sought to link Taipei's fortunes to those of Saigon. Thus during the John-

38. #180 McConaughy, Taipei, July 16, 1966, Thomson Papers, Box 11: Speeches/ National Security Staff, F: LBJ 7/12/66 White Sulphur Springs – Diplomatic Reactions, JFKL.
39. #1086 Hummel, Taipei, April 6, 1966, NSF Country File Box 239, F: China Cables Vol. VI 3/66–9/66, LBJL; #1240 May 7, 1966, ibid., LBJL.
40. #993 Hummel, Taipei, March 17, 1966, NSF Country File, Box 239, F: China Cables Vol. VI 3/66–9/66, LBJL; Memo Rusk to the President, n.d., NSF Country File, Bx 244–5, F: China – Visit of C. K. Yen 5/9–10/67 Briefing Book, LBJL.
41. Airgram Taipei to Washington, April 27, 1964, NSF Country File, Box 237–8, F: China memos Vol. I: 12/63–9/64, LBJL.

son administration he repeatedly proposed schemes targeting the southeastern provinces of China for an attack that would parallel U.S. operations in Vietnam.[42]

Such designs effectively challenged Beijing in a particularly sensitive area of concern. Not only did the communist authorities have to worry about Chiang's efforts to retake the mainland, but, more decisively, Mao had long believed that Korea, Taiwan, and Indochina provided vantage points from which American imperialism would confront China. Having sacrificed recently and heavily in Korea, he watched the other fronts with trepidation.[43]

On the other hand, few things in the mid-1960s could attract Lyndon Johnson's attention as could offers of help in southeast Asia. Although intelligence analysts quickly and consistently discounted the likelihood that an assault on southern China would destabilize Beijing and help bring the Vietnam conflict to a rapid conclusion, assistance in Vietnam could not be so easily dismissed.[44] In 1964 Johnson announced a program to solicit support from third countries, which suddenly made Chiang's importunings evoke eager anticipation rather than annoyance.[45] Harry Truman had avoided Chiang's embrace on the Korean peninsula, rejecting his repeated efforts to contribute troops to that war, but with different priorities Johnson gave participation of Nationalist forces in Vietnam serious consideration. It seemed a natural collaboration given Johnson's assumption that the Chinese communists were responsible for continuing North Vietnamese aggression. A February 1965 Harris poll showed 53 percent of respondents blaming China

42. Memcon Rusk and Chiang, April 16, 1964, NSF Country File, Vol. 4, Box 238, LBJL; Memo for the Record: Views of Ambassador Wright, May 12, 1964, Thomson Papers, F: Far East: Taiwan 1958, 1962–64, LBJL; Memo Jenkins to Rostow, March 7, 1967, NSF Country File, Box 241, F: China Memos, Vol. IX, 3/67–6/67, LBJL.

43. Wang Jisi, "From Kennedy to Nixon: America's East Asia and China Policy," *Beijing Review*, May 16–22, 1988. Zhang Shu Guang refers to this preoccupation as Mao's "three front concept." *Deterrence and Strategic Culture* (Ithaca, N.Y.: Cornell University Press, 1992), 174, 190. Re American conclusion that PRC fears were genuine see #1539 Rice, Hong Kong, February 19, 1966, NSF Country File, Box 239, F: China Cables Vol. 5, 10/65–1/66, LBJL.

44. SC No. 10078/65, CIA Office of Current Intelligence, "Probable Effects in China and Taiwan of a GRC Attack on the Mainland," August 18, 1965, NSF Country File Vietnam, Box 50–1, F: Vol. II: Special Intelligence Material 7/65–10/65, LBJL; LBJ Message for Chiang, NSF, Memos to the President, Box 14, F: Walt Rostow Vol. 23, 3/10–15/67 [1 of 2], LBJL.

45. Memorandum for the President, December 15, 1964, Memos to the President, Box 2: McGeorge Bundy, Vol. 7, 10/1–12/31/64 [1 of 2], LBJL.

for Viet Cong attacks whereas only 26 percent held the North Vietnamese accountable.[46] Moreover, South Vietnamese officials had urged Washington to enlist Chiang's troops as early as 1961.[47] Nevertheless advisers ultimately persuaded the president that uniformed Nationalist fighting men would be too provocative, arguing that other ways existed in which Chiang could be useful.[48]

The ways proved multiple if only marginally less dangerous. Nationalist soldiers carried out covert-action operations in cooperation with the CIA and American military intelligence; airmen flew transport and espionage missions and staffed technical maintenance teams.[49] A large contingent from Taiwan disguised as Vietnamese soldiers served in the Sea Swallows military unit, under the command of a Catholic priest and supported by American aid.[50] In Taiwan the Nationalists set up training programs and willingly provided staging areas; lengthened runways; stationed C-130 transport squadrons, KC-135 tankers, 13th Air Force fighter aircraft, and two fast reaction F-4 nuclear bombers; established repair facilities; and allowed the island to be used for ever larger deployments as well as armed forces rest and recreation.

In compensation for participation in the Vietnam effort as well as to strengthen self-defense capabilities on the island, the United States provided training and weapons to Nationalist forces throughout the Johnson presidency. The levels of such assistance, however, declined with the growing pressure of military expenditures on the U.S. budget and the development of a chronic balance-of-payments problem. In 1967 the U.S. Congress reduced the entire military assistance program, dropping Taiwan's share 50 percent. The U.S. embassy and

---

46. George McT. Kahin, *Intervention* (Garden City, N.Y.: Doubleday, 1987), 287.
47. U.S. Department of State, *Foreign Relations of the United States 1961–63*, Vol. I: *Vietnam 1961* (Washington: Government Printing Office, 1988), 91, 431–6. In 1966 they were still advocating in discussions with Japan that Chiang be supported in trying to return to the mainland. #3734 Johnson, Tokyo, November 19, 1966, NSF Country File Japan, Box 251, Vol. V, LBJL.
48. Warning against allowing Nationalist troops to fight in Vietnam came from various quarters: #129 Rice, Hong Kong, August 2, 1965, NSF Country File, Box 237–8, F: China Cables, Vol. IV 7/65–10/65, LBJL. In December 1966 Chiang told Rusk that he had reconsidered the idea of contributing uniformed troops lest settlement of the Taiwan question become part of the Vietnam denouement. Memo May 4, 1967, NSF Country File, Box 244–5, F: China – Visit of C. K. Yen 5/9–10/67 Briefing Book, LBJL.
49. #315 Hummel, Taipei, September 14, 1965, NSF Country File, Box 237–8, F: China Cables Vol. IV, LBJL; Interview with Ray Cline, May 1992.
50. Kahin, *Intervention*, 333.

the American Military Assistance Advisory Group used the contraction to renew entreaties to the Nationalist authorities to cut military spending before Taiwan's economic growth and social stability suffered. Military expenditures had consistently averaged 10 percent of GNP and more than 80 percent of the central government's annual budget.[51] Taipei put more money into the military than any other nation not actively at war and fielded the largest standing army, proportionately to population, in the world. The Nationalists obdurately resisted all pressure to decrease forces, making up for cuts in American military support with escalation of their own appropriations, until 1967. At that point Defense Minister Chiang Ching-kuo finally agreed to engage in discussions about the reorganization of the military with the combined goal of shrinking the numbers of men in uniform while maintaining security.[52]

In addition to military collaboration, Nationalist officials insisted on economic linkage to the Vietnam effort, particularly as U.S. aid programs began to be phased out in the mid-1960s. Taipei emphasized procurement for the war theater and created a Committee on Overseas Economic Promotion specifically designed to increase Taiwan's share of the U.S.-financed commercial import program for Vietnam. Until Washington restricted purchases to U.S. suppliers, Taiwan's trade profits soared. Nationalist technicians in agricultural, medical, and public works served in Vietnam largely through U.S. Agency for International Development financing, although Taipei also directly contributed a power substation, textbooks, seeds, fertilizer, prefabricated buildings, and more than $800,000 of commodity assistance.[53] Each of these programs, whether military or economic, tightened bonds between Washington and Taipei as well as giving the Nationalist regime greater visibility in world affairs.

Ironically, the termination of economic aid to Taiwan, rooted in the growing prosperity of the island, accelerated in response to American economic problems aggravated by the Vietnam commitment. Congressional cuts of 34 percent in the president's proposed

51. It consumed some 55 percent even of the consolidated central and provincial annual budget, which better reflected the unavoidable internal expenditures. *New York Times* (March 24, 1968), 5.
52. Administrative History of the Department of State, Vol. I, Chapter 7, pt D: Taiwan, LBJL.
53. Ibid.; Visit of C. K. Yen 5/9–10/67 Briefing Book, LBJL.

1964 foreign aid bill led officials to use Taiwan as an example of successful foreign assistance, declaring precipitously that no further allocations would be necessary after June 1965.[54]

To Taiwan's relief, aid did not terminate abruptly on June 30. The two governments through the Sino–American Fund for Economic and Social Development continued to apply the proceeds of established programs to development projects.[55] They negotiated new food aid agreements, under the Agricultural Trade Development and Assistance Act of 1954 (Public Law 480), facilitated scientific exchange that contributed to industrial modernization, and, above all, the United States continued to provide generous access to the American market.[56]

Taipei proved less able to use the Vietnam conflict to convince Washington of the need for a regional military alliance based on American financial support and the possible involvement of U.S. air and naval forces. Chiang Kai-shek's desire to draw Taiwan, South Korea, and other nations in the area together dated back to the late 1940s, when the concept of a Pacific Pact had been resisted by State Department officials who saw it as a perilous trap. In its new guise Chiang argued that such a grouping would counter growing Chinese militancy that, he insisted, had accompanied development of Beijing's atomic bomb.[57] But, although Walt Rostow favored regional integration and the president spoke of Asian unity in his Johns Hopkins University speech of April 7, 1965, they saw it as economic cooperation through agencies such as the Asian Development Bank and the Asian and Pacific Council, not as military association.[58]

54. *New York Times*, July 1, 1965, 1–2; Burton I. Kaufman, "Foreign Aid and the Balance-of-Payments Problem: Vietnam and Johnson's Foreign Economic Policy," in Robert A. Divine, ed., *The Johnson Years*, Vol. II (Lawrence: University Press of Kansas, 1987), 80–4.

55. Memo David Bell, AID, November 27, 1964, White House Central Files, Confidential File, CO 50–1 (Formosa), LBJL; T. H. Shen, *The Sino–American Joint Commission on Rural Reconstruction* (Ithaca, N.Y.: Cornell University Press, 1970), 251–2.

56. Maurice Scott, "Foreign Trade," in Walter Galenson, ed., *Economic Growth and Structural Change in Taiwan: The Postwar Experience of the Republic of China* (Ithaca, N.Y.: Cornell University Press, 1979), 348; Memo Donald Hornig, November 16, 1967, White House Central Files, Executive, Box 22, F: CO 50–1, 11/15/66, LBJL.

57. UPI despatch, August 2, 1965, NSF Memos to the President, Box 4, F: McGeorge Bundy Vol. 13, August 1965, LBJL.

58. *Public Papers of the Presidents: Lyndon B. Johnson, 1965* (Washington: Government Printing Office, 1966), 394–9; W. W. Rostow, *The Diffusion of Power* (New York: Macmillan, 1972), 426–9.

Japan

The Japanese also felt substantial and largely unwelcome pressure from Washington as it singlemindedly pursued the Vietnam effort. Ambassador Edwin O. Reischauer remarked retrospectively that "the Vietnam War . . . cast a dark shadow over all Japanese–American relations" in 1965 and 1966.[59] The Department of Defense, for instance, considered bribing Japan into increasing its aid to Vietnam by offering military equipment at "exceptionally favorable terms."[60] And Vice President Hubert Humphrey, traveling through Asia late in 1965 and early 1966 to sell Johnson's Vietnam peace offensive, urged more involvement politically and economically upon the Japanese. He optimistically reported to LBJ that if the United States continued "to prod them," the Japanese would comply. Humphrey insisted, moreover, not just on assistance for development, refugees, and medical care but also for a Japanese voice "in explaining our role in Vietnam to the international community."[61]

When Japanese resistance continued, so too did American duress. Lyndon Johnson, never a patient man and accustomed to forcing his administration to enact decisions quickly, had difficulty grasping the inability of Japan's prime minister to produce instant results. Although Sato Eisaku promised aid for the southeast Asian effort, generating consensus in his cabinet, the prerequisite for action, often proved a slow and arduous process.[62] In 1967 the State Department, still seeking ways to increase Tokyo's economic support for Saigon, suggested that the U.S. embassy provide encouragement by promising Japan the opportunity to participate in postwar rehabilitation and development.[63] Johnson, on the other hand, remained uncertain that verbal and economic support was

59. Edwin O. Reischauer, *My Life Between Japan and America* (New York: Harper & Row, 1986), 257.
60. #1889 Department telegram, January, 30, 1965, NSF Country File Japan, Box 250, Vol. III Cables September 1964–October 1965 (1), LBJL.
61. Memo Humphrey to Johnson, January 5, 1966, NSF, NSC Meetings, Vol. 3, Tab 37 1/5/66 Peace Offensive, Box 2, LBJL.
62. U. Alexis Johnson, *The Right Hand of Power* (Englewood Cliffs, N.J.: Prentice-Hall, 1984), 461–2.
63. #43782 Katzenbach, State to Embassy, Tokyo, September 26, 1967, NSF Country File Japan, Box 251, Vol. VI, LBJL.

sufficient, complaining to his foreign policy advisers in November 1967 that "what I am interested in is bodies."[64]

For the Japanese government, cooperation with Washington was more difficult than for authorities in Taipei because public opinion had long been critical of the U.S. war in Vietnam. The press tended, despite periods of moderate coverage, to see the American ground war as futile and fraught with abuses against the Vietnamese people.[65] American efforts to gauge public attitudes revealed that, of those Japanese who knew something about the Vietnam conflict, two-thirds disapproved of U.S. actions.[66] Demonstrations at the U.S. embassy in Tokyo became so frequent and massive that trucks of riot police had to be stationed in the vicinity throughout the spring of 1965.[67] Reischauer believed that "the Japanese equated the war with their own misadventure in China and as recent victims of American bombing identified with the North Vietnamese sufferers from American air attacks."[68] Government officials, though more positive, felt that the high costs of the war wasted resources that ought to be going toward economic development in the Asian region.[69] The United States made its greatest progress in winning over the Japanese when it spoke about fighting poverty and disease, as Johnson did in Baltimore in April 1965, or when it appeared to be sincere about seeking pathways to a peaceful resolution of the conflict as the 1966 peace offensive suggested.[70] Indeed, the Japanese government tried on several occasions to serve as an intermediary. But left-wing opponents of Japan's security relationship with the United States stridently insisted that Washington would eventually drag Tokyo into the Vietnam War, particularly given the use

64. Meeting Notes File, Box 2, F: November 4, 1967 Meeting with Foreign Policy Advisors, LBJL.
65. "Growing Severity of Japanese Press on U.S.-Related Issues," November 9, 1967, NSF Country File Japan, Box 252, F: Japan Memos, Vol. VII, October 1967–December 1968, LBJL.
66. United States Information Agency, "Some Recent Japanese Public Opinion Indications on Issues Affecting Japanese–American Relations," November 9, 1967, NSF Country File Japan, Box 252, Vol. VII, LBJL.
67. Reischauer, *My Life*, 285.
68. Edwin O. Reischauer, *The Japanese* (Cambridge, Mass.: Harvard University Press, 1977), 347.
69. #6011 Johnson, Tokyo, February 25, 1967, NSF Country File Japan, Box 251, Vol. V, LBJL.
70. #2828 Reischauer, Tokyo, February 14, 1966, NSF Country File, Japan, Box 251, F: Japan Cables, Vol. IV, 7/65–9/66 [1 of 2], LBJL.

of bases in Okinawa for bombing missions.[71] Indochina, a sensitive issue in and of itself, thus also became a factor in the continuing struggle over the alliance with the United States as 1970 – the year in which the security treaty became subject to amendment or termination – approached.

During the Johnson presidency the U.S. alliance with Japan, based on provisions of the 1952 and 1960 security treaties, dictated that Washington provide a nuclear umbrella and strategic guarantees to Tokyo. No longer a massive military presence, which in 1952 had encompassed 2,800 bases and facilities, American forces had declined to some 15,000 logistical troops in Japan proper, occupying by 1968 only 149 bases with additional units in Okinawa and on other Pacific islands. Nevertheless, utilization of the remaining naval maintenance and repair establishments "by making it unnecessary for Seventh Fleet vessels to return to Hawaii or the West Coast . . . save[d the United States] hundreds of millions of dollars a year in peace time and . . . [promised] even greater logistics value in certain kinds of war situations."[72] The U.S. Seventh Fleet, in fact, operated out of Yokosuka as its home port, and Japanese airfields provided integral support for American forces in Vietnam. The result proved to be a strategic and financial bonus for the United States while engendering a peculiar mixture of gratitude and irritation among the Japanese public.

Serious frictions surrounded America's occupation of Okinawa and the question of nuclear weapons in the possession of U.S. forces on Japanese territory, rather than the U.S. presence per se. Japanese opinion remained passionately antinuclear, and suspicions that American naval ships were bringing weapons into Japanese waters sparked repeated demonstrations. The general public believed that the security treaty banned such actions. In fact, the United States had the right, under an agreement signed confidentially in 1960, to carry nuclear weapons on board naval vessels and military aircraft transiting the nation, as this did not constitute in-

71. Originally the United States had been free also to use bases in Japan proper to launch attacks against third parties, but it had relinquished that right in the revised treaty signed January 19, 1960. Johnson, *Right Hand*, 449.
72. Department of State Policy Paper on "The Future of Japan," June 26, 1964, p. 4, NSF Country File Japan, Box 250, Vol. 2, LBJL.

troducing, storing, or installing them in Japan.[73] Since 1964 the United States had also been bringing nuclear-powered submarines to Japan. In 1967 the navy sought to broaden interpretations to include nuclear-powered surface vessels such as the U.S.S. *Enterprise,* sparking massive protests in Sasebo during January 1968.[74] The Japanese nuclear allergy also affected opinion regarding Okinawa, where U.S. forces possessed atomic capabilities not subject to monitoring by Japan.[75]

The issue of reversion of Okinawa, which had remained under U.S. control since 1945, became a popular symbol, beginning in the early 1960s, of Japan's desire for independence from U.S. tutelage. Increasing Japanese dissatisfaction with existing arrangements under Article 3 of the 1951 Peace Treaty made the U.S. embassy in Tokyo and the State Department conclude that compromise involving some restoration of administrative authority over the Ryukyu island chain, of which Okinawa was a part, would be necessary to keep the United States from being forced out of American bases entirely and to protect the security treaty. In fact, Ambassador U. Alexis Johnson argued that if Japan took control of Okinawa it would perforce have to assume greater responsibility for its own and regional defense, as it would have to consult with the United States routinely over the use of American facilities.[76] The Defense Department, in contrast, sought not to surrender any rights, insisting that a rising leftist tide in Japanese politics and the potential for communist Chinese influence made it essential to sustain the American position unalloyed.[77] The military insisted that unrestricted use of Okinawa, including basing of nuclear-capable

73. Reischauer, *My Life,* 250. Reischauer's public confirmation that the Japanese government had always known that nuclear weapons were transiting Japan caused a brief uproar in Japan in 1981. Richard Halloran, "Nuclear Agreement on Japan Reported," *New York Times,* May 19, 1981, A-5.
74. Talking Points for Sato Visit, n.d., NSF Country File Japan, Box 253, Sato Visit Briefing Book, November 1967, LBJL.
75. #2470 Rusk, February 24, 1966, NSF Country File Japan, Box 251, F: Japan Cables Vol. IV, 7/65–9/66 [2 of 2], LBJL.
76. Johnson, *Right Hand,* 453.
77. #4017 Reischauer, Tokyo, May 24, 1966, NSF Country File Japan, Box 251, F: Japan Cables Vol. IV, 7/65–9/66 [1 of 2], LBJL. The Department of State noted two contradictory trends operating in Japanese politics – that is, an increasingly leftist voting pattern contrasting with a shift in popular attitudes toward the right even within the Japanese Socialist Party. "The Future of Japan," 8–10.

air and sea power, had to be preserved to meet American responsibilities for Japan and throughout Asia.[78] U.S. installations on the island included two major airfields, hundreds of acres of storage facilities, training grounds, and housing and equipment for a full Marine Division.[79]

By the autumn of 1967 pressure from Japan had shifted the U.S. government significantly toward reversion. The Liberal Democratic Party made it clear that its fortunes would be severely compromised if the United States did not begin to share administrative control and indicate a serious intention of returning the territory in the not-too-distant future. Public opinion polls conducted by the Japanese press suggested considerable concern about Okinawa – a clear desire for a specific timetable for reversion and the eventual elimination of nuclear weapons from the islands even though bases would be likely to remain in use by the United States.[80] The prime minister set progress on this issue as the central goal for his November visit to Washington.[81]

In response, the United States offered a cautiously worded compromise. Reversion would occur, but Washington would not specify a date. Rather the time would be set "within a few years" by American and Japanese leaders. On the serious questions of nuclear weapons stockpiles and the ability to use Ryukyuan bases for operations elsewhere in Asia without prior consultation, the U.S. government refused to yield. Washington did agree to increase substantially Japanese participation in local control in the islands and to try to raise local standards of education and health care to Japan's level.[82]

78. #4238 Johnson, Tokyo, December 7, 1966, NSF Country File Japan, Box 251, Vol. V, LBJL; Memo for the Record, August 31, 1967, NSF National Security Council, F: US Meetings Vol. 4 Tab 56, August 30, 1967 US Relations with Japan, LBJL.
79. Johnson, *Right Hand*, 448.
80. REA-50, "Japanese/Okinawan Focus on Reversion," Intelligence and Research, November 1 ,1967, NSF Country File Japan, Box 253, Sato Visit, November 1967, LBJL.
81. Memo Benjamin R. Read, Executive Secretary to Walt Rostow, October 13, 1967, NSF Country File Japan, Box 253, Sato Visit, November 1967, LBJL; #5555 Rusk, State to Embassy, Tokyo, October 18, 1967, ibid., Box 251, Vol. VI, LBJL; SATO B-4: Ryukyu Islands, November 9, 1967, NSF Country File Japan, Box 253, Sato Visit Briefing Book, November 1967, LBJL. Giving impetus to Sato's concern was the crisis that had been generated around the security treaty revision in 1960 when his brother Kishi Nobusuke had been prime minister. Johnson, *Right Hand*, 465.
82. #58047 Rusk, State to Embassy, Tokyo, October 22, 1967, NSF Country File Japan, Box 251, Vol. VI, LBJL. In the end, under the November 21, 1969, agreement govern-

The White House, moreover, surrendered the Bonin islands despite exhortations by the Joint Chiefs of Staff to maintain American control over such Pacific islands so that U.S. naval forces would be in position to protect vital sea lanes. The JCS pointed out that under the 1960 Security Treaty obligations were not reciprocal, and Japan would not be compelled to utilize bases in the islands to defend any shipping other than its own.[83] Nevertheless, recognizing the primary importance of the Ryukyus and the absolute necessity of concessions, the United States told the Japanese that reversion of the Bonins could be expected the following year so long as the United States could retain control of long-range navigation stations (LORAN) on Iwo Jima and Marcus islands.[84]

For the Japanese government, dependence on American military strength for national protection had become less welcome in the mid-1960s as Japan's economic boom made it the third-ranking industrial state in the free world. Tokyo recognized that to secure political status commensurate with its economic power it would have to develop a more significant military capability, and some government leaders even discussed the acquisition of nuclear armaments.[85] After Japan assumed a seat on the United Nations Security Council in 1966 the issue was magnified by the expectation that Japan would participate in peacekeeping operations. Although the government asserted that Japan, constrained by Article 9 of its con-

ing reversion signed by Sato and President Richard Nixon, the United States agreed to put the Okinawa installations under the same restrictions covering bases in the rest of Japan. On April 23, 1993, when Emperor Akihito became the first Japanese emperor to visit Okinawa, there were still forty-five U.S. military installations on the island. The peculiar history of the territory was underlined by this sustained American presence as well as Japanese–Okinawan tensions rooted in World War II use of Okinawa as a battlefield (the bloodiest of the Pacific war) and induced by the domination of local culture by Japanese traditions after the 1972 reversion from U.S. control. T. R. Reid, "Emperor Takes Long-Sought Okinawa Trip," *Washington Post,* April 24, 1993, p. A21.

83. JCSM-568-67 Memo JCS to Secretary of Defense, undated, NSF Country File Japan, Box 251, Vol. VI, LBJL.

84. Memo Walt Rostow to Johnson, September 11, 1967, NSF Memos to the President, Box 22, F: WWR Vol. 41, September 11–14, 1967 [2 of 2], LBJL; #2913 Johnson, Tokyo, October 28, 1967, NSF Country File Japan, Box 251, Vol. VI, LBJL; Johnson, *Right Hand,* 447.

85. Although the United States assiduously encouraged an increase in Japan's defense capability, this did not include a nuclear capacity, and Washington urged Tokyo to abide by nonproliferation and rely on the United States. Rusk to Johnson re meeting with Sato, n.d., NSF Country File Japan, Box 253, F: Sato Visit Briefing Book, January 1965, LBJL.

stitution, could at least play a role in observer missions, considerable leftist opposition blocked efforts to reinterpret restrictions against using Japanese forces overseas. Moreover, CIA analysts concluded that in contrast to a government eager to raise its international profile, the Japanese people in general "prefer that the US guarantee their security and spare them the expense, risk, and responsibilities involved."[86]

Thus Defense Secretary Robert McNamara emphasized to President Johnson that Tokyo would have to be forced to accept more of the burden of defending the region, economically if not militarily. This would include allowing U.S. companies to compete on equal terms with Japanese manufacturers for defense contracts with the government. In mid-1967 that meant raising purchases of U.S. military equipment from just $60 million to $200 million, a figure still below half of what Washington was spending in Japan on joint defense projects. Without such cooperation the Japanese foreign minister should be told that Congress could not be expected, given balance-of-payments problems, to extend the security treaty or agree to protect Japan from U.S. Pacific ocean bases or with its nuclear umbrella.[87]

Ironically, the United States, having repeatedly been attacked in the media and by the public for its many bases in Japan, discovered in 1968 an unwillingness on the part of Japan's Self Defense Forces to take over facilities when Washington sought to return them. Late in the year the United States proposed releasing or relocating more than one-third of its remaining 149 bases, but Japan protested that it did not have the funds to run these posts. Ambassador Johnson had to coerce authorities to accept the offer, threatening to embarrass the government by publicizing its reluctance to

---

86. "Japan Rethinking Security Policy," NSF Country File Japan Box 251, F: Memos Vol. IV, CIA Report Sc No 00767/66B, April 29, 1966, LBJL. Although the United States did not want to carry the entire burden of Japan's defense, a more disturbing trend seemed reflected in a *Yomiuri* newspaper public opinion poll which indicated that the public preferred to rely on the United Nations or unarmed neutrality and only 12 percent looked to the U.S.–Japan Security Treaty. "Some Recent Japanese Public Opinion," 20.

87. Memo McNamara to Johnson, August 30, 1967, Memos to the President, WWR, Box 22, F: Vol. 41, September 11–14, 1967 [2 of 2], LBJL. This simply repeated the argument that had been made since the beginning of the Johnson administration. See, for instance, Memcon, "Japanese Defense Arrangement; US Redeployment," January 28, 1964, NSF Country File Japan, Box 250, F: Vol. I Memos, LBJL.

reclaim bases it had long demanded when trying to win votes from the people.[88]

American balance-of-payments problems also had serious implications for U.S.–Japanese trade. By the mid-1960s the United States and Japan had become each other's largest trading partners. After years of nurturing the Japanese economy, first to bring about recovery and then to trigger growth, the United States could no longer see the need for unequal access, which provided the Japanese with American consumers while Japan kept its domestic market protected. This determination gained impetus when in 1965 the balance of trade, which had been consistently in America's favor, swung to the Japanese side.[89] The United States began to insist upon freer trade and greater opportunities for investment. Washington officials pointed to slow and reluctant removal of import controls as violations of Japan's obligations under both the Organization for Economic Cooperation and Development (OECD) and the General Agreement on Tariffs and Trade (GATT) and complained about nontariff barriers that further frustrated would-be U.S. suppliers. In 1968 the United States notified Tokyo that unless it removed illegal import restrictions promptly the issue would be formally submitted to GATT for action.[90]

The Japanese responded grudgingly, fearing sentiment favoring protectionism in the United States, particularly in the areas of textiles and steel, but unwilling to do more than absolutely necessary.[91] Tokyo instituted "voluntary" export controls covering price, quantity, and quality on a range of commodities.[92] Japan also proved willing to hold foreign exchange reserves in dollars rather than insist upon purchases of gold from the U.S. Treasury.[93] LBJ's

88. Johnson, *Right Hand,* 506–7.   89. Japan Administrative History, LBJL.
90. Ibid.
91. Scope Paper for 6th Meeting of the Joint U.S.–Japan Committee on Trade and Economic Affairs, September 13–15, 1967, NSF Country File Japan, Box 251, Vol. VI, LBJL; Sato B-9: Post-Kennedy Round Trade Problems: Bilateral and Multilateral Problems, November 9, 1967, NSF Country File Japan, Box 253, Sato Visit Briefing Book, November 14–15, 1967, LBJL.
92. Minister of International Trade and Industry Fukuda maintained that many of these voluntary controls had been forced on Japan by U.S. business circles. KEA/R-4 Record of the Third Meeting of Joint U.S.–Japan Committee on Trade and Economic Affairs, January 24, 1964, 3. NSF Country File Japan, Box 250, F: Vol. I Memos, November 1963–April 1964, LBJL.
93. SATO/B-5 "US–Japan Financial Arrangements," November 9, 1967, NSF Country File Japan, Box 253, F: Sato Visit Briefing Book, November 1967, LBJL.

demands that the government help remedy American balance-of-payments difficulties occasioned an unenthusiastic reaction in part because of Japan's own imbalances during the mid-1960s, brought on by its need for imports, the high costs of shipping, insurance and interest on debts, the recession afflicting its trading partners, as well as reductions in U.S. assistance to Japan.[94] The Japanese even feared that Vietnam-related U.S. military procurement expenditures, initially a boon, could prove devastating if a peace settlement abruptly ended the purchases.[95] Consequently Japan argued successfully for an exemption, beginning in 1965, from one major program designed to stem the flow of U.S. dollars abroad: the interest equalization tax, which when announced in 1963 had shocked officials and businessmen and had led to the near-collapse of the stock market.[96] The Japanese argued, ultimately convincingly, that they needed an uninterrupted flow of capital to drive economic growth. During Prime Minister Sato's November 1967 visit to Washington the two governments agreed to establish a committee to examine the balance-of-payments situation and recommend targets for Japan's assistance to the United States between the Japanese low of $300 million and the American high of $500 million.[97]

The United States also urged Japan to increase its foreign aid commitments as a mechanism not only to decrease the burden on Washington but also to heighten Japanese prestige and involvement in the world. In the mid-1960s Japan ranked fifth among free-world nations providing assistance to less developed countries, and the United States believed that it could and should do more. With

94. Sato B-7: Japan's Political and Economic Situation, November 9, 1967, NSF Country File Japan, Box 253, Sato Visit Briefing Book, November 1967, LBJL; "The Future of Japan," 37.
95. Memo Sneider to Jorden, November 9, 1967, NSF Country File Japan, Box 252, F: Japan Memos Vol. VII October 1967–December 1968, LBJL.
96. This measure discouraged U.S. purchases of foreign securities by imposing a 1 percent tax. Canada immediately secured an exemption that was denied to Tokyo. The Japanese finally received in 1965 a $100 million exemption that was subsequently renewed. Kaufman, "Foreign Aid and the Balance-of-Payments Problem," 86–7; KEA/R-3 Record of the Third Meeting Joint U.S.–Japan Committee on Trade and Economic Affairs, January 27, 1964, NSF Country File Japan, Box 250, F: Vol. I Memos, November 1963–April 1964, LBJL; SAT/B-9 "Interest Equalization Tax," January 4, 1965, NSF Country File Japan, Box 253, F: Sato's Visit Briefing Book, January 11–14, 1965, LBJL.
97. "Balance of Payments Cooperation Between Japan and the United States," November 11, 1967, Box 82, Diary Backup (Presidential Appointments), F: Visit of Prime Minister Sato, LBJL.

American encouragement Japan began to take a leadership role in Asia, for example, providing a major contribution to help launch the Asian Development Bank in 1966 and supporting a Japanese financier to be its first president.[98] But Washington wanted Japan to look beyond South Vietnam and Asia to global participation such as helping to finance OECD aid to Turkey.[99] The Japanese nevertheless would logically concentrate their energies in the Asian region recognizing, at the same time, that they must avoid the suggestion that their efforts in Asia were designed to reassemble a co-prosperity sphere.[100]

Washington explained its pressures on Tokyo as part of an effort to build a partnership with Japan because the Japanese no longer staggered under the weight of rehabilitation and recovery. The U.S. government initiated regular pre–UN General Assembly consultations to parallel those already in existence between Washington and London as well as between Washington and Ottawa.[101] At Tokyo's request, the United States undertook regular security briefings beginning in May 1967 through the US–Japan Security Subcommittee of the US–Japan Security Consultative Committee, and these also exposed American participants to Tokyo's thinking.[102]

One issue upon which the Japanese sought to exert influence on American decision makers was the improvement in relations between the United States and the Soviet Union evinced in events such as the Glassboro Summit of June 1967. Although détente would be good for world peace and could facilitate a settlement in Vietnam, Prime Minister Sato urged the Americans to remember that the Soviets could not be trusted. Noting Moscow's continued occupation of Japan's northern territories, Sato warned that the preoccupation

98. Japan Administrative History, LBJL.
99. SAT/B-4 "Japan's Role in the OECD," January 4, 1965, NSF Country File Japan, Box 253, F: Sato's Visit Briefing Book, January 11–14, 1965, LBJL. Japan formally accepted membership in this grouping of industrialized nations in April 1964.
100. "The Future of Japan," pp. 79–82.
101. #6062 Johnson, Tokyo, February 27, 1967, NSF Country File Japan, Box 251, Vol. V, LBJL.
102. Japan Administrative History, LBJL. The US–Japan Security Consultative Committee originally was organized under the 1960 revision of the US–Japan Security Treaty to reassure the public that regular discussions on defense issues were occurring.

in Washington with Chinese communist threats should not blind policymakers to the Soviets' "basic nature [which] was dangerous and one could not really deal with them openly and sincerely." Tokyo, he observed, was watching developments carefully, fearing Soviet efforts to take land from the Chinese and to compromise Japan's position in Asia.[103] Suspicion, on the other hand, did not prevent modest advances in Russo–Japanese relations, including increased trade, the opening of a civil aviation route, and a consular treaty.[104]

As much as the Japanese tried to alert Washington to what they believed to be the evil intentions of the Soviets, American policymakers struggled to convince the Japanese to be more "mature and responsible . . . [about] the threat posed by the Chinese Communists."[105] The Japanese had consistently refused to accept the American characterization of the Beijing regime as malevolent, although they abided by the basic elements of American China policy: nonrecognition, strategic trade controls, preservation of Taiwan. Even the expansion of China's nuclear weapons capabilities coupled with the instability of the Cultural Revolution made Prime Minister Sato and others only moderately more critical of Beijing. Public opinion surveys indicated that nine of ten Japanese polled did not fear a Chinese nuclear attack, and sentiment favoring diplomatic recognition of China remained at a three-to-one margin.[106] The United States persisted in warning Tokyo against dependence on Chinese markets or the provision of disguised foreign aid through easy credit terms.[107] But, although Washington worried about efforts to improve Sino–Japanese relations, it could also rely upon Japan's sym-

103. #6063 Johnson, Tokyo, February 27, 1967, NSF Country File Japan, Box 251, Vol. V, LBJL. Sato's concern about the Soviet impact on Japan's standing was reported in cable 6126, March 1, 1967, and alluded to in a Walt Rostow memo to the president, March 1, 1967, NSF Memos to the President, Box 14, "Walt Rostow, Vol. XXII," LBJL.
104. Sato B-3, November 9, 1967, ibid.
105. Memo Rusk to Johnson, September 4, 1967, White House Central Files/Confidential Files (CO140) Box 10, F: CO141 Japan, LBJL.
106. Sato B-3: Japanese Foreign Policy: Vietnam, China and the Soviet Union, November 9, 1967, NSF Country File Japan, Box 253, Sato Visit Briefing Book, November 1967, LBJL; "Some Recent Japanese Public Opinion Indications on Issues Affecting Japanese–American Relations," November 9, 1967, 3–4, ibid., Box 252, Vol. VII, LBJL.
107. KEA/R-5 Record of the Meeting of Joint U.S.–Japan Committee on Trade and Economic Affairs, January 24, 1964, p. 4, NSF Country File Japan, Box 250, F: Vol. I Memos November 1963–April 1964, LBJL.

pathy for Taiwan self-determination to act as a bar to precipitous policy changes. Moreover, the United States accepted Japanese offers to try to bring about a negotiated settlement of the Vietnam war through indirect pressure on Hanoi.[108] Skeptical of Tokyo's likely ability to convince Beijing to curb the North Vietnamese, the Johnson administration nonetheless encouraged its efforts.

In the closing days of the Johnson presidency, as in the opening moments, Washington's preoccupation with Vietnam threatened to undermine relations with Tokyo. The announcement by Lyndon Johnson on March 31, 1968, that he would implement a partial bombing halt, desired negotiations, and did not intend to run for re-election stunned Japan. The speech produced the instant conclusion there that the United States had decided to repudiate its entire Vietnam policy. Prime Minister Sato's opponents saw this as an opportunity to call for his resignation because Sato had been identified so closely both with LBJ and with the war. Because Washington, not for the first or last time, had neglected to warn Tokyo of what was coming, Sato had been shocked by Johnson's decision and unprepared to fend off the assault on his own position.

America's perceived abandonment of Vietnam led the Japanese to feel suddenly very alone in the Pacific. But Sato weathered the storm, and Japan quickly came to see the de-escalation of Washington's commitment to the war in positive terms. Along with the partial resolution of the conflict over the Ryukyu and Bonin islands, the appearance of progress toward settlement in Vietnam, however fleeting, produced good feelings between the two nations as they planned for a different, more equal, future.

Korea

The major issues in U.S. relations with South Korea consisted of Vietnam troop commitments, settlement of Korean relations with Japan, as well as U.S. economic aid and security guarantees in the face of continuing threats from North Korea. Each proved intimately linked to the others, with American policymakers pursuing

---

108. #227 Department telegram, July 23, 1965, NSF Country File Japan, Box 250, Vol. III Cables September 1964–October 1965 (1), LBJL.

the sometimes contradictory objectives of increasing Korea's ability to function independently while retaining considerable control over Seoul's decision making.

After the Korean War Washington had provided the only substantial external military and economic aid to Seoul, attempting to rebuild a war-ravaged and inherently weak and imbalanced South Korean economy. Progress had been hampered by Syngman Rhee's indifference to long-range development strategies and unrelenting emphasis on anti-Japanese as well as anticommunist policies. Conditions for planning and productive utilization of assistance finally improved only with the ouster of Rhee and the short-lived, weak successor regime of Chang Myon in a 1961 military coup. Under pressure from John F. Kennedy, the resulting military junta was transformed into a civilian regime in 1963, prompting accelerated U.S. monetary and technical aid to spur local growth.[109] Korea shifted from an import substitution strategy to one of export promotion, undertook a series of centralizing reforms that consolidated a government–business alliance, and launched upon a sustained period of expansion, averaging growth of nearly 10 percent per year in gross national product – up from just over 4 percent from 1953 to 1960.[110]

To Lyndon Johnson the cost of the Korean commitment quickly became problematic. Facing mounting expenses in Indochina and pressures in the Congress to reduce foreign aid expenditures generally, Johnson sought alternatives to overseas outlays. In the case of South Korea the administration emphasized the development of bilateral trade and investment through private industry trade missions (e.g., the 1967 Ball Mission) and encouraged South Korean initiatives in establishing the Asian and Pacific Council in June 1966.[111]

109. Administrative History, Vol. I: chapter 7 East Asia, Section F Republic of Korea, 2–4, LBJL.
110. Frank Baldwin, ed., *Without Parallel: The American–Korean Relationship Since 1945* (New York: Pantheon, 1974), 20–1; Koo Youngnok and Suh Dae-sook, eds., *Korea and the United States: A Century of Cooperation* (Honolulu: University of Hawaii Press, 1984), 246–7; and see Stephan Haggard, Byung-Kook Kim, and Chung-in Moon, "The Transition to Export-led Growth in South Korea, 1954–1966," *Journal of Asian Studies* 50 (November 1991), 850–73.
111. The presidents of the United States and South Korea launched a concerted effort to involve private investors in Korean economic development at their November 1966 meeting in Seoul. The first organized group of Americans to go to Korea was the Investment and Trade Exploratory Mission, led by former Undersecretary of State

But a more promising solution appeared to be rapprochement between Seoul and Tokyo. Not only would reconciliation eliminate a bothersome point of tension in northeast Asia, but it also would make possible a larger Japanese role in Korea, enhancing Tokyo's contribution to Korean security and economic development. Already in 1962 a settlement of outstanding Korean property claims against Japan had yielded a $600 million package of credits, grants, and commercial financing.[112] The State Department estimated that a treaty would save Washington $1 billion between 1965 and 1975.[113]

The Johnson administration, therefore, heightened pressures on both Tokyo and Seoul to negotiate a treaty for which neither government had felt particular enthusiasm over the previous twelve years of sporadic discussions. In South Korea President Pak Chung-hui (Park Chung-hee) confronted public hostility to Japan and fear regarding American abandonment. Students emphasized the dire threat to national sovereignty of allowing the Japanese to renew their domination and exploitation of the country.[114] Many of Korea's government leaders including the president appeared tainted by close ties with the Japanese, Pak having served in the Imperial Army, and critics believed that they wanted to improve relations for purposes of private gain and for the financial support that would allow the government to stay in power.[115] Others rightly concluded that the reconciliation urged by the United States would

George W. Ball in March 1967. "U.S.–Korean Economic Relations and the American Private Sector," March 9, 1967, Briefing Paper for Visit of Prime Minister Il Kwon Chung, March 14–15, 1967, NSF Memos to the President, Box 14, F: Walt Rostow, Vol. 23, March 10–15, 1967 [1 of 2], LBJL.

112. Stephan Haggard, "The Politics of Industrialization in the Republic of Korea and Taiwan," in Helen Hughes, ed., *Achieving Industrialization in East Asia* (New York: Cambridge University Press, 1988), 270.

113. Memo Thomson to LBJ, January 11, 1965, NSF Country File Japan, Box 253, F: Sato Visit Briefing Book, January 1965, LBJL.

114. A long series of cables attested to student turmoil in the country, including: #1211 and 1213 Berger, Seoul, March 25, 1964, NSF Country File, Korea, Vol. I. Box 254, LBJL. Others made clear the connection to wider opposition to the government: #1277 Berger, Seoul, April 9, 1964, ibid.

115. The most widely hated figure, Kim Chong-pil, a longtime crony of Pak's and widely accused of corruption, finally departed the fray with an invitation to the Harvard Summer Seminar run by Henry Kissinger arranged by State Department personnel. #1660 Berger, Seoul, June 15, 1964, NSF Country File, Korea, Vol. I, Box 254, LBJL. The upheaval over the treaty was also an attempt by opposition forces to oust the ruling party.

permit the Americans to reduce their obligations, persuading Japan to step into the breach. Public protests surged through Seoul, provoking Pak to impose martial law, squash the demonstrations, blame Washington for insisting upon the arrangement, and ram the treaty through the legislature. But although more pragmatic than the opponents of the treaty and ready to capitulate, the Pak regime insisted upon explicit loan and other guarantees from Washington to extend beyond settlement of the Korea–Japan Treaty.[116] Evoking what seemed ancient history to present-minded Americans, the Korean prime minister told the deputy assistant secretary for Far Eastern Affairs that the United States had to take responsibility for having facilitated the 1905 Portsmouth Treaty, which had led to Japan's takeover of Korea, as well as for the division of the peninsula in the wake of World War II.[117]

Paralleling, complicating, and giving impetus to Washington's urgent desire to see Korea and Japan cooperate, Lyndon Johnson also sought a Korean presence in Vietnam. Initial offers of Korean support in Indochina had been politely rebuffed, coming before Washington policymakers could see the utility in such a commitment.[118] Seoul wanted to prove to the United States the value of Korea as an ally as well as to take a stand against communist expansion in the region. But Lyndon Johnson soon concluded that to sustain domestic support for the U.S. role in Vietnam there would have to be a broader multilateral presence waging the anticommunist crusade, and, therefore, he came to insist upon an active involvement of America's allies in the conflict.

The result, Johnson's "many flags campaign" inaugurated in 1964, however, shifted the dynamics of the situation so that Seoul became a dispenser of favors rather than a supplicant, and Washington paid dearly. The United States found itself obliged to funnel in massive amounts of assistance, supplying weapons, equipment, and logistical support as well as increasing the pay of Korean soldiers (as much as 20 times levels in South Korea) and even supply-

116. "ROK Economic Development and Foreign Economic Assistance Programs," Briefing Paper, May 17–19, 1965, NSF Country File, Korea, Park Visit Briefing Book, 5/65, Box 256, LBJL.
117. Memcon Yim Yun-yong, Prime Minister with Robert W. Barnett, Deputy Assistant Secretary of State, September 14, 1964, NSF Country File, "Korea, Vol. II," Box 254, LBJL.
118. #1128 Berger, Seoul, March 7, 1964, NSF Country File, Korea, Vol. I, Box 254, LBJL; #12 Rusk, July 3, 1964, ibid., Korea, vol. II, LBJL.

ing them with *kimchi* to eat. In 1965 President Pak declared it the moral duty of each Korean "to save his drowning friend."[119] But in 1968 Washington had to provide destroyers to Seoul in exchange for dispatch of a light division.[120] The Republic of Korea (ROK) total troop deployment ultimately numbered in excess of 300,000 men (with no more than 48,000 in Vietnam at any one time), the cost of which reached some $10 billion.

South Korea also demanded access to American procurement contracts and aid in making business contacts in South Vietnam, reasoning that the Korean War had brought prosperity to suppliers such as Japan and that Korea now wanted to benefit from Vietnam.[121] By 1969 South Koreans made up more than half of the foreign civilian employees in South Vietnam and had actually maneuvered Americans into granting them a concession to collect garbage in the streets of Saigon. Some 20 percent of Seoul's foreign currency earnings in that year were derived from Vietnam-related enterprises.[122]

In addition, Seoul exacted commitments from Johnson regarding the defense of South Korea. Unlike seemingly automatic guarantees through NATO in Europe, the United States explicitly reserved the right to consult Congress in the event of an attack on Korea before determining what obligations it would assume under the 1954 mutual defense treaty.[123] Thus in communiqués signed in 1965, 1966, and 1968, Johnson found himself compelled to reassure Seoul of U.S. support. More concretely the United States, throughout the Vietnam conflict, kept as many Americans on guard at the Korean frontier as Seoul dispatched soldiers to Vietnam, reversing plans formulated in Washington to reduce troop concentrations in Ko-

119. Koo and Suh, eds., *Korea and the United States,* 360.
120. #9693 Porter, Seoul, March 19, 1968, Papers of Clark Clifford, Korea, Box 17, LBJL.
121. Baldwin, *Without Parallel,* 29–30. Agreement to pay all ROK expenses and provide new equipment was embodied in a March 4, 1966 Memorandum.
122. Kahin, *Intervention,* 335. In 1992 Korean filmmakers launched two multimillion-dollar projects about Korean involvement in Vietnam, a war few younger Koreans know anything about because of earlier government efforts to keep details secret. James Sterngold, "South Korea's Vietnam Veterans Begin to Be Heard," *New York Times,* May 10, 1992, 6.
123. "U.S.–Korean Mutual Defense Treaty," Briefing Paper, March 14–15, 1967, NSF Country File, Korea, PM Chung Il-kwon Visit, 3/67, Box 256, LBJL. In fact, during congressional debate over the NATO commitment the Senate made clear that it would be subject to constitutional processes which triggered explicit language to that effect in subsequent treaties.

rea.[124] Nevertheless, South Korean security did fall victim to North Korean terrorism in 1968 when a commando raid on Seoul's executive mansion designed to assassinate President Pak was followed two days later by the seizure of a U.S. intelligence ship.

The capture of the *Pueblo* and its eighty-two crewmen occurred during a routine intelligence-gathering mission off the coast of North Korea.[125] The American embassy in Seoul concluded that the incident reflected Pyongyang's desire to frustrate U.S. espionage operations following the abortive assassination attempt on Pak as well as to reduce South Korean willingness to support Saigon and to distract Washington from the Vietnam theater.[126] When the Tet Offensive materialized shortly thereafter, the connection to Vietnam appeared confirmed. And, when Washington's concern seemed to focus too relentlessly on the *Pueblo* rather than on South Korea's vulnerability and nervousness, engendering some resentment in Seoul, Pyongyang also succeeded in straining bilateral relations. As Kim Il-sung, North Korea's revered leader, declared, the ultimate goal was "to tear off the left and right arms of U.S. imperialism."[127] For Lyndon Johnson, "The *Pueblo* incident formed the first link in a chain of events – of crisis, tragedy, and disappointment – that added up to one of the most agonizing years any President has ever spent in the White House."[128]

In fact, it took eleven painful months to secure the release of the crew, during which time Johnson was plagued by Tet, the siege of Khe Sanh, a balance-of-payments crisis, trouble over West Berlin, the Soviet invasion of Czechoslovakia, and domestic violence at the Democratic national convention as well as in the assassinations of

124. Lee Yur-bok and Wayne Patterson, eds., *One Hundred Years of Korean–American Relations, 1882–1982* (Tuscaloosa: University of Alabama Press, 1986), 109; Memo McNamara to President, November 15, 1963, NSF Country File, Korea, Boxes 256–7, F: filed by LBJ library, LBJL; #953 Berger, Seoul, January 21, 1964, NSF Country File, Korea, Vol. I, Box 254, LBJL.
125. Under the Geneva Convention of 1958 warships on the high seas were to be immune from seizure. Moreover, electronic eavesdropping of this kind had become common practice by Soviet, American, and other trawlers, with some thirty such Soviet ships at sea in 1968. Memo Leonard Meeker, Legal Adviser, to Secretary, January 24, 1968, NSF Country File, Korea, Pueblo Incident, Vol. I, pt A, 1/68, Box 257, LBJL; Papers of George Christian, Box 12, F: Pueblo Misc., LBJL.
126. #8517 Porter, Seoul, January 24, 1968, NSF Country File, Korea, Pueblo Incident, Vol. I, pt A, Box 257, LBJL.
127. Koo and Suh, eds., *Korea and the United States*, 179.
128. Johnson, *The Vantage Point*, 532.

Martin Luther King Jr. and Robert Kennedy. Although Washington contemplated mining North Korean harbors, interdicting coastal shipping, and even striking selected targets, Johnson worked instead through diplomatic channels, ultimately securing help from the Soviets, who disapproved of Pyongyang's belligerence.[129] Cyrus Vance, special envoy to President Pak, also pledged increased funding for modernization of the ROK military and annual defense consultations.[130] Ultimately, a bizarre deal between the United States and North Korea resulted in freedom for the crew. The North Koreans dictated an American apology for spying and intruding into their territorial waters. Simultaneously, Americans repudiated North Korean accusations, the government's apology, and confessions wrested from the crew.[131]

Conclusion

In many ways the *Pueblo* affair proved a fitting capstone for a troubled presidency. Walt Rostow's conviction that the United States was following a new path and fresh policies in Asia appeared extraordinarily misguided by the end of the administration. Although he subsequently wrote that "Asia in early 1969 was a different and more hopeful place" than it had been a few years earlier, there were few concrete achievements to point to.[132] Probably the most exciting developments rested in the growing prosperity of Taiwan and Japan, the achievements of which owed much to the United States, but less specifically to the Johnson administration. The Korean–Japanese Treaty boded well for the region, and

129. Memo Walt Rostow to President, January 26, 1968, NSF Country File, Korea, Pueblo Incident, Vol. I, pt B, Boxes 256–7, LBJL. Initial concern that the Soviets had instigated the incident passed quickly. Intelligence Note from Thomas Hughes, Intelligence and Research, January 24, 1968, NSF Country File, Korea, Pueblo Incident, Vol. I pt. B, Box 257, LBJL.
130. #4229 Rusk, February 14, 1968, NSF Country File, Korea, Pueblo Incident, Seoul Cables, Vol. II, Box 262, LBJL.
131. Memo, Under Secretary, December 17, 1968, NSF Country File, Korea, Pueblo Incident, Cactus V, Misc. Papers, Box 261, LBJL. Dean Rusk later speculated that Pyongyang wanted the signed confessions for internal distribution for a citizenry that would never hear the repudiation because of strictly controlled access to external sources of information. Rusk, *As I Saw It*, 395.
132. Rostow, *Diffusion*, 524.

progress in settling the dispute over Okinawa suggested a maturing of ties between Washington and Tokyo that would facilitate economic and security cooperation in the future.

But as the *Pueblo* seizure demonstrated, war in Vietnam clouded every horizon, twisted every relationship, providing opportunities for harassment by enemies and engendering opportunism and dismay among friends and allies. Washington might easily have slipped into armed conflict with China as its planes violated the Chinese border and its bombs threatened PLA troops supporting North Vietnam in the jungles. Although the environment within the United States suggested greater flexibility in the American image of and approach to Beijing, initiatives proved minimal. The internal disarray occasioned by the launching of the Great Proletarian Cultural Revolution (1966–76), of course, would most likely have made barriers to better relations insurmountable in any case, but Vietnam was a sufficient deterrent even without China's domestic turmoil. And even as the war antagonized nations already opposed to American policies in Asia, it also placed the United States in the uncomfortable position of having to beseech allies for support, often bribing them for commitments to a crusade they would have preferred to ignore. Far from the beginning of a new era, the Johnson administration left a legacy of ill-conceived policies with which Asians and Americans would be forced to wrestle.

5

Toward Disillusionment and Disengagement in South Asia

ROBERT J. McMAHON

When Lyndon B. Johnson was suddenly thrust into the Oval Office in November 1963, a daunting array of domestic and foreign policy issues competed for his attention. The direction of U.S. policy in the Indian subcontinent formed but one of those, and one that must have seemed far from urgent to a leader determined to concentrate his formidable energies on domestic affairs. Nonetheless, Lyndon Johnson could not long postpone a set of fundamental questions about the future American relationship with India and Pakistan, questions left unresolved at the time of his predecessor's assassination.[1]

Kennedy's chief foreign policy advisers, all of whom were retained by a man determined to carry forward the Kennedy legacy, were unsure precisely where the new chief executive stood on matters pertaining to South Asia. With JFK's strong backing and direct participation, they had helped engineer a major shift in America's South Asia priorities over the past two years. The Sino–Indian war of October 1962 seemed to offer the Kennedy administration a unique opportunity to draw non-aligned India closer to the West. Convinced that India represented a political and strategic asset of potentially great value to the United States, Kennedy had hurriedly dispatched emergency military aid to that embattled nation while holding out the prospect for a generous, long-term military assistance agreement. The initiative had stalled, however, largely because of Pakistan's vehement opposition. The administration's

---

1. Parts of this chapter appear in a slightly different form in Robert J. McMahon, *The Cold War on the Periphery: The United States, India, and Pakistan* (New York: Columbia University Press, 1994), Ch. 9.

attempt to ease Indo–Pakistani bitterness and hostility by helping to mediate an amicable resolution of the emotionally charged dispute over the disposition of the state of Kashmir had failed, and Pakistan had countered the American tilt toward its fractious neighbor by establishing close diplomatic ties with China. Kennedy delayed a final decision on the proposed Indo–American military connection because of a hesitance about further alienating Pakistan, a major recipient of U.S. military and economic aid, a nation formally aligned with the West under two anticommunist alliance systems (the Southeast Asia Treaty Organization [SEATO] and the Central Treaty Organization [CENTO]), and a site of important intelligence-collection facilities.[2]

Although Lyndon Johnson had not directly participated in any major South Asia policy decisions as vice president, he had formed strong impressions about India and Pakistan, and their respective leaders, during a brief trip to the subcontinent in May 1961. LBJ, who greatly prized personal relationships, had developed an instant rapport with Pakistani President Mohammed Ayub Khan during that trip and a much less favorable impression of the cooler and more aloof Indian Prime Minister, Jawaharlal Nehru. When Ayub arrived in the United States several months later for official talks, Johnson went so far as to host a lavish barbecue at his Texas ranch for the visitor, replete with his favorite country-and-western singer, a *mariachi* band, and an aquatic show put on by members of the University of Texas swimming team. The vice president also treated his Pakistani guest to personally guided tours of San Antonio, Austin, and the hill country of central Texas. By all accounts, the two men got along famously. According to one of his aides, the vice president considered the vigorous Ayub "very much a man's man" – Johnson's ultimate compliment.[3] "It is seldom that I have been so very much impressed by a man," LBJ wrote Ayub in Sep-

2. Ibid., Ch. 8; Robert J. McMahon, "Choosing Sides in South Asia," in Thomas G. Paterson, ed., *Kennedy's Quest for Victory: American Foreign Policy, 1961–1963* (New York: Oxford University Press, 1989), 198–222.
3. Liz Carpenter Oral History Interview, May 15, 1969, Lyndon B. Johnson Library, Austin, Texas (hereafter LBJL); Richard S. "Cactus" Pryor Oral History Interview, September 10, 1968, LBJL; Johnson to Kennedy, May 23, 1961, National Security File (hereafter NSF), India, John F. Kennedy Library, Boston, Massachusetts (hereafter JFKL).

tember 1961, "and I think I enjoyed your visit to my ranch as much as anything that has happened to me this year."[4]

During his trip to Karachi, Johnson also met by happenstance a Pakistani camel driver and, in the style of a barnstorming American politician, offhandedly invited him to visit the United States. Much to the amazement of observers in both countries, the illiterate Bashir Ahmed, with an assist from wealthy countrymen, actually managed to take Johnson up on his offer the next year. He, too, received the legendary Johnson treatment during a stay that included a visit to the LBJ ranch and a whirlwind tour of New York, Washington, and a variety of other sites. The bizarre visit attracted enormous media attention, almost all of it favorable, providing Johnson with a welcome public relations bonanza. The vice president subsequently insisted that the U.S. embassy in Pakistan keep an eye on "my camel driver," and Bashir and "Johnson sahib" became regular correspondents.[5]

National Security Council aide Robert Komer worried that those personal and emotional connections might make the new president "more pro-Pak" than Kennedy. He also fretted that the Pakistanis would view Johnson as likely to be more sympathetic to their needs and therefore might become "more intransigent than ever." An early presidential commitment to the much-discussed military assistance program for India, Komer wrote his boss, National Security Adviser McGeorge Bundy, would send an invaluable signal of policy continuity both to the Indians and the Pakistanis. The NSC aide who had played a prominent role in bringing about the Kennedy administration's tilt toward India understandably wanted to see the Johnson administration move in the same direction. "Unless we get the new President signed on now while he is still carrying out the Kennedy policy," Komer wrote Bundy just one day after the assassination, "we may lose a real opportunity."[6]

Although Johnson's cautious instincts militated against any early commitments on military aid levels for India or Pakistan, he

---

4. Johnson to Ayub, September 21, 1961, Ayub Khan 1 folder, Subject File, LBJ Archives, Box 91, LBJL. See also Johnson to Supreme Court Justice William O. Douglas, August 10 and September 8, 1961, ibid.
5. See the extensive documentation in the Bashir Ahmed file, ibid.
6. Komer to Bundy, November 23, 1963, NSC History of South Asia, NSF, LBJL.

quickly disabused the Pakistanis of the notion that the new American administration might prove more tolerant of their opening toward the Chinese than had the previous one. During his very first week in office, LBJ delivered that message personally to Pakistani Foreign Secretary Zulfikar Ali Bhutto, who was in Washington for the Kennedy funeral. In characteristically forceful language, Johnson warned Bhutto that Chinese Premier Zhou Enlai's upcoming state visit to Pakistan, slated for February 1964, would cause serious "public relations" problems for the United States. The president voiced concern that the visit would spark an adverse reaction from Congress and implied that this latest demonstration of Sino–Pakistani friendship might jeopardize congressional support for future U.S. economic and military aid to Pakistan. LBJ told Bhutto that he was a friend of Pakistan and would continue to be one – "if Pakistan would let him." According to Assistant Secretary of State for Near Eastern and South Asian Affairs Phillips Talbot, who was present at the meeting, the Pakistani diplomat appeared "deeply upset and disturbed" by Johnson's blunt words. Bhutto tried to defend the Pakistani–Chinese relationship as a protective measure necessitated by America's strengthening of India, which he said was "driving Pakistan to the wall." But his American interlocutors remained unmoved by what they considered a weak rationalization for an indefensible affront to American interests.[7] As the Pakistani foreign minister left the Oval Office, Undersecretary of State George Ball recalled, "He turned on me furiously" to complain about the "discourteous reception" he had received.[8] "Bhutto was asking for it," a White House aid remarked after the stormy session.[9]

The Johnson–Bhutto colloquy offers a glimpse into the gaping chasm that separated the world views of American and Pakistani leaders. As Bhutto so forthrightly acknowledged, Pakistan's overture toward China derived not from any ideological affinity for its communist neighbor; instead, it represented diplomatic pragma-

7. Rusk to the Embassy in Pakistan, December 2, 1963, ibid.; Komer to Johnson, September 9, 1965, ibid.
8. George W. Ball, *The Past Has Another Pattern: Memoirs* (New York: Norton, 1982), 314.
9. Quoted in Philip Geyelin, *Lyndon B. Johnson and the World* (New York: Praeger, 1966), 3.

tism of the highest order. Obsessed with the potential danger posed to their nation's security by a larger and more powerful India, Pakistani policymakers believed that an entente with China provided a greater degree of protection than their Western alliances alone could offer. Born of small-power insecurity conjoined with a deepening skepticism about the reliability of its principal ally, Pakistan's opening toward China serves as a classic case of geopolitical expediency overcoming ideological dissonance.[10]

From Washington's perspective, however, the opening stood as an egregious provocation. It violated the bedrock assumptions undergirding all of America's Cold War alliances. Further, it conferred a degree of respectability on what American policymakers contemptuously regarded as an outlaw state. The Kennedy administration's military commitment to India, after all, was driven primarily by American concern about the threat China posed to the noncommunist nations of South and Southeast Asia. In the view of American national security planners, China had become a near-demonic force in world affairs; the Sino–Soviet split, they were convinced, had just emboldened Beijing's leaders, making them more, rather than less, aggressive, adventuristic, and unpredictable. Kennedy's fixation with India's importance to the United States flowed largely from his belief that India could help contain an expansionist China. Pakistan's China gambit infuriated Johnson, as it had Kennedy, because it threatened to undermine that fundamental goal of U.S. diplomacy.[11]

On December 9 Johnson reiterated those concerns in a friendly but firm letter to Ayub. LBJ remarked that he had appreciated the opportunity to meet with Bhutto because "I could talk to him frankly about some things which have been disturbing me for some time." Chief among them, he emphasized, were a series of recent Pakistani actions "which redound to the advantage of Communist China," especially the state visit planned for February 1964. "Re-

10. Yaacov Vertzberger, *The Enduring Entente: Sino–Pakistani Relations, 1960–1980* (Washington: Center for Strategic and International Studies, 1983), 7–22.
11. Gordon H. Chang, *Friends and Enemies: The United States, China, and the Soviet Union, 1948–1972* (Stanford, Calif.: Stanford University Press, 1990), 228–52, 259–63; James Fetzer, "Clinging to Containment: China Policy," in Paterson, ed., *Kennedy's Quest for Victory,* 178–97; John Lewis Gaddis, *Strategies of Containment: A Critical Appraisal of Postwar American National Security Policy* (New York: Oxford University Press, 1982), 210–11.

gardless of Pakistan's motivations, which I understand but frankly cannot agree with," Johnson continued, "these actions undermine our efforts to uphold our common security interests in the face of an aggressive nation which has clearly and most explicitly announced its unswerving hostility to the Free World." He appealed to Ayub, in closing, to recognize that "Pakistan's interests are best served by doing everything possible to strengthen, not weaken, its ties with the Free World."[12]

Komer, his initial fear that LBJ might treat the Pakistanis too gently erased by the Bhutto meeting and the Ayub letter, applauded the president's tough approach. Speculating that "Ayub isn't really serious about the Chicoms" and was simply "conducting a pressure campaign," Komer advised that the administration "stop pampering" the Pakistani leader. An "aloof" response to Pakistan's China ploy, in his view, would ultimately prove most effective. "If we're not so apologetic," Komer smugly predicted, "Ayub will step in and call a halt to this nonsense."[13]

From his vantage point in Karachi, Ambassador Walter P. McConaughy looked at Pakistan's deepening ties to China with a more discerning eye. One of the government's most senior China specialists, the veteran diplomat found confirmation in recent events, most especially the invitation to Zhou Enlai, for his earlier forecast that Pakistan was moving toward a partial disengagement from its Western alliances. What most troubled McConaughy was the proposal, currently being debated in Washington, that called for the provision of at least $50 million in military aid to India over each of the next five years. Given Pakistan's "almost psychotic fears of India," he was certain that such an agreement would produce a grave setback for the U.S. position there and "force [a] major reconsideration and reorientation of Pakistan foreign and military policies." The conclusion of a multiyear military assistance pact with India at this hazardous juncture, McConaughy cautioned the State Department, would be like "injecting [a] flame into [an] already combustible subcontinent situation."[14]

12. Johnson to Ayub, December 9, 1963, NSC History of South Asia, NSF, LBJL; Komer to Johnson, September 9, 1965, ibid.
13. Komer to Bundy, December 13, 1963, ibid.; Ball to Johnson, December 12, 1963, ibid.
14. McConaughy to the State Department, December 9, 1963, NSF, India, Cables, vol. I, LBJL; McConaughy to the State Department, January 9, 1964, NSF, Pakistan, Memos, vol. III, LBJL.

Plainly the issue of how much military aid to provide India, and over how long a period of time, posed a series of vexing problems for the United States. Although sympathetic to the perspective of his counterpart in Karachi, Ambassador Chester Bowles argued vociferously from his post in New Delhi that the United States could not allow Pakistan's obsessions to divert it any longer from a "highly promising" opportunity "to achieve a breakthrough in Asia which is clearly in [the] interests of [the] United States." The Sino–Indian war afforded the United States a one-time chance to align India with the West, Bowles insisted, and to gain in the process a key ally in the struggle against Chinese expansion; further delay in reaching a decision would just leave a vacuum into which the Soviets would likely plunge. His recommendation: guarantee India $60 to $75 million in military assistance per annum over the next five years.[15] The State and Defense Departments for once found their thinking essentially in harmony with that of the notoriously pro-Indian Bowles, although they envisioned a slightly more modest program of $50 to $60 million per year. Just before the arrival in the subcontinent of a fact-finding mission headed by General Maxwell D. Taylor, the State Department authorized Bowles to inform Indian officials that Washington was currently preparing the details of a long-term military assistance pact. Fearing "a violent reaction" in Pakistan to the premature disclosure of U.S. plans, however, Secretary of State Dean Rusk recommended against providing the Indians in advance with as explicit a commitment as Bowles desired.[16]

The Taylor mission, which came at a critical juncture in the evolving, triangular relationship among the United States, India, and Pakistan, aimed at stabilizing the American position in the subcontinent. By dangling the carrot of long-term military assistance agreements in front of both Indian and Pakistani leaders, administration planners hoped that Taylor could check growing suspicions in both countries about American reliability. In New Delhi, Taylor sought to reassure the increasingly skeptical Indians by signaling American willingness to pursue the multiyear military aid pact that

15. Bowles to the State Department, December 19, 1963, NSF, India, Memos & Misc., vol. I, LBJL.
16. Ball to the U.S. Embassy in France, December 14, 1963, NSF, India, Cables, vol. I, LBJL; Rusk to Johnson, December 11, 1963, Memos & Misc., vol. I, ibid.

the two countries had been discussing ever since the Chinese military incursion of October 1962. The chairman of the Joint Chiefs of Staff carried a similar carrot to Pakistan but brought a thinly concealed stick as well. He sought to persuade Ayub and other Pakistani leaders that their fear of the Indian military threat was unwarranted; to inform them once again that the United States believed that China posed the real threat to the security of the subcontinent; to make clear that, regardless of Pakistani protests, Washington would continue to supply New Delhi with needed military assistance; and to remind Pakistani leaders that they must discharge their alliance responsibilities to SEATO and CENTO if they expected continued American aid.[17]

During a frank, private meeting with Ayub in the new, interim capital of Rawalpindi, the American general expressed "deep regret" over the "downward trend" in U.S.–Pakistani relations over the past year. Why, Taylor implored, could the two nations not simply "accept the existence of an honest difference of view as to the rightness of US military aid to India, cease the recriminations which have been souring our relations and move forward together toward common objectives?" The new Sino–Pakistani relationship of course offered the most obvious answer to Taylor's plaintive plea, and it once again provided the main stumbling block to mutual understanding. Ayub said that he "loved President Johnson more than a brother" and wanted Taylor to assure the American leader that the upcoming Zhou visit signified nothing more than Pakistan's natural desire to normalize relations with a potential enemy. Echoing Johnson's earlier cautionary words to Bhutto, Taylor emphasized that the visit created "a domestic problem" for the United States that might negatively affect future congressional support for Pakistan. "Ayub will be seen in close company with [Zhou] on every TV in the world," Taylor chided, "to the detriment of US/Pak relations."[18]

17. Scope Papers for Taylor Visits to India and Pakistan, December 1963, NSF, India, Memos & Misc., vol. I, LBJL; Bowles to the State Department, December 19, 1963, ibid.; Bundy to Taylor, December 14, 1964, NSF, Gen. Taylor folder, International Meetings and Travel File, LBJL.
18. Memorandum of conversation between Taylor and Ayub, December 20, 1963, NSF, India, Memos & Misc., vol. I, LBJL; McConaughy to the State Department, December 21, 1963, NSF, Gen. Taylor folder, International Meetings and Travel File, LBJL; Talking Points Paper for Taylor's Visit to India, November 27, 1963, prepared by the Depart-

Upon his return to Washington, Taylor quickly sent Johnson his impressions of the visit along with a detailed set of recommendations concerning future military assistance commitments to the two countries. He expressed his conviction that India and Pakistan, provided they met certain U.S. conditions, should be offered $50 to $60 million in military support over each of the next five years. On February 8, 1964, Johnson approved part of the Taylor program. He authorized "exploratory approaches" to India and Pakistan, looking toward the possible negotiation of five-year military aid packages. The president added some important caveats, however. "It seems to me premature," he informed Rusk and Secretary of Defense Robert S. McNamara, "to indicate to India or Pakistan how much military aid they might be able to count upon, regardless of how tentatively we put it." Johnson preferred to hold off any discussion of specific aid figures until the two countries prepared "austere" military plans. Further, he insisted that "we should make clear to both countries what we expect of them in return for prospective long-term military aid." In the case of India, that meant that the practice of diverting dollars earned through developmental assistance to the defense budget needed to be sharply curtailed. In the case of Pakistan, it meant "satisfactory performance with respect to its alliance obligations." Johnson added pointedly that the initial approach to Pakistan should be delayed until after the administration had had sufficient time to assess the results of the Zhou visit.[19] Then, the State Department alerted McConaughy, the White House intended "to use [the] prospect of continued military assistance both as a carrot to demonstrate [the] value of [a] continued alliance relationship and as a lever to get from Pakistan the necessary assurances that it will limit its relationship with Peiping and pursue policies in general which will not be adverse to US interests."[20]

ment of Defense, ibid.; Maxwell Taylor, *Swords and Ploughshares: A Memoir* (New York: Norton, 1978), 305–6.

19. Taylor to Johnson, December 23, 1963, NSF, India, Memos & Misc., vol. I, LBJL; NSAM No. 279, February 8, 1964, NSC History of South Asia, NSF, LBJL. See also Komer to Johnson, January 22, 1964, NSF, India, Memos & Misc., vol. VI, LBJL; Komer to Johnson, January 30, 1964, NSF, Pakistan, Memos & Misc., vol. I, LBJL.
20. Ball to the Embassy in Pakistan, February 21, 1964, NSF, NSAM 279 folder, National Security Action Memorandums, LBJL.

The Zhou trip to Pakistan weighed heavily on the mind of a president who saw "Red China," as he invariably called it, as the chief threat to global stability. By early 1964, LBJ, Rusk, McNamara, Bundy, and other top administration planners were convinced that Southeast Asia provided China with an especially tempting opportunity to extend its influence southward. The rapidly disintegrating political and security position of America's South Vietnamese client state, which Johnson was sure Beijing would capitalize on, had already begun to overshadow and color the president's response to all other foreign policy matters. As he pondered the difficult choices posed by the Saigon regime's desperate plight, Johnson must have blanched at the distasteful images presented by Ayub's meetings with Zhou. Although the Pakistanis took pains not to offend their erstwhile ally by too lavish a treatment of their Chinese visitors, the mere fact of the meetings served as a powerfully dissonant symbol. An American ally was greeting with great amiability the senior representatives of a nation that, according to Johnson and his top national security strategists, was guilty of fomenting aggression in Vietnam.[21] LBJ dispatched Talbot to Pakistan in March 1964 to inform Ayub sternly that his flirtation with China was rapidly approaching the limits of American tolerance.[22]

The Talbot trip, which also took the assistant secretary to India, came at a time when political and economic developments in the two countries were moving in very different directions. The political stability that had been the hallmark of the Nehru era was fast eroding in the wake of the prime minister's weakened physical condition. Nehru, who had not recovered fully from the stroke he had suffered in January, was no longer the robust leader of the past, a man who had placed his personal stamp on virtually all aspects of Indian political life. Indian politicians, recognizing that the prime minister's days were numbered, were already jockeying for advantage in what was shaping up as a divisive succession struggle. In addition to that budding political crisis, India was plagued by a renewed wave of communal violence throughout the country and a

21. Chang, *Friends and Enemies*, 253–6; Geyelin, *Johnson and the World*, 51–4; G. W. Choudhury, *India, Pakistan, Bangladesh, and the Major Powers: Politics of a Divided Subcontinent* (New York: Free Press, 1975), 183.
22. Bundy to Johnson, March 8, 1964, NSF, Name File, Komer, LBJL.

economy that continued to perform sluggishly. Ironically, Pakistan, a country beset by political instability and economic crises for more than a decade, now boasted a strong and popular leader in Ayub and showed signs of genuine economic progress. Talbot said that his trip to the subcontinent revealed "the sharpest contrast in years" in the "internal dynamics of India and Pakistan." He found in Pakistan a self-confidence and a "new-found buoyancy" that stood in stark contrast to the malaise so distressingly evident in India.[23]

Worried about the sense of drift in India, Komer urged Johnson to make a definite, long-term military commitment to India. Like Bowles, he invariably framed that case in terms of American grand strategy. "As the Sino–Soviet split widens," the NSC aide wrote Johnson, "Moscow has been making up for lost time." The "Soviets are now doing more than we to woo the Indian military establishment" while Indo–American relations were "sliding backwards from the high point reached as a result of our vigorous response to the Chicom attack in October 1962." That unfavorable trend posed a serious threat, in his view, to American global interests. "India, as the largest and potentially most powerful non-Communist Asian nation, is in fact the major prize for which we, the Soviets, and Chicoms are competing in Asia," Komer reminded the president. "With India heading into a succession crisis, we have to watch our step," he cautioned. "If India falls apart we are the losers. If India goes Communist, it will be a disaster comparable only to the loss of China." Given those risks, which were "not just Bowlesian hyperbole," he added pointedly, the Johnson administration could not allow its alliance with Pakistan "to stand in the way of a rational India policy"; Washington could not permit "the tail to wag the dog."[24]

Johnson remained ambivalent about completing the South Asia policy reorientation that his NSC staff was advocating with such

23. Talbot to Rusk, March 25, 1964, NSF, India, Cables, vol. I, LBJL; Komer to Johnson, March 27, 1964, NSF, India, Memos & Misc., vol. II, LBJL; Ball to the Embassy in Pakistan, February 21, 1964, NSF, NSAM 279 folder, National Security Action Memorandums, LBJL; Herbert Feldman, *From Crisis to Crisis: Pakistan, 1962–1969* (London: Oxford University Press, 1972), 34–67.
24. Komer to Johnson, February 24, 1964, NSC History of South Asia, NSF, LBJL; Komer to Johnson, March 27, 1964, NSF, India, Memos & Misc., vol. II, LBJL; Komer to Bundy, June 3, 1964, ibid. For Bowles's views, see especially Bowles to the State De-

vigor. On one level, he accepted the logic of the Komer–Bundy argument that India's prospective alignment with the West offered strategic benefits to the United States that far outweighed any likely damage to the Pakistani–American alliance. Confident in his ability to handle an ally that remained dependent on the United States for military and economic support, Johnson probably agreed with Komer's breezy assessment that, as a result of administration pressure, the "Paks are coming around."[25] Still, the president had no desire to push the Pakistanis further into the Chinese embrace, nor did he want to jeopardize by his own actions American access to intelligence installations that senior defense and intelligence aides highly valued. His instinctive prudence when faced with complex diplomatic decisions of uncertain consequence – a trait displayed in abundance during the agonizing policy debates about Vietnam being held at the very same time – militated against bold policy shifts and multiyear aid commitments.

In addition, the cautious chief executive harbored an instinctual skepticism about the political viability of America's expanding commitments in the subcontinent. As a man who had spent much of his adult life in the Congress and sensed its moods and concerns as well as anyone in Washington, Johnson fretted that a legislative revolt was brewing against the escalating costs of foreign aid. Sure to be targeted for pointed criticism were the administration's economic and military assistance programs for India and Pakistan, programs that absorbed nearly one-third of the entire foreign aid budget, brought little obvious return for America's sizable investment, and often worked at cross-purposes. Johnson worried that an administration guarantee to provide India with a specific level of aid over the next five years, in the absence of any significant movement toward an Indo–Pakistani rapprochement, might simply invite closer congressional scrutiny of American aid commitments in South Asia, precipitate a contentious public debate, and ultimately jeopardize future funding requests.

partment, February 20, 26, and 28 and March 12, 1964, NSF, India, Cables, vol. I, LBJL; Bowles to former Ambassador John Kenneth Galbraith, January 27, 1964, Galbraith folder, Box 330, Chester Bowles Papers, Sterling Library, Yale University, New Haven, Connecticut.
25. Komer to Bundy, May 28, 1964, NSF, Name File, Komer, LBJL.

Unlike Kennedy, moreover, Johnson sympathized with many of the complaints leveled at the foreign aid program by angry critics on Capitol Hill. He, too, tended to view as a foolish waste of resources any major expenditures that did not bring political or diplomatic benefits. Probably the most intensely political of twentieth-century American presidents, LBJ approached international affairs much as he did the rough-and-tumble arena of domestic politics. And one of his basic political rules held that favors must always be repaid in kind; if not, the recipient could hardly expect additional assistance from the benefactor. The Third World for Johnson increasingly seemed less the towering ideological challenge it had been for Kennedy and more just a mundane and bothersome collection of "countries that want something from us."[26] That palpable shift in attitudes and priorities bore important implications for India and for Pakistan.

Indian Defense Minister Y. B. Chavan, who arrived in the United States late in May 1964 with the hope of negotiating a long-term military aid agreement, quickly discovered the limits that Johnson's skepticism had imposed on the evolving security relationship between the two nations. Having produced the five-year defense plan urged by the United States, Chavan almost certainly expected the Johnson administration to propose a multiyear military assistance pact. It was not forthcoming. Instead, the United States offered to provide India with $50 million in military aid for fiscal year 1965 but withheld any definite commitment beyond that period. Given the tenor of previous discussions, and the positive signals conveyed by Bowles over the past several months, the circumscribed nature of the U.S. offer just confirmed the suspicions prevalent in Indian governing circles about the diminishing credibility of American promises. The blow was partially but not sufficiently softened by an American commitment to provide India with a $10 million credit for the purchase of U.S. military equipment during the remaining

---

26. Geyelin, *Johnson and the World*, 30, 271 (the quotation is from p. 271); Komer to Bundy, June 3, 1964, NSF, India, Memos & Misc., vol. II, LBJL; Komer to Bundy, November 27, 1964, NSF, India, Cables & Memos, vol. III, LBJL; Burton I. Kaufman, "Foreign Aid and the Balance-of-Payments Problem: Vietnam and Johnson's Foreign Economic Policy," in Robert A. Divine, ed., *The Johnson Years*, vol. 2: *Vietnam, the Environment, and Science* (Lawrence: University Press of Kansas, 1987), 80–1.

portion of the current fiscal year and the promise of a $50 million credit for fiscal year 1965. The sudden death of Nehru on May 24 added drama and suspense to the Chavan visit. The defense minister rushed home upon hearing the news, just prior to a scheduled meeting with Johnson. Only on June 6, after Chavan's return to Washington, did the White House publicly announce the details of this new military commitment to India.[27]

In a classic case of wishful thinking, Komer speculated that the Pakistani response to the announcement, although sure to be critical, would be limited "because we haven't given much yet."[28] He could not have been farther from the mark. The Pakistani reaction was angry, emotional, and explosive, at both official and non-official levels. News of the Indo–American military assistance pact unleashed a flood of anti-American demonstrations throughout the country. The knowledge that the United States was deliberately delaying future military aid commitments to Pakistan as a crude form of punishment for its China policy fueled the intensity of those protests. Pakistan's leaders found the differential treatment meted out by its erstwhile ally in Washington to a formally non-aligned state especially galling. U.S. policy is "based on opportunism and is devoid of moral quality," Ayub snapped during a press interview; "now Americans do not hesitate to let down their friends." The Pakistani leader also registered a vigorous, formal protest, notifying Johnson in a letter of July 7 that Pakistan might now have to reappraise its commitments to SEATO and CENTO.[29]

The quick-tempered Johnson was infuriated by the curt tone of Ayub's message and by the veiled threat that it contained. In a meeting with Ambassador Ghulam Ahmed, who personally delivered the letter to him, Johnson made no effort to hide his "considerable distress" with Ayub's complaints. Offering the standard defense of U.S. policy, he insisted that military aid to India served American – and Pakistani – interests by contributing to the con-

27. Draft memorandum of understanding, May 27, 1964, NSF, India, Memos & Misc., vol. II, LBJL; Komer to Bundy, September 9, 1965, NSC History of South Asia, NSF, LBJL; Nehru to Johnson, ibid.; Bundy to Johnson, May 16, 1964, White House Central File (hereafter WHCF), Country File 121, LBJL.
28. Komer to Bundy, June 23, 1964, NSC History of South Asia, NSF, LBJL.
29. Ball to Johnson, July 5, 1964, ibid.; Rusk to McConaughy, July 29, 1964, ibid.; CIA Special Report, "Pakistan and the Free World Alliance," July 10, 1964, NSF, Pakistan, Cables, vol. I, LBJL.

tainment of the communist threat to the subcontinent. It hardly offered proof that Washington was being "disloyal" to its Pakistani ally, as Ayub charged. The president turned the charge around. He implied that Pakistan, by dint of its relationship with China, was the real disloyal partner, especially in view of the grave threat that China currently posed to the noncommunist states of Southeast Asia. LBJ told the ambassador flatly that if Pakistan chose to reexamine its relationship with the United States, regrettable as it might be, the United States would have no choice but to reexamine its relationship with Pakistan.[30]

The following week, a still-fuming president met with Ambassador McConaughy. Johnson told his envoy, who had been urging the president to invite Ayub to Washington to clear the air, that there would be no invitation. The United States should take no action to placate the Pakistanis at this juncture, Johnson directed; he wanted a cooling-off period instead, during which U.S.–Pakistani relations would remain correct but aloof. LBJ instructed McConaughy, upon the latter's return to Karachi, to inform Ayub personally of his candid remarks to Ahmed, stress the "worrisome implications for the future" of the Pakistani–Chinese relationship, emphasize American concern with the threat of Chinese subversion and aggression in Southeast Asia, and impress upon Ayub the importance Washington attached to Pakistan's joining the "free world effort in Viet Nam and at least show[ing the] flag there."[31] Mused the ever-candid and irreverent Komer: "Pak policies have now succeeded in alienating two Presidents; if the Paks aren't careful, they may kill the goose that lays the golden egg. . . ."[32]

Born of frustration and anger, Johnson's confrontation with Ahmed and his blunt follow-up message to Ayub set the tone for U.S.–Pakistani relations over the next six months. It was a troubled and stormy period that witnessed a further acceleration of the trends first set in motion by the Chinese invasion of India in October 1962.

30. NSC, "Narrative and Guide to Documents," NSC History of South Asia, NSF, LBJL; Bundy to Jack Valenti, White House aide, July 6, 1964, 230 Pakistan, Confidential File, LBJ Papers, LBJL.
31. Rusk to McConaughy, July 29, 1964, NSC History of South Asia, NSF, LBJL; Rusk to Johnson, July 15, 1964, ibid.; Komer to Johnson, September 9, 1964, ibid.; "Narrative and Guide to Documents," ibid.; Rusk to the Embassy in Pakistan, July 15, 1964, NSF, Pakistan, Cables, vol. III, LBJL.
32. Komer to Bundy, July 24, 1964, NSF, Komer Name File, LBJL.

Pakistan expanded its ties with the non-aligned states of Asia and Africa (making a special effort to warm up to Sukarno's Indonesia), continued to pursue actively a closer connection with China, and steadily deemphasized its commitments to SEATO and CENTO. For its part, the United States maintained a cordial but distant relationship with its recalcitrant ally. When the pro-American Finance Minister Mohammed Shoaib visited Washington in September 1964, Bundy reminded him that fundamental differences over China posed the greatest obstacle to a constructive dialogue between Washington and Karachi.[33] The deepening crisis in South Vietnam during this same period, which preoccupied Johnson and his senior aides, only exacerbated U.S.–Pakistani tensions. As the Johnson administration moved to shore up the embattled Saigon regime, many of its leading analysts saw Beijing, more than either Hanoi or the Viet Cong guerrillas, as America's real foe in Southeast Asia. China's detonation of its first atomic device in October 1964 raised the specter of aggressive intentions being joined by alarming new capabilities – a dangerously combustible mix. In that explosive context, the Beijing–Karachi axis posed more than just a public relations embarrassment for Washington; it represented a repudiation of the core values and interests of American foreign policy. With the righteous arrogance of decision makers convinced that their view of world affairs could brook no responsible dissent, Johnson and his senior advisers condemned what they considered the reckless and irresponsible behavior of a once-loyal ally.

Although the United States and Pakistan appeared to be moving inexorably toward an ever more open clash as 1964 drew to a close, the bonds forged a decade earlier continued to yield significant benefits to both sides. Those served as a brake on any precipitous action by either nation aimed at severing the alliance altogether. Pakistan still required U.S. aid for critical development and defense priorities; and the United States still valued the intelligence-collection facilities that Pakistan permitted it to operate. "The Pakistani President knows that the strongest card he holds is the US communications facilities at Peshawar," the CIA speculated in an adroit analysis. "He almost certainly calculates that closing

---

33. NSC, "Narrative and Guide to Documents"; CIA report, "Pakistan and the Free World Alliance."

the facilities would bring a drastic reduction in the US military and economic assistance on which Pakistan is so heavily dependent and for which there is no alternative in sight."[34]

In order to reopen the stalled dialogue with Pakistan, in January 1965 Johnson approved a State Department recommendation that he invite Ayub to visit Washington that April. Johnson envisioned the meeting as an opportunity to persuade the Pakistani leader that, despite the chill that had beset Pakistani–American relations since July, a "basis for close and mutually beneficial ties" between the two countries continued to exist. He also intended to discuss frankly with Ayub the alarming gap that separated U.S. and Pakistani assessments of Chinese actions and intentions.[35] The State Department held relatively modest hopes for the visit. In a memorandum for the White House, approved by Rusk, it recommended that LBJ seek "*to halt the drift in our relations with Pakistan.*" He should make it clear that Pakistan's relationship with China could not "exceed the speed limits" imposed by the United States if it desired continued ties with Washington. "President Ayub should go away," the department offered, "with a clear appreciation of the relationship of our aid levels to a tolerable, if somewhat watered-down, alliance relationship."[36]

Had the scheduled meetings with Ayub proceeded as planned, it is doubtful that the Johnson administration could have achieved even those limited goals. Flushed with his personal triumph in the national elections of March 1965, which demonstrated overwhelming domestic support for Ayub and his new foreign policy direction, the Pakistani president could hardly have been expected to approach American officials in a compromising mood. His decision to reduce Pakistan's ties with the West to their bare essentials while simultaneously courting favor with Beijing and the non-aligned states of the Afro–Asian world not only enjoyed wide popular acclaim at home but comported with the diplomatic strategy advocated by most influential Pakistanis inside and outside the government. That strategy had, moreover, achieved a degree of success that even CIA analysts grudgingly recognized. Six months

34. CIA Report, "Pakistan and the Free World Alliance."
35. Rusk to the Embassy in Pakistan, January 11, 1965, NSF, Pakistan, Cables, vol. III, LBJL.
36. State Department Scope Paper, April 1, 1965, NSF, Pakistan, Memos, vol. III, LBJL.

of diplomatic coolness from Washington had consequently done nothing to shake Ayub's conviction that both vital national security considerations and domestic political imperatives validated the wisdom of the new international course he was charting.[37]

Just nine days before the Pakistani leader's scheduled arrival in Washington, to the shock and dismay of some of his own advisers, Johnson abruptly withdrew his invitation. The recent state visits by Ayub to Moscow and Beijing, especially the latter trip, lay behind the president's precipitous action. Much to Johnson's discomfiture, Ayub had greeted Mao Zedong, Zhou, and their compatriots with open arms. He had pledged "lasting friendship and fruitful cooperation" between Pakistan and China, openly criticized the escalation of the American commitment in Vietnam, and, according to a State Department intelligence assessment, even adopted "Afro–Asian jargon" in his speeches.[38] That "disturbing" behavior irritated and angered the thin-skinned Johnson. On April 6 he told his senior aides that Ayub's arrival in Washington would just focus attention on the Pakistani's unfortunate behavior and unfriendly statements in the two communist capitals, thus jeopardizing congressional action on the administration's foreign aid bill. In addition, Ayub would almost certainly feel compelled to make statements regarding Vietnam that would spark additional controversy with Congress and with the media.[39]

In an explanatory letter to the surprised Ayub, Johnson pulled few punches. After the obligatory professions of good will, the president came right to the point. He said that his long years of experience with Congress had led him "to the conclusion that your visit at this time would focus public attention on the differences between Pakistani and United States policy toward Communist China." Such an airing of differences, at the very moment that Congress was deliberating about the administration's foreign aid

---

37. CIA report, "Pakistan and the Free World Alliance"; William J. Barnds, *India, Pakistan, and the Great Powers* (New York: Praeger, 1972), 190–2.
38. Hughes to Rusk, March 6, 1965, NSF, Pakistan, Memos, vol. IV, LBJL.
39. Ball to Rusk, April 6, 1965, NSF, India, Cables, vol. IV, LBJL; memorandum of telephone conversation between Ball and the British Ambassador, April 13, 1965, India folder, George Ball Papers, LBJL; Bundy to Johnson, April 22, 1965, NSF Aides File, Bundy Memos to the President, vol. 10, LBJL; CIA Special Report, "India and Pakistan Remain at an Impasse," April 2, 1965, India, NSF, Memos & Misc., vol. IV, LBJL.

budget proposals, might "gravely affect" continued legislative support for Pakistan's development and defense efforts. "I cannot overstate the full depth of American feeling about Communist China," Johnson wrote. "The mounting number of American casualties in South Vietnam is having a profound effect upon American opinion. This is being felt in Congress just at the time when our foreign aid legislation is at the most sensitive point in the legislative cycle." Under the circumstances, Johnson concluded, a postponement of the visit until the fall, when it would likely generate less heat, appeared the wisest course of action.[40]

In order to maintain a rough parallelism in U.S. treatment of India and Pakistan, Johnson at the very same time postponed the first scheduled visit to the United States of the new Indian prime minister, Lal Bahadur Shastri. Ayub, not Shastri, was the prime target of Johnson's blunt signal. Nonetheless, the two visits were closely linked in American planning, and Johnson's advisers convinced him that a decision to postpone Ayub's trip and not Shastri's would have stood as an unforgivable affront in Pakistani eyes. The moderate Congress Party politician who had replaced Nehru the previous year had, in the judgment of ranking administration officials, done nothing even mildly comparable to Ayub's galling actions. True, Washington had its differences with the Shastri government. The new Indian leader's intransigence on Kashmir rankled American observers, some of whom had forecast hopefully that a change at the top might produce a more conciliatory Indian policy. Likewise, Shastri's insistence on continuing Nehru's foreign policy of non-alignment and his eagerness to accept military supplies from Moscow angered and frustrated U.S. planners; their dream of an American-armed India adopting an openly pro-Western orientation increasingly seemed a mirage. The Indian prime minister's lukewarm support for the American effort in Vietnam did little to soothe American misgivings about India's reliability. In spite of those continuing differences, however, the Indo–American relationship rested on a much sounder foundation than the Pakistani–American connection. A common fear of China had forged a strong sense of shared interests between India and the United

40. Johnson to Ayub, April 14, 1965, NSC History of South Asia, NSF, LBJL.

States, much as a profound cleavage over China policy had pulled Pakistan and the United States apart.[41]

Consequently, American officials had from the beginning seen the Shastri visit, originally scheduled for June, in a far more positive light than the Ayub visit. They viewed it primarily as an opportunity for the new Indian leader to establish a personal rapport with Johnson and for the American president to extend to Shastri firm reassurances about U.S. support. Those hopes, however, quickly dissipated in the wake of Johnson's decision to postpone the two scheduled visits.[42]

Both Ayub and Shastri expressed indignation at the abrupt cancellation of their invitations. The latter was especially angry and resentful; he complained to Bowles that the American announcement had unfairly linked the postponement of his planned visit with that of a man whose recent statements in Beijing had offended the Indians fully as much as they had offended the Americans. Komer, who closely monitored the velocity of "the inevitable furor" in India and Pakistan over the cancelations, recognized that the administration's decision had deeply embarrassed the Indians by bracketing them with "the misbehaving Paks." He confessed that he had "honestly underestimated the Indian sense of bewilderment and hurt."[43] *The Economist* observed with sardonic accuracy that the United States had managed to achieve "the unusual diplomatic feat of giving offence to both [India and Pakistan] simultaneously."[44] Komer admitted that the United States would probably suffer "short term lumps" as a result of Johnson's brusque decision. Inveterate opti-

41. State Department, "Scope Paper for Ayub and Shastri Visits to the United States," April 1, 1965, NSF, Pakistan, Memos, vol. III, LBJL.
42. Johnson to Shastri, April 15, 1965, NSC History of South Asia, NSF, LBJL; Ball to Rusk, April 14, 1965, NSF, India, Cables, vol. IV, LBJL; CIA Special Report, "India's Revamped Defense Posture," November 20, 1964, NSF, India, Cables and Memos, vol. III, LBJL; Rusk to the Embassy in India, December 18, 1964, NSF, India, Cables, vol. IV, LBJL.
43. Komer to Bundy, April 21, 1965, NSC History of South Asia, NSF, LBJL; Bowles to the State Department, April 15, 1965, NSF, India, Memos & Misc., vol. IV, LBJL; Bowles to the State Department, April 16, 1965, NSF, India, Cables, vol. IV, LBJL; Chester Bowles, Oral History Interview, November 11, 1969, LBJL. On Bowles, his policy recommendations, and his diminishing credibility with Johnson and other senior officials, see especially Howard B. Schaffer, *New Dealer in the Cold War: The Role of Chester Bowles in U.S. Foreign Policy* (Cambridge, Mass.: Harvard University Press, 1994), Ch. 16.
44. *The Economist,* April 24, 1965, p. 415.

mist that he was, the NSC aide also identified a string of possible benefits likely to flow from the double postponement as well: "(a) it reminds our friends that we too have feelings – especially about Vietnam; (b) Ayub got the signal, though we may need to remind him; and (c) the Indians too will end up a bit worried." Both countries, he said, now would be forced to "reflect on the moral that Uncle Sam should not just be regarded as a cornucopia of goodies, regardless of what they do or say."[45]

Once again, however, Komer seriously underestimated the impact of American heavyhandedness on the two countries – and on Indo–Pakistani relations. Johnson's announcement proved especially ill timed in the latter regard because at the very moment of his notification to Ayub and Shastri large-scale clashes between Indian and Pakistani troops were taking place. The clashes occurred in a desolate area abutting the Arabian Sea called the Rann of Kutch. India and Pakistan maintained overlapping border claims there, the symbolic significance of which far outweighed any material or strategic value either side attached to the land in question. The use by Pakistani troops of U.S.-supplied weapons raised awkward political questions for the United States. The fighting "has propelled us once more into the center of a subcontinental dispute," a State Department analysis noted, "at a moment when our leverage in both countries is at a low point." Pakistan, it speculated, might have precipitated the conflict in the hope that its use of U.S. military equipment would drive a wedge between India and the United States.[46] If that was the Pakistani intention, the ploy proved quite effective. Almost immediately, India lodged a vehement protest with the United States, reminding Washington of its repeated assurances that it would not allow Pakistan to use U.S. military equipment against India. Bowles urgently cabled the State Department that its response to this troubling affair would have a far-reaching effect on U.S.–Indian relations.[47]

45. Komer to Bundy, April 21, 1965, NSC History of South Asia, NSF, LBJL; Komer to Johnson, April 16, 1965, ibid.
46. Benjamin H. Read, Executive Secretary, State Department, to Bundy, April 24, 1965, NSF India, Memos & Misc., vol. IV, LBJL.
47. Memorandum of conversation between Rusk and B. K. Nehru, May 8, 1965, NSF, India, Memos & Misc., vol. IV, LBJL; Rusk to Bowles, May 8, 1965, ibid.; Bowles to the State Department, May 10, 1965, NSC, India, Cables, vol. IV, LBJL.

Under the circumstances, the Johnson administration believed that it had no choice but to inform Pakistan and India that it was prohibiting the use of any U.S. military materiel in the Rann. Pakistanis deeply resented this edict, characterizing it as yet another American capitulation to India. They considered the U.S. decision to prohibit the use by either side of its military equipment to be grossly unfair because virtually all of Pakistan's equipment came from the United States, whereas India acquired military hardware from a variety of sources. Foreign Minister Bhutto warned that the U.S. decision would have profoundly negative repercussions on Pakistani–American relations.[48]

The Rann of Kutch incident, although militarily insignificant, did have important diplomatic consequences. In its aftermath, confidence in the United States plummeted in both Rawalpindi and New Delhi – simultaneously. Shastri and his chief advisers, already stung by Johnson's disinvitation, felt betrayed by Pakistan's use of American equipment. America's repeated promises to them that it would deter Pakistani aggression now appeared empty. For their part, Pakistani leaders had their gravest suspicions confirmed by the U.S. response to the Rann of Kutch fighting; they were now convinced that previous U.S. pledges about restraining Indian aggression were meaningless. Its standing with the two parties was now so low that the United States lacked sufficient leverage to play even a minor mediatory role. Accordingly, it deferred to Great Britain, which managed to negotiate a cease-fire agreement that Ayub and Shastri signed in London on June 30. The Johnson administration could do little but applaud the British effort from the sidelines.[49]

Another leader might have sought to rebuild bridges at such an incendiary juncture. Not Lyndon Johnson. Convinced that any conciliatory moves could be read as a sign of weakness, Johnson opted instead to intensify American pressure on both Pakistan and India. Late in April, while the skirmishes in the Rann were still raging, he directed that all pending aid decisions regarding the two countries first be cleared with the White House. "The President's reluctance to move forward on India and Pakistan matters,"

48. Read to Bundy, May 12, 1965, NSC History of South Asia, NSF, LBJL; Hughes to the Acting Secretary of State, May 13, 1965, ibid.
49. Greene, Chargé in India, to the State Department, May 25, 1965, NSF, India, Memos & Misc., vol. IV, LBJL; Komer to Bundy, May 15, 1965, ibid.; Rusk to Johnson, May 19, 1965, NSC History of South Asia, NSF, LBJL.

Komer explained, "stems from his own deep instinct that we are not getting enough for our massive investment in either."[50] Indeed, on June 8 Johnson made those feelings absolutely clear in a terse handwritten note to Bundy. "I'm not for allocating or appropriating $1 now [for India or Pakistan]," he ordered, "unless I have already signed and agreed – if I have show me when and where."[51] Sensing a stagnation in the American approach toward the subcontinent, the results-oriented Johnson began to assume an unusual degree of personal control over the policy process. On June 9, during a meeting with Rusk, McNamara, and Agency for International Development (AID) administrator David E. Bell, he demanded a fundamental rethinking of American strategy and tactics in South Asia. Following the session, LBJ issued a blunt directive to the bureaucracy, ordering that "there be no additional decisions, authorizations, or announcements on loans to India or Pakistan without his approval, pending passage of the FY 1966 foreign aid appropriation." Additionally, he requested that the State Department and AID conduct a full-scale review of all U.S. economic aid programs to India and Pakistan in order to determine "(a) whether the US should be spending such large sums in either country; and (b) how to achieve more leverage for our money, in terms both of more effective self-help and of our political purposes."[52]

The impact of this tough new stance not accidentally hit Pakistan the hardest. The economic pressure that the aid slowdown placed on India, with the important exception of surplus food shipments under the Public Law 480 program, was not immediate. The India aid consortium had already held its annual pledging session, with the United States agreeing to maintain in fiscal year 1966 a level of economic support for India comparable to its commitment of the previous year. The Pakistan aid consortium had yet to meet. "To keep up the pressure" on Pakistan, Johnson postponed that annual pledging session, originally scheduled to convene on July 27, for two months.[53] The decision, he hoped, would deliver an unmistak-

---

50. Komer to Bundy, May 30, 1965, NSC History of South Asia, NSF, LBJL.
51. Bundy to LBJ, with LBJ handwritten note, June 8, 1965, NSF, Bundy Memos to the President, LBJL.
52. Bundy to Rusk, McNamara, and Bell, June 9, 1965, NSC History of South Asia, NSF, LBJL; Komer to Donald Cook, June 3, 1965, ibid.
53. Komer to Johnson, June 28, 1965, ibid.; Rusk to the Embassy in Pakistan, June 30, 1965, NSF, Pakistan, Cables, vol. III, LBJL.

able warning to the Pakistanis. According to a subsequent assessment by the NSC, "The postponement was designed to show Ayub that American aid was far from automatic, and to be a forceful reminder that his relations with China and other US–Pakistani difficulties could endanger his nation's economy."[54] In adopting this bruising tactic, Johnson was closely following a script written by his favorite South Asia expert. "We may lose Pakistan," Komer had advised him, "unless we can convince Ayub that he can't have his cake and eat it too. Pakistan's still desperate need for US aid gives us real leverage."[55]

Although it was couched in the usual diplomatic niceties, the consortium postponement aroused passionate resentments in Pakistan. McConaughy reported that "Ayub took the news quite hard – worse than I had anticipated."[56] Komer agreed. With a hint of arrogance, he informed Johnson that the consortium decision "was quite a shock to Ayub."[57] The Pakistani president publicly vented his anger with the United States. Speaking before a meeting of the Muslim League on July 14, Ayub declared that he had sought during his recent foreign travels to find "new friends, not new masters." He complained that Pakistan had tried on numerous occasions to explain its policy to the United States, but to no avail. The Americans, he charged, were "power drunk"; they did not listen to smaller countries. Massive anti-American rallies were staged in all major Pakistani cities following Ayub's inflammatory speech.[58]

According to an understated assessment by the State Department's intelligence bureau, "Pakistan apparently considers the postponement of the Consortium pledging session as a major crisis in US–Pakistani relations, and Ayub has probably come to believe that the US intends to use economic aid as a lever to force modifications of Pakistan foreign policy."[59] In fact, Pakistani disillusionment with the United States went far deeper than American analysts recog-

54. NSC, "Narrative and Guide to Documents."
55. Komer to Johnson, April 22, 1965, NSC History of South Asia, NSF, LBJL; Komer to Bundy, June 30, 1965, NSC History of Indian Famine, NSF, LBJL.
56. Komer to Johnson, September 9, 1965, NSC History of South Asia, NSF, LBJL.
57. Komer to Johnson, July 6, 1965, ibid.
58. Hughes to Rusk, NSF, Pakistan, July 28, 1965, Memos, vol. III, LBJL; Rusk to the Embassy in Pakistan, July 8, 1965, NSF, Pakistan, Cables, vol. III, LBJL; CIA Intelligence Information Cable, July 29, 1965, ibid.; Burke, *Pakistan's Foreign Policy*, 315–17.
59. Hughes to Rusk, July 28, 1965.

nized. LBJ had deliberately driven Ayub into a corner in the vain hope that increased pressure would bring him around to the American point of view. But Johnson's heavyhanded tactics failed to produce the desired effect. Tensions between the two nations continued to escalate throughout the summer of 1965, making it difficult for the United States even to keep open its channels of communication with Pakistan.[60]

At this dangerous juncture, with U.S.–Pakistani misunderstanding at an all-time high, American policymakers were suddenly faced with the most serious threat to the peace of the subcontinent since 1948. The crisis built slowly throughout August 1965, following Ayub's decision early that month to infiltrate Pakistani-trained guerrilla forces into Indian-occupied Kashmir. Most likely, Ayub sought to undermine the efforts of the Shastri government to integrate more fully into the Indian state the portions of Kashmir that it occupied. He probably calculated that by bringing the Kashmir problem to a head once more Pakistan could at least force India back to the bargaining table. Whatever Ayub's precise motivations, his high-stakes game soon backfired. India moved quickly to block Pakistani infiltration routes, leaving Ayub little choice but to up the ante by sending in regular army forces. On September 1 Pakistani armed forces invaded the extreme southern portion of Kashmir in the Chhamb sector. The drive, which featured the use of U.S.-supplied Patton tanks, aimed at severing the thin communications links between Indian-held Kashmir and India proper. UN Secretary General U Thant that same day issued an urgent appeal for a cease-fire and for the withdrawal of all armed personnel behind the previous cease-fire line established by the UN. At Johnson's directive, Arthur Goldberg, the U.S. ambassador to the United Nations, immediately endorsed the secretary general's appeal.[61]

The sudden outbreak of hostilities posed a series of potentially grave threats to American interests in South Asia – and beyond. When Bowles wired Johnson and Rusk on September 2 with the

60. Hughes to Rusk, September 4, 1965, NSC History of South Asia, LBJL.
61. Ibid.; NEA study, "The Indo-Pakistan War and Its Aftermath," enclosed in Eugene V. Rostow, Under Secretary of State for Political Affairs, to Walt Rostow, National Security Adviser, October 28, 1968, ibid.; U.S. Department of State *Bulletin* 53 (September 27, 1965), 527; Shivaji Ganguly, *U.S. Policy Toward South Asia* (Boulder, Colo.: Westview Press, 1990), 121–3.

warning that "we are face to face with the prospect of disaster in the subcontinent," that dire admonition reflected more than just the ambassador's trademark hyperbole.[62] For once, Rusk, McNamara, Bundy, Komer, Talbot, and other senior officials shared Bowles's fears. From the very inception of the conflict they worried that the use of U.S. military supplies by either or both sides would thrust Washington unavoidably into an embarrassing, center-stage position. India's early protests against Pakistan's use of American-supplied tanks and aircraft drove that point home forcefully. Even more ominously, American analysts feared that China might directly or indirectly offer Pakistan military support, thereby transforming a regional conflict into another theater of Cold War confrontation. The presence of Chinese Foreign Minister Chen Yi in Pakistan in early September, coupled with China's public condemnation of Indian aggression in Kashmir, accentuated those concerns. On September 2 Johnson decided that direct pressure on the two combatants would likely only further provoke their indignation with the United States. "It will be very hard to go beyond even-handed 'grave concern,'" fretted Komer, "without goring someone's ox."[63] The president consequently directed that the United States place primary reliance on UN peace efforts.[64]

On September 6 the conflict entered a new and more dangerous phase as four Indian divisions thrust across the international boundary in the Punjab, driving toward Lahore. Ayub immediately called in McConaughy to inform him of the Indian violation of Pakistan's territorial integrity. He presented the American ambassador with an *aide-mémoire* that called upon Washington to uphold the 1959 agreement between the United States and Pakistan and act immediately to "suppress and vacate" the Indian aggression.[65]

With the conflict rapidly escalating, Johnson and his top advisers realized that they could not long postpone a decision on U.S.

62. Bowles to Johnson and Rusk, September 2, 1965, NSF, India, Cables, vol. V, LBJL.
63. Komer memorandum, September 4, 1965, NSF, Pakistan, Memos, vol. IV, LBJL.
64. NEA, "The Indo–Pakistan War and Its Aftermath; Bowles to Johnson and Rusk, September 2, 1965, NSF, India, Cables, vol. V, LBJL; Rusk to the Embassies in Pakistan and India, NSF, Pakistan, Cables, vol. IV, LBJL; Rusk to Bowles, September 2, 1965, NSC History of South Asia, NSF, LBJL.
65. NEA, "The Indo–Pakistan War and Its Aftermath"; McConaughy to the State Department, September 6, 1965, NSC History of South Asia, NSF, LBJL; CIA cable to the White House Situation Room, September 7, 1965, NSF, India, Cables, vol. V, LBJL.

aid shipments to the two warring countries. Former Vice President Richard Nixon and Michigan's Republican Congressman Gerald R. Ford both called upon Johnson to terminate immediately all U.S. assistance to both India and Pakistan. Komer argued that the United States needed to halt deliveries of military equipment to India and Pakistan "on the simple ground that in the light of the UN appeals we cannot be in the position of adding fuel to the flames."[66] Furthermore, given mounting congressional anger with the counterproductive behavior of two of the world's leading recipients of U.S. aid, Komer and Bundy reasoned that an aid cutoff was necessary to save the administration's beleaguered foreign aid bill. "It will certainly be highly resented in both India and Pakistan," Komer acknowledged, "and risks pushing both even further off the deep end. On the other hand, it may well help bring home to both the consequences of their folly."[67]

On September 8 the administration publicly announced its decision. Rusk at the same time instructed Ambassadors Bowles and McConaughy to explain to Shastri and Ayub, respectively, that the U.S. decision to halt aid shipments was intended neither as a "punishment" nor as a "threat." Rather, "it is simply what US opinion requires in situation of *de facto* war where [the] US cannot be in position on one hand of supporting UN appeal for ceasefire and on other hand of providing equipment that might be used in further conflict." The administration, moreover, faced "a volcanic reaction in Congress to events in the subcontinent" that made this decision unavoidable.[68]

A Chinese ultimatum of September 17 caught the Johnson administration off guard, quickly elevating the crisis to a new level of danger. Beijing demanded that India dismantle within the next forty-eight hours a string of military structures along the Sikkim–Tibet border. Uncertain if the Chinese note represented a genuine threat or mere bluster, administration decision makers believed they had no choice but to plan for the worst. The ominous

66. Komer to Bundy, September 7, 1965, NSF, Pakistan, Memos, vol. IV, LBJL.
67. Komer to Johnson, September 7, 1965, NSF, Name File, Komer, LBJL; Komer memoranda to Johnson, September 7, 1965, NSC History of South Asia, NSF, LBJL.
68. Rusk to the Embassies in India and Pakistan, September 8, 1965, NSC History of South Asia, NSF, LBJL; memorandum of conversation between Rusk and members of the Senate Foreign Relations Committee, September 8, 1965, ibid.

tone of the Chinese ultimatum alarmed U.S. analysts; they feared that it could very well serve as both prelude to and pretext for active Chinese intervention. The Johnson administration, already seeking to contain the communist threat to Asia with a rapidly expanding contingent of American ground forces in Vietnam, viewed with extreme wariness the possibility of a Chinese military thrust into South Asia. Chinese intervention in the Indo–Pakistani war could pose a challenge of global dimensions to American interests and to American credibility.[69]

Johnson, in response to this frightening new twist, directed American policy along several parallel tracks. First, he ordered the Defense and State Departments to prepare military contingency plans for his review. Those plans presumably were to focus on U.S. military options in the event that a Chinese attack occurred and Indian security became endangered. Second, he pledged continued diplomatic support for UN Secretary General U Thant's efforts to bring about a cease-fire. Those efforts culminated on September 20 with a Security Council resolution that called upon the two parties to halt all military operations by September 22 and to begin withdrawing their forces to the positions occupied before the current fighting began. Third, LBJ sought to use whatever influence the United States still retained with New Delhi and Rawalpindi to gain their compliance with the UN resolution. Prompt Indian and Pakistani acceptance of the Security Council directive would, in the view of American experts, serve U.S. interests by obviating the rationale for Chinese involvement.[70]

Firm Pakistani resistance frustrated the American strategy. Although India, flushed with success on the battlefield, readily agreed to accept a cease-fire, Pakistan initially rebuffed the UN resolution. A Chinese decision to postpone until midnight, September 22, the deadline they had arbitraily imposed on India only partially eased the sense of impending crisis. The Johson administration feared that Pakistan's defiance of the UN order might yet encourage Chinese intervention. Consequently, upon urgent instructions from Washington, McConaughy forcefully lectured Ayub about the risks he was running. The American ambassador warned Ayub that Pakistan now faced a critical choice: If it should directly or indi-

69. NEA, "The Indo–Pakistan War and Its Aftermath."   70. Ibid.

rectly encourage Chinese entry into the conflict, Pakistan would alienate itself from the West, perhaps permanently. This was not a threat, McConaughy stressed, but a reality.[71]

After an awkward period of wavering, punctuated by additional U.S. pressure, Ayub on September 22 reluctantly acceded to the UN's cease-fire proposal. Given the difficult military prospects that Pakistani forces faced, Ayub almost certainly reasoned that the cease-fire represented the best Pakistan could expect under the circumstances. At least it avoided a complete break with the West, which would have served only to heighten Pakistan's isolation and its dependence on an external patron – in that case, ironically, China. Nonetheless, that calculation of *realpolitik* did not diminish Pakistani fury with the United States. Indeed, Pakistan's leaders and its masses were swept by an unprecedented tide of anti-Americanism. During a "stiff" meeting with the American ambassador on September 29, Ayub sharply upbraided the United States for its revocation of solemn pledges regarding defense support, decried the lack of cooperation by the United States and the lack of appreciation for Pakistani efforts to moderate Chinese policy toward Vietnam, and accused the United States of "bullying" a friendly nation. A series of widespread anti-American demonstrations in Pakistan – including the stoning of the U.S. embassy, the burning of a U.S. Information Service library, and mob attacks on the U.S. consulate in Lahore – provided stark testimony to the depth of anti-American sentiment in Pakistan.[72] "U.S. prestige" in Pakistan, Komer told Johnson, "is at an all-time low."[73]

Keenly aware of the mounting public and congressional demands that the administration justify the massive flow of dollars from the United States to South Asia, Bundy and Komer recognized that "as a simple fact it will be a long time before military assistance can begin again to either party."[74] Indeed, the Indo–Pakistani

71. Ibid.; Rusk to McConaughy, September 19, 1965, NSF, India, Cables, vol. V, LBJL; draft cable from Rusk to McConaughy, September 20, 1965, NSC History of South Asia, NSF, LBJL; India–Pakistan Working Group, "Situation Report," September 20, 1965, NSF, India, Memos & Misc., vol. V, LBJL.
72. CIA Special Memorandum, "The Indo–Pakistan War – A Preliminary Assessment," September 24, 1965, NSF, India, Memos & Misc., vol. V, LBJL; McConaughy to the State Department, September 21, 1965, NSF, Pakistan, Cables, vol. V, LBJL.
73. Komer to Johnson, October 1, 1965, NSC History of South Asia, NSF, LBJL.
74. Komer and Bundy to Johnson, ibid.

conflict impelled senior policy planners to begin a fundamental re-thinking of U.S. interests and policies in the subcontinent. The big questions that the president needed to address in the war's wake, according to Komer, included: "*What can we really accomplish in South Asia?* Are India and/or Pakistan worth the investment?" And, "Do we now have a major opportunity to re-sort our priorities in South Asia and get a lot more for our money?"[75]

Johnson, infuriated with the image of self-defeating fratricidal strife presented by the 1965 war, was certain that a different approach to South Asia was long overdue. The conflict embarrassed LBJ politically at the very time that he was seeking public and congressional backing for the expanded U.S. military effort in Vietnam. The unwillingness of either India or Pakistan to stand by the United States in Vietnam or to offer more than the most tepid support for what Johnson invariably portrayed as a defensive response to communist aggression further soured him on the South Asian powers. Convinced that previous administrations had exaggerated the importance of India and Pakistan to broader Cold War security interests, Johnson directed that the United States adopt a lowered profile in the subcontinent and pursue more limited policy objectives there.[76]

Johnson's backing for a Soviet mediation offer reveals just how radically the war had shaken long-held American policy assumptions about the region. Following the UN-sponsored cease-fire of September 1965, the Soviet Union offered to supply its good offices to both parties in order to help settle the conflict, proposing the central Asian city of Tashkent as a conference site. Washington, which had launched so many of its South Asia initiatives over the past decade because of a perceived need to contain Moscow, ironically welcomed the offer. Rusk later recalled that the administration encouraged the Soviet initiative because "we felt we had nothing to lose."[77] It was time to let the Soviets "break their lance" in the subcontinent, quipped Ball at a White House meeting.[78] By the end of 1965, Rusk, Ball, and other leading foreign

75. Komer memorandum, November 16, 1965, ibid.
76. NEA, "The Indo–Pakistan War and Its Aftermath."
77. Dean Rusk Oral History Interview, January 2, 1970, LBJL.
78. Briefing Meeting on Ayub Visit, December 14, 1965, Office of the President File, Valenti Meeting Notes, LBJ Papers, LBJL.

policy advisers calculated that Soviet and American interests in South Asia now ran along parallel lines. Both superpowers, they reasoned, were most anxious to end the present hostilities and to promote long-term Indo–Pakistani amity; both, moreover, saw China as the most destabilizing force in the region and consequently ranked the containment of Chinese influence as an overriding policy objective.[79]

Johnson soon conveyed to the Indians and the Pakistanis the fundamental shift that the war had induced in U.S. thinking about South Asia. The president met with Ayub in Washington in December 1965 and made clear to the Pakistani ruler that the alliance between the United States and Pakistan was now over. How soon the United States might resume economic aid and what kind of a relationship could be resurrected out of the ashes of the war with India were questions for the future. Plainly, whatever new relationship emerged would bear little resemblance to the alliance of the past. A blunt Johnson told Ayub that the resolution of those issues would hinge to a great extent on Pakistan's willingness to curtail its ties to China.[80] Much to Johnson's delight, the Pakistani president pursued a statesmanlike approach at the Tashkent negotiations, allowing the Soviets to achieve in January 1966 a diplomatic breakthrough that brought the Indo-Pakistani war to a close. Two months later Johnson met with newly appointed Indian Prime Minister Indira Gandhi in Washington; Nehru's daughter had just replaced the late Shastri, whose untimely death occurred just one day after he signed the Tashkent agreement. As he had during his earlier sessions with Ayub, Johnson emphasized to the Indian leader that the old relationship between Washington and New Delhi was now over. It was time to begin anew. The visit occurred, LBJ boasted to Komer, "with the slate wiped clean of previous commitments and India coming to us asking for a new relationship on the terms we want."[81] Johnson used almost identical language in a subsequent letter to Ayub. The old slate had been wiped clean

79. On the parallelism in U.S.–Soviet policy, see especially memorandum for the record by John W. Foster, NSC staff, January 9, 1969, NSC History of South Asia, NSF, LBJL.
80. Memorandum of Johnson's meetings with Ayub, December 15, 1965, ibid.; Komer to Johnson, December 14, 1965, ibid.
81. Komer to Johnson, March 27, 1966, NSC History of the Indian Famine, vol. II, NSF, LBJL.

in South Asia, LBJ emphasized to the man he had once characterized as America's staunchest friend in Asia.[82]

In the aftermath of the 1965 war, a disillusioned Johnson insisted upon more modest and more circumscribed relationships
with both India and Pakistan. He was convinced that his predecessors had vastly overrated the importance to the United States of
two impoverished nations situated on the periphery of world affairs. Now that he had a chance to begin anew, he was determined
not to repeat that mistake. Neither India nor Pakistan appeared vital, in Johnson's view, to core American interests. The growing
American military involvement in Vietnam, another peripheral
area, was in large part a function of commitments made earlier by
Dwight D. Eisenhower and Kennedy. LBJ believed that those commitments had put America's global credibility on the line and thus
made extrication from a land beset by a communist-led insurgency
politically and diplomatically imprudent. South Asia, on the other
hand, offered an opportunity for measured disengagement without
jeopardizing any fundamental American interests.

Johnson was not ready to write off South Asia entirely, to be
sure. His advisers persuaded him that such a course would be as
imprudent as the abandonment of Vietnam. Yet, according to the
president's senior national security advisers, communism posed a
much less direct and immediate threat to the subcontinent. "The
real threat to India," the NSC staff told Johnson in a thoughtful
reexamination of U.S. policy objectives, "is not invasion through
the Himalayas, but possible disintegration and fragmentation of
the as yet fragile Indian state." If India disintegrated and fragmented because of internal failures, a national communist regime
could emerge comparable to that which emerged in China in the
late 1940s – "and perhaps with comparable effects." Not only
would such a regime upset the Asian power balance, but it might
also trigger a "domino effect" among other noncommunist nations. "These dire possibilities may seem remote at present," the
paper conceded, "but the real question is whether they are sufficiently realistic to justify insurance commensurate with the risk."

82. Quoted in NSC, "Narrative and Guide to Documents."

Convinced that they were, the NSC staff urged Johnson to continue using U.S. economic assistance to help ensure the survival of a noncommunist India.[83]

Although LBJ accepted the essential logic of that position, he also believed strongly that the United States needed to exact more of a *quid pro quo* for its economic aid than it had in the past.[84] An increasingly ominous food shortage in India, which by the end of 1965 was reaching catastrophic proportions, provided Johnson with the leverage he sought. Beginning in the months leading up to Indira Gandhi's arrival in Washington, and continuing after her departure, the president placed a series of stringent controls on American food shipments to India. Abandoning the long-term PL 480 commodity agreements that had become so routine during the Eisenhower and Kennedy administrations, Johnson instead authorized the shipment of wheat to India for only two or three months at a time, and he conditioned future food aid on India's economic performance. Through this tough "short tether" policy, LBJ believed that he could force India to devote more of its resources to agriculture and eventually to achieve self-sufficiency in foodgrain production. The president was convinced that in the process India's dependence on the United States could be minimized and the future prospect of widespread famine and internal disorder averted. LBJ explained the rationale for the new aid program to Prime Minister Gandhi during their March 1966 meetings in Washington; after the sessions, Komer boasted that *"the message has gotten through loud and clear."* He added: "If India wants massive US support it has to be earned. Our holding up on aid has powerfully reinforced this tune."[85]

Over the next twelve months, Johnson stuck to his guns, even in the face of persistent bureaucratic opposition to the harshness of

83. NSC Staff, "A United States Assistance Strategy for India," November 8, 1965, NSC History of the Indian Famine, vol. II, NSF, LBJL. See also Komer to Johnson, January 12, 1966, Komer Name File, Memos vol. II, LBJL.
84. Komer to Johnson, March 26, 1966, NSC History of South Asia, NSF, LBJL; Harold Saunders, preface to NSC study, "The President and the Indian Famine, August 1966–February 1967," January 1, 1969, NSC History of the Indian Famine, vol. I, LBJL.
85. Komer to Johnson, March 21, 1966, Komer Name File, Memos vol. II, NSF, LBJL; summary record of conversation between Johnson and Gandhi, March 28, 1966, NSF, India, Memos & Misc., vol. VII, LBJL; Rusk to Johnson, March 26, 1966, NSC History of the Indian Famine, vol. II, LBJL.

the short-tether policy from the departments of State and Agriculture and from AID. An old poker player, the president felt confident that the United States held most of the cards in the high-stakes game it was playing with India. As a subsequent State Department history of the crisis noted: "India was destitute: the Indians knew it and we knew it. The only possible source of food to tide them over until the next harvest was the United States."[86] Well aware of that dependence, Johnson insisted that only after he received proof that India was pursuing more efficient agricultural policies would he authorize the shipment of additional food aid. In the spring of 1966, Gandhi bowed to American pressure by devaluating the rupee and relaxing India's import restriction laws, measures that ignited fiery protests from across the Indian political spectrum.[87]

When severe drought conditions during the following fall and winter raised the specter of widespread starvation once again, Johnson refused to ease the pressure. Rather, he kept U.S. wheat shipments to India on a short leash, continued to push for greater Indian agricultural self-sufficiency, and solicited food aid from other developing nations so that the burden of the famine relief effort could be more widely shared. At the same time, LBJ won congressional backing for his India aid program by emphasizing its new, tough-minded orientation. He sent a series of personal messages to Capitol Hill that combined humanitarian and practical appeals and dispatched to India a fact-finding delegation of congressmen and senators who proved effective lobbyists for the program upon their return. By February 1967 the monsoons returned, easing what had been the most severe Indian food crisis in a century.[88]

In the end, America's use of food as a diplomatic weapon achieved some, but certainly not all, of the results Johnson sought. The short-tether policy impelled Indian leaders to shift their development priorities toward the agricultural sector and placed the India aid program on more of a multilateral basis, changes that

86. State Department study, "India's Food Crisis, 1965–67," NSC History of the Indian Famine, vol. V, NSF, LBJL.
87. Ibid.; memorandum of conversation between Rostow and Indian Ambassador B. K. Nehru, August 12, 1966, vol. I, ibid.
88. "Narrative," NSC History of the Indian Food Crisis, vol. I, ibid.; State Department study, "India's Food Crisis, 1965–67," ibid.

served to diminish over time India's dependence on American commodity assistance. But those achievements exacted a hefty price on the overall Indo–American relationship. Still reeling from the 1965 war and the subsequent suspension of U.S. military and economic support, the relationship became further strained by Johnson's heavyhanded efforts to influence Indian internal policies. Indians of all political persuasions deeply resented a policy that forced them "to go begging for food." LBJ's willingness to withhold available American food reserves when millions of desperate Indian peasants were facing possible starvation did little to ease underlying tensions between the two countries.[89]

Indeed, Prime Minister Gandhi's frequent criticisms of American behavior in Vietnam and her continued reliance on Moscow for military support are suggestive of the fundamental differences that continued to bedevil Indo–American relations. The Indian ruler's friendly birthday message to North Vietnam's Ho Chi Minh in March 1967 brought them to the surface. "If she feels she must slant her 'non-alignment' in favor of the Communist world in order to keep her credentials clear with Moscow," an infuriated Rusk wired Bowles, "she cannot maintain her credentials with the US. The general mood in this country does not permit us to act like an old cow which continues to give milk, however often one kicks her in the flanks."[90]

The administration's efforts to place the postwar Pakistani–American relationship on a sounder footing than in the past proved no more effectual than its efforts with India. The 1965 conflict destroyed the Pakistani–American alliance, a reality recognized by Ayub and Johnson during their December 1965 talks in Washington. The key questions for Johnson and his top advisers following

89. For similar criticisms of the Johnson policy, see James Warner Bjorkman, "Public Law 480 and the Policies of Self-Help and Short-Tether: Indo–American Relations, 1965–68," in Lloyd I. Rudolph and Susanne Hoeber Rudolph, eds., *The Regional Imperative: The Administration of U.S. Foreign Policy Towards South Asian States Under Presidents Johnson and Nixon* (Atlantic Highlands, N.J.: Humanities Press, 1980), 201–40; and Carolyn Castore, "The United States and India: The Use of Food to Apply Economic Pressure, 1965–67," in Sidney Weintraub, ed., *Economic Coercion and U.S. Foreign Policy: Implications of Studies from the Johnson Administration* (Boulder, Colo.: Westview Press, 1982), 129–53. For Johnson's far more positive appraisal of his policy, see Lyndon B. Johnson, *The Vantage Point: Perspectives of the Presidency, 1963–1969* (New York: Holt, Rinehart & Winston, 1971).
90. Rusk to Bowles, May 18, 1967, NSF, India, Cables, vol. IX.

those talks concerned how much could be salvaged from the wreck-age. Above all, White House and State Department analysts agreed, the United States wanted Pakistan to curtail its relationship with China, permit continued utilization by U.S. personnel of the intelligence-gathering facilities at Peshawar and elsewhere, and up-hold its commitments to SEATO and CENTO.[91]

But what leverage did the United States retain that might facili-tate the achievement of those objectives? That daunting question defied easy resolution. Pakistan needed economic assistance and military materiel, especially spare parts for its American-equipped armed forces. Early in 1966, Johnson authorized the resumption of economic assistance. Much like the short-tether policy he had devised for India, the president insisted that economic aid for Paki-stan be used in a carrot-and-stick fashion: if Pakistan moved to-ward a reconciliation with India and toward a simultaneous curtailment of its ties with China, the United States would reward it with increased developmental aid. But the resumption of a mili-tary supply relationship proved much more problematic. No se-nior official wanted to resume military assistance to Pakistan; in addition, most harbored grave worries that even the cash sale of military supplies might spark another regional arms race. Yet Pakistan's insecurity vis-à-vis India made the acquisition of mili-tary materiel from some external source mandatory. American ex-perts fretted that if Washington refused to play that role, Ayub would turn to Beijing. Komer cautioned Johnson in March 1966 that Ayub was "clearly not ready to give up the Chicom string to his bow – at least until he knows where his next round of military hardware is coming from."[92]

The Johnson administration never resolved that vexing problem. On April 12, 1967, after a protracted review of American options that took nearly one year to complete, Washington finally an-nounced a new military supply policy for Pakistan and India. It per-mitted the cash sale of spare parts for previously supplied U.S.

91. Komer to Johnson, January 12, 1966, Komer Name File, Memos vol. II, LBJL; Komer to Johnson, January 24, 1966, ibid.; Ball to Johnson, April 19, 1966, NSF, Pakistan, Memos, vol. VI, LBJL.
92. Komer to Johnson, March 18, 1966, NSC History of South Asia, NSF, LBJL; Walt W. Rostow, National Security Adviser, to Johnson, April 18, 1966, NSC History of the In-dian Famine, vol. II, NSF, LBJL; Komer to Johnson, April 26, 1966, NSF, Pakistan, Memos, vol. III, LBJL; Rusk to Johnson, April 27, 1966, NSF, Pakistan, Memos, vol. VI.

equipment on a case-by-case basis, as well as the cash and limited credit sales of what the Pentagon called "non-lethal" military equipment.[93] The compromise policy satisfied neither Pakistan nor India. Instead, it demonstrated once again the limits of American leverage on both countries. Pakistan welcomed the opportunity to purchase American spare parts, but Washington's inability to meet Pakistan's broader defense needs propelled it toward even greater dependence on Beijing, much to the consternation of American officials. The Ayub government's decision, early in 1968, to terminate the U.S. lease on the Peshawar installation stripped away the last remaining vestige of the once-special relationship between the United States and Pakistan.[94]

As the Johnson administration came to a close, American relations with both India and Pakistan were suffused with bitterness, tension, and disappointment. Like his Oval Office predecessors, Johnson began his presidency with the belief that the United States could cultivate friendly relations with both of South Asia's major nations, using military and economic aid to transform them into loyal Cold War partners. The Indo–Pakistani war of 1965 decisively shattered that illusion, calling into question the assumptions that had guided U.S. policy toward South Asia for more than a decade. In the war's aftermath, Johnson moved to limit sharply America's commitments to a region that he increasingly viewed as of but secondary importance to overall national security priorities. Yet his policy of measured disengagement and careful evenhandedness proved no more effective than the hyper-involvement of the past. For all of Johnson's efforts to use food aid, developmental assistance, and military sales to regain some U.S. leverage with India and Pakistan, he could not prevent India from deepening its ties to the Soviet Union nor Pakistan from deepening its ties to China. Like South Vietnam, although in a much less costly and tragic fashion, India and Pakistan taught Lyndon Johnson an important lesson about the limits of American power.

93. Rostow to Johnson, March 16, 1967, Howard Wriggins Name File, Memos 1967, NSF, LBJL; Rusk to Johnson, March 17, 1967, ibid.; Rusk to the Embassies in India and Pakistan, April 6, 1967, NSF, India, Cables, vol. IX, LBJL.
94. Bowles to Rusk, March 8, 1968, Country File 121 India, Confidential File, WHCF, Box 9, LBJL; Ed Hamilton, NSC Staff, to Rostow, June 13, 1968, Hamilton Name File, NSF, LBJL.

6

Lyndon B. Johnson, Germany, and "the End of the Cold War"

FRANK COSTIGLIOLA

"I know my Germans," President Lyndon B. Johnson liked to say, having grown up with a German grandmother near German set-tlements in the Texas hill country.[1] For Johnson, this "knowing" denoted admiration, apprehension, and a touch of condescension for a powerful, talented people with dangerous tendencies. Re-membering from his youth an estranged German farmer who had hanged himself in a barn, LBJ told National Security Adviser Walt W. Rostow, "If you let the Germans isolate themselves, they will do crazy things."[2] Johnson determined to keep the Germans "by my side where I can count on them and where I can watch them."[3] Within weeks after becoming president, LBJ hosted Chancellor Ludwig Erhard at the Texas ranch, gave the German a cowboy hat, and announced, "I like simply everything about him." Erhard replied, "I love President Johnson, and he loves me."[4]

Johnson embraced the Germans out of fear as well as fondness. He saw divided Germany as a hobbled giant, with the horrific past of two world wars and the Holocaust. In 1922 and in 1939, the Germans had wrenched world politics by making sudden deals with the Soviets. Since the end of World War II, West Germany had nursed political and territorial grievances against the Soviet Union

---

1. Francis M. Bator, "President's Conversation with John McCloy Concerning U.S. Position in Trilateral Negotiations," 2 March 1967, Box 50, NSC, History of the Trilateral Negotiations, Lyndon Baines Johnson Presidential Library (hereafter LBJL).
2. Author's interview with Walt W. Rostow, 3 June 1992, Austin, Texas.
3. Arthur Krock, "Memorandum of Conversation with Lyndon B. Johnson, 15 December 1964," Box 1, Arthur Krock Papers, Mudd Library, Princeton University, Princeton, N.J.
4. Margarita Mathiopoulos, "The American President Seen Through German Eyes – Continuity and Change from the Adenauer to the Kohl Era," *Presidential Studies Quarterly* 15 (Summer 1985): 684.

and its allies. Viewing this turbulent history, Johnson declared that his "overwhelming interest was to make sure that the Germans did not get us into World War III."[5]

To keep the Germans tethered safely by America's side, the Johnson administration launched, in tandem, two extraordinary ventures – the multilateral force of nuclear missiles aimed at the Soviet Union and the "bridge building" campaign to bring about an eventual end to the Cold War. Although these two programs differed drastically in content, they both sought to manipulate German aspirations that seemed too dangerous or too difficult to satisfy.

Johnson and his advisers appreciated West Germany's central importance as America's trophy from World War II, as the chief prize and the front line in the Cold War, and as the object of America's competition with French President Charles de Gaulle. West Germany also stood out as an ally with a powerful army under U.S. command, as the base for 300,000 American troops and many nuclear weapons, as a key customer and business partner, as the creditor and arms purchaser that helped offset America's payments deficits, as an appreciative acolyte of American culture, and as the dependent ally whose limited sovereignty made it particularly receptive to U.S. influence.[6] In sum, Germany figured as the key nation in western Europe, and close ties with that region remained essential to American global power. As Vice President Hubert H. Humphrey put it, losing the Western alliance would "mean the loss of our diplomatic cards in dealing with the Russians."[7]

In the tradition of U.S. foreign policy since the late 1940s, Johnson believed that the Western alliance served a triple purpose: containing the Soviet Union, containing (with different tactics) the Federal Republic of Germany (FRG), and channeling the energies of the allies into constructive enterprises designated by the United States. If the alliance failed to "tie the Germans in," Johnson feared,

5. McGeorge Bundy, Memorandum for the Record, 7 December 1964, Box 18–19, Files of McGeorge Bundy, LBJL.
6. The Federal Republic had pledged not to produce or possess atomic, biological, or chemical arms; the West German *Bundeswehr* was integrated into NATO and subject in wartime to American command; and the World War II victor powers retained significant rights in the former enemy, including authority over German reunification. For all its economic clout, West Germany was not equal to the other Western allies and remained, as de Gaulle put it, a "juridically reduced nation." (Bohlen to Secretary of State, 30 October 1964, NSF Subject File, Box 24, LBJL.)
7. "Summary Notes of 566th NSC Meeting December 13, 1966, 12:10 P.M.," Box 2, NSC Meetings File, LBJL.

"there was some 17-year-old right now in Germany who would be a 20-year-old little Hitler in another three years." LBJ obviously regarded the Germans as both useful and dangerous. He reminded British Prime Minister Harold Wilson that they "had made rockets for the U.S. and the British, which proved they had brains, and they lent a lot of money to the UK, which showed they had money." "All they needed now was will," LBJ believed, fearing that West Germany might develop its own nuclear weapons or otherwise break free of its Western ties, "and that was what we had to prevent."[8]

Here the president pointed to a key challenge of his foreign policy. Somehow Washington had to tranquilize, co-opt, or otherwise manage West Germany's "will" for security, reunification, and equality because those nationalist strivings had the potential to destabilize Europe and trigger another war. Although he remained focused on Vietnam, Secretary of State Dean Rusk nevertheless believed that "the German question is probably the only question on which the Soviet Union and the United States might be drawn into a nuclear war."[9] Former Secretary of State Dean Acheson advised the solution of further "integrating and 'denationalizing' Germany" with NATO, the European Common Market, and other supranational institutions.[10] Walt Rostow agreed that Washington had to "to sink German nationalism and its [sic] national vulnerability" into such institutions or else face consequences "at best, ugly and, at worst, lethal."[11] Americans worried that Germans would become less "docile" as their guilt over World War II ebbed.[12]

The Johnson administration's efforts to contain Germany ran into competition from de Gaulle, who also wanted to limit the Germans and end the Cold War, but on French terms. De Gaulle sought the withdrawal of U.S. and Soviet troops from the heart of

8. Ibid.   9. Dean Rusk Oral History Transcript, 22, LBJL.
10. Acheson to Robert S. McNamara, 16 September 1963, Box 22, Dean Acheson Papers, Yale University Library, New Haven, Conn.
11. Rostow to William Tyler, 20 March 1965, Box 88, Dean Acheson Papers, Harry S. Truman Presidential Library (hereafter HSTL). Although U.S. officials regarded the Bonn republic as more resilient than the interwar Weimar government, they still feared for the future of German democracy. See, for example, "Memorandum of Conversation between French Foreign Minister Couve de Murville and Under Secretary Ball," 25 May 1963, Box 72, NSF, John F. Kennedy Presidential Library (hereafter JFKL).
12. Harold van B. Cleveland in Eleventh Meeting of the Steering Group, "Atlantic Policy Studies," 23 September 1964, Vol. 112, Records of Groups, Council on Foreign Relations Archives, New York City (hereafter RG, CFR); John J. McCloy in Thirteenth Meeting, 15 December 1964, ibid.

Europe and the integration of Germany (possibly reunified) into a Europe led by Paris and Moscow. In this scenario, the United States and NATO might provide a military balance to the Soviets, but Washington would have little political influence in Europe. Although Americans appreciated that Paris's ties with Bonn helped contain Germany, they opposed de Gaulle's ambitions and worried that his defiant nationalism set a dangerous example.[13] U.S. policy in Europe was also complicated by the Vietnam War, which aggravated a variety of problems: America's balance-of-payments deficits, America's need for German offset payments, pressures from Congress to withdraw troops from Germany, U.S. resentment of the allies' refusal to get involved, and European criticism of America's reflexive anticommunism.

The war also riveted the attention of Johnson, Rusk, and other key officials. During the 1966 European crisis precipitated by de Gaulle's withdrawal from NATO, *New York Times* columnist Cyrus R. Sulzberger interviewed the president for more than two hours. Johnson kept thumbing through a folder of papers while telling the journalist, "I'm spending most of my time on Europe these days." His administration had a global agenda, LBJ insisted, "despite Vietnam, despite what 'intellectuals' and the *New York Times* and those people in Georgetown say." But when he tried to talk to reporters about these other matters, "all they did was keep whining Veetnam, Veetnam, Veetnam," protested the president, himself imitating a whining baby. Sulzberger recorded that after this performance, Johnson "suddenly . . . opened the folder of papers he had been browsing over – and started to read a cable sent to him by [Ambassador Henry Cabot] Lodge in Saigon."[14] According to Francis M. Bator, the Deputy National Security Adviser and the White House expert on Europe, Rusk "was so preoccupied by Vietnam" that he "was basically not engaged" with Europe and "had gotten used to letting [Undersecretary of State George] Ball handle it."[15]

One of the administration's few skeptics on Vietnam, Ball aggressively pursued a European agenda that centered on Germany.

13. See Frank Costigliola, *France and the United States: The Cold War Alliance Since World War II* (New York: Twayne/Macmillan, 1992), 126–59.
14. Cyrus L. Sulzberger, *An Age of Mediocrity* (New York: Macmillan, 1973), 264–8.
15. Author interview with Francis M. Bator, 21 November 1992, Cambridge, Mass.

Ball had helped the Europeanist Jean Monnet set up the Common Market, and he drew from that experience the fervent belief that unless the FRG were tightly integrated into supranational organizations such as NATO and the proposed multilateral force, that frustrated country could fall to demagogic nationalists. Like Johnson and Rostow, Ball cared about the Germans while regarding them as dangerously emotional, anxious, and susceptible to extremism.

Ball and other U.S. officials often referred to West Germany with patronizing language connoting a nation that was subordinate despite its power and importance. A State Department analysis pointed out the "unspoken" assumption in U.S. policy "that the Germans may once again become the sick children of Europe, and that their care and feeding is a matter of nervous concern to us."[16] Ball thought it important to "keep" the West Germans "from getting off the reservation."[17] He agreed with the president that the FRG had to remain "on a leash."[18] A White House aide believed that for Bonn, "the truth is dangerous medicine. We will have to feed it to the Germans in very small doses and very gradually."[19] The metaphors used here suggested problem children, unruly natives, straying dogs, and frail patients. Despite the diversity of the images, they all indicated beings that are troublesome, diminished, and the objects of action by more rational superiors. Such negative stereotyping fed the belief among Americans that they had the right to control the alliance, and it encouraged them to manipulate rather than to address honestly the concerns and objections of the FRG. This patronizing attitude went beyond Germany. In general, American leaders had difficulty viewing as serious and legitimate allied points of view that challenged those of Washington. NATO expert Harold van B. Cleveland observed that U.S. officials often trivialized "the political fears and ambitions of our allies . . . as passing irrationalities."[20]

16. Walt Rostow to Bundy, "A Re-Examination of Premises on the German Problem," 10 December 1965, NSF Country File, Germany, Box 186–7, LBJL.
17. Ball telephone conversation with J. William Fulbright, 23 August 1965, Box 6, George Ball Papers, LBJL.
18. "Memorandum of Discussion of the MLF at the White House, at 5:30 P.M., April 10, 1964," NSF Subject File, Box 23, LBJL.
19. Bator to Bill Moyers, 15 March 1966, Box 3, Bator Papers.
20. Ninth Steering Committee Meeting, "Atlantic Policy Studies," 18 February 1964, 9, RG 111, CFR.

Americans never regarded their own fears and ambitions as trivial or irrational, in part because they controlled almost all of the West's nuclear weapons and they remained the chief interlocutor with the other nuclear superpower. Weapons of mass death and destruction and those who controlled them commanded attention and respect. Aside from deterring a Soviet attack, nuclear bombs solidified the Western alliance. NATO's stockpiling of nuclear weapons, the alliance's regular military exercises in using them, and its ongoing discussions of nuclear strategy all enhanced the group's sense of seriousness and purpose. The stockpiling of nuclear armaments in the allied countries reinforced their sense of a common fate, because those with such weapons would be targeted in a Soviet attack. And the weaponry helped perpetuate tensions between East and West, thereby justifying the alliance.

Nuclear weapons strengthened the Western alliance in another way. Both possession of these instruments of mass destruction and discussion about them created a kind of male homosocial bonding among American and European leaders. Cultural theorists have analyzed how language, the social construction of gender, and the psychological needs of those drawn to the study of science have reinforced the commonplace association of "hard" sciences – particularly the quintessentially abstract and "objective" science of physics – with domination and masculinity.[21] Striking images of male sexuality and males giving birth to males abound in the talk and writing of nuclear strategists, scientists, and other members of the self-styled "nuclear priesthood." Carol Cohn recounts, for example, descriptions of nuclear blasts as "shooting, seething and boiling in a white fury of creamy foam," invitations to those touring the Trident submarine to "pat the missile," and common references to the first atomic bomb as scientist Robert "Oppenheimer's baby" and to the first hydrogen weapon as Edward "Teller's baby." Unsure whether the first atomic bomb would in fact explode, scientists expressed their hopes that the baby would be a boy, and not a girl – that is, not a failure.[22]

21. See Evelyn Fox Keller, *Reflections on Gender and Science* (New Haven, Conn.: Yale University Press, 1985), 8–10, 42–4, 70–92, 123–30; Evelyn Fox Keller, "The Gender/Science System: or, Is Sex to Gender as Nature Is to Science?" *Hypatica* 2 (Fall 1987): 33–44; Brian Easlea, *Fathering the Unthinkable: Masculinity, Scientists, and the Nuclear Arms Race* (London: Pluto Press, 1983), 5–12, 146–72.
22. Carol Cohn, "Sex and Death in the Rational World of Defense Intellectuals," *Signs* 12 (1987): 694–701; see also Easlea, *Fathering the Unthinkable*, 81–116; Miriam Cooke

Such linkage of nuclear weapons with male sexuality appeared in discussions of how to prevent West Germany from building a national nuclear force. When Bonn resisted signing a treaty forbidding it to acquire nuclear weapons, the White House expert on Europe explained that "the Germans didn't want to renounce manhood."[23] "A strong and resurgent nation," Germany nevertheless "remains nuclearly impotent," observed State Department consultant Robert E. Osgood. Given the "dangerous frustrations of nuclear deprivation," the problem was how "to keep German energies flowing in a Westerly orientation."[24] Like Osgood, Johnson and many of his advisers favored the nuclear Multilateral Force (MLF) as the safest outlet for these "frustrations."

The Multilateral Force

During the 1960s, nuclear sharing and nuclear strategy became touchstone issues in U.S. relations with Western Europe. As the Soviets developed intercontinental ballistic missiles in the late 1950s, Western Europeans doubted that the United States would risk New York to defend Paris or Berlin. The allies pressed for more of a voice in Washington's nuclear decision making. The French built their own nuclear force, a step that undermined Washington's centralized management of the West's deterrent and Secretary of Defense Robert McNamara's preferred nuclear doctrine of flexible response (about which more follows). U.S. officials worried that the French example would inspire West Germany to build its own nuclear forces, despite its 1954 pledge not to do so. De Gaulle held out to Germans the prospect of uniting under French leadership and moving toward a European-controlled nuclear force independent of the United States.

Washington responded to these challenges with the MLF, a proposal to channel the nuclear aspirations of West Germany (and in the future, perhaps the weapons systems of Britain and France) into

and Angela Woollacott, eds., *Gendering War Talk* (Princeton, N.J.: Princeton University Press, 1993).

23. Edward Fried Oral History Transcript, 22, LBJL. Fried replaced Bator in the fall of 1967.

24. Robert E. Osgood, "The Case for the Multilateral Force" [1964], box 10, Livingston T. Merchant Papers, Mudd Library, Princeton University.

an American-controlled nuclear force. Although ostensibly a device for nuclear sharing, the MLF would continue western Europe's subordination to the United States. Like NATO itself, this nuclear extension of the alliance would reinforce and obscure the inequalities in the partnership by means of integration and intimate relations.

The MLF concept originated in 1960 largely out of the thinking of Robert Bowie, an Atlantic relations expert who served in the State Department during the Eisenhower and Johnson administrations. The proposal went through three cycles of international negotiation from 1963 until it faded away in 1966. Presidents Kennedy and then Johnson embraced the MLF as the answer to the problem of nuclear sharing within the alliance, then dropped the plan when its inherent contradictions and the steep opposition to it made the solution seem too costly, then revived it again because the nuclear sharing problem continued to fester. Although the MLF went through several permutations, the basic concept envisioned a fleet of some 25 ships, manned with multinational crews from the United States, Germany, Britain, and other NATO nations and armed with 200 nuclear-tipped missiles aimed at the Soviet Union. This multiple ownership and "mixed-manning" would supposedly give the Germans and other allies a finger near, but not on, the nuclear trigger. U.S. officials intended the MLF to convey to Europeans the feeling, but not the substance, of mutual decision making. Despite pretenses, however, the alliance would remain divided into the nuclear haves and have-nots because the MLF force could not be fired without the unanimous agreement of the participating nations. That requirement meant that in a crisis, any of the member nations could veto using the MLF, while the United States, Britain, and France still could launch their much larger, nationally owned nuclear forces, which remained outside the multinational system. Acknowledged as a "fraud" by Kennedy, the MLF was labeled the "multifarce" by its many domestic and foreign opponents and a Rube Goldberg contraption even by some of its supporters.[25]

25. Arthur M. Schlesinger, *A Thousand Days* (Boston: Houghton Mifflin, 1965), 872; Frank Costigliola, "The Pursuit of Atlantic Community: Nuclear Arms, Dollars, and Berlin," in Thomas Paterson, ed., *Kennedy's Quest for Victory* (New York: Oxford University Press, 1988), 51. The two best accounts of the MLF remain John D. Steinbruner, *The Cybernetic Theory of Decision* (Princeton, N.J.: Princeton University Press, 1974), and Philip Geyelin, *Lyndon B. Johnson and the World* (New York: Praeger, 1966), 159–80.

The fact that the MLF became such an easy target for criticism and ridicule illustrated Washington's increasing difficulty in directing the integration of western Europe. Its American architects expected that the MLF, like the Marshall Plan, NATO, and the abortive European Defense Community of the early 1950s, would contain the aspirations and rivalries of the allies, particularly those of West Germany, and channel the energies of those nations into a supranational structure dominated by the United States and directed against the Soviet Union. In the 1960s, however, European resistance, particularly from France, undercut two major U.S. initiatives, the MLF and Kennedy's Grand Design. The Grand Design would tighten economic integration in the Atlantic arena with the 1962 Trade Expansion Act and with the admission to the European Common Market of Britain, with its special relationship to the United States. Kennedy and his advisers calculated that with Britain in the Common Market, Europe would open its doors wide to U.S. trade and investment. But in January 1963 de Gaulle vetoed the British application, seeing it as the Trojan horse of the United States. The French leader also denounced London's special nuclear relationship with Washington and sought his own special ties with West Germany. Kennedy responded by pushing hard for the MLF, until then a proposal on the back burner. Then in June 1963 Kennedy eased off, particularly after an influential memorandum from National Security Adviser McGeorge Bundy pointed out that the MLF had only meager support on both sides of the Atlantic, that de Gaulle had failed to win over the Germans, and that Moscow, which strongly opposed the MLF, seemed ready to sign a nuclear test ban treaty.[26]

In April 1964 Johnson, determined to corral the Germans, recommitted his administration to getting the MLF by the end of the year.[27] A major victory for the fervent MLF advocates in the State Department, this renewed effort deepened the split within the Johnson administration. On one side in the dispute stood the MLF "theologians," true believers in European integration under American aegis: Ball, Rostow, Henry Owen, Robert Schaetzel, and

26. Bundy to President, 15 June 1963, Box 2, Aides Files, LBJL.
27. Memorandum of Discussion of the MLF at the White House, 10 April 1964, Box 23, NSF, LBJL.

Thomas Finletter, all connected with the State Department. They were assisted by former Secretary of State Dean Acheson and former High Commissioner for Germany John J. McCloy, both of whom had strong, though not steady, influence in the Johnson administration. Opposed to the State Department were William Foster and Adrian Fisher of the Arms Control and Disarmament Agency (ACDA), which aimed for global nuclear nonproliferation through a treaty negotiated in cooperation with the Soviets rather than through the Cold War–oriented MLF. This view gained currency in 1965–6, particularly as worry mounted that India, Israel, Japan, and other nations might respond to China's 1964 nuclear blast with nuclear programs of their own. Meanwhile, the Soviets – aghast at the possibility of a German finger anywhere close to a nuclear trigger – continued to protest vehemently against the MLF and press for a nonproliferation treaty. In between the pro- and anti-MLF stalwarts were Rusk, McNamara, and Bundy, who remained open-minded but skeptical about the proposal.[28] In Congress, both liberals and conservatives abhorred the idea of sharing America's nuclear weapons, particularly with Germans. Although Johnson valued the MLF as a means to contain German nuclear aspirations and to counter de Gaulle, he ultimately balked at fighting Congress over the issue, particularly with his Great Society legislation at stake. Despite the broad opposition to the MLF proposal at home and abroad, it seemed impossible to sink. U.S. officials kept resurfacing the MLF because it addressed their deep fears about Germany and because it fit their pattern of pacifying the allies with the semblance, and not the substance, of shared decision making.

Johnson administration officials complicated the inherent ambiguity and ambivalence of the MLF with deception. They tried to camouflage the purposes of the MLF, the division of power within it, and the very position of the U.S. government with regard to the scheme. A State Department memorandum explained to Johnson that although the MLF "has been described *publicly* as intended to meet European requests," "actually . . . it was developed to serve US interests."[29] The State Department hoped that the MLF would

28. Warren I. Cohen, *Dean Rusk* (Totowa, N.J.: Cooper Square, 1980), 297–300; Deborah Shapley, *Promise and Power: The Life and Times of Robert McNamara* (Boston: Little, Brown, 1993), 330–1.
29. "Notes on the MLF: Status and Needed Decisions," 6 December 1963, NSF, Box 23, LBJL.

ease German resentments, head off a German national nuclear force, thwart "De Gaulle's proposals for . . . inducing Germany to support the *force de frappe*," and help phase out the independent nuclear systems of Britain and France by creating "a powerful alternative force into which they might eventually be drawn." By "harnessing European resources," the MLF would get Europeans to pay "a part of [the] heavy US cost of nuclear weapons," the State Department calculated.[30] This cost sharing would extend to the nuclear arena the financial help that Washington was already getting from the allies, principally the FRG, to offset the costs of U.S. troops stationed in Europe.

To balance these substantive benefits for the United States, the Johnson administration offered the allies the possibility of an important concession, the "European clause." Such a provision would leave open the prospect that at some future time, perhaps when western Europe fully unified, the United States would relinquish its veto in the MLF, and the force would then become a European nuclear deterrent. As with other aspects of the MLF, Johnson officials layered the ambivalence with artifice. Senate aide John Newhouse observed that the Johnson administration was simultaneously assuring those opposed to nuclear proliferation that "the United States veto will assure its control over the force. But Europeans are being told that the MLF does represent a devolution of control and in time could become an independent European force."[31] Caught between McNamara's vehement opposition to giving up the U.S. veto and the German's desire for a substantive European clause, Ball – the consummate lawyer and the MLF's highest-ranking enthusiast – assured the Pentagon that "it was just a matter of working out words that do not give up our veto."[32]

At times the generated fog of such "words" became too thick. Talking with the Italian ambassador, the secretary of state blurted out that "there was an element of unreality" in all the discussions about the European clause. After reciting the standard formula – "the US is prepared to make nuclear decisions jointly with Europe"– Rusk laid out the conditions under which "jointly" meant, in effect, that Europe would make the choices that Washington wanted: "We

30. Ibid.
31. Newhouse, "Balancing the Risks in the MLF," 20 March 1964, Box 23, LBJL.
32. Memorandum of telephone conversation between Ball and McNaughton, 20 November 1964, 10:45 A.M., Box 5, George F. Ball Papers, LBJL.

do not want separate European and US decisions. We will not accept a situation in which Europe can in fact decide for us on the use of nuclear weapons, while we have 95% of the total alliance power. We do not concede that there can be separate nuclear action within an alliance."[33] In nuclear as in political matters, then, Rusk and other U.S. officials resisted almost any diminution in their authority over the alliance. They instead sought a partnership that would link western Europe more tightly to the United States and blur the unequal power relationship with "joint" decisions made by Washington.

Although ostensibly a military project, the MLF had an overwhelmingly political purpose. The supposed military rationale of the 200-missile force was to target Moscow's missiles aimed at western Europe. Yet U.S. and British submarines and other nuclear weapons based in the United States already deterred these Soviet forces. The MLF's military purpose remained so tangential that the extended discussions of the project rarely mentioned it. Doubts persisted whether multinational, "mixed-manned" crews could function effectively together and whether the missile-bearing ships would be easy targets in wartime.

Not surprisingly, supporters characterized the MLF as a primarily political device to counter centrifugal forces within the alliance. With the failure of Kennedy's Grand Design, the widening credibility gap over the U.S. nuclear umbrella, and the growing appeal of Europeanism even among opponents of de Gaulle, Atlantic-minded Americans looked anxiously for what a former ambassador to NATO described as "ways to work together with our European partners. The MLF is a perfectly logical step for our next efforts."[34] The State Department promised Johnson that the MLF would "strengthen ... [NATO] by creating a closely knit force in which ... members would take part and have pride."[35] Quite apart from any actual Soviet military threat, then, NATO needed shared purposes, some "work together," to sustain the personal bonding and common goals that cemented these otherwise sovereign countries in the

33. Memorandum of conversation between Ambassador Fenoaltea and Secretary Rusk, 24 October 1964, Box 23, NSF, LBJL.
34. Discussion following speech by Robert R. Bowie, "The Political Rationale of the Multi-Lateral Nuclear Force," 10 December 1963, R.M. Vol. 47, CFR.
35. "Notes on the MLF: Status and Needed Decisions," 6 December 1963, NSF, Box 23, LBJL.

U.S.-led alliance. West Germany remained the most critical ally to enlist in this work.

U.S. officials designed the MLF as a device to reassure and pacify Germany because they viewed the German people with mistrust and foreboding. Although analysts feared the consequences of neglecting German discontent, they saw little prospect for German reunification. Nor did they want to give West Germany real nuclear parity with Britain or France – except by folding the nuclear forces of those two nations into something like the MLF and thereby reducing Britain and France to Germany's status. U.S. officials hoped to escape this problem by "tranquiliz[ing] German nuclear ambitions" with a psychological pacifier, the MLF.[36] As Ball explained, the MLF had to give the Germans the "*feeling* that they are respected, first class members of the Atlantic Alliance" and the "*sense* that they are in on an equal basis."[37]

Launched in April 1964, the energetic sales campaign with the allies for the MLF won firm commitment only from Christian Democratic Chancellor Erhard; his Foreign Minister, Gerhard Schröder; and his Defense Minister, Kai Uwe von Hassel. Henry A. Kissinger, an unofficial adviser to Bundy, noted that these German officials "at our urging have staked their prestige" on the MLF.[38] Through nuclear sharing, the Erhard government hoped to tighten Washington's nuclear commitment to defend Germany, to gain a bargaining chip in negotiations with the Soviets over reunification, and to profit from civilian spinoffs from nuclear technology. Loudly opposed to Erhard were the Christian Democratic "Gaullists," who included former Chancellor Konrad Adenauer and Bavarian leaders Franz Josef Strauss and Freiherr zu Gutenberg. Inspired by de Gaulle's independent nationalism and Europeanism, these Gaullists found the MLF interesting only insofar as it might eventually lead, through a substantive European clause, to a German-led nuclear force, a prospect that terrified nearly everyone else.[39] As the Americans pushed harder for the MLF, France es-

36. "The Case Against Offering the Germans Ownership in Nuclear Hardware," 9 December 1965, Box 186–7, NSF, LBJL.
37. Ball to the President, 5 December 1964, no. 1978/431A, Declassified Documents Reference Service (hereafter DDRS) (emphases added).
38. Kissinger to Bundy, 27 November 1964, Box 15–16, Files of McGeorge Bundy, LBJL.
39. Walt Rostow, "Conversations with Germans at APAG Meeting," 19 October 1965, Box 36, NSF, LBJL; Günter Buchstab, "Zwischen 'Zauber und Donner' Die CDU/CSU und

calated its campaign against it. Ambassador Bohlen explained that the French objected to the MLF because it would "bind key members of the European Community to [the] United States in nuclear matters and in this sense foreclose even [the] possibility [for] French-style European unity centered around [the] Franco-German relationship."[40]

De Gaulle's opposition to Bonn's joining the MLF tightened the squeeze on Erhard, who had committed himself to the force, but who could not afford a complete break with Paris, especially with the pro-French German Gaullists loudly denouncing the chancellor's subservience to Washington. Moreover, Erhard faced another battle with de Gaulle over setting a unified Common Market price for grain products. Kissinger warned that in the German election coming up in September 1965, the Christian Democrats could split over the MLF, thereby throwing victory to the Social Democrats, who might then "veer into a more leftist and nationalistic course."[41] Apparently the German domino could fall to the right or to the left. If Washington postponed the final decision on whether to build the MLF until after the German elections, that postponement would ease the divisions within the Christian Democratic Party. Yet this turnaround would also deeply embarrass Erhard, who had publicly embraced Johnson's original timetable.[42] In Britain, Labour Prime Minister Harold Wilson came to power in October 1964 determined to resist what he termed the "fanatical pressures" for the MLF generated by Ball and Walt Rostow.[43]

Like London, Moscow worried that the MLF "will enable [the Germans] to put their finger on the nuclear rocket trigger at long last." While warning that creation of the MLF would be "a hostile

de Gaulle," in Wilfried Loth and Robert Picht, eds., *De Gaulle Deutschland und Europa* (Opladen, Germany: Leske and Budrich, 1991), 100–2.

40. Bohlen to Secretary of State, 28 October 1964, Box 24, NSF, LBJL. See also Summary of Discussion on MLF, Atlantic Defense and Related Matters, 31 October 1964, Box 38, ibid.; U.S. Information Agency, "Analysis of European Media Reaction to MLF," 2 December 1964, Box 23, ibid.

41. Kissinger to Bundy, 27 November 1964, Box 15–16, Files of McGeorge Bundy, LBJL. See also Hillenbrand to Secretary of State, 28 November 1964, Box 24, NSF, LBJL.

42. Hillenbrand to Secretary of State, 28 November 1964, Box 24, NSF, LBJL.

43. Harold Wilson, *The Labour Government, 1964–1970: A Personal Record* (London: Weidenfeld and Nicolson, 1971), 40–51; Gustav Schmidt, "Die sicherheitspolitischen und wirtschaftlichen Dimensionen der britisch-amerikanischen Beziehungen 1955–1967," *Militärgeschichtliche Mitteilungen* (February 1991): 122–3.

act," Soviet Foreign Minister Andrei Gromyko urged negotiations leading to a nuclear nonproliferation treaty.[44] Smaller NATO allies shared Soviet worries about West Germany, and they objected to Washington's attempt to set the direction of European integration by imposing the MLF.[45] By endorsing what Kissinger termed this "American project," Erhard and his government had isolated themselves from much of their party and from much of Europe. Then, in late 1964, Johnson himself walked away from the MLF, even while reaffirming his loyalty to it and to Erhard.[46]

With opposition to the MLF rising abroad and in the Congress, the Johnson administration – with the president and Bundy taking the lead – made the unambiguous decision to reverse the U.S. commitment to the plan. Characteristically, however, Johnson and his advisers shrouded their actions with ambiguity and artifice, made decisions without consulting the allies, and tried to pin responsibility for the change on the Europeans. Through all this deception and manipulation, Johnson officials sought to retain the trust and confidence of the FRG, which they feared might otherwise go off and seek refuge with the French or the Soviets or succumb to rabid nationalism.

In an influential memorandum on November 25, Bundy unequivocally stated "that the U.S. should now arrange to let the MLF sink out of sight. . . . [W]e should now ask the President for authority to work toward a future in which the MLF does not come into existence."[47] Although disappointed with the MLF's "failure . . . in Washington," Ball agreed with Bundy that they had to avoid "any suggestion [that] we were moving toward an abandonment ourselves – this is something we have to get the Germans to conclude in the atmosphere of studying the problem."[48] To make sure the Germans would "get" the right conclusion, Ball suggested

44. Thomas L. Hughes, "Soviet Opposition to Multilateral Force Is Intensified," 16 December 1964, Box 23, NSF, LBJL.
45. Thomas L. Hughes, "Review of Possible Modifications in the MLF to Take Account of West European Problems Revealed During the MLF Negotiations," 28 October 1964, Box 23, NSF, LBJL.
46. For the quotation, ibid.
47. Bundy to Secretary Rusk, Secretary McNamara, and Under Secretary Ball, 25 November 1964, Box 2, NSF, Aides Files, LBJL.
48. Telephone conversation between Walt Rostow and Ball, 24 November 1964, 10:30 A.M., Box 5, Ball Papers, LBJL; telephone conversation between Bundy and Ball, 25 November, 3:05 P.M., ibid.

bringing in the French, who fiercely opposed the MLF.[49] While Bundy doubted that de Gaulle could be maneuvered so easily, he did favor using the British to deflate German expectations. Ball and Bundy decided that "we should avoid getting into an MLF discussion with [German defense minister] von Hassel until after the British tackle him."[50] The tactic here was to withdraw U.S. leadership from the negotiations and so leave the hapless MLF to the British and Germans, who had fundamental disagreements over it. Although MLF enthusiasts such as Ball and Owen would continue to cherish hopes for such a "hardware solution," Johnson and his White House staff kept the actions of the "MLF-ites" under control and factored into the overall strategy for gradually deflating German hopes.

Just as the Johnson administration tried to shirk responsibility for its shift in policy, the president blamed his troubles with the MLF on the alleged incompetence of his advisers. Presidential adviser and scholar Richard E. Neustadt, who participated in these MLF discussions, later related that "Johnson had a fine eye for the human vulnerabilities of people he was working with and [he] looked for that soft spot and then turned the knife in it as a means of attaching people more securely." Johnson also exhibited "the Franklin Roosevelt streak, of just liking to pull the wings off flies."[51] At one of the meetings on the MLF switch, Johnson went around the room, verbally attacking each of his advisers, even Acheson, the "man who got us into war in Korea" and had to "get Eisenhower to get us out of it." Reportedly it was Acheson who ended this tirade by cutting in, "Mr. President, you don't pay these men enough to talk to them that way – even with the federal pay raise."[52]

At a White House meeting on December 7, 1964, Johnson inflicted the "treatment" on newly installed Prime Minister Wilson. This vulnerable leader hoped to develop a special relationship with

49. Ibid.
50. Telephone conversation between Ball and Bundy, 29 October 1964, Box 5, Ball Papers.
51. Richard Neustadt oral history interview, 9, LBJL.
52. Ibid.; Geyelin, *Johnson*, 162. According to Neustadt, Bundy escaped this brutality "because I don't think he ever had Mac calibrated, and people he didn't have calibrated he didn't beat up on" (Neustadt oral history, 8). The day after, Bundy commented that "he had never seen a man who made so much noise but that it didn't necessarily follow that he would not change his mind later on" (telephone conversation between Ball and Bundy, 26 November, 11:30, Box 5, Ball Papers).

the president, needed U.S. support for the faltering British pound, and hung on to a tiny parliamentary margin. LBJ, who had just won a smashing electoral victory, began the discussion by pulling off Wilson's wings. Complaining "about the troubles which [Wilson] had already given" him, Johnson warned that "our folks were damned tired of . . . solv[ing] all the world's problems . . . alone." He charged that Wilson's Labour budget "with its heavy emphasis on social security" increased the burden of bolstering the pound sterling and the speculative pressure on the dollar. This quick review of Wilson's vulnerabilities was a setup for the president's main point: unless Britain became more sensitive to Germany's nuclear aspirations, that frustrated nation might eventually start a third world war.[53] After this tough talk, Johnson backed away from any rigid demand as to the timing and details of a multinational nuclear force. The president even agreed to combine the MLF with Wilson's proposal for a watered-down version, the Atlantic Nuclear Force (ANF), as long as the plan included the key element of a "mixed-manned surface force."[54]

The point of Johnson's strategy was to impress upon the British the necessity of "tak[ing] very seriously" German arguments and expectations for nuclear sharing. LBJ maneuvered London and Bonn into a long negotiation that might or might not lead to something. But in the meantime the talks would, he hoped, defuse the MLF crisis, deflate German expectations, and get the United States off the hook of its commitment to the MLF. To ensure that the MLF negotiations would remain mired, Johnson picked up on Ball's earlier suggestion that the interests of France be considered in the European discussions.[55] The French noted approvingly that Johnson had marooned the MLF: "[W]hat is acceptable to [the] Germans is anathema to [the] British and vice versa."[56] Despite

53. Bundy, Memorandum for the record, 7 December 1964, Box 18–19, Bundy files, LBJL. See also Memorandum for Ambassador Bruce, 9 December 1964, Box 23, NSF, LBJL.
54. The British regarded the ANF as an interim proposal that could lead to the eventual sinking of all projects involving the sharing of nuclear "hardware" with West Germany. Johnson and Bundy appreciated the blurring effect of the ANF, whereas diehards such as Rostow hoped that the ANF scheme could eventually be transmuted back into the MLF. See "U.S. Comments on the UK Proposal of a Project for an Atlantic Nuclear Force," 8 December 1964, Box 23, NSF, LBJL.
55. Geyelin, *Johnson*, 175.
56. Bohlen to Secretary of State, 5 January 1965, Box 170, NSF, LBJL.

their rivalry, the Americans and the French understood each other's role in containing Germany, and they shared a predilection for manipulating the Germans.

Most Europeans felt relieved at Johnson's camouflaged turnaround, except those who had most faithfully followed Washington's lead. A top German diplomat confessed that he and his "fellow German Atlanticists" felt isolated and "not a little ridiculous."[57] From Bonn, U.S. Ambassador George McGhee reported a "tempest. . . . The atmosphere here is the worst I have encountered."[58] Germans worried that if the United States could so quickly reverse itself on the MLF, their protector might also suddenly strike a deal with Moscow or Paris at Germany's expense.

Such "German nervousness" annoyed Johnson. The president cabled that he did not "find it agreeable to have repeatedly renewed German questions about the firmness of [my] purpose or the direction of [my] policy." The language of McGhee's response expressed and reinforced the American stereotype of Germany as a reduced, excessively emotional nation: "During these periodic flurries the Germans behave in a very irrational and immature way. This is, however, their present nature, derived from their basic insecurity and lack of confidence in themselves and their future."[59] McGhee's phrase "periodic flurries" suggested that the crisis originated from some cyclical, natural cause rather than from Johnson's decisions; that it would quickly blow over; and that men sufficiently tough could weather it easily. Coding the Germans as "irrational and immature" made it easy, as Harold Cleveland has recognized, for Americans to trivialize Germany's concerns and differences with Washington. Most important, Johnson and his top advisers failed to see that their manipulation of Germany's desires for security, notably with the MLF proposal, aggravated that vulnerability toward which they were so condescending.

With the basic problems of Germany's discontent and other nations' distrust of Germany still festering, the rise and fall of the MLF (now combined with the ANF) went through another cycle in 1965. Assisted by Bundy, Johnson stifled any substantive revival of

57. Rivkin to Secretary of State, 14 January 1965, Box 25, NSF, LBJL.
58. McGhee to the President, 16 January 1965, Box 194, NSF, LBJL. See also McGhee to Secretary of State, 14 January 1965, no. 1978/285D, DDRS.
59. McGhee to the President, 16 January 1965, Box 194, NSF, LBJL.

MLF/ANF while he strung the Germans along so that they would not lose trust in the United States. The White House kept a tight rein on Rostow, Ball, Owen, and the other MLF enthusiasts while calibrating official statements so as to sustain German hopes while allowing the opposition to the MLF/ANF in Britain, France, the Soviet Union, and elsewhere to do its work. The day after the White House received a telegram from McGhee warning of the "grim mood" among Bonn officials fearing that the "US had lost interest" in the MLF/ANF, Johnson assured reporters that he was "still strongly in favor of a mixed-manned nuclear fleet."[60] Yet Johnson vetoed Rusk's proposal to help resolve the Anglo–German impasse. "We are about where we should be at the moment," the president observed.[61] While Bundy privately asserted that the MLF/ANF "is never going to be the right next step," Rusk assured the Germans that "there was no US policy change." Presumably with a straight face, Rusk lectured the German ambassador: "We must be very clear that [the] US shift on the MLF was based solely on expressed FRG desire to keep [the] matter quiet before elections and was strictly responsive to Bonn['s] wishes."[62]

After the September 19, 1965, German elections, in which Erhard, Schröder, and von Hassel won a victory, the German government once again pressed for MLF/ANF or some variant of this hardware solution. Two days after the German election, Martin Hillenbrand, a State Department analyst who was not an enthusiast, noted that since December 1964 German leaders "have been partly reassured by American official expressions of continuing interest in something along the lines of the ANF/MLF."[63] Johnson continued to manipulate rather than deal honestly with the supposedly fragile Germans, a tactic that only aggravated their insecurity. In late 1964, the administration had deployed British and French opposition to the MLF. In late 1965, the administration again decided "to let the Germans down gently" – this time by lur-

60. Geyelin, *Johnson,* 177; McGhee to Secretary of State, 14 January 1965, No. 1978/285D, DDRS; McGhee to Secretary of State, 15 January 1965, 1978/250C, ibid.
61. Telephone conversation between Rusk and Ball, 3 February 1965, Box 5, Ball Papers; Bundy to Secretary of State, 4 March 1965, Box 23, NSF, LBJL.
62. Ibid.; Department of State to American Embassy in Bonn, 9 July 1965, Box 190, NSF, LBJL.
63. Hillenbrand, "The Nuclear Problem of the Alliance," Box 2, Bator Papers.

ing them with McNamara's idea for a Nuclear Planning Group.[64] In April 1966, when a hardware solution had become highly unlikely, a front-page *New York Times* story asserted that the administration had asked the Germans to accept McNamara's planning group in place of MLF/ANF.[65] In essence, the story was true; McNamara believed that the new group "will end talk of the Multilateral Force."[66] Yet Ball burned the telephone lines in both the United States and in Europe trying to "knock down" this "flat lie" and "absolute and total nonsense."[67] Bator, no friend of the MLF, remembered the newspaper story as "very inconvenient because we were trying to play the Germans" by moving them away from MLF/ANF without "upset[ting] German politics." By this time, however, the MLF masquerade had become absorbed into the larger drama of trying to end the Cold War.

The "End of the Cold War"

The failure of the MLF demonstrated that traditional, Cold War solutions no longer fit the changing conditions of the mid-1960s. The standard operating procedure of keeping the Germans contained and the alliance busy with the task of confronting the "Soviet threat" – in this case by building a multinational force of 200 nuclear missiles aimed at the Soviet Union – no longer worked because the Russians appeared less threatening and the Germans seemed more formidable. Despite Moscow's nuclear arms buildup in the 1960s, the chance of a Soviet military attack on the West appeared increasingly remote.[68] The first thawings of spring in Romania, Hungary, and Czechoslovakia created both opportunities for the West and pressures to respond with positive policies. Moreover, the Eastern countries were not the only ones moving away from their hegemon.

64. Ibid.   65. *New York Times,* 27 April 1966.
66. "Summary Notes of 566th NSC Meeting December 13, 1966, 12:10 P.M.," Box 2, NSC Meetings File, LBJL.
67. Ball telephone conversation with James Reston, 27 April 1966, 9:20 A.M.; Ball telephone conversation with Heinrich Knappstein, 27 April 1966, 9:15 A.M.; Ball telephone conversation with Walt Rostow, 27 April 1966, 9:10 A.M. All in Box 4, Ball Papers.
68. Kermit Gordon, *Agenda for the Nation: Papers on Domestic and Foreign Policy Issues* (Washington: Brookings, 1968), p. 353.

In March 1966, de Gaulle announced that he was yanking French forces out of the NATO integrated command, and he demanded that NATO military forces and facilities leave France. "The really disturbing thing," Ball fretted, thinking about Germany, "is the effect of this kind of assertive nationalism on others. Even the good ones are beginning to beat their chests."[69] Then the general set another bad example. Journeying to Moscow in June 1966, de Gaulle invoked past French alliances with "eternal Russia" as he tried to sidestep ideology and reach an understanding with Moscow based on containing the Germans and securing French preeminence in western Europe. Although de Gaulle failed to win a commitment from Moscow, his actions helped crack the solidity of both the Cold War and the Western alliance.[70] Not daring to be left behind, U.S., German, and British leaders accelerated their contacts with eastern Europe, including the Soviet Union. Foreign Minister Schröder had already begun a policy of small steps to chip away at the barriers separating the FRG from East Germany and other Soviet bloc nations.[71] Although Johnson and his advisers were fighting the communists in Vietnam, they reached out to the communists in eastern Europe, believing that both efforts would weaken a hostile ideology while encouraging the growth of a moderate nationalism and modern technocracy receptive to American influence.

In the spring of 1966, the Johnson administration launched a policy of "bridge building" to eastern Europe and the Soviet Union. Johnson, Bator, Walt Rostow (the National Security Adviser after Bundy's departure in February 1966), Acheson, Eugene Rostow, and others expected that bridge building would open avenues of political, economic, and cultural contact with eastern Europe and the Soviet Union. They hoped that in the very long run, bridge building might even undermine communist ideology. More immediately, however, bridge building addressed the crisis in NATO sparked by de Gaulle's withdrawal and Germany's restiveness. Just as U.S. officials in 1948–9 developed the NATO treaty as a device to institu-

---

69. Ball telephone conversation with James Reston, 2 April 1966, Box 5, Ball Papers.
70. Zérapha Belooussova, "La visite du général de Gaulle en URSS em juin 1966" (Paper presented at conference, "De Gaulle en son siècle," 19–24 November 1990, Paris).
71. Wolfram F. Hanrieder, *Germany, America, Europe* (New Haven, Conn.: Yale University Press, 1989), 178–80.

tionalize the emerging Western bloc and align it against the Soviet Union, so too U.S. officials in 1966–8 promoted détente within the framework of the alliance as a means to involve western Europeans in a common, U.S.-led exploration of what Humphrey called the "Wild East." "We stand a far better chance of safely reaching" this new frontier, the vice president advised the allies, "if our wagons are in line, and if we mount a reliable shotgun guard, than if the wagons set out separately, each in its own direction."[72] Although the pursuit had shifted from Cold War to détente, Americans still assumed that they would be the ones to ride shotgun, decide what was "reliable," and lead the wagons.

This shift in tactics was epitomized by Dean Acheson, the father of the Cold War version of the Western alliance. Focusing on Europe rather than on Vietnam, Acheson in April 1966 urged Americans to rethink the "idea that all Communists are devils."[73] He suggested that NATO develop a "good neighbor policy" toward the Warsaw Pact, a formulation that recalled America's traditional predominance over its lesser-developed Latin neighbors.[74] Bator recalled that in the spring of 1966, when the administration was attempting a "careful growing out of the Cold War," Acheson became the "de facto Assistant Secretary for Europe."[75] Acheson accelerated State Department and White House thinking on alternatives to the dead-ended policies typified by the MLF.[76]

At his temporary office in the State Department, Acheson tackled the immediate question of how to respond to de Gaulle and the long-range challenge of keeping NATO vital – despite France's departure from the integrated military command, Germany's longing for reunification, and the Soviet bloc's eagerness to talk and trade

72. Humphrey, "A Mission to Europe," 21 April 1967, in U.S. Senate, Committee on Government Operations, "The Atlantic Alliance: Current Views," 90th Cong., 1st sess. (Washington: Government Printing Office, 1967), 24.
73. U.S. Senate, Committee on Government Operations, *The Atlantic Alliance,* 89th Cong., 2nd sess., 27 April 1966, 27.
74. Douglas Brinkley, *Dean Acheson: The Cold War Years, 1953–71* (New Haven, Conn.: Yale University Press, 1992), 232.
75. Author's interview with Francis M. Bator, Cambridge, Mass., 21 November 1992. Assistant Secretary of State John Leddy was suffering from a particularly severe bout of back trouble that spring.
76. Acheson was ably assisted by State Department European analyst Lawrence Eagleburger, who thereafter worked with Bator in the White House.

with the West.[77] Acheson, who had fathered the NATO organization, raged at de Gaulle's repudiation of it. Backed by Ball and Rusk, the elder statesman favored a public denunciation of de Gaulle's position. They calculated that an open confrontation would undercut de Gaulle's support in western Europe and among the French people. On the delicate issue of what should be the legal and military status of French troops in Germany after France had withdrawn from the NATO integrated command, Acheson and Ball wanted Bonn to take an uncompromising stance, even at the risk of damaging French–German relations.[78]

Although Johnson privately cursed de Gaulle, he rejected the idea of an uncurtained fight that might offend the French people. Like Eisenhower and Kennedy, who had had their own quarrels with the difficult French leader, Johnson shaded the animosity because he assumed that the "natural" pro-Americanism of the French people would outlast the nationalist spleen of their leader. "We love France and look on her with sorrow rather than with anger," Johnson declared; "the French will not always feel about us as their government now feels."[79] Johnson's tactic was to accede to de Gaulle's request to withdraw U.S. forces and NATO headquarters from France while denying him the prestige of an open debate with the world's foremost nation. When Acheson and Ball openly attacked de Gaulle, Johnson leaked his disapproval to the press.[80] Acheson, angry at his public humiliation and Johnson's public conciliation of France, cornered Bator at a dinner party and chided: "You made the greatest imperial power the world has ever seen kiss de Gaulle's ass."[81]

77. Acheson, "Broad Lines of Approach Toward Negotiations with France in NATO Crisis," 13 May 1966, Box 3, Bator Papers.
78. Walt Rostow and Bator to the President, 18 May 1966, Box 7, Rostow's Memoranda to the President, LJBL; Brinkley, *Acheson*, 228–35.
79. Sulzberger, *Age of Mediocrity*, 268; C. L. Sulzberger, "Foreign Affairs: Johnson and de Gaulle," *New York Times*, 5 June 1966. When polled in 1965 as to which side they favored in the Paris–Washington quarrel, the French picked their own government, 53 percent to 5 percent. See Costigliola, *France and the United States*, 138–9.
80. Brinkley in *Acheson*, 228–35, mistakes this tactical dispute between Acheson and Johnson for a major difference over strategy toward Europe.
81. Author's interview with Bator, 21 November 1992. The former secretary of state also thought that White House staff officials such as Bator were gaining too much of a role in policy making.

Washington had amassed that imperial power during the worst of the Cold War, when western Europe had huddled close to America for protection. Now with détente emerging, Acheson and Johnson agreed – despite the small tempest over de Gaulle – that bridge building could make the Cold War less dangerous and bolster the United States' influence in both western and eastern Europe.

Bridge building was a metaphor that emerged from a series of papers by Acheson, Bator, Rostow, and Zbigniew Brzezinski. It referred to a collage of U.S. initiatives, statements, and nuanced actions that cohered around the central theme of "actively develop[ing] areas of peaceful cooperation with the nations of Eastern Europe and the Soviet Union," as National Security Action Memorandum 352 expressed it. Signed by the president on July 8, 1966, this document directed the foreign policy bureaucracy to "help create an environment in which peaceful settlement of the division of Germany and of Europe will become possible."[82] Advocates such as Bator hoped to move forward with nuclear arms control while easing tensions in eastern Europe. Although the bridge-building initiatives focused on Europe, they also appealed to Johnson, Walt Rostow, and others preoccupied with Vietnam. The central question of the bridge-building policy was whether the initiatives would "enhance" Washington's "peace posture" and perhaps induce Moscow to broker a settlement of the war, as some officials hoped, or whether the escalating conflict would destroy this effort at détente.[83]

In terms of specific initiatives, bridge building encouraged improved (though limited) contacts between Bonn and the nations in the Soviet sphere. The policy sought to nudge the Germans away from MLF/ANF and toward the nuclear nonproliferation treaty and the Nuclear Planning Group, both acceptable to Moscow. It initiated what became the International Institute for Applied Systems Analysis. The United States upgraded its missions to Bulgaria and

---

82. National Security Memorandum No. 352, 8 July 1966, Box 8, NSAM File, LBJL.
83. Bator to the President, "Tactics on East–West Trade Bill," 21 April 1966, Rostow's memorandum to the President, Box 7; Walt Rostow to the President, 10 June 1966, Box 8, NSAM 345; W. Averell Harriman to the President and Secretary of State, 3 October 1966, Box 12, ibid.; Memorandum, 7 October 1966, Box 4, Bator Papers; Arthur Goldberg to Secretary of State, 10 December 1966, Box 55–56, NSC History, The Non-Proliferation Treaty. All in LBJL.

Hungary, increased cultural contacts with these and other Soviet bloc nations, and tried to eliminate petty irritants in east–west relations. A final and essential component of bridge building was increased east–west trade, which Johnson tried to secure through congressional legislation enabling him to grant most-favored-nation tariff status to goods from the Soviet Union and eastern Europe.[84]

The bridge-building policy rested on a key assumption, that Moscow's expected intransigence and Washington's enlightened leadership would together safely limit Bonn's reaching out to the East (what would later become known as *Ostpolitik*). On this basis, Acheson recommended that the U.S. "gently, subtly and through every channel . . . encourage the FRG to remove the obstacles to progress in better relations" with eastern Europe."[85] In a major speech on October 7, 1966, Johnson urged Bonn to soften its refusal to recognize officially the postwar loss of territories to Poland, Czechoslovakia, and the Soviet Union.[86] In his State of the Union address on January 10, 1967, the president declared that "our objective is not to continue the cold war, but to end it."[87] A background explanation to the press emphasized that NATO would become the institution through which the United States and western Europe would "seek together new, constructive relations with the governments and peoples of Eastern Europe and the Soviet Union."[88] In December 1967, NATO formally adopted the Harmel report, which made détente an equal priority with defense. Eugene V. Rostow, who succeeded Ball as undersecretary of state and who worked "for a long time" on Harmel, described its purpose "to generate wholly new political impulses . . . in the alliance."[89]

In reaching out to eastern Europe and the Soviet Union, Bator tried, in small ways, to create a sense of mutual interest in stabilizing Europe. When the Czech ambassador complained that Bonn refused to renounce the 1938 Munich agreement that had ceded

84. See *Public Papers of the Presidents of the United States 1966* (Washington: Government Printing Office, 1967), II, 1125–30; *Public Papers of the Presidents of the United States 1967* (Washington: Government Printing Office, 1968), I, 10; Bennett Kovrig, *Of Walls and Bridges* (New York: New York University Press, 1991), 108–11.
85. Quoted in Bator to the President, 13 October 1966, at 12:45 P.M., Box 4, Bator Papers.
86. *Public Papers 1966*, II, 1125–30.   87. *Public Papers 1967*, 10.
88. Rostow's Memoranda to the President, 10 January 1967, Box 12, LBJL.
89. Eugene V. Rostow Oral History Transcript, 22, LBJL; Lawrence S. Kaplan, "The U.S. and NATO in the Johnson Years" (unpublished essay), 28–31.

Czech territory to Nazi Germany, Bator, alluding to the American tactic of reforming the Germans, emphasized "our shared interest in helping Germany . . . evolve in a constructive direction."[90] When de Gaulle left for Moscow, Bator tried to cool the Frenchman's reception in the Soviet capital by emphasizing the common "responsibility" of the two superpowers. "We had to be very careful with the problems of Central Europe and Germany," Bator told a Soviet official, while guarding against de Gaulle's "propaganda tricks."[91] The president dealt with the annual Cold War tradition of Captive Nations Week by issuing, at Bator's suggestion, "a soft, *un*-cold-warish" proclamation.[92]

In discussing bridge building, Johnson administration officials frequently talked about generating the proper "atmosphere" and "environment." The policy involved actions on two levels: actually removing irritants that divided eastern and western Europe, and taking steps that made the reunification of Germany and Europe appear possible even if it never occurred. Acheson alluded to both aspects when he urged the "members of NATO to think what they could do to improve an environment in which a [European] settlement could take place."[93] The bridge builders hoped that the glimmer of reunification would offer the West Germans enough satisfaction so that they would not turn to nationalist demagogues.

Like Ball trying to maneuver German "feelings" about the MLF, Brzezinski, an adviser to the State Department's Policy Planning Council, believed that bridge building would give the Germans "a sense of direction" and "a feeling of participation" in closing the east–west gap and moving toward reunification. He argued that convincing the Germans that reunification would come only after gradual change in the east "might help to *acclimatize* them to the status quo . . . [and] thus reduce the likelihood of unilateral and

90. Bator, "Lunch with Czech Ambassador at his Residence," 24 August 1966, Box 3, Bator Papers. See also Bator, "Lunch with Counselor Vorontsov of the Soviet Embassy," 7 June 1967, Box 5, Bator Papers. In December 1966, Chancellor Kiesinger formally renounced the Munich agreement.
91. Bator, "Lunch with Minister Councelor [*sic*] Zinchuk of the Russian Embassy," 15 June 1966, Box 3, Bator Papers.
92. Bator to the President, 21 June 1966, Box 3, Bator Papers; Bator to the President, 11 July 1967, Box 6, ibid.
93. U.S. Senate, Committee on Government Operations, *The Atlantic Alliance*, 89th Cong., 2nd sess., 27 April 1966, 27.

potentially divisive German initiatives toward Moscow."[94] Another State Department paper reasoned that although Bonn's more active policy toward eastern Europe "is unlikely to have any decisive effect on advancing a German settlement . . . nevertheless, we ought to encourage it" because such steps might ease the Germans' "chronic distemper over being merely the 'object' of the policies of others."[95] Once again, American officials addressed their subordinate's discontents by treating the symptom – in this case "chronic distemper" – with a placebo that they did not expect would change the underlying conditions of Germany's status as an "object" and as a divided nation.

While using bridge building to sustain German faith and allegiance in the alliance, U.S. officials felt quite comfortable in their belief that Germany would not achieve reunification for a long time, if ever. When asked whether the Johnson administration had ever pushed for any quick progress toward renunification, John Leddy, the assistant secretary of state for European Affairs, replied in surprise: "No, no. Why would we do that?"[96] Like Leddy, Edward Fried, who in 1967 replaced Bator at the White House, believed that no change in Germany's division would occur "for the next 50 years." He added, "It isn't going to be settled by the West German moves toward East Germany."[97]

Frustration over the impasse on reunification encouraged the Erhard government to persist in its requests for MLF/ANF. By 1966, few Germans actually expected to get such a hardware solution. But many, particularly Christian Democrats, feared that abandoning this possibility would be giving away one of the few cards that Bonn had to bid with Moscow (and Washington) for progress on reunification.

German policy shifted after the resignation in November 1966 of the forlorn Erhard, abandoned by his allies at home and abroad.[98] Despite his past deference to the Americans, Erhard re-

94. Brzezinski, "The NATO Crisis and East–West Relations," 6 July 1966, Box 88, Acheson Papers, HSTL (emphasis added).
95. "A Re-Examination of Premises on the German Problem," 10 December 1965, Box 186-7, NSF, LBJL.
96. Transcript, John Leddy Oral History interview, 19–20, LBJL.
97. Transcript, Edward R. Fried Oral History interview, 23, LBJL.
98. George McGhee, *At the Creation of a New Germany* (New Haven, Conn.: Yale University Press, 1989), 188-9.

ceived little sympathy when he begged Johnson not to make him commit "political suicide."[99] Beset by a sharp recession, Erhard asked for a stretchout or reduction of Bonn's obligation to offset (with purchases of U.S. weapons) the dollar drain resulting from American troops in Germany. German willingness to buy U.S. weaponry was sapped further by a run of sixty-six accidents involving the controversial F-104 Starfighter jets that Bonn had already purchased.[100] Turned down by "his friend Johnson,"[101] Erhard endured taunts from other Christian Democrats: "This is your reward for being a model boy to the Americans."[102] After a governmental crisis in November–December 1966, Christian Democrat Kurt-Georg Kiesinger became chancellor, and Social Democrat Willy Brandt became foreign minister in a Grand Coalition government. In contrast to Erhard, who had looked primarily to Washington, the new government balanced its ties to the United States with improved relations with France. Although Kiesinger and other Christian Democrats still clung to Erhard's stance on nuclear weapons, Brandt believed that holding out for the MLF/ANF and opposing nuclear nonproliferation had become outmoded. He focused instead on utilizing Germany's economic strength to improve relations with the East.[103]

Also trying to shift from Cold War to détente, the Johnson administration in 1966 divided the two functions of the would-be MLF/ANF – containing and channeling German nuclear aspirations – and assigned the containing to the nuclear Nonproliferation Treaty (NPT) and the channeling to the Nuclear Planning Group (NPG). In contrast to the MLF/ANF, which would have forestalled a German nuclear force by allowing the Germans limited participation in a missile force aimed at the Soviet Union, the NPT flatly prohibited a German nuclear force (and national nuclear programs by other adherents to the treaty) and placed the Soviet Union by the side of the United States as co-sponsor of the covenant. Despite widespread fears that India, Japan, Israel, and

99. Memorandum, 30 August 1966, Box 193, NSF, LBJL.
100. McGhee, *Creation of a New Germany*, 189.
101. Mathiopoulos, "The American President Seen Through German Eyes," 684.
102. Memorandum, 30 August 1966, Box 193, NSF, LBJL. For the widespread German feeling that Erhard had been humiliated by the Americans, see *Der Spiegel* 20 (3 October 1966): 26–8.
103. Willy Brandt, "German Policy toward the East," *Foreign Affairs* 46 (April 1968): 476–86; Hanrieder, *Germany, America, Europe*, 182–90.

Egypt might build nuclear weapons, Germany stood out, particularly for the Soviets, as the main target of the NPT. Soviet negotiators repeatedly expressed "their concern about Germans having or getting their hands on U.S. nuclear weapons."[104] Americans understood this worry. "The Germans are the Germans," explained Fried; "they got us into two wars. . . . They're the one country that could most quickly develop a very potent and credible nuclear capability. Unfortunately they might well have the most cause to use one because they have a divided country. Now, those are the ingredients for the end of the world. It's as basic as that."[105]

Part of the rough transition from the Cold War to détente, the NPT negotiations predictably snagged on the issue of MLF/ANF. Although the Soviets agreed that a future united Europe could inherit the nuclear forces of Britain and/or France, they refused to permit creation of a new force such as MLF/ANF. When the German ambassador nervously protested that "accommodation of [the] USSR" should not supersede the "nuclear problems of the alliance" and Bonn's own aspirations, the acting secretary of state assured him that "there would be no agreement [with Moscow] without appropriate consultation with our allies."[106] In light of Washington's past unwillingness to consult seriously on major issues, the word *appropriate* probably did not ease German anxiety. In early December 1966, Soviet and American negotiators proposed the specific language that would become the heart of the treaty. Only then did Rusk invite the NATO allies to consult. Leddy recalled that "we were more or less saying" to the allies, 'We and the Soviets are in effect agreed on this thing; we don't know how we could change it.' "[107] Not surprisingly, many Germans felt betrayed; typically, too, the U.S. embassy characterized German concern as "emotional" and obsess[ive]."[108] When Kiesinger complained of the superpowers' "atomic complicity" and the lack of

104. Memorandum of Conversation between J. M. Vorontsov and George Bunn, 9 September 1966, Box 55–6, NSC History, The Non-Proliferation Treaty, LBJL; this is a recurring theme in Spurgeon M. Keeny, "The Non-Proliferation Treaty," 24 December 1968, ibid.

105. Edward Fried Oral History, 22–3, LBJL.

106. Department of State to American Embassy in Bonn, 26 October 1966, Box 55–6, NSC History, Non-Proliferation Treaty, LBJL.

107. Leddy Oral History Transcript, 15. See also Keeny, "The Non-Proliferation Treaty," 24 December 1968, box 55–6, NSC History, Non-Proliferation Treaty, LBJL.

108. Text of Cable from Bonn (8769), 30 January 1967, Box 12, Memos to the President, Rostow Papers. For German concern, see Hanrieder, *Germany, America, Europe*, 93.

consultation, LBJ retorted: "If I had a dollar for every time I consulted the Germans, I'd be a millionaire. . . . They have been over here every six months on every damned subject you can imagine."[109] Johnson was not the only U.S. official who assumed that informing the allies was consulting with them.

On the key question of whether the NPT did prohibit a new multilateral force, the treaty language was – in the tradition of the MLF – "gloriously ambiguous," as Bator judged it.[110] Several months after the United States, the Soviet Union, and fifty other nations formally approved NPT on July 1, 1968 (West Germany did not sign until November 1969), Rusk told an interviewer that the treaty prohibited MLF/ANF, though Leddy and Undersecretary of State Eugene Rostow testified that they saw no such prohibition.[111] Even as it faded away, the MLF/ANF remained a mix of ambivalence and artifice.

In moving from the Cold War to the more sophisticated policies demanded by détente, the Johnson administration on at least two issues promoted U.S. objectives by establishing the dominant discourse in which that issue was debated. (A discourse is the set of rules – the assumed conventions – about a body of knowledge that governs how specific issues are conceived, articulated, debated, and usually decided.[112]) The Johnson administration pioneered the Nuclear Planning Group (NPG) and the International Institute for Applied Systems Analysis (IIASA) as ostensibly nonpolitical, technical forums in which Americans' superior technical knowledge enabled them not only to dominate discussions but also to set the framework and rules of the debate. By controlling the discourse, Americans achieved political objectives that were difficult or impossible to pursue with a frontal political campaign. McNamara created the NPG to "educate" the principal allies to think as he did about nuclear weapons and to channel German nuclear aspirations blocked by the failure of the MLF/ANF and the success

109. Bator, Memorandum for the Record, 2 March 1967, Box 50, NSC, History of Trilateral Negotiations, NSF, LBJL.
110. Author interview with Bator, 21 November 1992.
111. Rusk Oral History Interview, 15; Eugene V. Rostow Oral History Transcript, 20–1; Leddy Oral History Transcript, 7. All in LBJL.
112. For an easily accessible discussion of discourse, see Joan W. Scott, "Deconstructing Equality-Versus-Difference: Or, the Uses of Poststructuralist Theory for Feminism," *Feminist Studies* 14 (Spring 1988): 35–6.

of the NPT. Bator, Bundy, and other Americans built the IIASA as a bridge of communication and influence with the rising technocrats of eastern Europe, including the Soviet Union. Unlike Cold War mechanisms that relied on power confrontations and hardware, the NPG and IIASA utilized America's superior expertise in science and management.

The concept of a dominant discourse is particularly useful in explaining McNamara's strategy in establishing the NPG. The very nature of nuclear issues – involving secret knowledge, a special vocabulary, exotic technology, godlike power, and cataclysmic destruction – encouraged a sense of the knowing in-group among the men whom McNamara inducted into the NPG priesthood. McNamara had earned the nickname "the Computer" because of his driving personality and his awesome grasp of the details of weaponry and strategy. U.S. Ambassador to NATO Harlan Cleveland observed how McNamara in four intense sessions "baptize[d] Europe's Defense Ministers, and through them their governments, by total immersion" in the technicalities of nuclear strategy and the horrors of nuclear warfare.[113] In place of MLF/ANF, McNamara's indoctrination offered the Germans participation in what Harlan Cleveland called a "new nuclear intimacy." In this communion, the defense ministers of Germany and of the other principal allies[114] could exercise influence only insofar as they spoke in an acceptably reasonable and knowledgeable way – that is, within the boundaries of what McNamara had established as the dominant discourse. Harlan Cleveland noted approvingly how the NPG developed "a framework of orderly and informed discussion."[115] As his biographer would later conclude, "now McNamara had a small, controlled forum in which he could lead the allies over time to his own views."[116] Like other NATO institutions, however, the

---

113. Cleveland, *Transatlantic Bargain*, 54; Paul Buteux, *The Politics of Nuclear Consultation in Nato, 1965–1980* (New York: Cambridge University Press, 1983), 50–6; Kurt Birrenbach, *Meine Sondermissionen* (Düsseldorf, Germany: Econ Verlag, 1984), 222–5.
114. Cleveland, *Transatlantic Bargain*, 56. Not willing to be constrained by this or other American mechanisms, the French declined to participate in the NPG.
115. Cleveland, *Transatlantic Bargain*, 65. Within each participating nation, the NPG helped shape debate on nuclear issues by enhancing the defense ministry's claim to significant, secret knowledge not available to others, particularly those challenging the dominant discourse.
116. Shapley, *McNamara*, 402.

NPG could only talk about shared decision making because U.S. officials reserved most actual decisions for themselves. Before one of the NPG sessions, Bator explained to LBJ that "the main result of the meeting – apart from general education – will be agreement on a series of further joint studies."[117] Years later, a senior Pentagon official observed that the NPG "was so inhibited by the US that it might have been better called the Nuclear 'Unplanning' Group. The US initiated it as a sop to Allied concerns."[118]

The NPG did more than make national and multilateral nuclear forces appear impractical and unnecessary. The group also educated the Europeans on the soundness of flexible response, McNamara's preferred nuclear strategy. Fearing that any war would devastate their homelands, the European allies had since the 1950s favored the doctrine of quick and massive nuclear retaliation – a horrific prospect, but one that they hoped would deter a Soviet assault. Since 1962, however, McNamara had pushed flexible response, which required the buildup of conventional forces in Europe so that in the event of Soviet aggression, NATO could delay or perhaps avoid the terrible destruction that would result from nuclear war. With the help of the NPG forum, McNamara in December 1967 won European acceptance of the flexible response doctrine.[119]

Although McNamara shaped the options perceived by Europeans within the alliance, he himself could not escape the boundaries imposed by the broader constraints of nuclear weapons and the Cold War. Despite his determination to reduce the allies' military and psychological dependence on U.S. tactical nuclear weapons in Europe, and despite his dominance of the NPG forum, McNamara did not dare bring into public debate the shared, unquestioned assumptions that underlay both the flexible response and the massive retaliation doctrines: that more nuclear weapons meant more safety, that the risks of accident and miscalculation

---

117. Bator to the President, 6 April 1967, Box 37, NSF, LBJL.
118. Justin Galen [pseudonym], "NATO's Theater Nuclear Dilemma: A New Set of Crucial Choices," *Armed Forces Journal International* 116 (January 1979): 20.
119. Jane E. Stromseth, *The Origins of Flexible Response* (New York: St. Martin's Press, 1988), 42–194; David N. Schwartz, *NATO's Nuclear Dilemmas* (Washington: Brookings, 1983), 136–92; Lawrence S. Kaplan, *NATO and the United States* (Boston: Twayne, 1988), 95–9.

with such weaponry remained negligible, that heavy armament remained the best means to head off a Soviet lunge into western Europe, and that a negotiated end to the Cold War was nearly impossible and not very desirable.[120] Instead, McNamara and his aides – like administration officials during the MLF/ANF charade– focused on trying to "pacify the allies and the military" and "get them [the Europeans] into the right mood" by continuing with the nuclear buildup begun by Eisenhower.[121] While acknowledging that "we don't need all these weapons over there," McNamara and his assistants oversaw a near-tripling to 7,200 in the number of tactical nuclear bombs in Europe.[122] Because he was focused on the war in Vietnam, McNamara further undercut flexible response by reducing U.S. conventional forces in Germany.[123] Imprisoned by his own sense of "responsible" and "reasonable" options, McNamara fed the nuclear arms buildup that undermined his preferred nuclear doctrine and, perhaps, the chances for bridge building. Years later, when the boundaries of the reasonable had become less confining, he regretfully concluded that "we should have stopped the increases."[124]

Unlike the NPG, the IIASA did not focus on the German problem. Yet IIASA sought in subtle ways to bridge east–west differences (largely by inducing the Soviets and their allies to accept Western points of view) and so create an environment in which a German settlement might eventually take place. Like the NPG, IIASA brought together – and in the process also created – experts, whose technical discussions had important political repercussions. Growing out of Acheson's recommendation for an East–West Institute of Management and Administration, IIASA was nurtured by

---

120. During the Johnson years there were accidents involving U.S. planes carrying nuclear weapons over Spain and over Greenland.

121. Stromseth, *Origins of Flexible Response*, 90–1.

122. Ibid.; Shapley, *McNamara*, 405.

123. McNamara would have pulled out more troops and air support if Johnson, Bator, McCloy, and others had not mounted a counter-campaign. The issue was complicated by Senator Mike Mansfield's congressional resolution calling for further troop withdrawals and a sharp dispute with Bonn over the level of German payments and weapons purchases to offset the balance-of-payments burden of stationing U.S. forces in the Federal Republic. In 1966-7, these matters were thrashed out in the Trilateral negotiations – an important issue but one outside the scope of this chapter. See Gregory F. Treverton, *The Dollar Drain and American Forces in Germany* (Athens: Ohio University Press, 1978); Schmidt, "Britisch-amerikanischen Beziehungen," 128–32.

124. Stromseth, *Origins of Flexible Response*, 94.

Bator, whose experience in government and as a professor at the
Massachusetts Institute of Technology had convinced him that "*all*
advanced economies – capitalist, socialist, communist – share the
problem of efficiently managing large programs and enterprises."[125] The push for IIASA reflected a widespread confidence in
the superiority and widespread applicability of the latest Western
techniques and technology, such as cybernetics, operations research, and systems analysis. Although describing the transfer of
this expertise as "technical and strictly non-political," Bator appreciated that it would expose "the rising and important class of
technocrats in Eastern Europe and the Soviet Union" to the advantages of Western-style economies.[126] Brzezinski, another advocate of bridge building, argued for packaging foreign aid in ways
"increasingly depoliticized in form, even if the ultimately underlying purpose remains political."[127] As *Fortune* magazine explained,
computer-aided systems analysis emphasized "market-like sensitivity" to changing goals and products, flexible and decentralized
decision making, and "an emphasis on information, prediction,
and persuasion, rather than on coercive or authoritarian power."[128]

Although systems analysis was a kind of planning, the governing discourse assumed that efficient, flexible production methods
had priority over the interests of workers, the party bureaucracy,
or the state. Bator told Johnson that IIASA could develop into "a
kind of neutral place in which the Russians and the Eastern Europeans will be able to draw on Western economists to give advice
on the process of how you make this complicated transition to
much more market, price system, decentralized economies."[129] Established in 1972 in Austria, with the national academies of science
of the United States, the Soviet Union, and most of eastern and
western Europe as members, IIASA had a charter that required
freedom of movement within countries wishing to host institute
functions.[130] With an American director, IIASA "succeeded ad-

125. Bator to the President, 30 November 1966, Box 4, Bator Papers.   126. Ibid.
127. Zbigniew Brzezinski, *Between Two Ages: America's Role in the Technetronic Era*
    (New York: Viking, 1970), 288.
128. Quoted in ibid., 203.
129. Author's interview with Francis M. Bator, 12 March 1993, Cambridge, Mass.
130. U.S. House of Representatives, Committee on Science, Space, and Technology, *U.S.
    Participation in the International Institute for Applied Systems Analysis (IIASA)*, 101st
    Cong., 2nd sess., 18 April 1990, 10–11, 211–24.

mirably, punching many small holes in the Iron Curtain," its leadership would later observe.[131]

Like LBJ's Great Society, the small, incremental steps in bridge building rested on two flawed assumptions: that time was on this administration's side, and that enlightened officials could shape the pace and direction of the changes they encouraged. Just as Johnson aimed to avoid a confrontation between frustrated African-Americans and angry conservative white Americans, he also hoped to avoid a clash between the aspirants for change in West Germany and eastern Europe and the hardline opponents to such progress in the Soviet Union. But in both arenas, LBJ's war in Vietnam undercut the possibilities for his reforms. The Johnson administration found that its foreign policies, however ameliorative and manipulative, could not manage the trick of fighting the communists in southeast Asia and making peace with those in Europe. Without the economic cement of expanded trade relations, the bridges between East and West were built on sand. Congress refused to budge when LBJ repeatedly asked for most-favored-nation tariff status for the Soviet Union and eastern Europe so that their goods could compete in U.S. markets. Legislators listened instead to their many constituents, who were outraged at the prospect of trading with communist nations who supplied North Vietnam with weapons to kill American boys. Rusk acknowledged that the east–west trade bill counted as another "casualty of Viet Nam."[132] As the Vietnam War illustrated, the pursuit of détente did not end Cold War assumptions and behavior.

Bridge building seemed heading for a high point with the announcement, set for August 21, 1968, that Johnson and Soviet President Alexei Kosygin would soon meet to launch negotiations toward banning anti-ballistic missiles. Moscow and Washington

131. International Institute for Applied Systems Analysis, *Annual Report* (1991), 3. Usually a Soviet citizen, the chairman of IIASA attended the twice-annual meetings while the American director was "responsible for Institute guidance." U.S. Congress, *U.S. Participation*, 11. See also David Collingridge, "Making the Impossible Possible," *Futures* 21 (April 1989): 201–3.
132. Rusk Oral History Transcript, 24, LBJL; Edward Skloot, "The Decision to Send East–West Trade Legislation to Congress, 1965–1966" in Commission on the Organization of the Government for the Conduct of Foreign Policy, *The Organization of the Government for the Conduct of Foreign Policy* (Washington: Government Printing Office, 1975), Appendices, vol. 3, 72–87; Kovrig, *Walls and Bridges,* 248–50.

had already signed the NPT and accords to demilitarize outer space and expand consular representation. In 1966–7, Czechoslovakia had established trade ties with West Germany and relations with the U.S. Export–Import Bank. In 1968, the "Prague Spring" government of Alexander Dubček abolished censorship and was seeking (as Bator had foreseen in pushing for the IIASA) a more flexible, technocratic alternative to the rigid communist party bureaucracy. But on August 20, 1968, Moscow hardliners, frightened that this liberalization could infect the rest of the Soviet bloc, crushed Prague Spring with a massive invasion by Warsaw Pact forces.[133] "The 'Cold War' is not over," Johnson sadly concluded.[134]

Although disappointed, LBJ and his advisers understood that Soviet military action disciplined not only Czechs but also those Americans and western Europeans who had pushed for military cutbacks. Kiesinger relayed the comment that "if the Russians had waited two years, nothing would have been left of NATO."[135] The invasion slashed the arguments of de Gaulle and other independent-minded western Europeans while enhancing Washington's leverage with anxious allies. After getting a Soviet pledge not to move against dissident Romania or Yugoslavia, U.S. officials discussed "how we can *use* the crisis to strengthen Western European defense and NATO" and "how we carry on our current business with the Russians and Eastern Europe."[136] Secretary of Defense Clark Clifford, who had taken over from McNamara in early March 1968, felt relieved "that the Czech crisis had saved a dangerous situation which was almost lost on the Hill," where the Mansfield Resolution and the Symington Amendment were trying to force the administration to withdraw troops from Europe.[137] After warning the

---

133. Evidently, Soviet Foreign Ministry officials who had been pursuing détente were overruled by leaders of the party, the military, and the secret police. Walter LaFeber, *America, Russia, and the Cold War, 1945–1992* (New York: McGraw-Hill, 1993), 259–60; Rusk Oral History Transcript, 28, LBJL.
134. Tom Johnson, Notes of 22 August Cabinet meeting, Box 3, Meeting Notes of W. Thomas Johnson, LBJL.
135. Memorandum of Conversation with Clifford and Kiesinger, 11 October 1968, Box 7, Clark Clifford Papers, LBJL. Claiming to be quoting an "unnamed European Prime Minister," Kiesinger may have been speaking for himself.
136. Rostow, "Order of Business for NSC Meeting on Issues Raised by the Czech Crisis," 4 September 1968, Box 3, Meeting Notes, LBJL (emphasis added).
137. "Meeting with the President, Monday, October 14, 9:40 A.M.," 16 October 1968, Box 3, Meeting Notes, LBJL.

Germans that the Soviet threat had become "exceedingly serious," Clifford pressed them to increase payments for the U.S. troops in Europe.[138] He reported back to LBJ that "we are now beginning at last to get 'some movement' out of the Germans. In the past there was talk; now there is action."[139] Recalling the MLF issue, Americans again aggravated German insecurities while trivializing them as "founded on emotionalism rather than fact."[140]

Although the Czech affair replayed some Cold War themes, this episode differed from the intense crises over Berlin or Cuba. The superpowers quickly resumed their talks on strategic missiles, with Johnson trying desperately in the last weeks of his administration to reschedule the summit with Kosygin.[141] In contrast to earlier emergencies, this crisis witnessed the widespread breakdown of the Cold War discourse that had cleanly separated the "Free World" from "Communism." Echoing de Gaulle, German press accounts of the invasion played heavily on the theme of "superpower complicity" in the division of Europe.[142] Many critics in the United States and around the world equated Moscow's invasion with Washington's war in Vietnam, a comparison that sparked angry, hurt exclamations in a cabinet meeting. Trying to sustain the Cold War discourse, Secretary of Labor Willard Wirtz explained the equation as resulting from "confusion in the people's minds."[143] When, however, Chicago police beat up protesters at the Democratic National Convention only days after the Soviet invasion, the parallel became unavoidable; placards read "Welcome to Czechago."[144] Although bridge building would resume in the 1970s under the rubric of détente, the policy yielded the Johnson administration only meager returns.

138. Memorandum of Conversation, 11 October 1968, Box 7, Clark Clifford Papers, LBJL.
139. "Meeting with the President, Monday, October 14, 9:40 A.M.," 16 October 1968, Box 3, Meeting Notes, LBJL; Memorandum of Conversation with Edouard Adorno and Paul H. Nitze, 9 December 1968, Box 7, Clifford Papers.
140. Diary Backup, Folder 4 September 1968, Box 109, LBJL.
141. See, for example, Memorandum, 7 September 1968, Box 11, Files of Walt Rostow, LBJL; Rostow to the President, 20 November 1968, ibid.; Rusk to American Embassy in Moscow, 9 December 1968, ibid.; Rostow to the President, 11 December 1968, ibid.
142. State Department Memorandum, 4 September 1968, Box 3, Meeting Notes, LBJL.
143. Tom Johnson, Notes of Cabinet Meeting, 22 August 1968, Box 3, W. Thomas Johnson Meeting Notes, LBJL.
144. George Katsiaficas, *The Imagination of the New Left: A Global Analysis of 1968* (Boston: South End Press, 1987), 62.

Bridge building and the MLF stand out as the defining policies in the Johnson administration's relations with Europe. Both policies had the larger purpose of keeping the Western alliance together, particularly by providing a creative yet controlled outlet for German aspirations. Even as the MLF plan would defuse German ambitions through the Cold War device of a weapons system aimed at the Soviet Union, bridge building would slowly defuse the Cold War itself and, not incidentally, safely channel German ambitions. Ironically, the MLF failed in part because the Cold War was winding down, whereas bridge building failed during the Johnson years because the Cold War was not yet over. Although U.S. officials talked a great deal about partnership with the allies, they were not inclined to practice it. Americans tried instead to manipulate the allies, especially the FRG, an effort that aggravated the Germans' insecurities and resentments. Although Johnson and his advisers deserve credit for thinking about an end to the Cold War, they remained imprisoned by the Cold War discourse that restricted even their most innovative policies. History has yet to judge whether LBJ was paranoid or prescient in his apprehensions about an unshackled Germany.

7

The Promise of Progress: U.S. Relations with Latin America During the Administration of Lyndon B. Johnson

JOSEPH S. TULCHIN

Perhaps in no region of the world was the death of John F. Kennedy felt more profoundly and more widely than in Latin America. The young, dashing president with the beautiful wife – the beautiful wife who spoke Spanish on behalf of her husband during their visits to countries in the region – had captured the imagination and the heart of people rich and poor, old and young, from Mexico to the Southern Cone. But it was not his youth alone that made Kennedy so attractive to Latin Americans. His style was appealing: how he carried himself, and what he said and how he said it. No president since Franklin D. Roosevelt had used language with such care and to such effect. His rhetorical flourishes, which seemed elaborate and even exaggerated to some Americans, only added to his image in Latin America as a leader.

While his call for sacrifice in his inaugural address and his challenge three months later to all in the hemisphere to join in an Alliance for Progress were greeted with enthusiasm in some quarters in the United States, they generated enormous, widespread anticipation in Latin America because of their timing. Many countries were in the process of shifting from authoritarian to civilian, democratic regimes. One observer referred to the period as "the twilight of the tyrants."[1] There even was a sense of community among the democratic governments, and a sense that they should stick together to defend themselves and to collaborate to bring down some of the remaining "tyrants." Such a feeling of solidarity among democratic regimes in the hemisphere had occurred only once before, during World War II, but it was confined to a few of the

1. Tad Szulc, *Twilight of the Tyrants* (New York: Holt, 1959).

smallest nations, led by Uruguay, while the presence of the military behind the throne in Argentina and Chile and the authoritarian nature of the Vargas regime in Brazil made appeals to democratic community sound hollow.

The Alliance generated such enthusiasm in Latin America for another reason. It seemed to be an unequivocal response to a growing chorus of voices of Latin American leaders calling for "aid, not trade" to help lift their nations from the cycle of underdevelopment. Ever since the end of World War II, Latin Americans had sniped at the United States for giving so much support to European recovery and for building a Marshall Plan while leaving Latin Americans to their own devices. George Marshall had told the Latin Americans at Bogotá in 1948 that they should expect "trade, not aid" from the United States.[2]

This did not go over well in Latin America, and through the 1950s there was increasing evidence that more and more Latin Americans blamed the United States for their problems while at the same time demanding help from the government in Washington. The culmination of the campaign was a joint declaration by the presidents of Brazil and Colombia, Juscelino Kubitschek and Alberto Lleras Camargo, calling for a joint hemispheric effort. Operación Panamericana, to stimulate the development of the region.[3] The Eisenhower government had decided at the very end of its administration to give in to the Latin Americans and set up an Inter-American Development Bank (IDB) and provide $500 million for a Social Progress Trust Fund. To some degree, then, the Kennedy administration was seizing an Eisenhower initiative and running with it.

But if the idea was not new, the way in which it was put forward certainly was, and that brings us back to personality. Kennedy was markedly different from his predecessor: almost 30 years younger, energetic, playing touch football in Hyannis Port with his extended family. The president's charisma, together with the idealism pro-

---

2. Robert Wagner, *United States Policy Toward Latin America: A Study in Domestic and International Politics* (Stanford, Calif.: Stanford University Press, 1970).
3. I have told this story previously, in greater detail, in "The United States and Latin America in the 1960s." *Journal of Interamerican Studies and World Affairs* 30, 1 (Spring 1988). See also Stephen Rabe, *Eisenhower and Latin America: The Foreign Policy of Anti-Communism* (Chapel Hill: University of North Carolina Press, 1988).

jected in the Kennedy rhetoric, seemed to define a new policy for the United States.

In his inaugural address, Kennedy promised Latin Americans an alliance in the quest for progress, "to assist free men and free governments in casting off the chains of poverty." But, he warned:

this peaceful revolution of hope cannot become the prey of hostile powers. Let all our neighbors know that we shall join them to oppose aggression or subversion in the Americas and let every other power know that this hemisphere intends to remain the master of its own house.[4]

Here was the central dilemma of the Kennedy policy in Latin America and in the Third World: how can you effect change without pitching the nations undergoing change into a condition of instability that invites subversion by communist agents? As Albert Hirschman warned in 1963: "To advocate reforms in Latin America without tolerating, accepting, and sometimes even welcoming and promoting the only kinds of pressures which have proven effective in getting reforms is to risk being accused of hypocrisy and deception."[5]

To some extent, the government expected change to be accompanied by instability. Secretary of Defense Robert McNamara noted,

Roughly 100 countries today are caught up in the difficult transition to modern societies. This sweeping surge of development has turned traditionally listless areas of the world into seething cauldrons of change. The years that lie ahead for the nations in the southern half of the globe are pregnant with violence. This would be true even if no threat of Communist subversion existed – as it clearly does.[6]

To contain this seeming contradiction, Kennedy proposed a dual approach of (1) supporting economic development and political reform while (2) providing military aid to facilitate counterinsurgency, to bring about a nonviolent revolution in Latin America. At the same time, his administration sponsored Project Camelot to identify the causes and patterns of instability in Latin America. In

4. *Public Papers of the Presidents of the United States,* 1961 (Washington: Government Printing Office, 1961), 170–75.
5. Albert Hirschman, *Journeys Toward Progress: Studies of Economic Policy-Making in Latin America* (New York: Greenwood Press, 1962), 260.
6. Michael Shafer, *Deadly Paradigms* (Princeton, N.J.: Princeton University Press, 1988), 80.

this way, he hoped to resolve the intellectual battle over the nature of development and change, as well as to avoid getting caught up in the political debate between those who considered direct military aid the best response to communist threats on the one hand, and those who considered economic development the best defense against subversion on the other – a debate that nearly had mired the Eisenhower administration in inaction.

In his inaugural address Kennedy gave voice to this dual approach[7] in describing his administration's attitude toward foreign aid:

To those peoples in the huts and villages of half the globe struggling to break the bonds of mass misery, we pledge our best efforts to help them help themselves . . . not because the Communists are doing it, not because we seek their votes, but because it is right. If a free society cannot help the many who are poor, it cannot save the few who are rich.[8]

A month after his inauguration, Kennedy summoned the representatives of the hemispheric nations in Washington to a meeting in the White House and called upon them to initiate a multilateral effort to put his new policy into effect. The hemispheric nations met in August 1961, at the beach resort of Punta Del Este (Uruguay), and declared themselves bound together in an Alliance for Progress. JFK sought to harness the power of democracy and the strength of the U.S. economy to the U.S. tradition of revolution in order to deny to communism, or the enemies of the United States more generally, the existence of misery or of social discontent as a weapon to be fielded against the United States.[9]

They drafted for the alliance a charter that enumerated all of the social, economic, and political goals of the hemisphere. It amounted to a litany of demands that Latin Americans had made over the preceding fifty years. The Alliance for Progress would attempt to improve and strengthen democratic institutions, to accelerate economic and social development, to carry out urban and rural housing programs, to encourage – in accordance with the characteristics of each country – programs of agrarian reform, to assure

7. Adolph A. Berle Jr., "Latin America: The Hidden Revolution," *Reporter*, xx, 11 (May 28, 1959), 17–20.
8. Theodore Sorenson, *Kennedy* (New York: Harper & Row, 1965), 245–8.
9. U.S. Department of State, *Bulletin*, August 1961, 1.

fair wages and satisfactory working conditions for all workers, to eliminate illiteracy and increase facilities for higher education, to press forward with programs of health and sanitation, to reform the tax laws (demanding more from those who had the most), to maintain monetary and fiscal policies that would protect the purchasing power of the people, to stimulate private enterprise in order to encourage economic development, to solve problems created by excessive price fluctuations and basic commodity exports, and finally, to accelerate the economic integration of Latin America.

John F. Kennedy committed the United States to a decisive role in the establishment and strengthening of free societies in the underdeveloped world. This commitment was an outgrowth of the global containment policy, intimately tied to national security policy, and a ringing endorsement of the dominant social science paradigms concerning the relationship between political organization and economic development. The United States called for a hemispheric commitment to spend $100 billion in a decade. Of that, 80 percent was supposed to come from Latin America. Half of the U.S. share ($20 billion) was to come from public money, half from private sources.[10]

The multilateral mechanisms to be employed were the crucial differences between the Alliance and earlier efforts. They were not part of any social science orthodoxy. They were a political response to pressure from the nations of the hemisphere and in other regions. They helped to create a sense of partnership with Latin America, one that was especially significant in the realm of intervening on behalf of good government. This was a major departure for Latin America as well, offering to join with the United States to ensure that democracy would reign in the hemisphere. No one would disagree with those goals in 1961. The idealistic rhetoric used and the nature of the goals won widespread support. It was a dream set in motion.

Unhappily, the reality was markedly different. From the very beginning the Alliance for Progress ran into difficulty. In retrospect it

10. For a convenient summary of the Alliance programs, see Jerome Levinson and Juan de Onís, *The Alliance That Lost Its Way* (Chicago: University of Chicago Press, 1970); and Inter-American Economic and Social Council, *Latin America's Development and the Alliance for Progress* (Washington: IESC, 1973). It is worth noting that population control was not one of the goals included in the charter.

is easy to see that it was an illusion, a quixotic adventure. It had so many structural deficiencies and flaws. It had obstacles on every side. To begin, it was the largest public program of aid for developing countries ever conceived by the United States, and there was no administrative machinery in existence to carry it out. The president attempted to create the machinery and ended by creating a layer of bureaucracy within the Agency for International Development (AID), then a part of the State Department. The new organization ran into competing groups within the bureaucracy at every turn.[11]

The project had opposition within the executive branch and in the Congress. It was opposed by those who feared granting to the executive the kind of long-term commitment – ten years – without which the planning function in the Alliance was unthinkable. It was opposed also by those in the United States who quite honestly felt that the promotion of social change in the language of revolution, however moderate and desirable such a revolution might be, was contrary to national security interests.

The private sector was never happy with the project. Peter Grace, chairman of the Commerce Committee for the Alliance for Progress, commented:

In its present size and form [the Alliance] cannot succeed. Investors are frightened away by the unfavorable business climate. . . . The U.S. should adopt a "carrot-and-stick approach" with grants and loans to encourage Latin Americans to enact laws more hospitable to private investment.[12]

David Rockefeller, who had been selected along with Grace by Kennedy as the most internationalist representatives of the business community, was no less critical. "In the long run," he said, "encouragement of private enterprise, local and foreign, must become the main thrust of the Alliance."[13]

The partnership features of the program made it harder to get rolling. The Latin Americans themselves were responsible for preparing "country plans" that would be submitted to the "Wise Men's Committee." That mechanism proved too weak and was replaced after the São Paulo meeting in November 1963, only a week

11. *Time*, September 20, 1963, 42–45. Veterans of the bureaucracy argue that by the end of the 1960s it was working quite well. Interview with Enrique Lerdan and Theodore Mesmer, January 11, 1994.
12. *Time*, February 15, 1963, 29.   13. Ibid.

before Kennedy's death by a new Inter-American Committee on the Alliance, known by its Spanish abbreviation, CIAP, operating through the Organization of American States (OAS). The IDB also had a role in evaluating the reform programs – in taxes, land, health, education, and public administration – that were the necessary prerequisites for distributing the aid provided under the program. It was an administrative tangle that was not straightened out until the end of the Johnson administration, by which time the U.S. aid dollars that made the whole thing work had begun to dry up.[14]

When Kennedy declared his support for democratic governments in the hemisphere and then, in his speech announcing the Alliance for Progress, linked democracy to economic and social reform and progress, he warmed the heart of every democratic politician in the hemisphere. But the Alliance for Progress was still in its infancy by November 1963. Kennedy had stumbled badly at the Bay of Pigs in 1961 and by mid-1963 had begun to have second thoughts about defending democracy against military *golpes*.

Moreover, the growing importance of counterinsurgency programs and military assistance programs designed as elements in the U.S. global strategy of containment of the Soviet threat created a powerful lobby within the U.S. government against making the defense of democracy or radical reforms the top priority of U.S. foreign policy.

In country after country, the military advisory group was poised to defend the free world while the Department of State and the executive attempted to coax reformist regimes into constructive channels of cooperation. In El Salvador and the Dominican Republic the result was civil war, in which the United States was implicated on the side of reaction, seriously undermining its claim to support democracy and social justice in the hemisphere. After 1963, when Thomas Mann became the dominant force in the formulation of U.S. policy toward Latin America, his severe doctrine of official nonintervention had the effect of giving even greater prominence or influence to the security forces operating in each country.

14. NSF, AH (Administrative History) State Department, 1–4; interview with Theodore Mesmer, CIAP staff person, December 12, 1992. For a more optimistic account of the administration, see the chapters by Lerdan and Upton in L. Ronald Scheman, ed., *The Alliance of Progress: A Retrospective* (New York: Praeger, 1988).

Despite these shortcomings – and others – some of which we see more clearly thirty years later than we did at the time, the image of Kennedy frozen in the memory of millions of Latin Americans was of a young, heroic, idealistic leader who understood them and had dedicated himself to helping them solve their problems.

Lyndon B. Johnson understood the burden of this legacy. His first official gathering in the White House was on November 27, 1963, when he addressed the ambassadors of the Latin American nations and assured them that he was committed to the ideals of the Alliance for Progress, that he would do everything in his power to expand the Alliance and make it work. He called on the ambassadors to join him in making the Alliance a living memorial to President Kennedy.[15] But to Johnson – the man of action, the pragmatist, the man who understood Congress – making the Alliance work meant ending the bureaucratic chaos that had beset the program and defining its goals in a clearer and more focused manner. The fancy ideals of social reform interested Johnson less. In fact, they made him nervous, because such social reform reminded him of the danger of the Cuban revolution. From the moment he stepped into the Oval Office, Johnson was mindful of the threat of another Cuba and the need to be vigilant against Cuban subversion of the hemisphere.[16] And this is not to imply that Johnson was more conservative than Kennedy. The Standing Group on Cuba had been created within the National Security Council in January 1963, and Kennedy was still president when it was decided that the Alliance for Progress was "not strong enough to serve as the first line of defense against subversion" in the hemisphere.[17]

On the other hand, Johnson was deeply interested in several specific goals of the Alliance and invested considerable effort in achieving them. He was concerned with infrastructure and much taken with a memorandum on the importance of infrastructure in preparing the way for economic development written by Walt W.

15. Department of State, *Bulletin*, November 27, 1963, 1.
16. NSF, Memos to the President, Box 1, v. l.
17. William Walker, "Mixing the Sweet with the Sour: Kennedy, Johnson and Latin America," in Diane B. Kunz, ed., *The Diplomacy of the Crucial Decade: American Foreign Policy in the 1960s* (New York: Columbia University Press, 1994), 29.

Rostow, who was then on the Policy Planning Board and the U.S. member of CIAP.[18] Johnson's enthusiasm for Rostow's ideas on physical and communications infrastructure was one factor in his decision to appoint Rostow to replace McGeorge Bundy as his National Security Adviser in 1965, and both Rostow and Johnson worked with enthusiasm to push these specific projects through the clumsy, slow bureaucracy of AID.

During the transition period, Johnson was careful to keep Kennedy's appointments and to give public support to them and their work. In Latin American policy, however, he made one of the most fateful personnel moves of his administration – one that, more than any other single decision, shifted the delicate balance among contending forces within the administration in discussion of Latin American affairs. He called his fellow Texan Thomas Mann, a senior foreign service officer with years of experience in Latin America, and asked him to leave his post as ambassador to Mexico and return to Washington to take over all aspects of U.S. policy toward Latin America.

At the risk of caricaturing complex historical processes, it is impossible to avoid the impression that Thomas Mann, together with the war in Vietnam, did more than anything or anyone else to shape Johnson's policy toward Latin America. Even at the time of his appointment, Mann was seen as a "pragmatist."[19] In a *U.S. News and World Report* article, Mann gave a good sense of his thinking on Latin American policy.

LBJ announced earlier this month, "I want Mr. Mann to be the one man in government to co-ordinate the policies of this Hemisphere." Mann is convinced that U.S. prestige in Latin America can never be high until the U.S. has shown it can cope with Cuba, which he called a "cancer" in the Hemisphere. "We need to isolate Cuba," he said. Mann believes the idea of the Alliance is sound but that aid can only be a catalyst for development. Public investment alone would be insufficient; we must create a healthy atmosphere for private investment. With reference to the Alliance for Progress, he said, "Too much was promised for too short a time." The problem is not lack of money, but the lack of proper atmosphere for de-

18. Rostow to the President, May 27, 1966, NSF, Memos to the President, Box 8, v. 5.
19. *Time*, January 31, 1964, 15–18.

velopment. Private investment has been frightened by nationalizations. The creation of a favorable atmosphere to produce a big influx of private capital is one of Mann's main objectives.[20]

The selection of Mann, which apparently Johnson decided soon after returning to Washington from Dallas, illustrates the delicacy of the transition period. At no time was the splendid burden of the presidency more lonely. Not only did Johnson have to step in and begin to govern immediately, but he had to do so surrounded by and dependent upon Kennedy's team of advisers. Gradually, he began to bring in people with whom he felt comfortable, but in replacing Kennedy people he was careful neither to give the public impression that he was making sweeping changes nor to offend the individuals involved, and he worked well with some Kennedy appointees, like Bundy and Lincoln Gordon.

At the same time that he appointed Mann, Johnson acted to shore up private-sector support for the Alliance, the lack of which was one of its greatest weaknesses in the eyes of the public. He created a Business Group for Latin America, chaired by David Rockefeller, which was to "meet with Government officials from time to time to consider matters of common interest relating to Latin America. It also hope[d] to work with similar organizations of businessmen in Latin America."[21]

In the area of foreign affairs, not one of his strengths, Johnson was in constant touch with and most heavily dependent upon McGeorge Bundy. For his part, Bundy was careful to preserve his relationship with the president. His numerous memoranda were respectful and detailed, and they always provided the president with options from which to choose. In the case of Mann's appointment, Bundy reminded the president that bringing in Mann as undersecretary for Latin American affairs would embarrass Ed Martin, the incumbent assistant secretary of state, and asked Johnson to remember Martin's "energetic and devoted work." Bundy thought a good solution might be to send Martin to "one of the agreeable smaller West European embassies."[22]

20. *U.S. News and World Report,* December 30, 1963, 32.
21. Office of the White House Press Secretary, January 31, 1964, NSF, Memos to the President, Box 1.
22. Bundy to the President, December 9, 1963, NSF, Memos to the President, Box 1, doc. 58.

Eventually, Mann's appointment pushed out several Kennedy people, all of them advocates of a policy of supporting democracy and of linking democracy at one and the same time to recognition of new governments and development aid. The Kennedy people who remained, like Bundy, were all of the realist or pragmatist school that respected power and security more than anything else and who accepted or even applauded Mann's insistence on sacrificing support for democracy to other priorities in the formulation of U.S. policy in specific cases or toward specific countries. Ironically, it was a Johnson confidant, Bill Moyers, who suggested that Mann might tone down his speech justifying the new policy. While indicating that "I admire Tom for trying to introduce *reason* into the debate on The U.S. and Representative Democracy in Latin America," he thought he was using unnecessarily strong language.[23]

Those who left the government seemed to take with them the determination to fight in the decision-making process to keep democracy and reform high on the list of U.S. policy priorities. Three men who had a great deal to do with Latin American policy under Kennedy and who left soon or lost visibility under Johnson were Arthur M. Schlesinger Jr., Richard Goodwin, and Ralph Dungan. Dungan, especially, remained hostile to Mann for years and blamed him for what he considered the dramatic changes in policy after Kennedy's death.[24] Bundy's comments on Dungan's departure make it clear how difficult the relationship between Mann and Dungan had become. And, although Bundy took Mann's side, he pushed Johnson to give Dungan an embassy in Latin America.[25] Johnson named Dungan ambassador to Chile.

In picking Dungan for the embassy in Santiago, Bundy sent a memo to Johnson that helps to make clear the delicate mix of fac-

---

23. Moyers to Bundy, June 4, 1964, NSF, Memos to the President, Box 1, Vol. 1.
24. Ralph Dungan, Oral History, Lyndon Baines Johnson Library (hereafter LBJL), p. 3. John Plank, senior analyst in INR, left the Department of State to go the Brookings Institution. He had been "in the dumps" after Kennedy's death, because as one NSC staffer reported, "he was afraid our Latin American policy would just not be the same." G. Chase to Bundy, April 30, 1964, NSF, CO, Box 1. Schlesinger twenty-five years later was more categorical. He said, "The *Alianza* came to an end with Kennedy's death," and he implied that the blame lay with Johnson and his top Latin American adviser, Mann. See Schlesinger chapter in Scheman, ed., *The Alliance for Progress*.
25. Bundy to the President, September 20, 1964, NSF, Memos to the President, Box 1.

tors that had gone into Kennedy's Latin American policy and to explain how the addition of a strong-willed, conservative person like Thomas Mann could make such a significant difference in the balance among those factors. It is as close to an explicit acknowledgment of Mann's role within the policymaking apparatus as we have.

Tom Mann will do a very good job on protecting our interests, but he is a little insensitive to the Chilean need for reform. So Dean Rusk and I both believe that a progressive and imaginative Ambassador will be needed as a counterweight, and that Dungan would be an excellent choice. This situation is much like that in Panama, where [Jack Hood] Vaughn is doing an excellent job of producing new ideas, while Tom Mann keeps an eye on the brakes.

Ralph Dungan is a liberal Catholic with strong convictions on the need for progressive policies. He is also a realist.

Ralph is not absolutely ideal for this job – it would be better if he had some business reputation and better also if he spoke Spanish. . . . But against any presently available businessman, Ralph has the great advantages of prestige in your Administration, proven sympathy for the progressive anti-Communist effort in Latin America, and a close personal relationship with Frei.[26]

Earlier, in March, Bundy had told Mann that the president "strongly agrees that you should make important public statements at an early date on the major general problems of our policy in Latin America." He went on to say that the president wants to see drafts of the statements so that there is coordination in the statements and so that it is plain "that they have his personal backing."[27] In June, Mann delivered through Jack Valenti a report to the president on "Progress Made in Latin America" since his appointment: "growing alertness to the threat of subversion; increased capabilities of internal security; and forward movement under the Alliance for Progress." Democracy was not even mentioned.[28]

At the same time, it is important to note that many competent observers, Kennedy appointees and Johnson appointees alike, insisted at the time and in numerous interviews after the fact that the administrations' Latin American policies had been essentially the same. Bundy himself was an important element of continuity between the two administrations, and he was in complete agreement

26. Ibid.   27. Bundy to Mann, March 25, 1964, NSF, CO, Box 1.
28. Mann to Valenti, June 17, 1964, NSF, Memos to the President, Box 7.

with Mann on the relative weights of democracy, stability, security, and development.

The comments about Mann in the oral histories deposited by Johnson appointees in the Johnson Library may exaggerate his conservatism and his impact on policy, but they certainly reflect the hostility felt by people who believed that they had "lost" in the policy debates that followed Kennedy's death.[29] Lincoln Gordon felt that Mann represented a "shift in policy," although Gordon focused on the fact that Mann gave the Alliance for Progress less attention than had his predecessor, Ed Martin. Gordon said, "Mann always felt that [the Alliance] was greatly oversold in rhetoric and to some extent a diversion from the more earthly problems."[30]

As Kennedy enjoyed brio in debate, Johnson preferred the weighty argument of politics – who counted, and what mattered? What policy would produce results; which option could he sell in Congress? In foreign affairs, except for Vietnam, Cuba, and the Dominican Republic, he insisted that his advisers convince him to act. Unless it was absolutely necessary, he preferred a cautious approach.

Johnson took piles and piles of papers with him each night to his private quarters and asked that every file carry a summary memorandum by the National Security Adviser in which the president's decision options were specified. He spent most of each day meeting with people. He was a master networker and dealt with people, all sorts of people, on instinct, in his down-home, folksy manner. But he was profoundly uncomfortable with foreigners and demanded that his staff justify every visit with a foreign dignitary.[31] Bundy chided him on his unwillingness to see foreign visitors.[32]

29. For example, see John Bartlow Martin, David Bell, George Ball, Ralph Dungan, and Lincoln Gordon, all Oral History, LBJL.
30. Lincoln Gordon, Oral History, LBJL, 14. Contemporary observers thought Gordon as assistant secretary of state "tends to follow the same line. . . . Besides, Gordon and other Washington officials argue that any question of a policy switch is really a matter of words and style rather than substance. But style moves Latins more than it does pragmatic North Americans." In Juan Cameron, "Threatening Weather in South America," *Fortune,* October 1969, 128.
31. Bundy to the President, February 11, 1964, NSF, Memos to the President, Box 1. Bundy asked for two hours a week of visits and settled for one hour. He also asked that all foreign visitors be coordinated through his office, which was done, at least for a short while.
32. Bundy to the President, May 14, 1964, ibid. On the accompanying list, the only Latin American Johnson had seen one on one – aside from a ceremonial fifteen-minute conversation with the new chair of the Inter-American Committee on the Alliance for Progress, Carlos Sanz de Santamaria – was Mexican President Lopez Mateos.

I get such a needle from you on this subject that I thought you might be interested in records provided to me from the Appointment Office with respect to all the foreigners for whose visits I am responsible over the 12-week period from February 11 to May 5 [1964].

The official records show that in that 12-week period you averaged 32 minutes a week with people who are my fault. . . . So you see how extraordinarily restrained we have been.

What this means, of course, is that under the terms of our treaty you may be hit at any moment by five hours and 33 minutes of accumulated overdue visitors from nearly everywhere. But I am much too kind for that, and the truth is that we can keep up our good work in limiting your foreign callers. . . .

Johnson warmed up a bit in 1965 and 1966, but he always was more comfortable on his ranch and would ask Bundy or Rostow that meetings they asked him to hold be held in Texas.[33] By 1967, as he became increasingly obsessed with Vietnam, he withdrew further and avoided seeing foreign visitors whenever he could.[34]

He was most at ease with people he trusted, and he trusted people he felt he understood. He trusted Mann. He thought Mann understood Latin America – as he, a Texan felt he understood Latin America better than other staff in the White House. Richard Goodwin, after all, the primary drafter of Kennedy's Alliance for Progress speech, had never been in Latin America. Johnson's personal experience as a teacher of young Mexican-Americans had left him with the sense that he understood Mexicans and, by extension, all Latin Americans, and that he owed the poor of Latin America a special obligation. That obligation was only increased by the legacy that Kennedy had left him.[35]

He differed markedly from Kennedy also in his management style. Where Kennedy was dynamic and charismatic and operated with a high degree of rhetorical flourish, Lyndon B. Johnson was neither of those things. His political strength always had been quiet manipulation of groups, the brilliant orchestration of political

33. Johnson felt most at home on his ranch entertaining Mexicans. Antonio Carrillo Flores, Mexican foreign minister, wrote on May 12, 1966, to thank Johnson for a lovely few days at the ranch. He recognized "the terrible solitude of the presidency." NSF, Memos to the President, Box 7.
34. On one occasion, he scribbled on Rostow's memo recommending that he see a visitor, "Do I have to?" NSF, Memos to the President, Rostow to the President, March 21, 1967, Box 7.
35. NSF, Administrative Histories, Department of State, Latin America, 1.

forces, particularly in the Congress. Johnson had little interest in the sweeping reforms that underlay the Alliance for Progress and gradually removed the warriors most identified with Kennedy in the quixotic episode of drafting the Alliance. He preferred to work with professionals who adopted a more formal, cautious approach to the region, including several Kennedy appointees, such as Lincoln Gordon. Thereafter, he left policymaking to those advisers, much as Eisenhower had. He never attempted to achieve the same command of detail as he did on domestic issues, nor did he evidence the same intellectual interest that Kennedy had in the foreign policy issues themselves.

Sometimes, however, Johnson did get involved with detailed decisions. David Bell of AID complained that he butted in all the time, where Kennedy never would have done so. Bell reported that Johnson actually followed the detailed negotiations of loans under the Alliance for Progress.[36] This appears to be an exaggeration by a loyal but frustrated administrator. George Ball said of Johnson during the Dominican crisis that he "became the Dominican desk officer."[37]

Johnson and his staff were sensitive to comments in the press about the transition, and they went to great lengths to plant stories emphasizing the continuity of policy and personnel.[38] Bundy, while addressing the National Press Association, became quite irritated by repeated questions aimed at documenting changes in foreign policy and, especially, changes in attitudes toward foreign policy. But his most passionate response was to a question suggesting that Johnson did not understand foreign affairs:

But if you mean to suggest that this is not a man who understands the world, or if above all you meant to suggest that the President is not aware of the degree to which he and the other holder of strategic power in the nuclear age have a shared responsibility, then I would say that is not so. The thing that most impressed me in the immediate process of the first few days, was the rapidity with which the President [communicated] with Mikoyan.[39]

36. David Bell, Oral History, LBJL, 4.   37. George Ball, Oral History, LBJL, 6.
38. Bromly Smith to the President, "Suggested points to be made to Roscoe Drummond," January 31, 1964, NSF, Memos to the President, Box 1.
39. The text of Bundy's talk is in his memo to the President, March 10, 1964, Memos to the President, Box 1, Vol. 2.

The press continued to be a source of concern to Johnson throughout his presidency. When word of an appointment was leaked to the press, Johnson frequently would refuse to make it, even if that meant losing the best-qualified person for the job. He would at the very least delay announcing something if he felt that the press was taking advantage of him or someone in his administration.[40] Leaks to the press were an obsession from his first days in the White House.[41]

On the other hand, he, Bundy, and Rostow went to great lengths to get their version of the story to selected journalists. On one occasion, Bundy reported to Johnson that "we have had indications that the Soviets would find it easier to keep [Fidel] Castro under some control if you were to reaffirm our intention not to launch an invasion of Cuba." So they planted a question to which Johnson could give an appropriate answer at his next press conference.[42] When recommending Dungan for the embassy in Chile, Bundy suggested, "If you do designate Dungan, I think we can get cordial and responsive notices from the [New York] *Times* and the [Washington] *Post,* and also from other less doctrinaire observers of the Latin American scene."[43] Johnson, Bundy, and, later, Rostow, were easily irritated by what they considered "mistakes" by correspondents for the *New York Times* or *Washington Post.* Rostow took it upon himself to chastise Tom Wicker of the *Times* for "sloppy" citation of sources, but when Wicker asked Rostow for an interview to clear up some things, Rostow told him that he was trying to minimize the time he spent with the press. However, he told Johnson that he would see Wicker if Bill Moyers "thought it helpful."[44]

Walter Lippmann and Drew Pearson were two of their favorite journalists, but, because neither cared much about Latin America, there were few opportunities to get the administration's policy toward the region into print, except at moments of crisis. That dearth of opportunity would be a source of concern to Johnson until the very end of his term. As the years went by, and the public and Congress turned against him because of Vietnam or because of U.S. in-

40. Lincoln Gordon, Oral History, LBJL, 5.
41. Bundy to the President January 6, 1964, Memos to the President, Box 1, Vol. 1.
42. Bundy to the President, June 2, 1964, Memos to the President, Box 2.
43. Bundy to the President, September 20, 1964, Memos to the President, Box 1.
44. Rostow to the President, April 27, 1966, Memos to the President, Box 7.

tervention in the Dominican Republic, he became more and more anxious to get people to pay attention to the "real" accomplishments in the hemisphere, the concrete accomplishments he attributed to the Alliance for Progress.[45]

Johnson wanted Mann to control the various facets of Latin American policy so that he might end the bureaucratic disorder that had plagued the policy since Kennedy's inauguration. As Kennedy had before him, he ordered a shift in the reporting lines dealing with Latin America, but Johnson backed up the administrative order by vesting real power in his personal representative for Latin America, Thomas Mann. Even so, the State Department was hard to change. The department's official history of the Alliance admits rather meekly that the changes had little effect and that the Alliance had rough going in part at least because of administrative difficulties in Washington.[46] This suggests that Johnson actually wanted to get something done in Latin America. He authorized Mann to coordinate Latin American policy, hoping to make the Alliance work, but then, in a decision that would typify his administration's experience in Latin America, he immediately sent him to Panama to solve the crisis there.

No matter how much time and energy Johnson and his advisers might devote over the succeeding four years to the Alliance for Progress or to careful and considered reflection on how the U.S. might improve its relations with Latin America, U.S. policy was driven by spasmodic reactions to crises in the Caribbean Basin, long referred to as the Caribbean Danger Zone and by an overpowering fear that instability would lead to "another Cuba" in the hemisphere. That fear and that style of crisis management through damage control would slowly, inexorably reduce the options Johnson was willing to consider in U.S. relations with the hemisphere. His posture toward the region became increasingly defensive during his administration. Of course, his growing commitment to Vietnam had a great deal to do with the shift in his priorities, but

45. On concern for "getting the story out," see G. Chase to Bundy, July 27, 1964, NSF, CO, Box 2; Bob Sayre to Bundy, August 18, 1964, ibid., reporting on Mann's response to Johnson's request for a two-month "action plan" to communicate with the press. Later, Johnson showed similar concern in trying to explain the 1967 Latin American Summit Meeting; see Johnson to Rostow, October 14, 1967, NSF, CO, Latin America, Box 3, Vol. 6.
46. NSF, AH, Chapter 6, B. "The Alliance for Progress," 1–4 and 10–11.

dealing with the crises of instability in the hemisphere might have pushed him in the same direction even had Vietnam not existed. Panama was the first crisis he faced as president.

In his visit to Washington in 1962, President Roberto Chiari of Panama had called on the Kennedy administration to renegotiate the treaties that gave the United States virtually sovereign status in the Canal Zone. Kennedy said that he could not do so until the United States had completed feasibility studies for an alternative route across the isthmus, but he agreed to create a bilateral commission to consider differences between the two nations and admitted privately that it might be necessary to revise the treaties before the feasibility studies were completed.[47] As a result of those conversations, the United States agreed to have the U.S. and Panamanian flags fly together at certain points in the Canal Zone, adopting "a policy that would not [be] hung up on formalisms of sovereignty, but concentrate on meeting the legitimate Panama complaints while maintaining . . . our military activities in the Zone."[48] In January 1964, a confrontation occurred between Panamanian nationals and residents of the Canal Zone over the flying of the Panamanian flag. Violence erupted, and more than twenty people were killed.

Virtually as soon as he arrived in Washington, President Johnson asked Mann to head a "powerful" delegation to Panama to attempt to resolve the "explosive situation." Embassy staff were being evacuated, classified documents and code machines were being destroyed, while "left wing agitators [were] going all out to stir further violence."[49] Chiari demanded that the United States renegotiate the treaties. Johnson refused. He instructed Mann to take the position that the United States would not negotiate under pressure but that it was prepared to discuss all issues with the Panamanian government. It is worth noting that in an earlier discussion of the issue in the White House, McGeorge Bundy had noted that the United States undoubtedly would have to make some concessions to Panama and that gestures to enhance Panama's sovereignty and satisfy its national pride would not undermine the U.S.

47. NSC Memorandum #152, April 30, 1962, NSF, NSAMS, Box 1.
48. NSC Memorandum #164, June 15, 1962, NSF, NSAMS, Box 1.
49. Bundy to the President, January 10, 1964, Memos to the President, Box 1, Vol. 1.

presence in the Canal Zone. That same memorandum indicated that it might be necessary to begin looking for alternatives to the canal. However, when the crisis erupted, Bundy took as hard a line as anyone and never wavered. When former Supreme Court Justice Felix Frankfurter wrote to Johnson to encourage him to renegotiate the treaties, quoting Edmund Burke, "Not the least of the arts of statesmanship is gracefully to grant what eventually cannot be withheld," Bundy added, "I am sure that this thought is not a stranger to you, but I am equally sure that, as I told [columnist] Drew Pearson yesterday, we cannot let our foreign policy be governed by Molotov cocktails."[50]

Later in the month, Mike Mansfield, an old Johnson colleague in the Senate, wrote a long memorandum urging the president to negotiate the minor differences that separated the two countries. Remember, he told Johnson, local problems created the pressure for social change, which "comes primarily from the inside." Then, alluding to the central debate of Latin American policy during the Cold War, he added, "Don't credit Castro for the problems; they existed before Castro and will continue to exist as long as the canal is there."[51]

Bundy saw no reason to give in to the Panamanians unless domestic U.S. politics compelled the administration to do so. He agreed with Secretary of State Dean Rusk in February 1964 that it "would be good to get Panama off the stage for the present, if we can do so without retreat." Bundy had always felt that they could give in on minor issues "without giving way on gut issues" such as the perpetuity clause or "our own ultimate responsibility for the security and effectiveness of the Canal." And, he went on,

Your choice of Vaughn as your prospective Ambassador shows your own readiness to pick a man who has much more basic sympathy for the Panamanians than for the conservative Americans in the Canal Zone (Almost too much so, in my judgment).[52]

By November 1964, the Office of the Legal Adviser in the Department of State had prepared a draft agreement that provided for ab-

50. Bundy to the President, January 17, 1964, Memos to the President, Box 1, Vol. 1.
51. Mansfield to Johnson, Jan. 31, 1964, NSF, Memos to the President, Box 1, Vol. 1. Bundy covered the letter with a memo suggesting that "Except for the difference in emphasis between you and him, much of Mansfield's memo on Panama makes good sense."
52. Bundy to the President, February 25, 1964, Memos to the President, Box 1.

rogation of existing treaties, negotiation of new ones that explicitly recognized Panamanian sovereignty and that had a termination date, and that while effectively eliminating the Canal Zone, provided for safeguarding the lives and interests of its residents. Negotiations dragged on into 1967 and treaties were actually completed, when they were suspended because of the onset of the Panamanian presidential election campaign.[53] They were not resumed until 1977, during the presidency of Jimmy Carter.

That experience and his own ideas about Latin America led Mann to request permission as early as February 1964 to declare or clarify U.S. policy. On March 18, 1964, he announced his interpretation of U.S. policy, immediately known as the Mann Doctrine, which downplayed democracy and democratic government in Latin America. Stability would be the top priority in order to protect the hemisphere from subversion.[54]

That would be the central theme of the Johnson administration's policy, a theme that would dominate and obscure from public view the sincere and energetic efforts to accomplish something under the rubric of the Alliance for Progress. The consistently hard, even harsh response to crises in the region dominated the headlines and occupied the president's time. That consistent response in search of stability to prevent communist incursions (which, on occasion, pushed the quest for democracy or social change out of the policy spotlight) blended into the much more dominant theme of Vietnam and made it hard for observers at the time – or since – to appreciate anything else that was accomplished by the administration in the hemisphere. In retrospect, we can see that the foundations were laid during the Johnson administration for the successful operation of the Inter-American Development Bank, that the development process was legitimized during his government, and that a great deal of valuable work was done to ameliorate the conditions of underdevelopment because of Johnson's policies. The detailed history of this good work has yet to be written.[55]

53. LBJL, NSF, NSC History, Box 1, "Panama."
54. *Time*, March 27, 1964, p. 29; and May 15, 1964, p. 48; U.S. Department of State, *Bulletin*, April 1964, 1.
55. Interviews with Theodore Mesmer, December 12, 1992, and with Enrique Lerdan and Mesmer, January 11, 1994. Mesmer and Lerdan make two points in convincing fashion. First, during the Johnson years much solid, effective work was done on Latin American

It was not that democracy disappeared from the discussions of policy; it simply did not enjoy the same priority it had earlier. Aside from the early statements by Mann and Bundy's private memos indicating his approval of the shift in priorities, there is no evidence that a systematic reevaluation of policy had occurred. In commenting to Bundy on a story in the press concerning the policy change represented by Mann's appointment, Gilbert Chase, the Latin Americanist on Bundy's staff, remarked, "I assume that there is, in fact, no change in our policy and that we are still opposed to dictatorships in Latin America (at least publicly and at least in places where we have leverage)."[56]

Of course there *had* been a change in policy, a subtle but significant one. Democracy was no longer the goal of importance; it was part of the pattern of relations that the United States would seek. At the end of 1964, Bundy himself recommended that Johnson take a trip to Brasilia in 1965 to meet with presidents of several South American countries who are "a more appetizing group right now than they have been any time in recent years." The current government of Brazil, while military, "is also progressive."[57]

Rostow seems to have put a higher value on democracy than Bundy. Two years later, in reporting to the president that Julio César Mendez Montenegro, head of the "moderate, left-of-center Revolutionary Party," had won the recent Guatemalan elections, he fairly gushed.

The assumption of power by Mendez will represent an impressive victory for democracy in this hemisphere. The formula for civilian, reform-minded presidents with the political knack for reaching practical working relationships with the military and other conservative elements is one which I hope will continue to prosper in this hemisphere. It is a formula for short-term political stability which allows the government to concentrate on development and reform.[58]

---

development through the machinery of the Alliance; and, second, that much good can be done for the people of Latin America through economic development even in conditions of imperfect political democracy. Lincoln Gordon Oral History, LBJL 35; NSF, AH, Department of State, Alliance for Progress, 22–6. See also Scheman, ed. *The Alliance for Progress.*

56. Chase to Bundy, March 16, 1964, NSF, CO, Box 1.
57. Bundy to the President, December 26, 1964, NSF, Memos to the President, Box 2.
58. Rostow to the President, April 5, 1966, Memos to the President, Box 7.

Later that same year, he advised the president against receiving Nicaraguan President René Schick because, although Nicaragua had "been good" on Vietnam and the Dominican Republic, it "does not enjoy a democratic image in the hemisphere. . . . You will get no domestic benefit from receiving him."[59] That same week he urged the president to write to Argentine President Arturo Illia on a minor matter because "President Illia is passing through another season of military plotting against him and a favorable response from you now will bolster his position. . . . The importance of the conference and the Argentine domestic angle persuade me that Secretary [of Education John W.] Gardner should go for a few days."[60]

The point is that democracy, as a policy objective in the region, had to compete with other policy objectives, and that in the bureaucratic discussions that accompanied the response to specific episodes, some members of the president's Latin American team took one position and others took a different position with regard to the relative weight of different goals. At no time, except in moments of great crisis, such as the disturbance in the Dominican Republic, did support for democracy become submerged as a policy goal under the weight of arguments referring to communist subversion and the fear of instability.

Lincoln Gordon, who served as Assistant Secretary of State for Inter-American Affairs from February 1966 to June 1967, insists that support for democracy was constant.[61]

During my sixteen months as Assistant Secretary, there was only one coup – the overthrow of [Arturo] Illia in Argentina. Ed Martin as Ambassador, Senator [Jacob] Javits, in a highly publicized Buenos Aires speech, and I in several actions and pronouncements all made clear our support for preserving Argentine democracy (such as it was at the time), but we had no effective leverage with the Argentine military. In Guatemala, where we did have leverage, Ambassador [John Gordon] Mein was instructed in vigorous terms to warn the military to desist from much-discussed action against Mendez Montenegro; that pro-democratic intervention was successful. We heaped assistance on [Eduardo] Frei in Chile, [Fernando] Belaunde [Terry] in Peru, and Carlos Lleras Resptrepo

59. Bundy to the President, June 2, 1966; Memos to the President, Box 8.
60. Rostow to the President, June 8, 1966, Memos to the President, Box 8.
61. Gordon to the author, July 27, 1993.

in Colombia. In Peru, with support from Johnson and Dean Rusk, I reversed Tom Mann's policy against suspending aid until any threat of oil nationalization was withdrawn. And, in the Dominican Republic, we held the ring for a heavily observed free and fair election in June 1966, when [Joaquin] Balaguer prevailed over [Juan] Bosch. [Ellsworth Bunker and I met] in the White House ten days or so before the election in which LBJ acknowledged that we would have to accept a Bosch victory if the electorate so decided.

With regard to the Brazilian coup, Gordon points out,

A fair review of all the pertinent documents will show that during the last quarter of 1963 I became increasingly concerned about indications that [João] Goulart was desirous of mounting a [Getulio] Vargas-like coup that would establish him as a populist dictator (what I then christened as "supervision" or "overmining"). But I also favored actions to help hold things together under the 1946 constitution until the 1965 presidential elections, which I expected [Juscelino] Kubitschek (a dedicated democrat) to win. I stated repeatedly that that would be the best possible outcome. The actions included relief to the balance of payments through debt rescheduling and the maintenance of a substantial aid program (not limited to anti-Goulart state governors).

After March 13, 1964, and especially through his support for the mutinous navy petty officers, Goulart foreclosed the democratic option. It then became a choice between his coup or a military coup. Between the two, we preferred the latter, partly because of my concern that a successful Goulart coup might quickly be followed by a more radical – and very likely communist-led – coup against Goulart . . . and partly because I believed (mistakenly, as things turned out) that the military would restore democracy after a relatively short period of purging and constitutional reform.

The crisis management of Latin American policy pushed Mann from Panama to Brazil the very same year and then, in 1965, to the defining episode of the administration, the intervention in the Dominican Republic.[62] The problem was that in dealing with crises of

---

62. On the Dominican Republic episode, see John Bartlow Martin, *Overtaken by Events* (New York: Doubleday, 1966); Abraham F. Lowenthal, *The Dominican Intervention* (Cambridge, Mass.: Harvard University Press, 1972). On the Brazilian coup, see Thomas E. Skidmore, see *Politics in Brazil*, 3rd ed. (New York: Oxford University Press, 1988); Jan Knippers Black, *United States Penetration of Brazil* (Philadelphia: University of Pennsylvania Press, 1977); and Ruth Leacock, *Requiem for Revolution: The United States and Brazil, 1961–1969* (Kent, Ohio: Kent State University Press, 1990). Gordon

stability, the administration could focus only on the threat of communist advantage and allowed democracy and development to slip from view. And, yet, when there was no crisis to manage, it was impossible to gain the president's attention and impossible, therefore, to make development and democracy such high priorities that they would push aside political difficulties in the Congress or convince members of the cabinet to subordinate trade or fiscal policy to the needs of the Alliance for Progress or the interests of one or more countries in Latin America.

The United States had been deeply involved in the politics of the Dominican Republic ever since 1904, when a breakdown in public order had led the government to suspend payments on its foreign debt, which suspension had prompted European bondholders to appeal to their respective governments for help in collecting their bond payments. President Theodore Roosevelt decided that it was not in the nation's interests to allow Europeans to intervene in the Caribbean basin, but, as it was imperative to uphold the rules of "civilized nations," the United States would have to become the policeman of the Caribbean if it did not want the Europeans to intervene. The U.S. government had dispatched marines to the Dominican Republic in 1905 to enforce the dictates of civilian advisers attempting to restore public order and fiscal responsibility in the republic. Marines were sent back in 1916 and remained until 1924, when their work was considered done and democracy established. Of course, the result of this exporting of democracy was the dictatorship of Rafael L. Trujillo, who ruled the country until he was gunned down by a group of opponents in 1961.[63] Trujillo, with Anastasio Somoza in Nicaragua and Fulgencio Batista in Cuba, had been one of the worst dictators in Latin America, and support of his regime by the

answered Leacock in a review article in the *Journal of Latin American Studies* (December 1990). In a separate communication to me (December 29, 1993), Enrique Lerdan, who was associated with the CIAP at the time, points out that most governments in Latin America at the time were extremely nervous about Goulart and that U.S. support for the coup actually won us some friends in the region.

63. The history of U.S. relations with the Dominican Republic is told in Sumner Welles, *Naboth's Vineyard: The Dominican Republic 1844–1924* (2 vols., New York: Payson and Starke, 1928); Joseph S. Tulchin, *The Aftermath of War* (New York: New York University Press, 1971); George P. Atkins and Larman C. Wilson, *The United States and Trujillo* (New Brunswick, N.J.: Rutgers University Press, 1973).

U.S. government offended democrats throughout the hemisphere. Kennedy let it be known that he was not happy with Trujillo, and Richard Goodwin developed a close relationship with several social democratic labor leaders who supported a budding democracy movement in the Dominican Republic. When, on May 31, 1961, Trujillo was gunned down, the United States was rid of an embarrassment. The story of CIA involvement in the assassination has been told in many versions but is no longer disputed.[64]

The United States used warships stationed off the coast to prevent the return to power of members of Trujillo's family, who held a sizable portion of the Dominican economy and had close ties with elements of the military. The Dominican military exercised authority in the country until elections in December 1962 – the first free elections in more than thirty years, which were won by one of the region's most prominent social democrats, Juan Bosch. Bosch, as it turned out, was not an effective ruler, and factional disputes soon undermined his government. To make matters worse, he blamed his political troubles on U.S. support of his military critics, became hostile toward the United States, and made frequent public statements sympathetic toward the Castro regime in Cuba. Kennedy and his advisers were more concerned about the threat of instability in the country than by Bosch's radicalism or the new constitution that he promulgated shortly after taking office. But in any event they were not upset when the military ousted him in September 1963, this ouster a direct result of Bosch's efforts to force the military to reduce its role in politics, and they made it clear that they would not welcome Bosch's return to power.

Bosch continued to rail against the United States from his exile and called on his supporters to remain loyal to him. Jealousies among the military leaders and the absence of any strong civilian alternatives to Bosch made the transition back to civilian rule very complicated. A triumvirate turned power over to Donald Reid Cabral, who tried to restore order and impose an economic austerity plan. Things seemed to be under control and new elections

64. See, for example, Thomas Powers, *The Man Who Kept the Secrets: Richard Helms and the CIA* (New York: Pocket Books, 1981), pp. 184–6; Darrell Garwood, *Under Cover: Thirty-Five Years of CIA Deception* (New York: Grove Press, 1985), pp. 104–17; William Colby, *Honorable Men: My Life in the CIA* (New York: Simon and Schuster, 1978), 340, 428.

not far off when, on April 24, 1965, a faction of the military calling itself "constitutionalists" tried to seize power in order to restore Bosch to the presidency. In the next few days, Johnson made a series of decisions that led, on April 28, to the landing of 500 Marines, followed within a week by 23,000 more. The reason given at first for landing U.S. troops was the need to protect American citizens. By the second day, as the troop buildup continued, the principal reason for the U.S. intervention was stated to be the restoration of public order and ending the civil strife. Today, we can see that from the very beginning, the central objective of U.S. policy was to prevent "another Cuba," and that the widespread distrust for Bosch set off the series of responses to the uprising on his behalf in order to prevent his return to power and, what proved to be much more difficult than Johnson had anticipated, to provide for a transition to civilian rule that would effectively eliminate Bosch from the running. All along Johnson exaggerated the danger to U.S. lives.[65] He used the gambit of Communist subversion in an attempt to win support in the court of U.S. domestic public opinion, but he succeeded only in confusing many people who would have been happy to support him.

In the end, he was disgusted with what he saw as the "venality" of Dominican politicians and with the corruption and deceit of the military leaders. Once it became clear that Bosch was not going to return to power, Johnson lost interest in the Dominican Republic and instructed his foreign policy people to get the OAS involved as a cover for the U.S. intervention and to get U.S. troops out as fast as they could.

After the Dominican crisis, relations with Latin America became a case of damage control, of trying to salvage something from the ashes of the dream. Mann left the government early in 1967 to join the private sector. Johnson became increasingly involved in the details of the war in Vietnam, and when he did pay any attention at

---

65. Robert H. Estabrook, former editorial page writer for the *Washington Post*, noted, " . . . in announcing the dispatch of U.S. marines to the Dominican Republic, President Johnson made an emotional broadcast relating that the American ambassador had had to shield himself under his desk to fend off his bullets. I happened to know the ambassador, Tapley Bennett, who told me during a visit a couple of months later that Johnson's histrionics were based very largely on fiction." SHAFR *Newsletter,* v. 23, No. 4 (December 1992), 25.

all to Latin America, it was to focus on specific, uncontroversial development projects, such as roads. Improving the physical infrastructure in the region became his mantra in conversations with visitors from Latin America.

But, before the Dominican crisis, there still was an effort to link development and the struggle against communist subversion. In September 1964, Johnson met with the ambassadors from Latin America and the key figures in the OAS, the CIAP, and the Inter-American Development Bank. To prepare for that meeting, Bundy met with Mann and agreed to an agenda that Bundy then outlined for Johnson. Aside from general pieties, there were only two items on the agenda: Cuba and the Alliance for Progress.[66]

. . .

(2) The last year has been a good one for the American Republics, and a bad one for the opponents of freedom. In one country after another the Communists and their supporters have been set back and the devotion of free peoples to freedom has been demonstrated.

(3) At the same time the conspiratorial aggressions of Castro have been exposed and understood more widely than ever, and we have been able to take increasingly effective action together in the OAS (the score is now 19 to 1 in the execution of that resolution, but you will want to avoid rudeness to Mexico).

(4) Cuba itself shows plainly the failure of Communism in action. . . . The people of the hemisphere recognize Castroism more and more as the shabby failure that it is.

(5) The Alliance for Progress is moving steadily forward. 16 countries have taken steps to improve their collection of taxes. Latin American countries are spending 25% more on public education than they did before the Alliance. 12 countries have introduced or passed agrarian reform laws. 12 have created new land reform institutions.

(6) American commitments under the Alliance are moving rapidly forward. We committed more in the first six months of 1964 than in the whole 12 months of 1963. . . .

(7) In our private sector too there is renewed confidence in the future of Latin America. We have reversed a trend away from investment by Americans in the growth of the hemisphere so that in the first quarter of this year, for the first time since 1961, there was an increase in direct new investment of private American funds in the future of Latin America.

66. Bundy to the President, September 10, 1964, NSF, Memos to the President, Box 1.

(8) Most important of all, we understand more and more our common commitment to progress and freedom, and our mutual obligation of loyalty and cooperation. The Alliance is on its way.

Bundy also prepared the president for difficult questions that might be asked. He took a fairly realistic posture on the Alliance – a lot had yet to be accomplished, and most of the problems were on the Latin American side – the Latins had failed to use the money appropriated, they had been slow in creating reform institutions, and so on, but progress was being made. The major problem was U.S. trade policy, and on that "we are conscious of Latin American interest and worked hard for . . . acceptable compromises. . . . We will continue to work for trade policies that will take into account Latin America[n] interests."[67] Now, ironically, the Latin Americans wanted trade as well as aid!

As the years went by, Johnson gradually lost his ability to push through Congress aid bills critical to the success of the Alliance for Progress. More damning, Johnson refused to become involved in intramural disputes over conflicts between those in the State Department and CIAP who tried to protect Latin American trade interests and those, such as Secretary of the Treasury Henry Fowler, who insisted on preserving general policy with regard to "tying" exports – the practice by which the U.S. government credits were required to be used to purchase goods from the United States – even though Latin American interests were sacrificed in almost every case.[68] No wonder Latin Americans became disillusioned with the United States!

At the end of his term Johnson made one last effort to revive the Alliance and to achieve public recognition of what he considered the very real accomplishments of his administration in the region by agreeing to attend a hemispheric summit meeting. Originally proposed by Arturo Illia as a way of shoring up his failing government, the gathering was postponed and delayed until Johnson was sure that there was a consensus among his Latin American col-

---

67. Ibid.
68. Lincoln Gordon, Oral History, LBJL, 8–15, tells a devastating story of how the entire administration failed to push the aid bill through the Senate because of Senator William Fulbright's opposition to Johnson's policy in Vietnam and because Johnson would not get directly involved in the struggle for votes. Gordon to Rostow, May 3, 1967, NSF, CO, Box 3; Copy of C. Oliver's testimony, in NSC Meeting 583, March 6, 1968, NSF,

leagues on their agenda. The key, for Johnson, was to celebrate what had been achieved and not to open the door to gratuitous complaints about what had not been done.

Preparations were careful, even meticulous. Lincoln Gordon and Sol Linowitz, former CEO of the Xerox corporation and newly appointed ambassador to the OAS, were dispatched to South America to consult with leaders from various countries. Rusk attended a preliminary meeting of foreign ministers to hammer out the agenda. The most difficult task for the White House staff in the months prior to the conference was controlling the State Department's efforts to get the president to meet with every ruler in the hemisphere, although he ultimately did meet with them.[69]

The U.S. press considered the summit a success, and Johnson went to great lengths to ensure that the promises he had made in Punta del Este were kept.[70] He asked Rusk to prepare a monthly "scorecard" on the follow-up. Each month, the Department of State submitted a report in which each promise was listed and action taken on it specified. Assistant Secretaries Gordon and Covey Oliver put a great deal of effort into these reports and on the actions they required. In the end, however, they were able to accomplish only minor goals. Major goals required presidential intervention in the policy process, and Johnson simply had no time or lacked the will to become involved.[71] The discussion over the congressional appropriation for the Alliance for fiscal year 1968 suggests that Johnson simply did not want to expend any political capital on Latin America. He refused to call over to the Capitol to win votes in the Senate Committee on Foreign Relations, even when it was clear that anything less meant failure to get the appropriations bill out of committee.[72] Once he had declared his intention not to seek reelection, Johnson made himself available to a number of

NSC Meetings File, Box 1; Fowler to Rostow, August 11, 1968; NSF, CO, Latin America, Box 4–5, Vol. 7. Gordon's recollection was that the main issue was not tying but rather whether there should be preferential tariff levels for imports from Latin America. Gordon to the author, July 27, 1993.

69. A detailed chronology of the summit is in NSF, NSC History, OAS Summit Meeting, Box, 12, LBJL.

70. For a sample of press comment, see *Time*, August 12, 1967, pp. 4–5.

71. A sample of the reports is Rusk to the President, October 14, 1967, NSF, CO, Latin America, Box 3, v. 6.

72. Both the Linowitz and Gordon oral histories tell this story, and it can be followed in the NSF, Memos to the President, Box 5.

public ceremonies that celebrated successes of the Alliance. There is a sad quality to these events, the valedictories of a beaten warrior trying to write the historical record of his accomplishments.[73]

Although it is tempting to explain the changes in U.S. policy during the 1960s in terms of presidential personality and leadership, an accumulation of evidence suggests that the Alliance for Progress could never have accomplished all that was attempted in its name, and that Kennedy himself had become disillusioned with the Wilsonian policy of intervention on the side of democracy. The basic concerns of the Cold War were as high on his agenda as they were on Johnson's. Would Kennedy have intervened in the Dominican Republic in 1965? We cannot say with any certainty. We can say, however, that the episode was a spasmodic response to domestic political concerns over "another Cuba."[74] Kennedy was at least as vulnerable as Johnson to such domestic pressures. Those advisers who might have taken a different view of reformers in the Caribbean than did the military advisers, or Thomas Mann and the others around Johnson, either had been cowed and chastened by the Bay of Pigs or had lost their access to the president. McGeorge Bundy actually visited Santo Domingo to try to settle the internal disputes behind the violence. He failed and became an advocate of a harder policy line. What is important, however, is that he went to the Dominican Republic with an intelligence briefing that judged Juan Bosch to be a bumbler at best and anti-American, and quite possibly something worse. Given the decisions concerning the Brazilian coup a year earlier, when a determination that Goulart was "allowing" Brazil to slide toward chaos or toward the left was ample justification to support the generals who overthrew him, the intelligence report on Bosch really was a delicate equivalent of the kiss of death.[75]

73. See Rostow to the President, December 5 and 15, 1968, NSF, Memos to the President, Boxes 4 and 5.
74. Lester Langley, *The United States and the Caribbean in the Twentieth Century* (Athens: University of Georgia Press, 1982); Joseph S. Tulchin, "Inhibitions Affecting the Formulation and Execution of the Latin American Policy of the United States," *Ventures* VII, (Fall 1967).
75. The CIA estimates on the Dominican Republic are April 1, 1964, in NSF, CO, Latin America, Box 1. For some harsh comments by Rusk to congressional leaders on the Goulart government justifying the military coup, see NSC Report, April 3, 1964, NSF, NSC Meetings File, Box 1.

Kennedy gave no more evidence than Johnson of his ability to use the nation's power in a restrained manner. His disposition to cooperate with Latin American nations, the most distinguishing feature of his policy, had begun to weaken by 1963. If anything, Kennedy was even more in thrall to the paradigm of counterinsurgency and stability than was Johnson. On balance, Kennedy supporters who would have us believe that things would have been different had he lived make an unconvincing case.

Of course, as the decade wore on, events outside the hemisphere came to assume transcendent importance in U.S. policy planning, so that Johnson, having once broken away from the lead of John F. Kennedy, was content to leave the hemisphere to its own devices. He maintained the high level of direct public aid, but, in effect, Latin America returned to the position of low priority on the U.S. policy agenda that it had held prior to 1958. Events in Asia, beginning with the Gulf of Tonkin episode, quickly took the attention of the U.S. administration away from the Western Hemisphere and skewed U.S. policy so as to redefine national security in terms of the experience in southeast Asia and its impact on the policy of containment. After 1966 U.S. foreign policy debate focused so obsessively upon events in Asia as to change totally the perspective on national security that had shaped policy since World War II. That obsession so haunted President Johnson that it finally drove him from office.

By the end of the decade the United States was thoroughly embittered by the threats to its security from within the hemisphere and by the sense of having its sphere of influence violated and destroyed by external influences without any constructive cooperation from the other nations in the hemisphere. On the other hand, from the Latin American perspective, their alienation from the United States had become so complete that there was almost no disposition on their part to cooperate with the United States in multilateral efforts or to sympathize with the U.S. perception of national security issues.

Another consequence of the events of the decade was that the issue of development became central to discussion of foreign policy and, more specifically, to discussion of national security, although there remained a glaring asymmetry in the perception, north and south, of the linkage between the two. Despite the fact that the 1960s were relatively good years for economic growth in Latin America, it was falling behind the developed countries.[76] They expressed their disillusionment with the United States and their conviction concerning the necessity for development in the public statements following the foreign ministers' meeting at Viña del Mar in May 1969. Similarly, in the ongoing work of AID and the growing influence of the Inter-American Development Bank, the Alliance left a permanent legacy that would live on and strive to achieve the goals first given such eloquent expression at Punta del Este in 1961.

Although its influence was already on the wane by the end of the 1960s, and many governments feared Cuban subversion, Castro's Cuba was still seen by many in Latin America as an alternative model of national development. The fierce, almost compulsive U.S. rejection of Cuban initiatives, wherever they might be encountered, contributed by the end of the decade to another consequence that would have staggered Kennedy or Johnson, had either of them understood it: the United States was seen by many people in the hemisphere not as a force for change, reform, and democracy but as a counterrevolutionary power, a reactionary force in hemispheric affairs. That is perhaps the most painful irony in the evolution of U.S.–Latin American relations in the decade of the 1960s. Having begun as the champion of change, in a ringing challenge to the nations of the hemisphere to join in a cooperative venture to seek the benefits of progress and democracy, the United States had ended the decade as an obstinent opponent of progressive regimes and an equally clumsy supporter of military regimes whose only claim to legitimacy was fervent anticommunism and the violent suppression of dissidents.

The reasons for this change were (1) the confusion between the short-term goal of anticommunism and the long-term elimination of conditions assumed to invite communist subversion, (2) an inability to use power in a restrained manner, (3) an inability to consider the region's development except as an element in the national

---

76. Samuel L. Baily, *The United States and the Development of South America, 1945–1975* (New York: Watts, 1976) Ch. 1; and Inter-American Development Bank, *Economic and Social Progress in Latin America* (Washington: IDB, 1988), 540.

security of the United States alone, rather than in the broader context of the entire hemisphere, and (4) Johnson's obsession with Vietnam and his inability to summon the political energy or will to do anything such as push his favorite programs within the Alliance for Progress.

8

Keeping Africa off the Agenda

TERRENCE LYONS

Lyndon Johnson assumed the presidency in November 1963 with a crowded agenda of difficult and challenging issues both at home and abroad. Africa occupied a peripheral position on Johnson's list of priorities, and the president sought to avoid the diversion of attention or resources to the continent. The euphoria and optimism of the early 1960s as dozens of new states achieved independence, ready to play an important role in John Kennedy's New Frontier, had faded. From Johnson's perspective, Africa was best kept on the back burner, handled by the State Department bureaucracy or ignored as much as possible. Africa was the farthest corner of the world to Johnson, the place to threaten to send indiscreet officials who drew his ire.[1] The Great Society at home, the obsession with fighting the war in Vietnam, and other more important areas of the world all deserved and received greater attention. As one official put it, Africa was "the last issue considered, the first aid budget cut."[2] Only occasionally – such as when the Congo threatened to erupt into a major crisis in 1964, when African issues required a decision at the United Nations, or when domestic interest groups generated enough attention to make an issue salient – did Johnson have to face decisions regarding the continent. Otherwise, the administration successfully kept Africa off the agenda.

Johnson's first priority on the morning after Kennedy's assassination, he would later recall, was "to try to display to the world that

1. David Halberstam, *The Best and the Brightest* (New York: Random House, 1972), p. 587.
2. Roger Morris, *Uncertain Greatness: Henry Kissinger and American Foreign Policy* (New York: Harper & Row, 1977), p. 17, quoting an unnamed official speaking in the context of the mid-1960s. See also Arnold Rivkin, "Lost Goals in Africa," *Foreign Affairs* 44:1 (October 1965), p. 113.

we could have continuity and transition, that the program of President Kennedy would be carried on."[3] In Africa, that meant trying to maintain the special relationship the young and dynamic Kennedy had had with a number of African leaders.[4] Johnson could never copy what one commentator labeled Kennedy's "special glow" in Africa but followed through on most of Kennedy's policies.[5]

Kennedy's style and personal attention to the new African leaders, the mystique of the Peace Corps, and the appointment of several dynamic ambassadors gave many the impression that the continent played an important part in Kennedy's view of the world. In southern Africa, Kennedy ended past hostility toward anti-colonial leaders. European interests and domestic budgetary constraints, however, inhibited new activities. In the end, the Kennedy legacy in Africa amounted to a temporary change of focus.[6]

By the time Johnson assumed the presidency, American liberals had become disenchanted with and uninterested in Africa. Deterioration and instability on the continent undermined their hopes that African nationalism would serve as a force for development. Growing doubt and cynicism replaced the optimism that had marked the first years of the decade, both in Africa and in the United States. The belief of U.S. liberals that "all good things go together" came up against increased evidence that there might be tradeoffs between development and democracy, nationalism and human rights.[7]

Johnson could afford to evade African issues because U.S. interests there were rarely vital. According to Arnold Rivkin, "Africa has come to be an area of residual interest for the United States."[8] Former colonial powers controlled most of the trade and invest-

3. Quoted in Tom Wicker, *JFK and LBJ: The Influence of Personality upon Politics* (New York: Morrow, 1968), p. 161.
4. Thomas J. Noer, "New Frontiers and Old Priorities in Africa," in Thomas G. Paterson, ed., *Kennedy's Quest for Victory: American Foreign Policy, 1961–1963* (New York: Oxford University Press, 1989), pp. 253–83.
5. Rupert Emerson, *Africa and United States Policy* (Englewood Cliffs, N.J.: Prentice-Hall, 1967), p. 95.
6. Noer, "New Frontiers and Old Priorities in Africa," p. 282.
7. Martin Staniland, *American Intellectuals and African Nationalists, 1955–1970* (New Haven, Conn.: Yale University Press, 1991), Ch. 4; Robert A. Packenham, *Liberal America and the Third World: Political Development Ideas in Foreign Aid and Social Science* (Princeton, N.J.: Princeton University Press, 1973), pp. 123–9.
8. Rivkin, "Lost Goals in Africa," p. 113.

ment, although access to certain strategic minerals in southern Africa merited attention. The United States had access agreements, space tracking stations, and other facilities in several states that motivated patronage, but few of these facilities were irreplaceable. Global policies such as containing communism applied to Africa, of course, but the Soviet threat seemed to subside after the initial Cold War confrontation over the Congo under Kennedy. China became more involved, and the administration was alarmed when Zhou Enlai visited Africa and proclaimed the continent "ripe for revolution." Washington saw the hands of the "Chicoms," as the cables always labeled them, behind rebellion in Zanzibar, the Congo, and elsewhere but never regarded the threat as sufficient to require major commitments.[9] Assistant Secretary of State for African Affairs G. Mennen Williams argued that nationalism and the commitment of the new states to independence would limit Soviet or Chinese influence because communism demanded subjugation to foreign powers.[10]

Johnson had little diplomatic experience when he assumed the presidency, and he was never comfortable with people who were "not like folks you were reared with."[11] His exposure to sub-Saharan Africa was limited to a ceremonial trip as vice president to attend the independence celebration in Senegal.[12] Johnson's report on his mission indicates his feeling that the key to success in Africa (as elsewhere) was to shake as many hands, kiss as many babies, and promise as much government largess as possible. According to Johnson, the Soviet emissary to the celebration

intended to be "the politician" – handshaker, backslapper, etc. It was my decision to outdo him at his own game – and the evidence, as suggested by the press accounts, indicates some success in that competitive enterprise.[13]

9. William Brubeck, NSC African specialist, to Johnson, "Chicom Activity in Africa," January 29, 1964, National Security Files (hereafter NSF), Box 77, Lyndon Baines Johnson Library (hereafter LBJL).
10. G. Mennen Williams, "Africa's Problems and Progress," March 1, 1964, in *Department of State Bulletin* (hereafter DSB) 50 (March 30, 1964), pp. 501–6.
11. Quoted in Philip Geyelin, *Lyndon B. Johnson and the World* (New York: Praeger, 1966), p. 15. See also Chester Bowles, *Promises to Keep: My Years in Public Life, 1949–1969* (New York: Harper & Row, 1971), pp. 533–5.
12. Lyndon Baines Johnson, *The Vantage Point: Perspectives of the Presidency, 1963–1969* (New York: Holt, Rinehart and Winston, 1971), pp. 351–2.
13. Report from Johnson to Kennedy, "Re: Mission to Africa, Europe," April 15, 1961, Vice-Presidential Security File, Box 1, LBJL.

Johnson "campaigned Senegal as he might have campaigned Texas" and at one point even promised the chief of a village a new outboard motor for his fishing boat.[14] Johnson enjoyed the glad-handing so much that he canceled a stop in Spain in order to spend more time in Senegal.

Johnson's preoccupation with Vietnam limited his options and slanted his perceptions regarding Africa. The administration and the Congress recognized the United States' unwillingness to become deeply involved in additional controversies far from home. Africa could do little to help Johnson in the war and therefore did not interest the president. Johnson and his staff occasionally lobbied African diplomats for support relative to Vietnam, but Africans had different concerns.[15] As Philip Geyelin suggests, Johnson's foreign policy derived from a belief that politics must be based on mutual self-interest and exchange of support.[16] From this perspective, Africa could not offer much and consequently earned little attention.

As a consequence of U.S. overextension in southeast Asia and following long-standing practice, Johnson explicitly urged former European colonial powers to take more responsibility for Africa. Secretary of State Dean Rusk wanted to play the junior partner to Europe. "We shouldn't play 'Mr. Big' in every African capital," he said.[17] In the case of Francophone Africa, Charles de Gaulle was more than willing to accept the predominant role, even to the extent of resenting any U.S. involvement at all.[18] The British and

14. G. Mennen Williams, Oral History (hereafter OH), LBJL; A-56, Dakar, "Visit of Vice President Johnson and Discussion of U.S. Aid," April 10, 1965, Vice-Presidential Security File, Box 1, LBJL.
15. Briefing Papers for White House Luncheon with African Ambassadors, "Africa and Viet-Nam," July 30, 1965, Declassified Documents Reference System (hereafter DDRS), 1985 (2351); Department of State Memorandum of Conversation, "U.S. Position on Viet-Nam," March 26, 1965, NSF, Box 76, LBJL; Thomas L. Hughes, Director of Intelligence and Research, to Rusk, "Africans on Peace Offensive in Viet-Nam," August 4, 1965, DDRS 1976 (171D).
16. Geyelin, *Lyndon B. Johnson and the World*, p. 39.
17. Dean Rusk, *As I Saw It* (New York: Penguin, 1991), pp. 196, 273; Williams, March 18, 1965, in *DSB*, April 12, 1965.
18. Charles F. Darlington and Alice B. Darlington, *African Betrayal* (New York: David McKay, 1968); Russell Warren Howe, *Along the Afric Shore: An Historic Review of Two Centuries of U.S.-African Relations* (New York: Barnes and Noble, 1975), pp. 151–7; Williams to Rusk, "Major Conclusions of Visit to Five West and Central African Countries, May 8–20, 1964," NSF, Box 76, LBJL.

Belgians, however, had to be prodded to accept the burden and to act as forcefully as Johnson desired. Rusk tells the story of Belgian Foreign Minister Paul-Henri Spaak leaving a cabinet meeting in Brussels during the Stanleyville hostage crisis and calling Rusk to ask the American view. Rusk answered that Washington would support Brussels in whatever decision it made. Spaak was shocked and replied, "That's incredible. No decision affecting Belgium has ever been made in Belgium before."[19] Portugal, on the other hand, habitually created problems for Washington, particularly in the United Nations, by its steadfast refusal to move its colonies toward independence.[20]

Initially Johnson kept Kennedy's principal African policymakers in place. Rusk had interest in the developing world from his time at the Rockefeller Foundation but rarely had the time as secretary to focus on Africa. G. Mennen "Soapy" Williams, the colorful former governor of Michigan who had opposed Johnson's nomination as vice president in 1960, remained as assistant secretary of state for Africa. Johnson phoned Williams after the transition and assured him that Africa would remain as important as before and that Williams would have direct access to the president whenever he wished.[21] Adlai Stevenson continued to represent Washington at the United Nations until his death in 1965. The large and increasingly vocal African bloc at the UN led him to take the lead in defending the administration on U.S. policy toward the Congo and other issues important to the continent. The National Security Council staff also included several who wanted a more vigorous policy toward Africa but disagreed with Williams over goals and means. NSC staffer Robert W. Komer supported an aggressive policy in Africa from an anticommunist perspective until Johnson sent him to Vietnam. Ulric Haynes, a man National Security Adviser McGeorge Bundy called "the ablest young Negro I have met in ten years of fairly constant looking," also actively covered African issues for the NSC.[22]

19. Rusk, *As I Saw It*, p. 279.
20. Witney Wright Schneidman, "American Foreign Policy and the Fall of the Portuguese Empire, 1961–1976," Ph.D. diss., University of Southern California, 1987.
21. Thomas J. Noer, *Cold War and Black Liberation: The United States and White Rule in Africa, 1948–1968* (Columbia, Mo.: University of Missouri Press, 1985), p. 106.
22. John Prados, *Keepers of the Keys: A History of the National Security Council from Truman to Bush* (New York: Morrow, 1991), p. 170.

As early as 1964, however, Johnson began to make personnel changes designed to stifle innovative policymaking that would divert his attention from more pressing matters. He wanted to keep African issues in the Department of State and off his desk. In April 1964 Johnson designated former New York Governor W. Averell Harriman ambassador-at-large with special responsibility for Africa in order to handle issues that could not be settled at the assistant secretary level and thereby to "keep them away from the secretary."[23] Harriman's credentials as a Cold Warrior allowed him to advocate increased assistance without being dismissed as idealistic like Williams.[24]

Williams continued to fight a losing battle for a more vigorous African policy but, as Waldemar Nielsen has noted, Williams "had neither the taste nor the talent for the fine épée work required in day-to-day internal staff debate."[25] Over time, Williams lost influence in the administration, and leaks that he was about to resign subverted his effectiveness.[26] Johnson no longer needed Kennedy's men to bolster his prestige after his own landslide election in 1964. By 1965 Williams had to beg for even a few minutes of the president's time. Bundy apologized to Johnson for forwarding the request but explained, "I know the problem he represents, but I think it is important that while he is Assistant Secretary he be seen as *your* Assistant Secretary."[27]

After Williams resigned in 1966 to run unsuccessfully for the Senate, Johnson appointed Joseph Palmer, a careful career diplomat, in his place to regularize policy. During the last few years of the administration, few new initiatives developed in the State Department's Africa Bureau. Arthur Goldberg, Johnson's close friend and former Supreme Court justice, replaced Stevenson. He had the

---

23. Warren I. Cohen, *Dean Rusk* (Totowa, N.J.: Cooper Square, 1980), p. 229; Bundy to Johnson, "Your Luncheon with Secretaries Rusk and McNamara," February 4, 1964; Rudy Abramson, *Spanning the Century: The Life of W. Averell Harriman, 1891–1986* (New York: Morrow, 1992), pp. 635–42.
24. Stephen R. Weissman, *American Foreign Policy in the Congo, 1960–1964* (Ithaca, N.Y.: Cornell University Press, 1974), pp. 223–5.
25. Waldemar Nielson, *The Great Powers and Africa* (New York: Praeger, 1969), p. 293.
26. Letter from Williams to Robert F. Kennedy, January 26, 1965, G. Mennen Williams collection, National Archives (hereafter GMW-NA).
27. Bundy to Johnson, "Two Requests for Brief Meetings," February 12, 1965, NSF, Aides File, Box 2, LBJL.

ability to act as an independent channel for new ideas on Africa and played an important role concerning southern Africa.[28]

Dealing with Conflict and Radicalism

By early 1964, a number of events in Africa began to accumulate to raise questions about the quick development of liberal, modern states on the continent. A series of coups in west Africa and military mutinies in the east forced American observers to question the prospects for liberalism. As Russell Warren Howe notes, these events "gave Africa a different 'taste' in the mouth of official America."[29] Soviet arms to Somalia, Chinese involvement in the revolution in Zanzibar, and radical anti-Americanism in Ghana made Africa a disquieting region for a preoccupied administration.

In general, increasing involvement in southeast Asia cooled any desire to seek tests of strength or arenas for superpower conflict in Africa in late 1963 and 1964. Even when an African leader began to move toward the communist bloc the administration remained relatively calm and tried to avoid unnecessary confrontation. In Somalia, Zanzibar, and Ghana, the administration decided that since it lacked either the interest or ability to alter developments on the ground, it was best to encourage others to take the lead, remain quietly engaged, and hope for the best outcome at low cost and low risk. Williams and the Africa Bureau reinforced these constraints by articulating the liberal belief in the power of nationalism in Africa: "We should never consider a country lost to communism, however bleak the picture may seem. We must hang on, never despair, never give up our presence."[30]

The Horn of Africa briefly reached policymakers' attention after Somalia rejected a U.S. military assistance agreement and signed a more generous Soviet offer in November 1963. The United States had an important communications facility in Ethiopia, Somalia's neighbor and rival, and believed that Emperor Haile Selassie served

---

28. Martin Mayer, "Goldberg Represents Lyndon Johnson," *New York Times Magazine*, February 6, 1966, pp. 16–24.
29. Howe, *Along the Afric Shore*, pp. 147–51.
30. G. Mennen Williams, *Africa for the Africans* (Grand Rapids, Mich.: Eerdmans, 1969), p. 84.

an important role moderating African politics.[31] The new threat to Ethiopia's security and U.S. interests raised the possibility that Johnson would have to increase his involvement in Africa. Unlike the rest of Africa, Ethiopia had no ex-colonial power to which Johnson could pass the problem. A serious border conflict between Ethiopia and Somalia broke out in late 1963, but the administration at first kept its distance.[32] American observers worried more about an arms race and did not want to let an obscure local skirmish escalate into superpower competition. When the Ethiopian minister of defense threatened that if the United States did not give him the assistance he needed then Addis Ababa "might have to deal with the Devil himself to save our country," Washington eventually relented.[33] The Ethiopian threat to end the patron–client relationship, rather than Soviet assistance to Somalia itself, persuaded Washington to accede to Addis Ababa's demands.

As the Ethiopia–Somalia conflict died down, a more dramatic and potentially unsettling development drew Washington's attention to the newly independent island of Zanzibar. An obscure Ugandan laborer and self-styled "Field Marshall" named John Okello seized power on January 12, 1964, and revolutionaries with past connections to communist China moved into the government.[34] The State Department faced the prospect that a radical state would consolidate itself just off the shore of east Africa.[35] The U.S. media emphasized the external involvement and raised the alarm that communists would create "another Cuba."[36]

The United States had little leverage with the new Zanzibari leadership, although Harriman urged the administration to make

31. Department of State Administrative History, Volume I, Chapter 5 (Africa), Section C, Part 4, "The Horn of Africa," LBJL.
32. Ted Gurr, "Tensions in the Horn of Africa," in Feliks Gross, ed., *World Politics and Tension Areas* (New York: New York University Press, 1966), pp. 316–34; Terrence Lyons, "Reaction to Revolution: United States–Ethiopia Relations, 1974–1977," Ph.D. diss., Johns Hopkins University, 1991, Chapter 2.
33. A-295 (Addis Ababa), "Transmittal of Memorandum of Conversation between Representatives of IEG Ministry of Defense and Members of the Country Team," December 11, 1963, document released pursuant to Freedom of Information Act request.
34. Keith Kyle, "Coup in Zanzibar," *Africa Report* 9:2 (February 1964): 18–20.
35. Hughes to Rusk, "The Communist Specter Looms in Zanzibar," January 13, 1964, NSF, Box 103, LBJL; Paul Grimes, "Coup in Zanzibar Stirs U.S. Concern," *New York Times*, January 14, 1964, p. 1.
36. "A Cuba Off Africa?" (editorial), *New York Times*, January 14, 1964; John Peer Nugent, *Call Africa 999* (New York: Coward-McCann, 1965), pp. 113–49.

every attempt to "prevent [a] commie takeover."[37] Unwilling to obstruct the new leadership from consolidating power, the administration saw few options but to remain engaged in a low-key manner and try to demonstrate the value of good relations with the West. When the government in Zanzibar ordered Chargé d'Affaires Frank Carlucci to dismantle a NASA tracking station, he did so without objection and even presented the generator to the government as a gift.[38] By March 1964, however, Carlucci had concluded that President Abeid Karume had surrounded himself with radicals and that there was little the United States could do to stop Zanzibar from becoming a communist state.[39]

Despite the threat of "another Cuba," Washington considered Zanzibar a problem for east African leaders and the British. Without major interests or influence, the administration kept its distance and avoided unnecessary involvement. In April 1964 Tanganyikan President Julius Nyerere merged Zanzibar into his state and changed the name to Tanzania, thereby preventing any outpost of instability off his shore. The U.S. government hailed Nyerere's decision as a good example of how Africans could solve their own problems and breathed a sigh of relief – another potential crisis had been avoided without U.S. involvement.[40]

The perils of radicalism bedeviled the administration in west Africa as well in 1964. In Ghana, Johnson continued – despite some misgivings – to provide assistance for a large hydroelectric dam on the Volta River originally supported by Kennedy.[41] Washington hoped that such assistance would moderate the mercurial Ghanaian leader Kwame Nkrumah.[42] As one of the most outspoken radicals in Africa, Nkrumah acted as a lightning rod for congressional critics of U.S. assistance to "socialist" states, particularly after anti-American protests in February 1964.[43]

37. Embtel 212 (Leopoldville), March 28, 1964, NSF, Box 30, LBJL.
38. Brubeck to Bundy, "Zanzibar," April 7, 1964, NSF, Box 103, LBJL; William Attwood, *The Reds and the Blacks: A Personal Adventure* (New York: Harper & Row, 1967), p. 164.
39. Embtel 212 (Zanzibar), March 26, 1964, NSF, Box 103, LBJL.
40. Williams speech, June 18, 1964, in *DSB*, 51 (July 13, 1964), pp. 51–4.
41. Thomas J. Noer, "The New Frontier and African Neutralism: Kennedy, Nkrumah, and the Volta River Project," *Diplomatic History* 8 (Winter 1984): 61–80.
42. W. Scott Thompson, *Ghana's Foreign Policy, 1957–1966: Diplomacy, Ideology, and the New State* (Princeton, N.J.: Princeton University Press, 1969).
43. Rusk to LBJ, "The Volta Problem," February 13, 1964, NSF, Box 89, LBJL; Kenneth

In response to the widely publicized demonstrations, Johnson recalled his ambassador in Accra, invited the Ghanian ambassador to the White House for some personal persuasion, and insisted that Nkrumah live up to his commitments.[44] Johnson sent Harriman to Ghana in April and May 1964 to emphasize that if Nkrumah continued to cause trouble, congressional pressures would force Johnson to withdraw from the Volta Dam project.[45] Harriman told Nkrumah that he could not "hammer away at [the] U.S. government and expect us to continue our help to Ghana."[46] Although Johnson resented having to deal with someone like Nkrumah, he concluded that the best course was to remain engaged but low key, a "holding operation" in anticipation of the day when moderates would assume leadership.[47] The Volta Dam was completed, but the United States otherwise disengaged from Ghana. In February 1966, a military coup overthrew Nkrumah and thereby removed one of the African thorns in Johnson's side. Although available evidence suggests that it had not orchestrated the coup, Nkrumah's removal pleased the administration. Washington immediately offered generous assistance to the new leader.[48]

In the Horn, Zanzibar, and Ghana, Johnson demonstrated in the early months of his administration that he viewed African issues as problems to be avoided whenever possible. He was willing to accept a certain level of communist involvement or radical leadership in Africa rather than increase U.S. involvement. In these three areas local dynamics kept the problems in check and thereby allowed Washington to keep its distance without risking vital interests.

W. Grundy and J. P. Falchi, "The United States and Socialism in Africa," *Journal of Asian and African Studies* 4:4 (October 1969), p. 302.

44. Brubeck, "Meeting with the President on Ghana," February 26, 1964, NSF, Box 89, LBJL; Memorandum of Conversation, "President Johnson's Meeting with Ghanian Ambassador," March 11, 1964, NSF, Box 90, LBJL.

45. Brubeck, "Meeting with President re Governor Harriman's Report on Trip to Ghana, Nigeria and Congo – April 3, 1964." NSC Meetings, Vol. 1, Tab 7, 4/3/64 – Various Topics, LBJL.

46. Telegram, "Governor Harriman's Meeting with Nkrumah," May 24, 1964, DDRS, 1977 (230F).

47. Department of State Administrative History, Vol. I, Chapter 5, Africa, Section A, LBJL.

48. Memorandum for Deputy Director of Central Intelligence, "Recent OCI Reporting on Ghana," February 25, 1966, NSF, Box 90, LBJL; Abdoulaye S. M. Saine, "The Ascent of Lyndon B. Johnson and the Demise of Kwame Nkrumah: A Drama of Political Subterfuge," paper presented at the 33rd Annual Meeting of the African Studies Association, Baltimore, Md., November1–4, 1990.

Crisis in the Congo

In contrast to the relatively contained dangers in the Horn, Zanzibar, and Ghana, the Congo represented a potential quagmire on the scale of Vietnam if mishandled. Here was a large country in the heart of Africa, a Cold War battlefield earlier in the 1960s when Kennedy and Nikita Khrushchev had sparred by proxy, a state in which the United Nations had become deeply and contentiously ensnared. The Congo ranked with Cuba and Vietnam in the early 1960s as top foreign policy trouble spots.[49] Given Kennedy's earlier involvement, Johnson felt that he could not allow the Congo to collapse so early in his own administration. Furthermore, the United States suspected Chinese involvement in the continuing political instability and worried that a rebel victory would undermine fragile governments across the continent. The Congo's minerals made Western business interests more involved than elsewhere on the continent.[50] Preventing chaos that might draw the United States into greater commitment required careful and high-level attention. Johnson authorized both covert and overt assistance to the Congo in the hope of keeping the conflict contained. When rebels took U.S. embassy officials and civilians hostage, however, the crisis escalated. Washington and Brussels launched a rescue operation that unleashed a stinging attack from Africa on the administration's motives. This criticism reinforced Johnson's perception that Africa represented more controversy than it was worth.

During the Kennedy administration, the Congo problem had centered on the secessionist province of Katanga and the struggle to manage a UN peacekeeping operation.[51] By 1964 the Katanga question seemed solved, and UN troops were scheduled to return home. A series of new and uncoordinated rebellions, however, broke out in the provinces of Kwilu and Kivu, and observers feared a new round of turmoil and conflict.[52] The United States attained an extension of the UN presence until June 1964, but the Con-

49. Williams, *Africa for the Africans*, p. 86.
50. David N. Gibbs, *The Political Economy of Third World Intervention: Mines, Money, and U.S. Policy in the Congo Crisis* (Chicago: University of Chicago Press, 1992).
51. Ernest W. Lefever, *Crisis in the Congo: A United Nations Force in Action* (Washington: Brookings Institution, 1965).
52. Crawford Young, "The Congo Rebellion," *Africa Report* 10:5 (April 1965): 6–11.

golese National Army (Armeé Nationale Congolaise, or ANC) still lacked the capacity to meet the challenge of facing the rebels alone. Robert Komer, the African analyst on the NSC, understood the challenge and potential danger clearly by January 1964. Because the Congolese military could not contain rebel advances, he urged a political settlement involving the Organization of African Unity (OAU) as soon as possible rather than waiting and being forced inevitably into a military confrontation. Komer warned his superiors that "unless we can draw some political umbrella over the Congo soon, we're either going to be sucked into another war, or have to retreat ignominiously."[53]

Johnson decided to try to shore up Congolese Prime Minister Cyrille Adoula in the hope of avoiding Komer's ominous scenario. He authorized supplemental military assistance, offered subsidies to any African country willing to provide troops, and sent Harriman to the Congo on a fact-finding trip.[54] In addition, Washington aided Adoula covertly, using CIA-recruited Cubans to run an "instant air force" that provided critical support for the ANC.[55] The administration believed that the stakes in the Congo were higher than in Ghana or Zanzibar and was prepared to take necessary actions short of direct military intervention to prevent a rebel victory.

On June 30, 1964, Adoula resigned, and Moïse Tshombe, the leader of the Katangan secession who had brought the Congo to the verge of disintegration just a few years before, returned to become prime minister. Tshombe's return resulted from complex, factional politics within the Congo and pressures applied by Belgian financial interests.[56] Washington was "not screaming against" his return but let developments play out on their own and supported Tshombe once he was in control.[57] Johnson, who never appreciated liberal antipathy toward Tshombe, continued military assistance so long as

53. Komer to Harriman and Bundy, January 12, 1964, DDRS, 1979 (159C).
54. Harriman to Johnson, April 20, 1964, NSF, Box 81, LBJL; Brubeck, "Meeting with President re Governor Harriman's Report on Trip to Ghana, Nigeria and Congo – April 3, 1964," Files of McGeorge Bundy, Box 18, LBJL.
55. Vance to Harriman, April 20, 1964, NSF, Box 81, LBJL; Weissman, *American Foreign Policy in the Congo*, pp. 229–30; Tom Wicker et al., "How C.I.A. Put 'Instant Air Force' Into Congo," *New York Times*, April 26, 1966, p. 1.
56. Gibbs, *The Political Economy of Third World Intervention*, pp. 152–6.
57. Weissman, *American Foreign Policy in the Congo*, p. 234; G. Mennen Williams, "US Objectives in the Congo, 1960–65," *Africa Report* 10:8 (August 1965), p. 18; *New York Times*, July 25, 1964.

the new leader professed his commitment to unity. Most Africans, however, regarded Tshombe as a traitor, an agent of foreign imperialists, and the murderer of Patrice Lumumba, a martyr of African nationalism. U.S. support for Tshombe therefore put at risk relations with most of the rest of the continent. A rebel government established itself in Stanleyville and proclaimed its independence. Tshombe responded by reactivating his old Katanganese gendarmes and recruiting foreign mercenaries (mostly from South Africa and Rhodesia) to lead the campaign against the rebels. The Congo crisis was escalating and threatening to divide Africa.

The White House plan called for a U.S.–Belgian effort to organize "3,000 former Katanga gendarmerie officered by military technicians (mercenaries)."[58] Harriman traveled to Brussels immediately after the fall of Stanleyville in August to prod his old colleague Paul-Henri Spaak, the Belgian Minister for Foreign Affairs, to provide more assistance. Harriman briefed the president upon his return, and Johnson noted with foreboding that "time is running out and the Congo must be saved"[59] The administration publicly accused the Congolese rebels of receiving assistance from communist China, but its own intelligence reports pointed out that the rebellion was "not so much organized insurrection as spreading anarchy."[60]

The ANC began to push the rebels back, thanks to U.S. and European military support, the CIA-sponsored air force, and the ruthless efficiency of the Katanganese units led by white mercenaries. In a move to buy time and allow for delivery of military assistance from Egypt, Ghana, and other radical African states, the rebels threatened to execute Europeans in Stanleyville if the mercenary advance did not halt.[61] The rebels abused and terrorized their hostages and sentenced Paul Carlson, an American missionary doctor, to death as a spy.

58. Harriman to Bundy, "The Congo," August 11, 1964, NSF, Box 81, LBJL; Williams to Rusk, "A New and Longer Term Approach to the Congo," August 7, 1964, GMW-NA, Box 29.
59. Memorandum for the Files, NSC Meeting on the Congo, August 11, 1964, NSC Meeting File, Box 2, LBJL. The Congo was also discussed at the NSC Meeting on August 25.
60. Harriman, "United States Policy and Africa," *DSB* 51 (September 7, 1964), p. 333; Embtel 283 (Leopoldville), July 31, 1964; Hughes to Rusk, "Appraisal of Congolese Insurgency," August 7, 1964. Both NSF, Box 81, LBJL.
61. David Reed, *111 Days in Stanleyville* (New York: Harper & Row, 1965).

The OAU appointed an ad hoc committee chaired by Kenya's Jomo Kenyatta to try to mediate an end to the crisis. Ambassador William Attwood in Nairobi met with the rebel representative and Kenyatta in a series of inconclusive talks. The rebels demanded an end to U.S. assistance and a cease-fire while Attwood insisted that the question of the hostages be treated separately and first.[62] The talks continued in a desultory fashion while the United States and Belgium took steps for a military rescue operation code named Dragon Rouge. By late November, the execution date approached, Attwood's talks bogged down, the mercenary armies converged on Stanleyville, and American planes prepared to fly Belgian paratroopers to the Congo.[63]

Washington and Brussels received reports of the rebels' killing some of their hostages as mercenary troops approached and decided to launch Dragon Rouge on November 24.[64] As the Belgian paratroopers began to land, Radio Stanleyville broadcast, "Take your machetes and kill the white people. Kill the white people!"[65] In the chaos that followed, twenty Belgian and two American civilians, including Carlson, were killed. Sixteen hundred foreigners were evacuated. In addition, the paratroopers opened the way for the ANC and mercenaries to take Stanleyville, a secondary but planned supplement to the rescue operation.[66] The ANC rampaged through town, looting and killing untold thousands of rebels, sympathizers, and innocents. An often murderous mopping up resulted in the death of a number of other foreign hostages and the wide-scale terrorizing of the Congolese countryside.

Washington calculated in advance that African reaction to Dragon Rouge "would be serious, but not catastrophic nor necessarily irreversible over time."[67] The fury of the response, however, greatly exceeded expectations. To much of Africa, the operation

---

62. Attwood, *The Reds and the Blacks,* Chapter 16.
63. Bundy to Johnson, "Congo Situation," November 16, 1964, NSF, Box 83, LBJL.
64. United States Cooperates with Belgium in Rescue of Hostages from the Congo," *DSB* 51 (December 14, 1964): 838–45; Thomas P. Odom, *Dragon Operations: Hostage Rescues in the Congo, 1964–1965* (Ft. Leavenworth, Kansas: Leavenworth Papers No. 14, 1988).
65. Reed, *111 Days,* p. 250.
66. Weissman, *American Foreign Policy in the Congo,* pp. 249–52. See also Paul F. Semonin, "Killing Them Definitively," *The Nation,* January 31, 1966, pp. 129–32.
67. INR Research Memorandum RAF-57, "Dragon Rouge: African Reactions and Other Estimates," November 18, 1964, NSF, Box 83, LBJL.

smacked of neo-imperialist interference in support of the detested Tshombe. Anti-American demonstrations broke out across Africa, "Hang Johnson" signs appeared in Nairobi, and rioters burned the official United States Information Service library in Cairo.[68] The anger threw the administration on the defensive, and administration officials began releasing statements and documents to back up their contention that the operation was purely humanitarian and was launched only after every other option had been exhausted.[69] Johnson spoke from his ranch on November 28 and insisted that "the United States has no political goals to impose upon the Congo. . . . We went in solely for humanitarian reasons."[70]

Africa's anger exploded at the United Nations, where rancorous and angry debate occupied the Security Council for three weeks in December.[71] Most African representatives (along with the Soviet Union) argued that the operation was a shameless attempt to reestablish colonial rule, questioned Tshombe's legitimacy, and considered the operation an insult to the OAU. The representative from Congo-Brazzaville, for example, stated that

the famous humanitarian operation of Stanleyville has now proved to us that a white, especially if his name is Carlson, or if he is an American, a Belgian, or an Englishman, is worth thousands upon thousands of blacks. Thus . . . the most ruthless and most scandalous aggression of our era has just been committed.[72]

Even generally moderate Kenya attacked, disputing Ambassador Stevenson's claim that every peaceful means had been exhausted prior to the launching of the rescue operation.[73]

Stevenson's anger reached the surface, and he responded with intemperate words of his own:

Never before have I heard such irrational, irresponsible, insulting and repugnant language in these chambers; and language used, if you please, to contemptuously impugn and slander a gallant and successful effort to

68. Reed, *111 Days*, p. 269; Attwood, *The Reds and the Blacks*, pp. 218–29.
69. Interview of Under Secretary Ball on NBC Television, November 24, in *DSB* 51 (December 14, 1964), p. 843.
70. *Public Papers of the Presidents: Lyndon B. Johnson, 1963–64* (Washington: Government Printing Office, 1965), pp. 1612, 1618.
71. *Yearbook of the United Nations, 1964*, pp. 95–100.
72. UN Security Council Meeting No. 1184, December 23, 1964, p. 24.   73. Ibid., p. 2.

save human lives of many nationalities and colors. . . . We have no apolo-
gies to make to any state appearing before this council. We are proud of
our part in saving human lives imperiled by the civil war in the Congo.[74]

Stevenson went so far as to attack his critics for engaging in "black
racism." Even liberals in the administration reacted with shock at
what they perceived as unwarranted denunciation.

Johnson believed that he could not allow the Congo to fall but
did not want extensive, open involvement to distract his administration from more important questions. He relied upon covert
assistance, endorsed Tshombe's use of mercenaries, and encouraged greater Belgian participation. When the hostage crisis in
Stanleyville drew Johnson into direct military action, the ensuing
controversy led the administration to retreat further from Africa's
problems. Although the heat and emotions generated by the rescue
operation cooled before too long, the impact on Africa's image in
the United States endured. It seemed as if Stanleyville represented
the nadir of U.S. policy in Africa.[75] U.S. liberals lost their self-
assurance that progress in Africa would be easy and inevitable and
began to view the continent with greater apprehension. Murray
Kempton wrote, "Africa hollers rape against us and does not
even know that we no longer even care, let alone lust, and that our
only reaction is to say, well, that's that and who's got a job for
Soapy Williams."[76]

The Development of a Johnson Policy Toward Africa

As Johnson took the oath of office following his landslide victory
in 1964, his inclination to avoid African problems had been reinforced by the turmoil engendered by Stanleyville. Williams and his
allies, on the other hand, believed that the difficulties in U.S. relations with the continent resulted from a lack of sustained attention
and insufficient assistance. The State Department's Africa Bureau
wanted to develop a distinctive "Johnson policy toward Africa"

74. *DSB*, January 4, 1965, p. 15.
75. Emerson, *Africa and United States Policy*, pp. 1–2; Kenneth W. Grundy, "The Stanleyville Rescue: American Policy in the Congo," *Yale Review* 56:2 (Winter 1967), p. 244.
76. Murray Kempton, "The End of Africa," *New Republic*, January 28, 1965, p. 12.

designed to bring order to the ad hoc and reactive policy and to make Africa an integral part of U.S. foreign policy. Williams also hoped that by putting Johnson's personal stamp on African policy he would have more leverage in bureaucratic battles for resources and attention. In this effort the Africa Bureau conducted a full-year review that culminated in a May 1966 speech by the president on the occasion of the third anniversary of the OAU.

After a slow review and many bureaucratic delays, the president eventually agreed to make the speech for several reasons. As a public relations gesture, the speech would show Johnson's personal concern about Africa's problems without having to make new commitments. In the bureaucratic struggle over policy toward white rule in Rhodesia, liberals convinced Johnson that strong and principled statements would translate into valuable good will on the continent. Johnson's political advisers, most notably Bill Moyers and Arthur Goldberg, presented the speech as an opportunity to make a symbolic gesture to the civil rights community and prevent others – particularly Senator Robert F. Kennedy – from using Africa against him.[77] Despite Williams's initial motivation, the speech did not represent increased high-level attention or lead to more resources for the continent. Instead, it placed the spotlight on Africa for a brief evening only to show the fundamental lack of interest that constrained policy and kept Africa off the agenda.

Williams began circulating a draft for a new Africa policy in April 1965 and discussed the idea with Johnson in May. The assistant secretary reported to all U.S. embassies and missions that the president had encouraged him "to shape future U.S. policy toward Africa with [the] same energy and imagination that generated programs of 'The Great Society' at home."[78] Williams's original draft, however, seemed to promise something for everyone while remaining silent on specifics, especially with regard to funding.[79] All of this set off warning bells for Ulric Haynes, the NSC member responsible for Africa, who considered the draft "long, vague, and

77. This account of the OAU speech is based on the National Security Council History compiled by Roger Morris. NSC Histories, President's Speech on Third Anniversary of Organization for African Unity, May 26, 1966, NSF, Box 14, LBJL.
78. Deptel Circular 2156, May 6, 1965, NSF, Box 76, LBJL.
79. Williams Memorandum to Ambassadors and Certain Principal Officers, May 10, 1965, NSF, Box 76, LBJL.

platitudinous." Haynes wrote Bundy that "I'm still skeptical that the 'New Program' . . . can be pulled down from way up there in the clouds" and warned that Williams was ignoring Johnson's stipulation that new substantial expenditures were impossible.[80]

Williams, not at all dissuaded, made the New Program for Africa his major policy initiative during the summer of 1965.[81] The program, he contended, would "imprint African policy with the LBJ brand."[82] Rusk forwarded the proposal to Johnson in October and justified increased spending as a means to prevent

[c]ommunist encroachments (perhaps "Wars of Liberation") in Africa. This liberal, responsive concept of our relations with Africa would be a particularly appropriate foreign policy counterpart of the Great Society.[83]

The NSC did not share State's enthusiasm for the plan. Komer long had argued for a new strategy and supported Williams's call for a presidential speech.[84] Komer, however, believed that the position Johnson took on political issues would matter more than additional aid dollars. The NSC wanted Johnson deliberately to show greater sympathy for the liberation movements in southern Africa "even if it breaks some crockery. A few rousing speeches will buy us more than $200 million in aid."[85] Komer believed that State missed this critical point and sat on the Rusk–Williams proposal for five weeks. When he finally forwarded it his covering note stated, "You will recall that this is what you 'asked' Soapy for last spring. We have held it up briefly, so as not to burden you with what is regrettably rather a mouse."[86] Johnson approved the plan but added Komer's concerns about budget review and the need to emphasize political issues.[87] Williams drafted a revised speech and

80. Haynes to Komer and Bundy, " 'Soapy's' Johnson Plan for Africa," April 28, 1965; Haynes to Bundy, "New Program for Africa," May 13, 1965; Haynes to Moyers, "Governor Williams' Johnson Plan for Africa," May 3, 1965. All NSF, Box 76, LBJL.
81. Haynes to Bundy, "AF Chief of Mission Conference – New Policy for Africa," June 5, 1965, NSF, Box 76, LBJL.
82. Williams to Rusk, "Strengthened African Program – Action Memorandum," September 17, 1965, NSF, Box 14, LBJL.
83. Rusk to Johnson, "Strengthened African Program," October 14, 1965, NSF, Box 14, LBJL.
84. Haynes to Bundy, "Improving U.S. Relations with Africa," March 8, 1965, NSF, Box 76, LBJL.
85. Komer to Bundy, "Draft Memo to President on Africa Policy," June 16, 1965, NSF, Box 76, LBJL.
86. Komer to Johnson, November 23, 1965, NSF, Box 14, LBJL. This memo was signed by Bundy.
87. Johnson to Rusk, "Strengthened African Program," November 28, 1965, NSF, Box 14, LBJL.

recommended several occasions for delivery in late 1965 and early 1966, but the memos did not get to Johnson.[88]

The Strengthened African Program seemed to languish for lack of attention at the highest levels of State or the White House for months. Williams eventually resigned from the Africa Bureau with the proposal still under review. The idea received an important boost in April 1966, however, when UN Ambassador Arthur J. Goldberg stepped in to champion the plan. Goldberg argued that the time was opportune for a Johnson plan because such a new initiative would show the world that, despite Vietnam, the United States still could act vigorously in foreign policy. Goldberg, echoing Komer, emphasized the political dimensions and noted that "it is on how firmly we support truly representative government and the termination of racial rule in Africa that the Africans will make their basic judgments about the United States over the next few years."[89]

With Goldberg providing the political rationale, Johnson immediately decided to give the speech. Bill Moyers finalized the draft during the night of May 25–6. Moyers made clear in a cover memo to Johnson what he believed the speech accomplished. He thought the statement on self-determination would "splash big headlines" except in "South Africa and Rhodesia and other outposts of injustice." In addition, Moyers made sure to point out the domestic benefits of the speech: "I think it is important to speak out this once on the subject for foreign policy reasons as well as for its impact on the civil rights people at home; it is a cheap way to keep them quiet on at least one issue." An additional domestic benefit related to Johnson's political nemesis Robert Kennedy, who was leaving for South Africa that week. Moyers stated that Kennedy "will try to get ahead of you on the question of political liberty for Negro Africans. Your speech prempts [*sic*] the stage."[90]

Johnson delivered the speech in the East Room of the White House to an audience that included the ambassadors of the 36 member states of the OAU and some 300 guests. Johnson's speech itself was relatively short. The most important section on Rhodesia stated that

88. Williams to Rusk, "Strengthened African Program," December 23, 1965, NSF, Box 14, LBJL, was updated and resubmitted on March 9, 1966.
89. Goldberg to Johnson, April 23, 1966, NSF, Box 14, LBJL.
90. Moyers to LBJ, May 26, 1966, NSF, Box 76, LBJL.

[a]s a basic part of our national tradition we support self-determination and an orderly transition to majority rule in every quarter of the globe. . . . Only when this is accomplished can steps be taken to open the full power and responsibility of nationhood to all the people of Rhodesia – not just 6 percent of them.[91]

The speech went on to discuss development issues and the need for greater regional cooperation but lacked detailed new programs. On the critical question of increased spending, the controversial issue throughout the review process, the president resorted to the hoary but useful stratagem of appointing a blue-ribbon committee to review the question. Johnson named Edward Korry, the ambassador to Ethiopia, to chair the panel.

Johnson agreed to make the speech after advisers pointed out it would help him deal with the civil rights community and undercut Kennedy and other liberal opponents. The speech did not translate into a new policy toward Africa, however, because Johnson was unwilling to fight for greater expenditures or risk controversial involvement on the continent while Vietnam absorbed so much money and attention.

The principal result of the year-long review and formulation of options that culminated in the speech was the establishment of Korry's study team on the future of economic assistance to Africa. The programs funded through the Agency for International Development (AID) and the Peace Corps were the primary instruments available to protect and promote U.S. interests in Africa.[92] Liberal policymakers in Washington perceived encouraging economic and political development as an important means to prevent radicalism and opportunities for Soviet or Chinese involvement. In addition, aid built good will toward the United States, and every ambassador wanted an assistance budget – even if it was only a token – in order to validate his or her presence in a developing state and to create the inevitable photo opportunities occasioned by opening new schools or other public works.

Getting the AID budget through Congress was never an easy matter nor one that the administration was willing to spend much polit-

91. *Public Papers of the Presidents: Lyndon B. Johnson, 1968* (Washington: Government Printing Office, 1967), pp. 556–7.
92. Joan M. Nelson, *Aid, Influence, and Foreign Policy* (New York: Macmillan, 1968), p. 1.

ical capital to accomplish.[93] AID always provided the Appropriations Committees with ample opportunities to score points by blasting assistance to independently minded states. Johnson submitted AID budget requests that he claimed had already been cut to the bone and tried to hold the line rather than pad the budgets and let Congress chop away. The process became even more difficult as anti-Vietnam members of Congress turned against foreign assistance.[94] Democratic Senator J. William Fulbright of Arkansas, for example, called foreign aid "a dubious instrument of national policy" and "a vehicle toward commitments which exceed both American interests and American material and intellectual resources."[95]

The Korry report began by accepting the fact that aid to Africa was limited by the constraints imposed by more pressing concerns elsewhere in the world.[96] The report called for a reduction in the number of African states receiving bilateral aid from thirty-five to ten or so selected on the basis of developmental potential.[97] Korry argued that "the fact that an eloquent case can be made setting forth a need does not mean that it is the responsibility of the United States to satisfy that need."[98] In place of small, scattered bilateral programs, greater emphasis would be given to multilateral institutions such as the World Bank and to regional projects. Much of this was not new, since the bulk of U.S. bilateral assistance already went to a handful of countries.[99] Johnson's total U.S. AID budget request for fiscal year 1968 (the first year after the Korry report) amounted to $195 million, about the same as that for fiscal year 1967.

The White House was pleased with Korry's work, although officials recommended not releasing the report publicly because of its sometimes blunt evaluations.[100] Implementation of the recommendations proved more troublesome. Although Korry supported an increase in annual AID appropriations, the report did little to build

93. Rusk, *As I Saw It*, p. 540   94. Gaud, OH, LBJL.
95. J. William Fulbright, *The Arrogance of Power* (New York: Random House, 1966), pp. 223, 232.
96. *Review of African Development* (hereafter Korry Report), July 22, 1966, NSF, Box 77, LBJL.
97. USAID, *FY 1968 Congressional Presentation*, p. 3.   98. Korry Report, p. 11.
99. Anthony Astrachan, "AID Reslices the Pie," *Africa Report* 12:6 (June 1967), p. 10.
100. Ball to Johnson, "Review of African Development Policies and Programs Pursuant to Your Speech of May 26," August 8, 1966; Rostow to Johnson, "The Korry Report on Development Policies and Programs in Africa," August 9, 1966. Both NSF, Box 14, LBJL.

a rationale for additional expenditures. The report separated the economic aspects of development from political considerations and thereby risked undermining the rationale for assistance.[101] The report's criticism of bilateral aid further eroded the political basis of the program. As Charles Darlington, the U.S. ambassador to Gabon, stated, "As a general matter give me bilateral aid; that is where the United States gets leverage."[102]

Constituencies and Southern Africa

Johnson gave the OAU anniversary speech to demonstrate to his detractors that his administration was capable of new foreign policy initiatives.[103] The high-level attention occasioned by the speech, however, soon faded, and the preoccupation with southeast Asia left Johnson's lofty rhetoric unfulfilled. While Williams and the NSC debated the outline of a Johnson policy toward Africa in 1965 and 1966, the White House avoided most other African issues and left the State Department to manage them on its own. Following the speech and the Korry report, the administration focused on the continent only when crises or extraneous concerns related an African issue to other more salient interests.

Johnson's policies toward decolonization in southern Africa – the "white redoubt" that included the Portuguese colonies of Angola and Mozambique, the British colony of Southern Rhodesia, South Africa, and the South African controlled territory of South-West Africa – illustrated the administration's reluctance to take the lead in Africa. The region could not be ignored, however, because the issues of racial, economic, and political justice resembled those in the United States, and inactivity in Southern Africa raised doubts about commitments at home.[104]

Williams and the Africa Bureau, often with the support of Goldberg at the UN and Komer and Haynes in the NSC, recognized that if Johnson did not position himself in support of liberation, all

---

101. Korry Report, pp. 20, 70.
102. Darlington and Darlington, *African Betrayal*, p. 97.
103. Goldberg to Johnson, April 23, 1966, NSF, Box 14, LBJL.
104. John Marcum, "Southern Africa and United States Policy: A Consideration of Alternatives," *Africa Today* 14:5 (October 1967), p. 5.

other African policies would be undermined. On the other hand, Europeanists such as Undersecretary of State George Ball, military strategists involved in building European support for Vietnam, NASA protecting its tracking stations in the region, and Department of Commerce officials interested in U.S. trade with the region believed that the United States would gain little and potentially lose much by being in the forefront of opposition to white rule in southern Africa.

The differences between Williams and Ball and their supporters bottled up new initiatives in endless bureaucratic meetings – a deadlock that suited Johnson and Rusk, who were uninterested or absorbed with more pressing matters elsewhere. As a result, policy toward southern Africa became a concoction of ad hoc reactions, shaped by non-African concerns such as diplomacy at the United Nations, European interests, and the irregular entreaties of interest groups. On occasion, such as the administration's actions in the UN on South-West Africa and Rhodesia, individuals were able to take action despite the lack of high-level interest. Otherwise Johnson tried to avoid potentially controversial and expensive involvement by making symbolic gestures and leaving the initiative to others.

Europeanists in the administration were particularly successful in stymieing policies in support of decolonization in Portuguese Africa. Johnson faced the dilemma of trying to balance the desire to build good relations with independent African states while maintaining close ties with Portugal, a NATO ally that controlled the strategically important Azores.[105] The administration tried to pursue these antithetical goals simultaneously and ended up angering both sides. The Africa Bureau wanted increased U.S. support for the nationalists, particularly in Angola, to prevent them from moving toward the communist bloc.[106] By 1965, Vietnam and Ball's opposition to policies that pressured Portugal made initiatives that risked U.S. military access to the Azores impossible.

Johnson had more room to maneuver in response to the November 11, 1965, Unilateral Declaration of Independence (UDI) by

105. Schneidman, "American Foreign Policy and the Fall of the Portuguese Empire," Ch. 3; Noer, *Cold War and Black Liberation*, Ch. 5.
106. Bureau of African Affairs, "Action Memorandum: Portuguese African Territories," April 29, 1964, NSF: Portugal, Box 1, LBJL.

the white government in the British colony of Rhodesia. African states viewed UDI as an outrage, and the United States could heed these concerns because it had few other interests in Rhodesia. Even this relative consideration, however, compared with other African issues, did not capture significant high-level attention. As one State Department official recalled, most officials regarded the crisis as "just a little mess the British had on their hands" in a year when Vietnam and the Dominican Republic dominated the agenda.[107]

The administration followed London's lead at first, reflecting both the "special relationship" with the United Kingdom and the propensity to encourage the involvement of former colonial powers in Africa. Rusk, for example, told Johnson that he regarded UDI as "first a UK problem, then a UN problem, and only then is it a U.S. problem.[108] The lack of consensus within the administration about an alternative policy reinforced this preference for European action.

This strategy, however, came under fire by both liberals and conservatives as Washington became disillusioned with London's inability to handle the crisis.[109] By 1966 Rhodesia had become a matter of considerable domestic debate. Johnson made specific condemnation of Rhodesia the centerpiece of his May 1966 speech on Africa. As Rhodesia continued to defy Great Britain, the Commonwealth pressured London to support mandatory sanctions at the United Nations. Washington also voted in favor of the resolution that passed on December 16, 1966, after receiving assurances that the action did not apply to South Africa or Portugal and that it did not imply the use of force. Support for sanctions helped diffuse some of the criticism from Africa of U.S. inaction. Given that the new policy continued to follow Britain and that U.S. business interests in Rhodesia were minor, however, the vote risked little. Europeanists in the administration, nevertheless, opposed even this largely symbolic vote. Ball, for example, dismissed sanctions as a "romantic delusion."[110]

---

107. Quoted in Anthony Lake, *The "Tar Baby" Option: American Policy Toward Southern Rhodesia* (New York: Columbia University Press, 1976), p. 61.
108. Summary Notes of the 567th NSC Meeting, January 25, 1967, NSC Meetings File, Box 2; Stevenson in *DSB* 53 (June 28, 1965), 1061–6; Williams in *DSB* 53 (June 12, 1965).
109. Noer, *Cold War and Black Liberation*, Ch. 9.
110. George Ball, *The Discipline of Power* (Boston: Little, Brown, 1968), p. 245.

The sanction vote stimulated an unusual amount of public comment and controversy. Former Secretary of State Dean Acheson publicly criticized the vote in a December 11, 1966, letter to the *Washington Post*. Acheson argued that the domestic policies of Rhodesia were not a "threat to peace" and therefore concerned neither the UN nor the United States.[111] Ambassador Goldberg responded and made the case in international law for sanctions against Rhodesia.[112] The two exchanged arguments and debating points though 1967 without resolving their fundamental differences. In the end, Goldberg saw little more to gain from the exchange and told a reporter that Acheson was "a very distinguished man, but what he has said [on Rhodesia] is sheer nonsense."[113]

South Africa had the symbolic potency to draw the attention of U.S. interest groups, and hence Johnson's notice, because its racial policies seemed somewhat analogous to domestic racial divisions. South African Prime Minister Hendrik Verwoerd regularly attacked the United States to protect his position in the National Party.[114] These provocations and inevitable American responses generated a degree of attention but did little to create a consensus for action. Verwoerd, for example, protested the American embassy's multiracial guest lists and stated that it would not allow black personnel at NASA's tracking station. When the aircraft carrier *Independence* wanted to refuel in Capetown the South African government denied shore leave for black crew members. Members of Congress arose in self-righteous opposition, and, following a meeting between members of Congress and Pentagon officials, all shore leave was canceled.[115]

These provocations provided fertile territory for U.S. politicians looking to build support in the civil rights community at home. Senator Robert Kennedy of New York traveled to Capetown in June 1966, for example, and used the setting to deliver a speech on

111. Dean Acheson, letter to the editor, *Washington Post*, December 11, 1966. See also Charles Burton Marshall, *Crisis Over Rhodesia: A Skeptical View* (Baltimore: Johns Hopkins University Press, 1967).
112. Arthur Goldberg, letter to the editor, *Washington Post*, January 8, 1967.
113. Quoted in Lake, *The "Tar Baby" Option*, p. 116.
114. Vernon McKay, "South African Propaganda: Methods and Media," *Africa Report* 11:2 (February 1966), pp. 42–3; Philip W. Quigg, "South African Problems and Prospects," *Africa Report* 10:1 (January 1965), pp. 9–11.
115. "Apartheid Keeps Crew on US Ship," *New York Times*, February 5, 1967, p. 1.

racial harmony that was addressed as much to the United States as
to South Africa.[116] Johnson regarded this trip as an effort to court
black voters for a Kennedy presidential campaign in 1968.

The competing concerns of different interests in Johnson's administration and in the broader public left his policy toward South
Africa lifeless. Williams and the Africa Bureau could not even get
the administration to accept a policy that would officially "discourage" new American investments in South Africa.[117] The administration continued to oppose economic sanctions and therefore
had few options other than symbolic disapproval to encourage reform. Strategic and economic concerns continued to undercut U.S.
political interests in seeking an end to apartheid, despite Williams's
attempt to camouflage with low-cost rhetoric the essential immo-
bility of U.S. policy in congressional testimony.[118]

Sometimes African issues could not be kept off the agenda because African leaders forced consideration at the United Nations.
The decision by the International Court of Justice (ICJ) to dismiss
the case against South African rule in South-West Africa required
a response from the White House. The protracted ICJ case had allowed the administration to avoid difficult choices in the region for
several years, but the court had thrown the issue back on the international agenda. For months the administration had developed
and reviewed contingency plans on the assumption that the court
would rule against South Africa and that Pretoria would resist the
decision.[119] The administration had few good options and expected
that the decision would inevitably "trouble Africa's relations with
the West."[120]

All these plans had to be scrapped and the administration scram-
bled for a new strategy when the court surprised almost everyone

116. *New York Times,* June 7, 1966; Arthur M. Schlesinger Jr., *Robert Kennedy and His
     Times* (Boston: Houghton Mifflin, 1978), pp. 743–9.
117. NSC, "Memorandum for Mr. Bundy," December 10, 1963, NSF: South Africa, Box
     2, LBJL.
118. Richard Eder, "Williams Backs Apartheid Fight," *New York Times,* March 2, 1966,
     p. A17.
119. "Briefing for NSC Standing Group: South Africa and South West Africa," March 10,
     1964, NSF, Box 76, LBJL; National Security Council Action Memorandum No. 295,
     "U.S. Policy Toward South Africa," April 29, 1964; NSC Meetings, Vol. 3, Tab 43,
     7/14/66 – Southwest Africa.
120. Special National Intelligence Estimate No. 70–66, "Probable Repercussions of the
     South-West Africa Issue," June 2, 1966, National Intelligence Estimates, LBJL.

and dismissed the case on July 18, 1966, after six years of litigation, on the grounds that the plaintiffs, Liberia and Ethiopia, lacked legal standing.[121] The Afro-Asian bloc at the United Nations reacted with immediate anger. It wanted the UN to terminate South African control and impose sanctions if Pretoria resisted despite the nondecision by the ICJ. Officials in Washington groaned that they risked a divisive battle regardless of their policy. Once the court's decision lobbed the issue back on the United Nations' agenda, however, the administration had to take a stand.

UN Ambassador Arthur Goldberg recognized the importance of the issue for U.S. standing in New York and almost singlehandedly pushed through a policy more responsive to African demands but that avoided mandatory sanctions. With Goldberg's support, the UN passed a resolution declaring that South Africa had forfeited its rights to continue to administer the territory and that a UN commission would propose additional actions. Goldberg was clearly Johnson's man and therefore had the ability to sidestep the preoccupied State Department and communicate with the president directly.[122] According to Waldemar Nielsen, Africans regarded Goldberg's initiative as "the finest performance by an American head of delegation in years."[123]

Each of the opposing factions of foreign policy professionals on southern Africa had the support of domestic constituencies and pressure groups. Conservatives, the old Katanga lobby, Southern politicians, and some business groups believed that support for the colonial governments served as the best guarantee of stability, anticommunism, and favorable trade. The Friends of Rhodesian Independence and the American–Southern African Council, for example, orchestrated letter-writing campaigns and successfully lobbied the press for favorable coverage.[124]

On the other hand, the civil rights community, some church groups, and many liberal and leftist organizations had by 1966

121. *New York Times,* July 20, 1966.
122. Mayer, "Goldberg Represents Lyndon Johnson," p. 16; Arnold Beichman, *The "Other" State Department: The United States Mission to the United Nations – Its Role in the Making of Foreign Policy* (New York: Basic Books, 1967), pp. 164–72.
123. Nielsen, *The Great Powers and Africa,* p. 317.
124. Vernon McKay, "The Domino Theory of the Rhodesian Lobby," *Africa Report* 12:6 (June 1967), pp. 55–8.

added support for African liberation to their critique of administration policies.[125] One of the most active groups was the American
Committee on Africa (ACOA), but this group had limited impact
because it tended to focus on the UN and the Africa Bureau rather
than on the source of opposition to new policies in the Pentagon
and European Bureau.[126] The administration met with these interest groups in an effort to quiet them with symbolic actions. For
example, both Bundy and Rusk met with delegations from the
National Conference on the South Africa Crisis and American
Action in order to avoid a "flap."[127]

The American Negro Leadership Conference on Africa
(ANLCA) was formed in 1961 and led by a committee that included the major figures in the civil rights movement. ANLCA
worked for greater emphasis on liberation and development and
attention to the OAU and the UN.[128] Johnson discouraged this
group, arguing that he did not want "an integrated domestic policy and a segregated foreign policy."[129] Domestic policy concerns,
not surprisingly, remained the principal mobilizing issue of civil
rights leaders, and ANLCA soon dissolved.[130]

During the final two years of the administration, Johnson's preoccupation with Vietnam resulted in the almost complete neglect of
Africa. The Africa Bureau shifted from Williams to Joseph Palmer,
a career diplomat designated because of his abilities as a careful administrator. Few in the administration sought to push Africa onto
the agenda. Vice President Hubert Humphrey toured the continent
in late 1967 and early 1968, but this high-level visit produced no
momentum. With the exceptions of a brief flurry in July 1967 when
a decision to support the government in the Congo led to a flap with
Congress and the public attention in late 1968 to the Biafran catastrophe, which prompted humanitarian relief, few developments on
the continent induced a reaction from Washington.

125. Noer, *Cold War and Black Liberation*, pp. 169–70.
126. Lake, *The "Tar Baby" Option*, pp. 70–1.
127. Haynes to Bundy, March 4, 1965; Memorandum of Conversation, "Secretary's Meet-
    ing with Delegation from the 'National Conference on the South African Crisis and
    American Actions,' " March 23, 1965. Both in NSF, Box 76, LBJL.
128. John A. Davis, "Black Americans and United States Policy Toward Africa," *Journal of
    International Affairs* 23:2 (1969), pp. 241–3.
129. Bundy to Rusk, January 7, 1965, NSF, Box 76, LBJL.
130. Komer and Haynes to Bundy, March 30, 1965, NSF, Box 76, LBJL.

Congress did not provide an alternative source of African policy during the Johnson years. As an issue outside the scope of most members' principal concerns, the continent could serve as a symbolic issue to express their disapproval of Johnson's policy elsewhere. For example, development assistance to Africa became a victim of congressional displeasure with the war in Vietnam. Proponents of civil rights criticized Johnson's resistance to sanctions against South Africa while anticommunist members complained that he favored radials such as Nkrumah.

Congressional criticism of Johnson's decision to send transport planes to the Congo indicates how members of Congress used Africa to send a message about Vietnam. In July 1967 white mercenary units rebelled and seized several cities in Western Congo. Johnson agreed to send the Congolese government three C-130 transport planes with American crews in the hope of preventing another round of chaos and to demonstrate that Washington supported the Congo whether under threat from "Maoist" guerrillas in 1964 or reactionary white mercenaries in 1967.[131]

When Congress heard of the decision, the White House received a flood of criticism as members voiced their opposition to Johnson's failure to consult and raised the specter of "another Vietnam" once again.[132] The Department of State cabled Kinshasa and informed the ambassador that the "highest levels in USG [are] interested in finding [a] humanitarian mission for [the] C-130s to perform" in order to furnish additional political cover.[133] Johnson chewed out his staff for failing to brief Congress adequately, although Rusk insisted that he had informed Senators Fulbright and Richard Russell, the latter a Georgia Democrat.[134] Rusk received a grilling by the Senate Foreign Relations Committee on July 11, but State stoically understood that the umbrage was the result of racial

---

131. Congo C-130 Crisis, July 1967, National Security Council History (hereafter NSCH), Box 15, LBJL.
132. Letter from 18 Senators to Johnson, July 27, 1967, NSCH, Box 15, LBJL.
133. Deptel 4338 (to Kinshasa), July 11, 1967; Rostow to Johnson, "Congo Situation Report," July 12, 1967, NSCH, Box 15, LBJL.
134. Tom Johnson's Notes of Meetings of the President with Secretary Rusk, Secretary McNamara, Walt Rostow, George Christian, Tom Johnson, July 12, 1967; NSC Meetings, Vol. 4, Tab 54, 7/13/67 – African Problems: Summary Notes of the 572nd NSC Meeting, July 13, 1967; Tom Johnson's Notes on the President's Meeting with the Cabinet, July 19, 1967; Rusk, *As I Saw It*, pp. 280–1, 543.

attitudes and a hesitancy to get involved anywhere in the world as a result of Vietnam.[135]

Africa attracted the attention of the general public and hence forced African issues onto the president's agenda. The sensational reports of savagery, cannibalism, and mercenary activities that surrounded the Stanleyville rescue mission made for good copy in 1964. Rhodesia's UDI in November 1965 generated attention as a story parallel to America's own break from England, on the one hand, or as a tale of gross racial discrimination, on the other. In 1968, as Johnson's days as president wound down and few new issues received attention, pictures of starving children in Biafra generated unprecedented and broad public outrage that obliged the administration to act.

Nigeria had been a favored recipient of U.S. economic assistance and served as a model of a moderate African state in the early 1960s.[136] By 1967, however, Nigeria's domestic divisions had created instability and civil war. Washington could do little to influence the escalating conflict as the eastern section declared its independence as the state of Biafra. Johnson, as usual, looked to Great Britain to take the lead in its former colony. Washington responded to the civil war by merely announcing its neutrality and instituting an arms embargo against both sides. The conflict risked taking on a Cold War dimension when the Nigerian Federal Government turned to the Soviet Union for military assistance. The State Department called the arms agreement "a matter of regret" but did not escalate its own involvement to match Moscow's.[137]

Famine broke out in Biafra following the Nigerian Federal Government's blockade of the region. Advocates of the Biafran cause as well as nonpolitical relief groups generated a compelling public campaign by using heartbreaking pictures of starving children to symbolize the need for action. Religious, civil rights, and labor groups sent telegrams to the president urging a massive airlift. A

---

135. Tom Johnson's Notes of the President's Meeting with the National Security Council Staff, July 13, 1967.
136. Robert B. Shepard, *Nigeria, Africa, and the United States: From Kennedy to Reagan* (Bloomington: Indiana University Press, 1991).
137. "Soviet Decision to Supply Arms to Nigeria," *DSB* (September 11, 1967), p. 320; Herbert Ekwe-Ekwe, *Conflict and Intervention in Africa: Nigeria, Angola, Zaire* (New York: St. Martin's Press, 1990), pp. 47–51.

full-page advertisement in the *New York Times* pictured a dead Biafran child and asked the reader to send the page to Johnson.[138] As one letter to the editor put it,

> I've seen nothing more compelling since I began reading newspapers than the article on the dying Biafra babies. . . . I pray that President Johnson will send aid. We have the pilots, the planes, and the parachutes to put food where it is needed most.[139]

Liberal Democratic senators such as Edward Kennedy of Massachusetts, Eugene McCarthy of Minnesota, and George McGovern of South Dakota attacked Johnson for his inaction and used the issue to differentiate themselves from his "immoral" administration.[140] Republican presidential candidate Richard M. Nixon also criticized Johnson for delay, and Mrs. Nixon appeared on the steps of St. Patrick's Cathedral soliciting donations.

Public pressure for action mounted until, according to Roger Morris, an NSC staffer at the time, Johnson ordered the State Department to "get those nigger babies off my TV set."[141] Johnson urged the Nigerian Federal Government to allow relief flights, encouraged Emperor Haile Selassie and the OAU to take action, but never advocated international recognition of Biafra as an independent state.[142] The administration provided funds and planes for the International Committee of the Red Cross when it began humanitarian flights to Biafra. Undersecretary of State Nicholas Katzenbach outlined both the humanitarian and domestic reasons for deciding to increase aid: "It will save lives, cost us next to nothing, and decrease Congressional heat here at home."[143] Johnson pointed out in a public statement that "the political dispute underlying this war is a Nigerian and an African problem – not an American one."[144]

138. *New York Times*, August 15, 1968.
139. Letter to the editor from Alphonso H. Caser to the *New York Times*, August 7, 1968.
140. E. W. Kenworthy, "M'Carthy Bids U.S. Ask Biafra Relief," *New York Times*, September 3, 1968, p. A1. Statement by Senator McGovern before the Senate, *Congressional Record*, August 2, 1968, pp. S10133–4; Kennedy, *Congressional Record*, September 23, 1968, pp. S1227–8.
141. Morris, *Uncertain Greatness*, p. 42.
142. Rostow to Johnson, August 15, 1968, NSF, Box 96, LBJL; *DSB*, October 7, 1968, p. 356; *Public Papers of the Presidents: Lyndon B. Johnson, 1968–1969* (Washington: Government Printing Office, 1970) p. 805, 875.
143. Katzenbach to Johnson, "Aircraft for Nigerian Relief," December 24, 1968, NSF, Box 96, LBJL; Katzenbach, *DSB* (December 23, 1968), pp. 654–8.
144. *Public Papers of the Presidents: Lyndon B. Johnson, 1968–1969*, p. 1115.

U.S. humanitarian assistance undoubtedly saved lives, but Washington lacked the leverage to resolve the underlying civil conflict. Johnson urged constraint on the Nigerian Federal Government, encouraged African mediation efforts, but never seriously considered recognizing Biafra. The White House avoided taking sides and did not increase U.S. involvement to match Soviet military shipments, thereby preventing Cold War considerations from complicating the local conflict. Biafra, however, came to Johnson's attention primarily as an issue of domestic public opinion, and his decision to send humanitarian aid was in reaction to this sentiment rather than to foreign policy goals.

In general, the public lobbying from domestic interest groups tended to reenforce Johnson's reluctance to become involved in Africa. Decisions seemed to generate controversy rather than additional support. Without clear options that would redound to the president's advantage, the lack of vital U.S. interests, the bureaucratic divisions reinforced by opposing public pressure groups, and the urgency of more pressing problems elsewhere in the world led Johnson to conclude that there was little to be gained by addressing African issues.

Conclusion

The constraints imposed by the lack of vital interests in Africa, Johnson's preoccupation with issues he perceived as more salient both at home and abroad, the decline of liberal interest in the continent by 1964, and the absence of a dependable and mobilized constituency for action kept Africa off the president's agenda for most of his administration. Once the war in Vietnam grew to dominate the time and attention of high-level policymakers, marginal areas of interest such as Africa had little chance to receive consideration. Bureaucratic divisions that stifled initiative and the belief by Williams and other liberals that communism did not represent a threat in Africa because of the power of nationalism reinforced Johnson's desire to avoid complicated and potentially risky involvement.

In 1964, Johnson kept his administration on the sidelines during the Ethiopia–Somalia border war and the revolution in Zanzibar despite the role of Soviet arms in the former and Chinese support in the latter. He sent emissaries to warn Ghana to tone down its anti-American campaigns but otherwise ignored Nkrumah and continued to fund the Volta Dam. Washington believed that European states should take the lead in these areas and that U.S. interests did not justify greater action.

Johnson perceived the Congo crisis of 1964 as far more serious. Kennedy had already established U.S. involvement, and Johnson simply could not ignore the clear signs of the Congo's unraveling. Victory for rebels with connections to China represented a graver threat in the Congo than in isolated Zanzibar. Western hostages, white mercenaries, and the role of the controversial Tshombe all made the Congo crisis too hot to ignore. Johnson still tried to keep involvement limited by keeping much of U.S. assistance covert, encouraging Europeans and the OAU to take the lead, and trying to shore up the central government without committing U.S. troops. The White House saw the Stanleyville operation as a limited rescue mission and quickly withdrew U.S. planes as soon as the Western hostages were free. Furthermore, the angry and, in U.S. eyes, unjustified reaction by African states to Stanleyville reinforced the administration's predilection to keep Africa on the margins of policy.

Williams and the Africa Bureau tried to forge a more activist policy, but the process of review that resulted in the OAU anniversary speech and the Korry report indicated the inherent constraints on African policy. Johnson never accepted the need for greater assistance given his other budget priorities both abroad and at home. His political advisers convinced him that a speech that put the president on record against UDI in Rhodesia would pay dividends in Africa and, more important, in domestic politics, but the rhetoric never translated into a sustained new policy direction.

Groups outside the administration occasionally forced African issues onto the agenda, but no sustained constituency for action emerged. Civil rights and liberal groups lobbied for tougher measures in support of liberation in southern Africa. Counterpressures from Europeanists, strategic and economic considerations, and the constraints imposed by overextension in Asia, however, led the administration to make symbolic gestures rather than costly or controversial actions. The marginality of Africa to Washington allowed Congress to use the continent as a symbol to display its concerns about Vietnam by cutting AID budgets or protesting the delivering of aircraft to the Congo. The broad general public focused on Africa only during the final months of Johnson's term, when pictures of famine victims in Biafra generated an outpouring of sympathy. Otherwise, Africa remained securely within the purview of the Africa Bureau, which could do little without additional resources or leadership from above.

Despite these constraints, the Johnson administration did rather well on several occasions when faced with concrete questions to which it would apply "pragmatic" solutions. The predisposition to avoid involvement in Zanzibar and Ghana prevented the imposition of Cold War concerns from distorting the local dynamics that worked on their own to limit any threat to U.S. interests. Goldberg's leadership in the UN regarding South-West Africa, Johnson's clear statement against UDI and support for sanctions against Rhodesia, the effective response to the mercenary rebellion in the Congo in 1967, and the skill with which Johnson maintained neutrality on the emotionally charged Biafran issue all represented effective policies despite the constraints of low priority and meager resources.[145] These small steps, however, did not begin to alter the overall lack of interest in Africa during the Johnson administration.

I wish to thank Jodi Nelson, Michael Matthews, and Kirsten Soule for their research assistance and Witney Schneidman and Donald Rothchild for their helpful criticisms of an earlier draft of my chapter on Africa. I also appreciate the financial support of the Lyndon B. Johnson Foundation.

145. Nielson, *The Great Powers and Africa*, pp. 327–9.

9

Balancing American Interests in the Middle East: Lyndon Baines Johnson vs. Gamal Abdul Nasser

WARREN I. COHEN

The men who advised Lyndon Johnson on issues relating to the Middle East perceived three important American interests there. First, the influence of the Soviet Union had to be contained. Second, Israel's right to exist had to be protected. And third, the flow of the region's oil, upon which the industry of the European and Japanese allies of the United States was dependent, had to be maintained. In November 1963, all three fronts were relatively quiet, and the Middle East could not command the attention of senior officials struggling with recurring crises in Vietnam. Only in late May and early June of 1967 did Johnson and his principal aides turn from the torments of southeast Asia to focus their attention on an Arab–Israeli crisis that might have triggered World War III.

The central role in the Middle Eastern drama, from November 1963 to January 1969, was played by Gamal Abdul Nasser, Egyptian president of the United Arab Republic (UAR).[1] Virtually every event of consequence bore his imprint as he rallied Arab masses, manipulated American presidents and Soviet premiers, terrified local potentates, and ranted against Israel. Only in the crisis in Cyprus was he peripheral – and even there his existence increased American anxiety. Important supporting roles were played by Johnson, Archbishop Makarios in Cyprus, King Faisal of Saudi

1. The United Arab Republic was the name given to the union of Egypt and Syria, under Nasser's leadership, consummated in March 1958 as a step toward Arab unity. The Syrians withdrew in September 1961, but Nasser, hoping for reunification, retained the name for the Egyptian remnant. See George Lenczowski, *The Middle East in World Affairs*, 4th ed. (Ithaca, N.Y.: Cornell University Press, 1980), 536–42, 545–9, for a brief sketch of the process. I have used the names *Egypt* and *UAR* interchangeably.

Arabia, Levi Eshkol, prime minister of Israel, the shah of Iran, and the men in the Kremlin.

The charismatic, mercurial, and volatile Nasser was the one great leader who had been able to rally Arab intellectuals, soldiers, shopkeepers, and peasants across northern Africa, through the fertile crescent, and on to the Arabian peninsula. In the twentieth century, he was the one man who might have united the many states into which the Arabic-speaking peoples had been separated. But however appealing his radical nationalist vision may have been to the great mass of Arabs, it was frightening to the kings and colonels who wielded power in existing Arab regimes, to the shah of Iran, and to the Israelis, who depended on Arab disunity for their survival. His dream of leading a Pan-Arab movement that would free itself from the remaining vestiges of European imperialism and desert feudalism was thwarted by conservative Arab rulers such as King Faisal, and by radicals elsewhere in the Middle East, as in Iraq and Syria, with egos equal to his own. He was also frustrated by the limits of his understanding of the problems of economic development and the sources of modern power, and by the trouble he brought upon himself through frequent rhetorical and military excesses. Like most leaders capable of mesmerizing their followers, he was often the victim of autohypnosis. He was, in the classic sense, a tragic figure, a victim of hubris. John F. Kennedy found him attractive and interesting. Lyndon B. Johnson did not.

Soviet pressures on Iran and Turkey and concerns about the Greek civil war had elicited sharp American responses in the late 1940s. The Arab nations had been drawn into the Cold War in the mid-1950s by the American effort to link the "northern tier" states of Turkey, Iraq, Iran, and Pakistan to the western alliance against the Soviet Union. Iraq's accession to the Baghdad Pact so angered Nasser, both as a betrayal of Arab nationalism and as a threat to his leadership, that he made common cause with the Soviets. Soviet influence consequently increased in the region, but the Middle East had been relatively quiet since American forces intervened in civil strife in Lebanon in 1958, and interest had declined in Washington. Technological advances in missile development, submarine launchers, and airborne refueling allowed the distant Americans to depreciate the strategic importance of the area. Should war come, the United States could strike at the Soviet Union without bases on the Soviet periphery.

The commitment to Israel had been strengthened notably in the early 1960s by John F. Kennedy. Privately and publicly he assured the Israelis that the United States would come to their aid if they were invaded. In 1962 he approved the sale of Hawk missiles to the Israelis. But Israel had faced little danger in the late 1950s and early 1960s. Its Arab enemies were disunited and riven with internal power struggles. Egypt, the largest and most powerful Arab nation, had demonstrated remarkable prudence in its actions toward Israel and, beginning in late 1962, had become deeply engaged in a war in Yemen.

The oil for which the region was famous remained important, although primarily to American friends rather than to the United States itself. American Middle East specialists talked and wrote of oil as an economic rather than a strategic concern, but Kennedy was quick to warn Nasser away from Saudi Arabia when the Egyptians and Saudis backed opposing contenders in Yemen and Egyptian planes bombed Saudi staging areas. The oil kept flowing to the industrial states that needed it, and there was no reason to doubt that it would keep flowing for the foreseeable future.

In brief, when Lyndon Johnson took the oath of office as president, there were no pressing issues in the Middle East. He was immediately preoccupied with domestic reform, the election campaign of 1964, and Vietnam. He had little time or inclination to dabble in the area. He expected his secretary of state and his National Security Adviser to manage Middle Eastern affairs and to keep problems from reaching his desk. For the most part, they and their subordinates succeeded, until May 1967, when the president had to take charge.

Johnson attempted in the Middle East as elsewhere to hold to the course Kennedy had chosen. Long a supporter of Israel,[2] in January 1964 he sent assurances to the Israelis that he would honor

2. Louis S. Gomolak in "Prologue: LBJ's Foreign Affairs Background, 1908–1948" (Ph.D. dissertation, University of Texas, 1989) argues that Johnson's grandfather and aunt, as well as LBJ personally, had strong commitments to Jews and to Israel. Members of the

Kennedy's commitment to them.[3] The Israelis were Lyndon Johnson's kind of people – brash, aggressive, unforgiving – and he admired them enormously. Ephraim "Effie" Evron, minister of the Israeli Embassy in Washington, became a close personal friend, a relationship probably unmatched by anything since the days of Teddy Roosevelt and the British diplomat Cecil Spring-Rice.[4]

Johnson's admiration for Israel was reinforced by his close ties, personal and political, to American Jews, to men such as Abe Fortas, Arthur Krim, Ed Weisel, Abe Feinberg, and Arthur Goldberg. He was extraordinarily well connected to Israeli leaders and to the American Jewish community. To Abba Eban, the Israeli foreign minister, he announced in October 1967 that he obtained much comfort from American Jews, that a recent New York poll showed Jewish voters favoring him by a ratio of eighty-one to seven, which, he declared, "proves you are still the smartest people in the world."[5] Johnson was continually troubled, however, by the failure of Israelis or American Jews to support his war in Vietnam, to share his conviction that the defense of Vietnam and the defense of Israel were analogous. Toward the end of his days in Washington, he was irritated by Israeli inflexibility over the Arab lands they claimed and by the political pressure they were able to bring to bear on him.

His relationship with Nasser, on the other hand, deteriorated rapidly. Tensions had arisen between Egypt and the United States over Egyptian intervention in the Yemeni civil war, but Nasser had persisted in perceiving Kennedy as friendly. Congress, however, had tired of Kennedy's efforts to woo Nasser with food aid, and Johnson was not going to invite trouble with the men and women

Austin Jewish community told Gomolak of LBJ's playing an important role in the rescue of European Jews from Hitler from 1938 to 1940. For evidence of Johnson's efforts on behalf of Israel – working with Dean Acheson against John Foster Dulles's threat to apply sanctions against Israel after the Suez crisis of 1956 – see Senate Papers/Office Files of George Reedy, 1956–1957/Box 421/Mid-East, LBJ Papers, LBJ Library, Austin, Texas. See also Thomas M. Gaskin, "Senator Lyndon B. Johnson and United States Foreign Policy," Ph.D. dissertation, University of Washington, 1989.

3. LBJ to Levi Eshkol [Israeli prime minister], January 2, 1964, WHCF/CF/Box 9/ CO 126 Israel (1964–1965).

4. Harry McPherson Oral History, LBJ Papers. McPherson, White House Special Counsel, served as Johnson's contact with the American Jewish community.

5. Notes on the President's Meeting with Abba Eban, FM, et al., October 24, 1967/Meeting Notes file/Box 2/October 24, 1967, Meeting with Abba Eban and others, LBJ Papers.

of Capitol Hill on behalf of a man he viewed as anti-American. Nasser was quickly convinced that Johnson was hostile and in a series of speeches and actions in 1964 undermined what little support he had in the United States. Arabists in the Department of State warned of trouble if Nasser was not pacified, but the Egyptian leader's abusive anti-American rhetoric left few in Washington willing to feed the hand that bit them. Nasser's behavior, at least as much as Johnson's proclivities, caused American policy in the mid-1960s to seem ever less sympathetic to the Arab cause.

In December 1963, Robert Komer, the National Security Council (NSC) staff member responsible for Middle East affairs, pressed his boss, McGeorge Bundy, to call the president's attention to the situation in Yemen.[6] Komer thought the United States was "probably in for real trouble there." An army coup in September 1962 had overthrown the new imam, hereditary ruler of Yemen, and replaced his government with a pro-Egyptian republican regime. The imam took to the hills and quickly obtained Saudi, Jordanian, and eventually Iranian support. American intelligence also suspected the British of aiding the royalists,[7] whose forces held out despite Egyptian military intervention on behalf of the republicans. Before long Nasser had sent 70,000 Soviet-equipped troops, planes, and tanks, to no avail. The United States recognized the republican regime in December 1962 in an attempt to match Soviet diplomatic activity and avoid being stigmatized as the champion of reaction – irritating the Saudis and Israelis, both of whom opposed the extension of Nasser's influence. An April 1963 U.S.–UN brokered agreement to end the civil war never took hold. By July, Kennedy's advisers began to worry about the threat to Saudi oil and persuaded the president to send a squadron of jets to reassure the Saudis and warn off the Egyptians. Komer noted in December that the fighting continued; that Nasser seemed unable to let go; that the United States was committed to withdraw its jets in the likely event that the Saudis resumed supplying the royalists with arms;

6. Komer to Bundy, December 3, 1963, NSF, Name File, Box 6, Komer vol. I [2], LBJ Papers.
7. Rusk suspected the British of providing covert aid to the royalists and of being less than frank with the United States on the matter. See Rusk Oral History Interview, JFK Papers, JFK Library, Cambridge, Massachusetts.

that Congress would cut off aid to Egypt as soon as it realized what the Egyptians were doing in Yemen.

Everything Komer feared would happen, did happen, with minimal consequences for the United States. Johnson, Bundy, Secretary of State Dean Rusk, and Secretary of Defense Robert McNamara may not have known how to get out of Vietnam, but they knew better than to involve the United States in Yemeni affairs. When the Egyptians could no longer sustain their effort years later, the Soviets rushed in to support the Yemen Republic, gaining little for themselves at enormous cost.

While Komer was fretting about Yemen, a much more dangerous crisis was developing on the island of Cyprus in the eastern Mediterranean. The Cypriots had won their independence from Great Britain in 1959 with an accord that rejected union with the Greek mainland and guaranteed the Turkish minority a share of governmental power. Archbishop Makarios, the Greek–Cypriot president of Cyprus, announced in December 1963 that he would disregard the agreement to share power and the relevant provisions of the Cypriot constitution. Before the month was out, Greek–Cypriots massacred 300 Turkish–Cypriots in the capital city of Nicosia. Turkey immediately threatened to invade the island to protect ethnic Turks. The machinations of Makarios promised to draw two NATO allies, Greece and Turkey, into a war, with potentially disastrous effects on the Western alliance. Apprised of the danger, Johnson quickly sent Undersecretary of State George Ball to Cyprus to defuse the crisis.

Ball was an able man, but he achieved nothing trying to reason with Makarios. Ralph Bunche, the superb UN troubleshooter, failed, as did former Secretary of State Dean Acheson, Democratic Senator J. William Fulbright of Arkansas, and Cyrus Vance of the U.S. Department of Defense in a succession of efforts throughout 1964. Makarios flirted with Nikita Khrushchev and Nasser, both of whom noised supportively. Khrushchev did a little more, warning the Turks to stay out and secretly sending arms to the Greek–Cypriots. Nonetheless, in August 1964 he rejected Makarios's request for Soviet intervention after Turkish planes strafed Greek–Cypriot villages in retaliation for attacks on Turkish–Cypriot villages. A UN peacekeeping force did what it could beginning in March.

In June 1964, Rusk drafted and Johnson signed a harsh note to Turkey, warning that the United States might not come to Turkey's rescue if it invaded Cyprus and provoked a Soviet response. Turkish leaders were angered, but they understood the message and held back. In Washington, Cyprus was high on the agenda of the National Security Council in July and August, but the president explicitly stated that he wanted no radical action before the November election. He did not need another war in September or October 1964.[8]

On Cyprus the problem festered, the murderous Makarios and mainland Greeks tormented the Turkish minority as best they could, but somehow a Greco–Turkish war was averted. The Turks came very close to invading the island in 1967, but Vance was able to negotiate a settlement that endured until the mid-1970s. Conditions improved in the spring of 1968, but there was little hope for an enduring peace on Cyprus as long as Makarios lived.

Cyprus never became a major issue for Lyndon Johnson. His fear of losing some Greek–American votes in 1964 may have been realized, but he managed quite well without them. Soviet restraint kept the Cyprus crisis from being burdened with all of the baggage of the Cold War. The Soviets were nonetheless beneficiaries of the trouble Makarios stirred. American relations with Greece and Turkey were strained, as were relations between Greece and Turkey. NATO's southeastern flank had been weakened, and the Turks underscored the point by effecting a rapprochement with the Soviets in the mid-1960s.

Iran, too, grew dissatisfied with American support in the 1960s and took steps to demonstrate its independence by improving relations with Moscow. The Kennedy administration had pressed for political reforms and economic development to immunize the

8. See minutes, notes, and memoranda for NSC meetings 535 (July 3, 1964), 536 (July 28, 1964), 537 (August 4, 1967), 540 (August 19, 1964), and 541 (August 25, 1964), NSF/NSC Meeting File/Box 1, LBJ Papers; McGeorge Bundy memorandum for the record, September 8, 1964, NSF/Files of McGeorge Bundy/Box 19/Luncheons with the President, vol. 1 [Part 1], LBJ Papers.

country against communism. Vice President Lyndon Johnson had visited Tehran in 1962 to drive home the message. Not surprisingly, the shah was irritated by American demands, fearful that the Americans might prefer democratic government in Iran to his autocracy, and troubled by what he perceived as American pandering to radical Arab nationalists such as Nasser. In September 1962 he delighted the Soviets by announcing that he would not permit foreign missiles to be based in Iran, the first such assurances the Soviets had received from an ally of the United States.[9] In November 1963, on the eve of Kennedy's assassination, Khrushchev sent Soviet President Leonid Brezhnev and his wife to visit Tehran. In 1964 a Moscow–Tehran air link was opened. In 1965, the shah traveled to Moscow, and the Soviet Union and Iran negotiated an economic agreement in which the Soviets offered to build a major metallurgical complex in exchange for Iranian natural gas. And in 1966 the shah purchased $110 million worth of Soviet military equipment.[10] The message was not very subtle.

Johnson as president continued Kennedy's efforts to direct Iran toward constructive economic development, attempting to limit arms sales and to make them contingent on political and economic reform.[11] His aides took the shah's opening to Moscow with equanimity, explaining to one another that the shah would still be dependent on the United States for sophisticated weaponry and that distancing himself a little from Washington would undermine those of his opponents who contended that he had become an American puppet.[12] McNamara resented the shah's transparent efforts to blackmail the United States, and Rusk, uneasy about the extent of the American commitment to the shah, argued for loosening the ties.[13] The CIA reduced its role in Iran, allowing the

9. James A. Bill, *The Eagle and the Lion* (New Haven, Conn.: Yale University Press, 1988), 150.
10. Ibid., 177; Lenczowski, *Middle East in World Affairs*, 216.
11. Barry Rubin, *Paved with Good Intentions: The American Experience and Iran* (New York: Penguin, 1981), 116.
12. National Intelligence Estimate 34–66, March 24, 1966, NSF/NIE/Box 6/34; W. W. Rostow memorandum for Vice-President Hubert H. Humphrey, February 13, 1967. NSF/Name File/Box 7/Rostow/2 of 2, LBJ Papers.
13. W. W. Rostow memorandum for LBJ, July 29, 1966, NSF/Memos to the President/W. W. Rostow/Box 9, LBJ Papers.

Israeli Mossad to take over the training of the shah's secret police, the dreaded SAVAK.[14]

A brouhaha late in 1964 over a routine status-of-forces agreement, granting American military personnel in Iran immunity from local prosecution, was perceived correctly by analysts in Washington as an effort by opposition fundamentalist forces, led by the Ayatollah Ruhollah Khomeini, to embarrass the government.[15] The U.S. government did not take fundamentalist reactionaries in Iran very seriously, especially after Khomeini was deported. The shah was in frequent contact with Johnson; his regime appeared stable, friendly to the United States and to Israel; and the oil kept coming. The Johnson administration tried with little success to persuade the shah to spend less of his oil revenue on arms but was consoled by the knowledge that every million he spent in the United States did not go to Moscow and served to alleviate American balance-of-payments difficulties.[16] It did not push him very hard and acquiesced in his efforts to reduce American contacts with his political opponents. Given the administration's obsession with the war in Vietnam, the president and his advisers had little inclination to trouble themselves about Iran.

It was Nasser, always Nasser, who made it impossible for Johnson to ignore the Middle East. If he seemed subdued for a moment in Yemen, he was soon meddling in Cyprus, or the Congo, or telling the Libyans to throw the Americans out of Wheelus Air Force Base. And he had the audacity to complain about the quantity of American food aid to Egypt!

In January 1964, John Badeau, the popular American ambassador in Cairo, sent a nine-page report to Johnson, advising him that all was well and contending that there had been a major increase in American influence in Egypt since 1956, primarily at the expense of the Soviet Union. Badeau, former president of the

14. Mark J. Gasiorowski, *U.S. Foreign Policy and the Shah: Building a Client State in Iran* (Ithaca, N.Y.: Cornell University Press, 1991), 118.
15. Rubin, *Paved with Good Intentions*, 111–14. See also Bill, *Eagle and Lion*, 158–61.
16. W. W. Rostow memorandum for LBJ, November 8, 1966. NSF/Name File/Box 3/Fulbright, LBJ Papers.

American University in Cairo, whose appointment had signaled Kennedy's desire for rapprochement with Nasser, was arguing for the continuation of food aid authorized by Congress under Public Law 480 (PL 480). He noted that Nasser had been quiet about Israel and claimed that he had been more moderate in his dealings with Arab leaders friendly to the United States. The UAR remained heavily dependent on Moscow for military aid, but Western aid helped keep it out of the Soviet camp. If the movement in Congress to cut off food aid succeeded, Nasser would not be chastened but more likely would respond in ways detrimental to American interests, nullifying recent gains.[17]

For the next several months, Arabists in and out of the government lobbied hard to persuade the president and Congress of the effectiveness of food aid and the importance of continuing it. They professed pleasure with results of an Arab summit in Cairo in January 1964, claiming that Nasser had isolated the extremists and produced a communiqué that was "statesmanlike relative to the Arab norm." UAR moderation was attributed to the desire "to continue to orient its economy toward the West and to insure U.S. economic assistance over the next critical years." They warned that Nasser would remain difficult, that he would never become "our creature," but that the existing level of aid had been successful in getting him to "moderate his positions so that they remain below the level of real danger to our interests."[18] Rusk was unimpressed, informing the NSC in April 1964 that the United States had received little in return for its assistance. Indeed, he quickly provided a list of Egyptian transgressions against American interests and indicated that the State Department was reexamining policy.[19]

But the situation was already spinning out of control. Nineteen-sixty-four was a presidential election year, and everybody knew it – Johnson's foreign policy bureaucracy, the friends of Israel, and Gamal Abdul Nasser. They knew that the American electorate was

17. John Badeau to LBJ, January 3, 1964 (with one-page summary), NSF/Country file/ME/UAR/Box 158/UAR vol. I Cables 11/63–5/64, LBJ Papers.
18. Benjamin H. Read memorandum for McGeorge Bundy, February 12, 1964, and W. W. Rostow to LBJ April 14, 1964, enclosing memorandum by William R. Polk, April 7, 1964, NSF/Country file/ME/UAR/Box 158/UAR vol. I Memos 11/63–5/64, LBJ Papers.
19. Summary Record of NSC Meeting 525, April 2, 1964, NSF/NSC Meetings file/Box 1, LBJ Papers.

overwhelmingly pro-Israel and that presidential candidates as well as members of Congress would be competing to demonstrate their support for Israel. In February, Komer reminded Bundy of the difficulty of obtaining support for a loan to the UAR in an election year and urged that the issue be decided by the president.[20] Trying to explain Nasser's decision to resume criticism of Libya for allowing an American air base on its territory, Badeau reported that the Egyptian leader suspected that because of the coming election, the United States was about to make a grand gesture toward Israel, like providing it with tanks.[21] Egyptian intelligence had doubtless learned of an Israeli request for tanks, and Nasser was reminding the Americans of his capacity for doing mischief to their interests.

Nasser suspected Johnson of being an unrepentant pro-Zionist, Badeau's protestations to the contrary notwithstanding. Badeau's resignation in May 1964 confirmed Nasser's assumption that Johnson was changing course.[22] In fact, Nasser and Johnson were trapped like the legendary two scorpions in a bottle. Israel, engaged in an arms race against the UAR and other hostile Arab countries, wanted stronger support from the United States. Johnson and many in Congress were sympathetic but in an odd-numbered year might well have found arguments about the need to pacify Nasser compelling. Indeed, the administration tried desperately to get the Germans to provide the tanks the Israelis wanted, tried desperately to avoid becoming Israel's principal arms supplier. It succeeded at substantial cost in keeping food aid flowing to Egypt. But in an election year, the power of American friends of Israel was inescapable. Johnson had to make a series of gestures toward Israel, and these would almost certainly include a less sensitive approach to Nasser.

The only conceivable way Nasser might have preempted obvious pro-Israeli behavior on the part of the American government, might have increased American aid to Egypt, would have been to take demonstrably friendly action toward Israel, like offering to

---

20. Robert Komer memorandum to McGeorge Bundy, February 24, 1964, NSF/Country file/ME/UAR/Box 158/UAR vol. I Cables 11/63–5/64.
21. Badeau to Secretary of State, April 5, 1964, NSF/Country file/ME/UAR/Box 158/UAR vol. I Cables 11/63–5/64.
22. In fact, Johnson urged Badeau to stay at his post, but he appears to have been eager to return to academic life.

recognize and sign a peace treaty with the Jewish state. To have done so, however, would have been to forfeit his claim to leadership in the Arab world and to sign his own death warrant. Such an extraordinary shift in his behavior was unimaginable, and it was not forthcoming. Instead, he yanked at the eagle's feathers, a performance much more in keeping with his personality and style. Every yank angered Lyndon Johnson a little more, making it harder for friends of Egypt to justify aid to Cairo, to justify the denial of support for Israel. An election year was no time to twit Lyndon Johnson.

In addition to meddling in American relations with Libya, Nasser spoke out in support of Makarios and invited Khrushchev to Egypt. The Egyptian government allowed Congolese students in Cairo to burn down the USIA library in protest against the American role in the Congo, and Egyptian jets shot down a private American plane owned by a friend of Johnson's. American protests were handled disagreeably by the Egyptian foreign ministry. When Nasser, in December 1964, concluded mistakenly that the American ambassador had rejected his request for additional food aid, he declared in a public speech, in the presence of a Soviet delegation, that the United States could "go drink in the sea," an Arabic variant of a scatological Yiddish epithet. Congress got the message and cut off aid to Egypt.[23]

In fact, Ball and Rusk were persuaded of the importance of keeping lines open to Cairo, fearful of surrendering any semblance of leverage with Nasser. They had acquiesced in the delay of aid to Nasser until after the election but had every intention of fulfilling existing American aid commitments to Egypt that ran through 1965. In January they began to lobby intensively, with Congress and with the president. Rusk informed Johnson that the UAR wanted to improve relations with the United States and reminded the president that the United States wanted Nasser's help with the Congo crisis.[24] The American negotiators needed a "carrot" to draw the UAR into a more cooperative posture. Food aid was the answer. Assiduously he explained the importance of good relations

23. Ethan Nadelmann, "Setting the Stage: American Policy Toward the Middle East, 1961–1966," *International Journal of Middle East Studies* 14(1982): 446–7.
24. Rusk memorandum for LBJ, January 22, 1965, NSF/Country file/ME/UAR/Box 159/UAR vol II Cables 6/64–12/64, LBJ Papers.

with the UAR, stressing the harm Nasser could do and arguing that
"none of our major interests" in the region had been damaged since
1958. In a top-secret executive session with the Senate Foreign Relations Committee, Rusk replayed the same arguments, warning
the committee that failure to meet U.S. commitments on food aid
to the UAR might lead to irrational actions by Nasser that would
result in American troops fighting in the Middle East.[25] Ball also
played the game, enlisting prominent Jewish-American leaders and
pro-Israeli groups, contending that aid to pacify Nasser was in Israel's interests.[26]

The administration ultimately won authority to resume aid shipments, but it was mid-1965 before it was satisfied with Nasser's responses. And then it took a series of very forceful presentations to
convince an extremely reluctant Johnson to allow the remaining
food promised to the UAR to be shipped.[27] Nasser made a series of
friendly gestures in the course of the year, but it was too late to win
over LBJ. Intensive efforts by Rusk and others to gain permission
to negotiate a new agreement with the UAR were rejected angrily
by the president.[28] Nasser had brought him grief; Nasser had endangered his presidency. Grudgingly Johnson agreed to fulfill the
commitment for 1965, concluding a three-year agreement. There
would not be a new one.

Throughout 1966, Komer at the NSC and Luke Battle and David
Nes at the American embassy in Cairo, those officials working
most closely on American relations with the UAR, were profoundly
apprehensive about the danger of Nasser's responding violently to
the decline in Washington's efforts to appease him. Nes, in partic-

25. U.S. Senate Committee on Foreign Relations, Executive Session, Top Secret, January 27,
   1965, "Briefing by Secretary of State Dean Rusk on Relationship Between the United
   Arab Republic and the United States," Papers of the U.S. Senate Committee on Foreign
   Relations (hereafter SFRC Papers).
26. Ball–Christian Herter Jr. conversation, January 27, 1965, Box 2/Congress, III
   8/3/64–10/8/65; and Ball–LBJ conversation, February 3, 1965, Jordan/Box 4, Papers of
   George W. Ball, LBJ Library.
27. Komer memorandum for Bundy, April 6, 1965, and Ambassador Lucius Battle to secretary of state, May 31, 1965, NSF/Country file/ME/UAR/Box 159 UAR vol. III Memos
   11/64–6/65; Komer and Bundy to LBJ, June 17, 1965, NSF/Country file/ME/UAR/Box
   159/UAR vol. IV Memos 6/65–6/66 [2 of 2]; Battle to secretary of state, June 21, 1965,
   NSF/Country file/ME/UAR/Box 159, UAR vol. IV Cables 6/65–6/66.
28. Rusk memorandum for LBJ, September 23, 1965, enclosures, NSF/Country File/ME/
   UAR/Box 159 UAR Vol. IV Memos 6/65–6/66 [2 of 2] LBJ Papers; U.S. Senate Committee on Foreign Relations, Executive Session, Secret, October 13, 1965.

ular, was persuaded that Nasser threatened no vital interest of the
United States and that achievement of his goals would be consistent with "our national security and really key global preoccupa-
tions," from which he implicitly excluded concern for Israel. He
condemned the manipulation of food aid and argued for a positive
gesture of support for Egypt.[29] When Nasser's Yemeni surrogates
seized two American AID officials in April 1967 and held them for
three weeks while their offices were ransacked and classified documents confiscated, Nes wrote, "We seem to have driven Nasser
to a degree of irrationality bordering on madness, fed, of course,
by the frustrations and fears generated by his failures domestic and
foreign." He anticipated further attacks designed to destroy the
friends of the United States in the region and to eliminate every vestige of Western political and economic influence.[30]

The principal opponents of aid to Nasser were the Israelis and
the Saudis.[31] Pro-Israeli forces in Congress were formidable on their
own. Supported by pro-Saudi lobbyists, they were unbeatable in
the absence of powerful presidential opposition to their objectives.
It is important to note that Saudi and Iranian hostility to radical
Arab nationalism, to Nasser especially, meant that oil interests unsympathetic to Israel could usually be found aligned with the
friends of Israel in the efforts to undermine the Egyptian leader
throughout the corridors of Washington.

Israeli ties to the United States were strengthened significantly
during the Johnson administration, in large part because Israel
could not find elsewhere military aid equivalent to that which the
Soviets were providing the UAR and Syria. Efforts to redirect requests from Tel Aviv for tanks and planes to the British, French, and
Germans, to deflect the inevitable Arab backlash, failed. Reluctantly, but with a sense that domestic political exigencies allowed
no alternative, the United States became the principal supplier of

29. David G. Nes to Rodger P. Davis [deputy assistant secretary of state for Near East and
    South Asian Affairs], October 17, 1966, Papers of David G. Nes, LBJ Library.
30. Nes to Davis, May 11, 1967, Papers of David G. Nes.
31. See Harold Wriggins [NSC staff] to W. W. Rostow, March 8, 1967, for an example of
    Saudi influence in the Senate posing an obstacle to food aid to the UAR. NSF/Country
    file/Middle East/UAR/Box 160 UAR vol. V, Memos 9/66–5/67, LBJ Papers.

Israeli military equipment. Perhaps most striking was the inability of American diplomats, even the redoubtable Averell Harriman, to exact concessions from the Israelis in return. In 1964, the primary Israeli demand was for tanks. In 1965 it was for fighter planes. Johnson's advisers knew what would happen if the United States responded favorably: the Arab media would attack the United States for upsetting the regional balance and for preparing Israel to attack Arab nations; the UAR would lead a campaign to undermine Arab moderates, to force cancellation of oil leases, to drive the United States out of Wheelus Air Force Base in Libya; Arab countries would turn to the Soviet Union and China for superior arms. Rusk advised the American ambassador in Tel Aviv that there was a "clear consensus contrary to US interests to sell military aircraft to Israel." But pressure from the friends of Israel was irresistible.[32]

To minimize the damage likely to follow from major subsidized arms sales to Israel, Johnson's advisers attempted to gain Israeli cooperation in coping with several related issues. They pleaded for Israeli forbearance in retaliatory attacks on Arab countries suspected of harboring terrorists, for Israeli restraint in its conflict with Syria and Jordan over the diversion of the waters of the Jordan River, the most of all they fought for an Israeli commitment not to develop nuclear weapons and to allow the International Atomic Energy Agency to inspect Israel's nuclear facility at Dimona.[33] Perhaps most extraordinary was the American plea that Israel allow the United States to strengthen its relations with the Arab nations of the region. In a memorandum to LBJ that McGeorge Bundy called "absolutely first-rate," Komer advised the president to assure

32. Memorandum, Carl T. Rowan [Director, USIA] for LBJ, March 25, 1964, NSF/Country file/Middle East, NE, Afghanistan, Ceylon/Box 116/NE vol. I 3/64–8/67; Rusk to Tel Aviv, June 5, 1965, NSF/Country file/Middle East/Israel vol. IV/Box 139 Cables 2/65–11/65; Memorandum, Meyer Feldman for LBJ, May 11, 1964, NSF/Country file/Middle East/Israel Tanks vol. I 12/63 – 5/64; Komer to Bundy, February 8, 1966 (. . . There's no doubt whatsoever in my mind that Hill and Zionist pressure will sooner or later force us to sell planes to Israel"), NSF/Name file/Box 6/Komer vol. 2 [1], LBJ Papers.
33. Administrative History of the Department of State, vol. I, Ch. 4, H.2, Jordan Waters Issue; Rusk to Ambassador, Tel Aviv, March 21, 1965, April 21, 1965, May 19, 1965, June 5, 1965, NSF/Country file/Middle East/Israel vol. IV Cables 2/65–11/65 [1 of 2], Box 139; Komer memorandum for the record, October 18, 1965, NSF/Name file/Box 6/Komer vol. 2 [2]; Rusk memorandum for LBJ, May 21, 1966, enclosure, WHCF/CF/Box9/CO126 Israel 1966, LBJ Papers.

Israeli Prime Minister Levi Eshkol of American support and to tell him that "*The one thing we ask of Israel* is not to keep trying to force us to an all-out pro-Israel policy." The United States had to keep "a superficial balance" in its public posture to protect its oil interests and to keep the Soviets out of the Middle East. Would the Israelis please try to understand that it was in their interest for the United States to keep good relations with the Arabs?[34]

In February 1965, as it became increasingly clear that the United States would be obliged to provide Israel with the tanks it wanted and to become its principal arms supplier, Harriman flew to Tel Aviv to gain Israel's acceptance of the sale of U.S. tanks to Jordan as well. Harriman attempted to attach other conditions to the deal, such as restraints on Israel's use of American equipment. The Israelis replied that "there could be no prohibition on Israel's right to use its arms" and rejected the argument on behalf of tank sales to Jordan. At a subsequent meeting between the Israeli ambassador to the United States and the assistant secretary of state for Near Eastern and South Asian Affairs, Ambassador Avraham Harman brushed aside as irrelevant all American efforts to link arms sales and deliveries to border incidents and Israeli water diversion schemes. Refusing to accept any agreement that would make military aid contingent upon Israeli behavior, Harman demanded to see the secretary of state.[35]

Washington had no more luck trying to win Israeli assistance somewhat farther afield, for American policy toward Vietnam. Little subtlety was attempted. In February 1966, LBJ personally pressed Abba Eban, the Israeli foreign minister. When two weeks had passed without an Israeli response, Rusk instructed the American ambassador in Tel Aviv to call attention to the fact that "the United States is being most helpful to Israel currently, and that reciprocal gestures would be well received in Washington." In April, the ambassador reported telling the Israelis that "Vietnam is now [the] touchstone of

34. Memorandum, Komer for LBJ, May 28, 1964 (see also similar memorandum dated June 2, 1964), NSF/Country file/Middle East/Israel/Box 143 Israel Eshkol Visit 6/1–3/64 [1 of 2], LBJ Papers.
35. Memorandum of Conversation, February 26, 1965, "Harriman Mission to Israel," dated March 19, 1965, and Memcon "Israel Arms Procurement," May 19, 1965, NSF/Country file/Middle East/Israel/Box 139/Israel vol. IV, Memos and misc. 2/65–11/65; Rusk to Ambassador, Tel Aviv, May 19, 1965, NSF/Country file/Middle East/Israel vol. IV, Cables 2/65–11/65 [1 of 2], Box 139, LBJ Papers.

American foreign policy" and that the United States thought Israel and the Saigon regime should have closer relations. A few days later, Johnson wanted the Israelis informed of his disappointment at their failure to make any gesture toward Vietnam.[36]

Israel's ability to ignore or at most offer nominal deference to American concerns reflected its confidence in the power of its supporters in the United States. The Johnson administration persistently demonstrated its recognition of that power by seeking to persuade Israel's friends that the United States was straining to do all it could for Israel. In August 1965, the president instructed Mc-George Bundy to brief Israel's congressional supporters so that they would allow him to protect American interests in the Arab world. They were told that Israel received loans, grants, and credits on concessionary terms, far exceeding what could be justified by AID economic criteria. The United States was providing for Israel's military needs, either directly or by brokering arms deals with other powers, and by training Israeli military personnel. The United States was assuring Israel access to Jordan River waters and enhancing Israel's technological edge, including nuclear research. American assistance to Arabs, such as aid to Jordan, support for refugees, and steps to maintain ties to the UAR and Syria, were all designed to maintain stability in the region and keep the Soviets and Chinese out, all in Israel's interest. Plaintive hopes that Israel would desist from "premature retaliatory raids" and from developing nuclear weapons were to be repeated.[37]

In June 1966, recognition of Israel's influence in the United States was demonstrated quite differently. Concerned more about the Vietnam-related erosion of his domestic support than the sensibilities of Arabs, LBJ asked Abraham Feinberg, chairman of the executive committee of the American Bank and Trust Company, to have major Israeli figures speak favorably about Johnson's policy toward Israel.[38] When Johnson prepared for a meeting with Fein-

---

36. Rusk to Ambassador, Tel Aviv, February 26, 1966; Ambassador Walworth Barbour to the secretary of state, April 26, 1966; and Harold Saunders [National Security Council staff] to W. W. Rostow, May 2, 1966, NSF/Country file/Middle East/Israel/Box 139/Israel vol. V Cables 12/65–9/66, LBJ Papers.
37. Komer memorandum for Bundy, August 10, 1965, NSF/Name file/Box 6/Komer vol. I, LBJ Papers.
38. Abraham Feinberg to W. W. Rostow, June 16, 1966, WHCF/CF/Box 9/CO 126 Israel (1966).

berg in February 1967, Walt Rostow, Bundy's successor as National Security Adviser, detailed for the president all the United States had done for Israel in the 1960s – and how little the United States had received in return. Not only did the Israelis refuse to make any significant concessions on the Arab–Israeli dispute, reject an American initiative to solve the refugee problem, and rebuff efforts to establish international safeguards at their nuclear research plant at Dimona, but they also would not stop "stirring concern and agitation among Israel's supporters in the U.S. on our N.E. policies, particularly those policies designed to maintain the U.S. position in the Arab world."[39] American–Israeli relations provided a wonderful example of the tail wagging the dog.

Vietnam consumed the time and energies of Johnson and the men with whom he took counsel. Ambivalent about the importance of the Middle East and frustrated by the failure of food aid to achieve political objectives, specifically to make Nasser more responsive to American concerns, they lost interest in the region. In this context, domestic political considerations overcame caution and allowed the United States to align itself increasingly with Israel, openly becoming that nation's arsenal despite the fact that the Israelis were hardly more amenable to American pressure and manipulation than was Nasser. Ultimately, the marked tilt toward Tel Aviv was rationalized by casting Israel as a strategic asset in the Cold War, a valuable friend in the struggle to contain the Soviet Union.

Since the mid-1950s the Soviets had been active in the radical Arab states, arming them, training their forces, exploiting the Arab–Israeli conflict to increase their influence in the Middle East. In the mid-1960s, with their American adversaries preoccupied in southeast Asia, the Soviets challenged the supremacy of the U.S. Navy in the region. Determined not to allow the United States to dominate the Middle East, accepting Mahan's dictates on the importance of seapower, the Kremlin leadership committed itself to the creation of a blue-water navy and began a major buildup of naval forces in the

39. W. W. Rostow memorandum for LBJ, enclosure, February 13, 1967, NSF/Country file/Middle East/Israel/Box 140 Israel vol. VI 12/66–7/67, LBJ Papers.

Mediterranean. An opportunity to displace Western influence existed, and the Soviets moved gingerly to seize it.[40]

As the Soviet Union armed the radical Arab states and the United States grudgingly tried to maintain Israeli military superiority – Israeli deterrent capability in the area – the potential for an explosion grew. The Syrian government that seized power in a bloody coup in February 1966, unstable, endangered from within, strengthened ties with the Soviet Union, obtained additional arms, and supported a series of provocative Palestinian raids against Israel. To Israeli threats to retaliate, the Soviets responded with appropriate promises of support for Syria. In November 1966, following a raid by Syrian-based Palestinian commandos, Israel sent 3,000 troops across the border to attack the village of Es Samu in Jordan, a response much of the rest of the world, including the United States, considered disproportionate and inappropriate.[41] In the early months of 1967, Syrian-based terrorist attacks against Israel continued, marked by a sharp increase in the sophistication of the operations. In April six Syrian MiGs were shot down by Israeli fighters they intercepted while the latter were attacking Syrian positions in the Golan Heights. Tension increased, and further Israeli retaliation seemed imminent.

Into this volatile mixture the Soviets inexplicably threw a match. They informed the Syrians that Soviet intelligence had determined that the Israelis were about to launch a massive invasion of Syria. The Soviet report was a fabrication. The Israelis almost certainly were planning some sort of punitive mission against Syria, but there was no evidence that they planned an invasion. When the Syrians began broadcasting pleas for help and the Soviets warned the Israelis, the Israelis invited the Soviet ambassador to inspect the area where they were alleged to be massing their forces, but he refused. Neither UN observers nor a high-level Egyptian military

---

40. There is a vast literature on the superpower rivalry in the Middle East in the 1960s. See, for example, Paul Y. Hammond and Sidney S. Alexander, eds., *Political Dynamics in the Middle East* (New York: American Elsevier, 1972), especially essays by Arnold L. Horelick, Jacob C. Hurewitz, Malcolm H. Kerr, and William B. Quandt. See also J. C. Hurewitz, ed., *Soviet–American Rivalry in the Middle East* (New York: Praeger, 1969).
41. W. W. Rostow memorandum for LBJ, November 14, 1966, NSF/Country file, Middle East/Israel/Box 140 Israel vol. VI Memos 12/66–7/67, LBJ Papers.

mission, dispatched to investigate, found any indication that Israeli forces were preparing to invade Syria. But it was too late.[42]

The war that came on June 5, 1967, the Six Day War, was a self-inflicted disaster for Gamal Abdul Nasser, probably the most damaging failure of judgment in his career. At a time when his troops were still bogged down in Yemen, he provoked a war with Israel, persuading himself first that the Israelis would allow him a political victory without war and then that he and his allies could defeat Israel and eliminate the Western cancer in the Arab nation.

Taunted by his rivals, most notably King Faisal of Saudi Arabia, for his failure to aid either Jordan or Syria against the Israelis after Es Samu in November 1966 or the Syrian–Israeli air battle in April 1967, Nasser was eager to demonstrate his bona fides as the man who would lead the Arab masses against the Israelis and their Western supporters. Informed by the Syrians and Soviets of the danger to Syria, on May 14, 1967, he put Egyptian forces on alert, warning the Israelis that if they started a war they would have to fight Egypt as well as Syria. Presumably Nasser imagined he would thus deter the Israelis and claim credit for having averted a war. But the taunts continued: Egypt was protected from Israel by a UN force that had been posted on its territory since the Suez crisis of 1956. On May 16, Egypt asked that the UN troops on its border with Israel be redeployed to the Gaza Strip. When advised by UN Secretary General U Thant that Egypt could ask that UN peacekeepers be ordered out of Egypt but could not dictate their deployment within Egypt, Nasser asked that they be removed. Quickly, arguably too quickly, U Thant complied – and there was no longer a buffer between Israel and Egypt. Moreover, Egyptian troops rapidly reoccupied Sharm el-Sheikh at the southern tip of the Sinai peninsula, a point from which they controlled the Strait of Tiran, entrance to the Gulf of Aqaba, Israel's outlet to the Red Sea, Asia, and the east coast of Africa.

---

42. Harold Saunders memorandum for McGeorge Bundy [undated], NSF/NSC History/ Middle East Crisis May 12–June 19, 1967, Box 17, LBJ Papers; Richard B. Parker, "The June 1967 War: Some Mysteries Explored," *Middle East Journal* 46 (1992): 177–97. Parker reports that most Soviet officials and scholars now admit the report was false and that the Egyptians knew by May 15 that there were no Israeli troop concentrations on the Syrian border. He was unpersuaded by any of the Soviet explanations for the false report. Clearly they had not anticipated the results.

The critical question was whether Nasser would dare to close the strait to Israeli shipping. The Israelis had taken his initial moves with surprising equanimity but left no doubt that they would fight rather than acquiesce in loss of the right of free passage guaranteed to them by the United States when they withdrew their forces from Sharm el-Sheikh in 1957. American diplomatists, preoccupied with Vietnam, were strikingly inactive in the critical week of May 14–21, neither consulting with U Thant about the disposition of UN forces nor warning Nasser against taking action in the Gulf. To their horror and to that of Europeans dependent on Middle East oil and fearful of a war that would interfere with supplies, Nasser announced on May 22 that he was closing the Gulf of Aqaba to Israel.

Almost immediately, Washington was forced to look toward the Middle East. Johnson condemned the blockade. Mindful of the American obligation to maintain free passage of the Gulf of Aqaba, policymakers in Washington dreaded the possibility of being drawn into another military action. Most uneasy was the U.S. Department of Defense, its resources already stretched by the endless war in southeast Asia. Congressional leaders, however sympathetic they may have been to Israel – and some, such as Fulbright, the man who had become Johnson's nemesis over American military action in the Dominican Republic and Vietnam, were not – expressed reservations about unilateral American action.[43] Johnson wanted the crisis in the Middle East to go away.

Obligated by the Eisenhower administration's 1957 commitment to keep the Gulf of Aqaba open, fully cognizant that if the Israelis went to war domestic pressures would require the United States to aid Israel, Johnson and his advisers groped feverishly for a way out. Communications between Johnson and Soviet Premier Alexei Kosygin suggested that the Soviets also thought Nasser had gone too far and that they would cooperate in efforts to prevent war.[44] Assuming that the Egyptians would not initiate hostilities,

---

43. Interview with Dean Rusk, April 9, 1977.
44. Hedrick Smith, *New York Times*, May 29, 1967, p. 2. There are indications in the LBJ Papers that Johnson and Kosygin, using the "hotline" inaugurated by Kennedy and Khrushchev, exchanged as many as twenty messages in the course of the crisis. See W. W. Rostow to LBJ, May 28, 1967, with draft message from Rusk to Gromyko, NSF/NSC History/ME Crisis May–June 67/Box 17; and Harold Saunders, memorandum for the record, October 22, 1968, "Hot Line Meeting June 10, 1967," Box 19, LBJ Papers.

the Americans searched for a way to restrain the Israelis. The key was to end the blockade of the Gulf before demands in Tel Aviv for a preemptive strike overwhelmed the Eshkol government.

Johnson asked the Israelis to do nothing for forty-eight hours while the United States attempted a peaceful resolution of the crisis. The Israelis agreed to wait and sent Eban to Washington via Paris and London to explain their concerns and to determine the degree of external support they could muster. The best plan Johnson's men could devise, however, was a variation on a British scheme for an international naval force to enter the gulf and open it to Israeli shipping. It was a plan for which there was little support in the world and that many of Johnson's advisers, especially his military advisers, had difficulty taking seriously. General Earle Wheeler, chairman of the Joint Chiefs of Staff, thought it would be weeks before an adequate antisubmarine unit could be brought from Singapore to make the operation feasible. Wheeler did not believe that the United States could spare forces adequate to assure the success of the operation in the face of full-scale Egyptian opposition.[45] In the absence of a better idea, the State Department, driven by Undersecretary Eugene Rostow, kept working on it.

Johnson implored Israel to wait. He gave Eban an explicit promise that the United States would find a way to open the Gulf of Aqaba and assurances of American support if Israel was attacked. The critical phrase, devised by Rusk, was that Israel would not be alone unless it went alone. The United States did not want a preemptive strike. But Johnson had not promised Eban enough to permit the Eshkol government to hold off Israeli warhawks – and he knew it. Still, given the level of support the United States was giving Israel, Johnson hoped that the Israelis would give him two weeks in which to find a peaceful solution.[46] They did not.

Eban was able to persuade the Israeli cabinet to wait one week, but Arab rhetoric and actions, added to the growing certainty that American efforts would fail, persuaded even the most reluctant

45. Record of National Security Council Meeting, May 24, 1967; and Earle G. Wheeler to Mc-Namara, June 2, 1967, NSF/NSC History/ME Crisis May–June 67, Box 18, LBJ Papers.
46. Rusk memorandum for LBJ, May 26, 1967, re: pending conversation with Eban, NSF/NSC History/ME Crisis May–June 67/Box 17, LBJ Papers; Abba Eban, *An Autobiography* (New York: Random House, 1977), 360ff; William B. Quandt, *Decade of Decisions: American Policy Toward the Arab–Israeli Conflict, 1967–1979* (Berkeley: University of California Press, 1977), 47–54.

Israeli leaders that the time for action had come. Nasser was no longer limiting his flights of fancy to humiliating the Israelis. He had resumed the terrifying rhetoric of threatening to liberate Palestine, to destroy the Israeli state. On May 30, King Hussein of Jordan, one of Nasser's bitterest enemies, flew to Cairo for a reconciliation and put his forces under Egyptian command. Israel now faced a three-front war for its survival. The Israelis could be reined in only by unmistakable evidence that the United States would force Nasser to retreat – or that the United States would punish Israel severely if it struck first. Israeli intelligence determined that the United States could not intervene against Nasser and would not act against Israel. Johnson never gave the Israelis a "green light" to attack, but as William Quandt suggests, Eshkol and his colleagues perceived by June 1 that they had at the very least a "yellow light," that the Americans would acquiesce in a preemptive strike.[47]

There is little reason to doubt that Rusk and the State Department's Middle East specialists would have preferred Israeli restraint. Their institutional concerns dictated diplomatic solutions and, in this instance, solutions that would preserve American influence with Arab countries and maintain the flow of oil to Europe. But they were exasperated with Nasser and knew that they had not offered the Israelis enough, that the clock was running out on them.[48] McNamara, Wheeler, and their respective staffs at the Department of Defense, on the other hand, were interested primarily in avoiding American involvement in the crisis. Defense intelligence analysts and the CIA argued that Israel could defeat the Arabs on all three fronts easily and rapidly.[49] Anticipating a quick Israeli victory, they were less convinced of the need to urge restraint – and did not argue against a preemptive strike with their Israeli counterparts.[50]

Had the Israelis ever questioned their support among Americans, the State Department analysis of the mail it received during the cri-

47. Eban, *Autobiography*, 385–403; William B. Quandt, "Lyndon Johnson and the June 1967 War: What Color Was the Light?" *Middle East Journal* 46 (1992): 198–288.
48. Harold Saunders memorandum for W. W. Rostow, June 1, 1967, indicates doubt that the Israelis will wait the fifteen to eighteen additional days needed to obtain the vessels to test the blockade. NSF/NSC History/ME crisis May–June 67, Box 18, LBJ Papers.
49. See Wheeler remarks in Record of NSC Meeting, May 24, 1967, NSF/NSC History/ME Crisis May 12–June 19, 1967, Box 17, LBJ Papers; Cyrus Sulzberger, *Age of Mediocrity* (New York: Macmillan, 1973), 346.
50. Quandt, *Decade of Decisions*, 56; Eban, *Autobiography*, 385.

sis would have reassured them. From May 29 to June 1, 17,444 pieces of mail were processed, 95 percent of it pro-Israel, 4.5 percent anti-intervention, and 0.5 percent pro-Arab.[51] Department analysts recognized an effective, organized campaign, but more than half the letters were less suspect. Doubtless most Americans were significantly more anti-interventionist than those stirred to write, but there was no gainsaying the enormous support the Israelis enjoyed among Americans – little democratic David threatened by the Soviet-supported Arab Goliath.

To the men and women responsible for Israel's decision, it was apparent by June 1 that neither the United States nor any other power or group of powers would act vigorously on their behalf. The American public was strongly behind them, especially if they could do the job without the help of American forces. American leaders appeared divided between those who still hoped for a peaceful solution and those willing to have the Israelis do what was required. And most important, Eshkol and Eban believed that Lyndon Johnson was satisfied with the restraint they had shown and asked no more of them[52] – they could act as they deemed necessary to counter the Arab threat to their survival.

Did Johnson signal his acceptance of an Israeli preemptive attack? The evidence is not conclusive. In later years Johnson and Rusk argued that they thought the Israelis had agreed to give them more time, until June 11, to find a peaceful solution, and that the Israelis had acted unreasonably, damaging relations with the United States.[53] William Quandt, however, argues persuasively that on June 1 Abe Fortas, known to be Johnson's close friend and adviser, indicated to Ephraim Evron, minister of the Israeli embassy in Washington, that Johnson's sympathy was assured, that there was no need for further Israeli restraint.[54] In an earlier work, Quandt noted that if Johnson was really irritated by the Israeli decision to strike preemptively, "his subsequent actions revealed few

---

51. Dixon Donnelley memorandum for Rusk, June 2, 1967, NSF/Country file/Box 107/Middle East crisis vol. IV Memos 6/67 [1 of 2].
52. Eban, *Autobiography*, 385–403.
53. Interview with Dean Rusk, April 9, 1977; Lyndon Baines Johnson, *The Vantage Point: Perspectives of the Presidency 1963–1969* (New York: Holt, Rinehart & Winston, 1971), 296–7.
54. Quandt, "Johnson and the June 1967 War," 212–19.

signs of this irritation."[55] Quandt's point is substantiated by Johnson's support of Israel, both diplomatic and military, after war began. The United States protected Israel's interests in the United Nations throughout the crisis and in its aftermath. When on June 10 the Soviets threatened Israel if it continued its advance against Syria, Johnson ordered the Sixth Fleet to stop circling and to head eastward in a show of support for Israel.[56]

There is, however, evidence to indicate that Johnson was genuinely upset by Israel's preemptive action. At an NSC meeting June 7, the third day of the war, Rusk and CIA director Richard Helms gloated over Nasser's "stunning loss," Soviet miscalculations, and Arab disillusionment with the Soviets. Johnson would have none of it. He was worried: the Russians would not just say that they had made a mistake and walk away. He warned that the war would cause problems that would make Americans wish it had never happened.[57] Two days later, when Rusk asked Johnson to send Eshkol a message in an attempt to restrain the Israelis, Johnson replied, "I had a firm commitment from Eshkol and he blew it. . . . That old coot isn't going to pay any attention to any imperialist pressures."[58] In a meeting with Eban several months after the war, colored to be sure by mounting irritation over Israeli intransigence in postwar peace efforts, Johnson was brusquely critical of Israel for ignoring his advice. He told Eban that the Israelis had been unwise to go to war and that he doubted that they would achieve any long-term gains.[59]

Nevertheless, Fortas almost certainly was correct in divining a change in Johnson's attitude between May 26, when he met with Eban, and June 1. In those few days the president had recognized the unlikelihood of a sufficient American or international response on Israel's behalf. He was pained by the inability of the United

55. William B. Quandt, "The Arab–Israeli Conflict in American Foreign Policy," in Itamar Rabinovich and Haim Shaked, eds., *From June to October: The Middle East Between 1967 and 1973* (New Brunswick, N.J.: Transaction Books, 1978), 3.
56. Harold Saunders, memorandum for the record, October 22, 1968, "Hot Line Meeting June 10, 1967," NSF/NSC History/ME crisis May–June 67/Box 19, LBJ Papers.
57. Harold Saunders memorandum for the record, January 7, 1969, based on his notes of June 7, 1967, NSC meeting, NSF/NSC Meeting File/Box 2.
58. Unsigned notes [probably Harold Saunders] dated June 9, 1967, NSF/NSC History/ME Crisis May–June 67/Box 19, LBJ Papers.
59. Memcon, "The Middle East," October 24, 1967, NSF/Country file/Middle East/Israel/Box 143 Israel vol. XII 1965–68, LBJ Papers.

States to honor its commitment to open the Gulf of Aqaba. He understood the pressures on Eshkol as Israeli militants forced him to reorganize his cabinet, to surrender the defense portfolio to Moshe Dayan, and as the chimera of Arab unity flashed across the Middle East. He appreciated Israeli understanding of his predicament and the deference Eshkol had paid to his wishes, to his needs. He could ask no more of the men and women under siege in Tel Aviv. Still, he hoped they could find a way to wait for the miraculous peaceful solution he sought, thus far in vain. War would surely endanger American interests in the region, and he did not want it. He could not approve of preemptive action, but he was intensely sympathetic to the Israeli cause. If they had to fight, he would support them as best he could. God speed. And that Eshkol understood Lyndon Johnson was evident in the message he sent the president through Arthur Goldberg, U.S. ambassador to the UN, after Israeli planes took to the air:

Eshkol strongly hopes that we will take no action that would limit Israeli action in achieving freedom of passage through the Gulf of Aqaba. They understand your difficulties in achieving this result; and are prepared to handle the matter themselves.[60]

Johnson was probably the best friend Israel ever had in the White House, but he never lost sight of the fact that Israeli and American interests were not identical. Had he ever thought otherwise, the Israeli attack on the U.S.S. *Liberty* in the midst of the Six Day War would have disabused him. Mistrustful of the American "spy" ship, the Israeli military launched a series of air and sea attacks against the vessel, disabling it and inflicting heavy casualties on the crew. It was an incident analogous to the Japanese attack on the U.S.S. *Panay* in 1937, but Israel and the United States were supposedly friendly countries, and the United States was providing considerable material and diplomatic support to the Israelis. Johnson, outraged, ordered that a stiff protest be sent to Eshkol and demanded the punishment of those responsible.[61] The Israelis

---

60. W. W. Rostow memorandum for LBJ, June 6, 1967, NSF/NSC History/ME crisis May–June 67/Box 18, LBJ Papers. Eshkol's message was received by Goldberg in a call from Jerusalem from a friend who was Israel's chief justice.

61. Unsigned notes [probably Harold Saunders] of meeting of NSC Special Committee [chaired by McGeorge Bundy] dated June 9, 1967, NSF/NSC History/ME crisis May–June 67/Box 19; "Diplomatic Activity in Connection with S.S. Liberty Incident"

claimed, of course, that the action had been accidental, a claim that was absurd given the circumstances of the action, but it was in the interests of both countries to settle the matter quickly and quietly, which they did.[62]

In the months that followed, the United States continued to protect Israel's interests in the United Nations, insisting that the Arabs agree to a general peace settlement before the Israelis were required to surrender the lands they had conquered during the war. At the same time, the Johnson administration privately expressed apprehension to the Israeli government over signs that Israel intended to annex and settle some of that territory. Ultimately, the United States and the Soviet Union supported UN Resolution 242, necessarily worded vaguely in order to gain Arab and Israeli acceptance but clearly embracing the principle of land for peace.[63] As best it could, the administration left negotiation with the belligerents to the United Nations. Rusk's effort in May 1968 to energize Johnson toward a more active role for the United States fell short of its goal.[64]

In the last year of the Johnson administration, despite the president's strong pro-Israeli sympathies, Israeli–American relations deteriorated. Johnson and his advisers were angered by overwhelming evidence that the Israelis planned to keep considerable part of the land they had occupied in the course of the war, utterly indifferent to UN strictures to the contrary or to the problems they created for the United States. The Israelis ignored American requests that they refrain from unilateral acts in Jerusalem, continuing to expropriate Arab property without regard for the American position, without informing or consulting the United States.[65]

undated and *aide-mémoir*, U.S. to Israel, June 10, 1967, NSF/Country file/Middle East/Box 107/Middle East crisis vol. IV, Memos [1 of 2] 6/67, LBJ Papers.

62. For a brief, angry report of the "coverup," see George Lenczowski, *American Presidents and the Middle East* (Durham, N.C.: Duke University Press, 1990), 110–12.
63. Quandt, *Decade of Decisions*, 64–8, is excellent on the Johnson administration's postwar approach. For evidence of American apprehension about Israeli territorial aggrandizement, see Harold Saunders memorandum for McGeorge Bundy, June 7, 1967, NSF/Country file/Box 107/Middle East crisis/vol. IV, Memos 6/67 [2 of 2], Department of State Circular Telegram, June 8, 1967 (209168), NSF/Country file/Box 107/Middle East crisis/vol. IV, Cables 6/67 [2 of 2], Summary Notes of 575th NSC Meeting September 13, 1967, NSF/NSC Meeting File/Box 2, LBJ Papers.
64. Rusk memorandum for LBJ, May 23, 1968, WHCF/Confidential File/Box 6/ME/NE, LBJ Papers.
65. Lucius Battle memorandum for W. W. Rostow, May 14, 1968, NSF/Country File/ Middle East Israel/Box 141/Israel vol. IX Memos 3/68–5/68, LBJ Papers.

Nonetheless, when Arab complaints were raised in the UN Security Council, the Israelis expected American support.

The Israelis, on the other hand, were angered by American pressure to relinquish land many of them thought part of their sacred heritage, land they had just rewon with their own blood. They would do nothing to enable the United States to improve its relations with the Arab states and were infuriated by indications that the Americans were courting Nasser again in 1968. Johnson administration efforts to use an Israeli request for F-4 Phantom jets to exact promises from the Israelis not to develop nuclear weapons or to obtain promises on territorial questions further displeased the Israelis without gaining any concessions. The Israelis knew that in an election year, Johnson would have to give them what they wanted, and, indeed, Congress forced his hand on the sale of the jets.[66]

The last issue on which Israel and Lyndon Johnson confronted each other also ended in bitterness. On December 28, 1968, Israeli commandos raided Beirut International Airport and destroyed thirteen Lebanese civilian aircraft, apparently in retaliation for a Palestinian attack on an El Al (Israeli) plane in Athens. The United States quickly condemned the Israeli action, more forcefully than it had condemned the Palestinian, to the intense dissatisfaction of the Israelis and major American Jewish organizations. Ernest Goldstein, a White House staffer in contact with American friends of Israel, reported that "the general view is that for the first time in your presidency even handed justice has not been dispensed."[67] At the end, strained relations had Johnson grumbling that the United States was not about to become an Israeli satellite. William Quandt suggests that it was with some relief, as well as apprehension, that the Israelis "welcomed the presidency of Richard Nixon."[68]

One interesting and revealing episode during Johnson's last year in office involved an attempt by Nasser to effect a reconciliation with

---

66. Robert McNamara memorandum for LBJ, February 6, 1968, and Ernest Goldstein [White House staff] memorandum for LBJ, August 21, 1968, WHCF/CF/Box 9/CO 126 Israel (1967–1968); W. W. Rostow memorandum for LBJ, October 8, 1968, and "Talking Points for The Secretary's Meeting with Israeli Foreign Minister Eban October 22," undated [October 1968], NSF/Country file/ME/Israel/Box 142 Israel vol. X Memos 6/68–11/68 [1 of 2], LBJ Papers.
67. Goldstein memorandum for LBJ, January 2, 1969, WCHF/CF/Box 9/CO 126 Israel (1967–1968), LBJ Papers.
68. Quandt, "The Arab–Israeli Conflict in American Foreign Policy," 7.

the United States. During the Six Day War, Nasser had charged that U.S. planes had participated in the attacks on Egypt, a charge widely accepted in the Arab world as an explanation for the crushing defeat inflicted by the Israelis. Enraged by the lie, Johnson and Rusk were more hostile than ever to Nasser.

In the autumn of 1967, however, hints that Nasser had repented surfaced. Stories circulated that the speed with which Israeli pilots refueled and returned to attack Egyptian targets had misled Nasser into thinking that American planes were supplementing the Israeli air force. In December, Nasser invited an American lawyer to meet with him in Cairo and used him to relay a verbal message to Johnson. He wanted to revive ties to the United States, which he claimed were essential to enable him to resist Soviet pressures for the use of Alexandria for housing Soviet naval personnel and refueling Soviet ships. He was willing to accept nonbelligerency with Israel and exchange ambassadors with Tel Aviv if the Israelis would make a gesture toward the Palestinian refugees, offer them just compensation for their lost lands.[69]

Rusk responded warily, noting that the United States had made overtures to Cairo and required an official statement of Nasser's interest before it would go further. It also wanted compensation for property damaged during the war and withdrawal of the charges that it had been a participant. In February 1968, while Johnson was still reeling from the impact of the Tet offensive, the issue came up at a meeting of the NSC. Recollections of problems Nasser had caused the United States in the past quickly surfaced. Johnson interrupted and remarked that Eugene Black, one of the few men in the world respected by both Nasser and Johnson, had reported that the U.S. position in the Middle East was deteriorating rapidly and had recommended more contact with Nasser. Black had apparently urged Johnson to accept the idea that Nasser was misinformed when he levied false charges against the United States. Johnson accepted the argument that Nasser had to take the initiative, but at the conclusion of the meeting he directed the Department of State to pursue the improvement of relations with the UAR.[70]

69. Ambassador, Cairo, to Secretary of State, December 10, 1967, NSF/Country file/ME/ UAR/Box 160 UAR vol. VI Memos 8/67–7/68, LBJ Papers.
70. Harold Saunders memorandum, February 26, 1968, on NSC Meeting February 21, 1968, NSF/NSC Meeting File, Box 2, LBJ Papers.

In April, after he had announced that he would not be a candidate for reelection, Johnson told a small group of trusted advisers that he wanted an opening to Nasser and was willing to take the political flak that such talks were likely to provoke. The alternative, Johnson warned, was another war in the Middle East and a further erosion of American influence in the region. But Nasser, conciliatory, even flirtatious, argued that he had severe internal problems. He wanted to restore relations with the United States, but elements in the military and the public generally were not ready. He needed a signal from the Americans that they wanted to see UN Resolution 242 implemented. The dance went on to the end of Johnson's presidency. Nonetheless, Johnson's recognition of Nasser's importance and his willingness to reach out to the Egyptian leader were apparent.[71]

At the conclusion of Johnson's five-year administration, American interests in the Middle East were arguably in greater danger than they had been when he took office in November 1963. Soviet influence appeared to be ascending, as the Kremlin rejected American efforts to prevent an arms race in the area and poured billions of dollars in military equipment into the radical Arab states, especially Egypt, Syria, and Iraq, after the Six Day War. Anger toward the United States for its support of Israel raged among Arabs everywhere. The Soviet navy had established its presence in the Mediterranean and was attempting to develop port facilities to enhance its effort to counter the U.S. Sixth Fleet, long hegemon of the area's waters. Western influence in the region had been doomed in any event, given the increasing political mobilization of Arab peoples and the intense nationalism that provided its focus. But the American relationship with Israel, not least as manifested by the congressional supporters of Israel who hindered efforts to buy Arab friends, hurt the country as it competed with the Soviets for Arab

71. Secretary of State to Ambassador, Cairo, January 24, 1968, and Robert Anderson to Secretary of State [report of conversation with Nasser], May 6, 1968, NSF/Country file/ME/UAR/Box UAR 160 vol. VI Memos 8/67–7/68; Harold Saunders memorandum February 26, 1968 [on NSC meeting February 21], NSF/NSC Meeting File/Box 2, LBJ Papers; Clark Clifford notes on talk with LBJ, Rusk, W. W. Rostow, and John McCloy, April 28, 1968, Clifford Papers, Vietnam Files Box 1.

favor. The Soviets had become a force to be reckoned with in the Middle East. The United States could not keep them out. Johnson's aides consoled themselves with the idea that it was "normal" for both superpowers to operate in the Middle East and with the bromide that there were "natural limitations on Soviet ability to increase influence in the area."[72]

On the other hand, if dominance in the Middle East was not an end in itself but rather the means of maintaining the flow of oil and preserving the existence of the state of Israel, matters were far less bleak. The oil kept flowing, and the major oil-producing states remained friendly enough. And the Israelis, prickly and sometimes abusive friends, seemed more secure than at any time in their history.

Johnson claimed no expert knowledge of the Middle East and had little interest in the area. The opposition to Soviet expansion that he practiced elsewhere on the globe he deemed appropriate there as well. He offered carrots to those who supported the United States and was unwilling to reward those he perceived as supporters of the Soviet Union. In general he left policy toward the region to the Department of State and the NSC staff, intervening only when a domestic political issue was involved, usually when the friends of Israel sounded an alarm. He understood the need to reach out to Arab leaders like Nasser but demanded respect for his country in return. In its absence, there was no reason for him to act contrary to domestic political imperatives. When, after the Six Day War, Nasser seemed contrite and the Israelis ungrateful, Johnson was willing to work with Nasser. Lyndon Johnson had been bloodied in Vietnam and New Hampshire. In 1968 he was able to empathize with Nasser. They were both heroic figures: Lyndon Johnson, the leader of the most powerful nation the world had ever known, and Gamal Abdul Nasser, leader of an impoverished Egypt, who nonetheless set the agenda in the Middle East during Johnson's years in the White House.

72. Nicholas Katzenbach speaking at NSC Meeting, cited in Harold Saunders memorandum February 26, 1968, NSF/NSC Meeting File/Box 2, LBJ Papers.

10

Lyndon Johnson:
A Final Reckoning

NANCY BERNKOPF TUCKER

In contrast to histories written about presidents such as John F. Kennedy and Dwight D. Eisenhower, this volume assessing LBJ and his administration has not tried to tell the reader that there abided a different man behind the brash, crude, often insensitive exterior that the public knew as Lyndon Johnson. In fact, the president was vulgar, demanding, vain, and combative, if also brilliant, determined, and filled with what seemed to be inextinguishable energy. He proved to be dominated by the Cold War stereotypes of his time, filled with the conviction that the world could be transformed through judicious applications of Franklin Roosevelt's New Deal thinking, and committed to fulfillment of some of the most assertive portions of the Kennedy legacy. Indeed, as much as those who fashioned the Kennedy legend would have hated the comparison, Lyndon Johnson proved remarkably like JFK in his pragmatism, dedication to nation building, concern about credibility, discomfort with revolutionary change, and arrogant assumption that American interpretations of democracy and development provided appropriate models for all nations. Where he differed, ironically, may have been in displaying a greater degree of prudence than Kennedy's youth, boldness, and activism could tolerate.[1] Johnson really was the man he seemed to be, really did lose his way in the jungles of Vietnam, and, in the end, really could not perceive why his vision for a Great Society in America and for American leadership in the world had gone astray.

But although the assessments in this volume are not broadly revisionist, they do transform our understanding of the foreign pol-

1. Thomas G. Paterson, ed., *Kennedy's Quest for Victory* (New York: Oxford, 1989), 3–23.

icy of the Johnson administration. As the first comprehensive examination of foreign policymaking in the Johnson years, this study provides a wealth of detail and insight that extends and deepens the analysis of this critical period. It is, for instance, striking to note the degree to which areas so often dismissed as peripheral to American concerns had come to preoccupy decision makers. Although the greatest threat to American security may have continued to come from nuclear weapons and the Soviet autocrats who wielded them, Warren Cohen correctly emphasizes the administration belief that there were no reasons for and little likelihood of a superpower war. This freed Washington to take the Third World more seriously – arguably a tragic awakening.

Foreign policy as crafted by Lyndon B. Johnson and his international affairs advisers reflected the unsettled times as well as the uncertain direction that an inexperienced president imposed upon it. If this was an era without an acute confrontation between the United States and the Soviet Union, it could not be characterized as a time of peace given the pernicious influence of the grinding struggle in Vietnam, which played a role in every region and intruded upon virtually every decision the administration made. Absent a cataclysm, Johnson still faced a series of emergencies ranging from turmoil in the Congo to war in the Middle East to a perceived communist challenge in the Caribbean to a lingering hostage crisis in Asia.

Early in his presidency Johnson reflected upon his discomfort in the international arena with the quip that "foreigners are not like the folks I am used to."[2] Joseph Tulchin notes that McGeorge Bundy deemed it his responsibility to see to it that few foreign dignitaries made it into the Oval Office. White House staff member and historian Eric Goldman remembered that Johnson felt "foreign policy was something you had, like measles, and got over ... as quickly as possible."[3] Reminiscent of Harry Truman, who also came to the office unexpectedly and with a conspicuous domestic bias, Johnson would have preferred to concentrate on his Great Society agenda and leave external relations to his secretaries of state and defense. But Johnson could not tolerate not being in command,

2. Eric F. Goldman, *The Tragedy of Lyndon Johnson* (New York: Dell, 1969), 447.
3. Ibid., 625.

and so he tackled problems he did not always understand. His schooling had been poor, his travels overseas severely limited, his reading even more so, leaving him, in Waldo Heinrichs' assessment, "culture-bound and vulnerable to clichés and stereotypes." Lacking a sophisticated perception of international relations, Johnson, not surprisingly, remained captive of Cold War illusions shaped by a Munich analogy where distinctions between fascism and communism blurred and a strong America always ready to counter aggression was essential. Extremely cautious in decision making, except where choices concerned Vietnam, once persuaded of the route the nation should take, "grimly, no holds barred, and at times utterly pell-mell, he went for the jugular."[4]

As the essays in this volume demonstrate repeatedly, Johnson empathized more easily with Third World nations that might benefit most from American largess rather than with states whose power demanded collaboration. Frank Costigliola makes clear that Johnson did not respond well to European demands for a partnership in policy formulation, preferring to give the Europeans an illusion of cooperation through a mechanism such as the multilateral force. In contrast, he relished the idea of creating a Tennessee Valley–style river development project for Vietnam's Mekong Basin and, as Tulchin details, displayed considerable enthusiasm for Walt Rostow's plans to improve infrastructure in Latin America even as he remained critical of John F. Kennedy's Alliance for Progress. His "Alamo instincts" led him to sympathize with the plight of Israeli leaders confronted by a hostile Arab community. Unlike the foreigners he customarily shunned, the Israelis were "Lyndon Johnson's kind of people – brash, aggressive, unforgiving," and he became "probably the best friend Israel ever had in the White House," argues Warren Cohen. Still, Johnson "never lost sight of the fact that Israeli and American interests were not identical," and, as Robert McMahon and I make apparent, Johnson seemed convinced that such countries inevitably wanted something from the United States, a condition that could be personally irritating and politically dangerous.

The men who assisted Johnson in devising solutions for the nation's foreign relations dilemmas largely shared the president's pri-

4. Ibid., 452.

orities. He retained most of Kennedy's staff after his sudden assumption of leadership, and some, such as Dean Rusk, Robert McNamara, and McGeorge Bundy, stayed on, serving the new president loyally. Later Walt Rostow would replace Bundy, and Clark Clifford would become secretary of defense when McNamara departed. This core group proved especially compatible because all shared Johnson's Cold War vision and favored pragmatic tactics. For instance, when LBJ gradually abandoned Kennedy's emphasis on nationalism and democracy in Africa and Latin America, as Terrence Lyons and Joseph Tulchin demonstrate, they agreed that such idealistic policies jeopardized larger U.S. interests. Above all, until late in the administration, these men reinforced the president's commitment to war in Vietnam.

If fear of communist aggression was the common concern motivating Johnson and his advisers, Vietnam proved to be their joint obsession. The importance of southeast Asia for LBJ need hardly be emphasized, but the essays in this volume show clearly for the first time the enormous toll that their fixation took, dominating virtually all other foreign policy discussions. All of the authors who have contributed to this review of Johnson-era diplomacy have remarked that Vietnam governed choices made, expenditures apportioned, challenges accepted in their disparate parts of the globe. Most obviously, the war interfered with prospects for better relations between the United States and the Soviet Union as Washington and Moscow lined up on opposing sides of the conflict. Nikita Khrushchev had made it plain in 1961 that Moscow would assist wars of national liberation, and Vietnam, as the pivotal battleground for challenging that threat, helped to stymie any serious U.S. efforts at détente. Frank Costigliola also asserts that policy toward western Europe was complicated by the continuing dissipation of U.S. resources in Vietnam. It magnified "America's balance-of-payments deficits, America's need for German offset payments, pressures from Congress to withdraw troops from Germany, U.S. resentment of the allies' refusal to get involved, and European criticism of America's reflexive anticommunism."

In Asia, as I have argued, Johnson saw a nation's willingness to support the United States as the primary test of its eligibility for assistance. Thus the United States made mercenaries of its allies and had difficulty focusing on interests they avowed that had nothing to do with Vietnam. Moreover, in determining policy toward China, movement toward improvement of relations was frustrated by the perception of Beijing as supplier and supporter of the North Vietnamese.

Even as far afield as Africa, the Middle East, and Latin America, Vietnam played a role. In Africa, Lyons shows, disillusionment with newly independent states whose governments failed to produce stability and prosperity was compounded by a preference to avoid tests of strength, despite Chinese and Soviet involvement, because the United States had enough to do in southeast Asia against the same adversaries. Johnson avoided African problems and stifled African initiatives. On one of the few occasions that he spoke publicly on African issues, his objective was to establish that his administration could act vigorously on questions other than the Vietnam War. Warren Cohen makes a similar case, showing that increasing amounts of time and attention given to Vietnam appeared to justify ignoring, as much as possible, intractable problems in the Middle East. In contrast to Africa, however, where no likely donor to the war effort emerged, Cohen remarks upon the tensions generated by Johnson's efforts to force the Israeli government to provide support in Vietnam in exchange for increasing American deliveries of military equipment. For Latin America the financial encumbrance of the war, on the other hand, reduced sums available for programs already circumscribed by small budgets, reflecting the administration's growing disinterest in the region.

At home, of course, as Waldo Heinrichs and Walter LaFeber make clear, the Vietnam imbroglio increasingly fractured politics and made of Lyndon Johnson an anxious, suspicious, and morose figure. The controversy over the war brought out many of LBJ's worst characteristics and possibly, as LaFeber contends, also the most debilitating features of American democracy. Harking back to Alexis de Tocqueville's critique of the American system, LaFeber emphasizes the inability of the nation to be patient with a long and difficult commitment as well as the contradiction between effective diplomacy and the resistance of an open society to the secrecy that government leaders and diplomats believe they require to formulate and carry out foreign policy. The president struggled with a hostile print press, alienated by his inept efforts to manipulate it, as well as the credibility gap between what reporters observed and the government tried to tell them. Johnson found intellectuals almost as alien as foreigners and failed to neutralize them while progressively losing the confidence of business leaders and finally, with the Tet offensive, Congress. Although the majority of the American people supported the war effort until almost the end of the administration, high casualties ensured that the public would defect and that Johnson would not be able to bludgeon or cajole the nation into staying the course.

However much American officials focused on the Vietnam conflict, their devotion of energy and intelligence did not simplify the problems or reduce the frustrations. Richard Immerman, who examines the war obsession in detail, tells a tale of indecision, confusion, and ultimate defeat. Although Johnson escalated involvement slowly and hesitantly, in the end he was primarily responsible for prolonging the war and, therefore, amassing higher and higher tolls in American and Vietnamese lives. Walt Rostow, in particular, bolstered Johnson's determination even after McNamara became disenchanted and Clifford began to try to steer the president toward serious negotiations. Ultimately, although Rusk remained reluctant to abandon the fight and opposed Clifford's pessimism, his proposal to stop the bombing proved decisive.

As difficult as it was to persuade Washington's policymaking core to focus on issues outside of southeast Asia, the essays in this volume do highlight the disparate pressures and opportunities with which foreign affairs confronted the administration. For instance, Robert McMahon argues that in south Asia lessons about limitations on the uses of American power should not derive simply from the Vietnam War. The United States, having shifted its priorities during the Kennedy years from exclusive support for Pakistan to trying to entice India into a closer relationship with the West, failed under Johnson to cope adequately with the unyielding religious and national conflicts of the subcontinent, managed to alienate both the Pakistanis and the Indians, and finally found itself forced to invite Moscow into the arena to settle conflicts beyond Washington's control.

Among the critical factors that McMahon emphasizes was administration concern regarding Chinese initiatives in South Asia, and it is with Johnson policy toward China that I launched my exploration of U.S.–East Asian relations in the era. Although elements within the administration and the public increasingly advocated a reassessment of China policy, the combination of confrontation over Vietnam and China's domestic preoccupation with the Cultural Revolution rendered significant change impossible. Johnson administration successes in the region were limited to facilitating a treaty between South Korea and Japan, moving toward a resolution of conflicts with Japan regarding Okinawa and the Bonin Islands, and presiding over Taiwan's graduation from economic aid programs. But in this sphere, too, crisis demonstrated that American might had a limited reach as Washington proved unable to prevent terrorist efforts to assassinate Korea's president or the successful seizure of an American intelligence ship.

Warren Cohen portrays a mixed legacy for Johnson's successor. The oil kept flowing out of the Arab states, and Israel's position was, if anything, strengthened. But America's struggle to prevent Soviet influence from penetrating the area and establishing a solid presence floundered as Moscow supplied radical Arab governments with military equipment in the wake of the Six Day War and anti-Americanism burgeoned.

The portrait of American power under siege is relieved somewhat by the essays contributed by Costigliola, Lyons, and Tulchin. In its relations with Europe the United States continued to prescribe the terms on which interaction would proceed, going so far as to dictate the language through which opinions and criticisms had to be expressed for an individual or government to be taken seriously. But even here alliance unity was fraying, and it took the Soviet invasion of Czechoslovakia in 1968 to restore power and consensus to NATO. Among Latin American nations, Joseph Tulchin indicates the perpetuation of patterns that kept the United States a distant and dominant force rather than the helpful friend that visionaries had hoped it would become when they inaugurated the Alliance for Progress. American leaders never understood the dynamics of the region and invariably put anticommunist politics

ahead of respect for national sovereignty or economic development. Africa because of its unimportance to the Johnson administration, according to Lyons, taxed the nation's resources least of
all. Africans remained supplicants, and the administration, for the
most part, ignored their needs. When their interests clashed with
those of current or former colonial powers, countries that happened also to be U.S. allies, Johnson was less likely than Kennedy
to criticize the Europeans.

Lyndon Johnson presided over an administration dedicated to
the proposition that the United States could champion democracy,
defend the national security, and undermine the spread of communism throughout the world. It would do these things first by
taking a firm stand in Vietnam and demonstrating American resolve, credibility, and even altruism. The adventure proved costly
in countless ways. It derailed Johnson's domestic agenda, it
plunged the American economy into deficits and imbalances that
would plague it for decades to come, and it divided the American
people. In Vietnam it led to tens of thousands of American victims
dead and disfigured, but also hundreds of thousands of casualties
and environmental devastation in Laos and Cambodia as well as
Vietnam – North and South.

Less often remarked upon were the costs incurred for foreign policy broadly conceived. The essays in this volume attest to the difficulties that the Johnson administration had balancing its responsibilities
and understanding its commitments beyond Indochina. Its persistence
in pursuing an often unidimensional foreign policy severely limited its
accomplishments elsewhere, strained friendships, aggravated ani-
mosities, and left a problematic legacy for subsequent occupants of decision-making posts in the White House, State Department, and
Department of Defense.

Indeed in 1993 as the Clinton administration assumed the responsibilities of foreign policy management it confronted a post–Cold
War world that reflected many of the problems that had burdened
Lyndon Johnson's presidency, making evident that some of the solutions employed in the 1960s did not work. In Europe Germany remained a central issue, as it was for Johnson, whose fear of and
fondness for Germany rendered him especially sensitive to growing
German power and the need to craft policies to deal with it. Clinton

also emphasized Israel in the Middle East, if not quite as determinedly as Johnson, reportedly being more interested in the possibilities of a land-for-peace solution but not willing to strain relations with Israel to accomplish that goal.

Outlining approaches to Africa and Latin America, government spokesmen pledged to fill broken promises of the past. Anthony Lake, Bill Clinton's National Security Adviser, in remarks concerning the foreign policy objectives of the new administration, declared that Washington would pay more attention to Africa. "There has been a sense that some administrations have taken years to figure out where Africa is on the map," but the Clinton team not only "knows where Africa is" but also wants to accelerate progress toward "where it is going" in the spheres of economic reform and democratization. Thus, Lake suggested as an example, the United States would work with Belgium and France to try to pressure Mobutu Sese Seko, who came to power in 1965 with CIA assistance, to liberalize Zaire's repressive domestic politics.[5] Similarly reversing the tone of Johnson pragmatism, as well as the anticommunism of the Reagan years and other intervening administrations, Latin American policy would, according to then–Deputy Secretary of State Clifton R. Wharton, once again emphasize human rights and democracy.[6]

Asia also had changed and remained the same. Although relations with China were far better than any scenario imagined during the Johnson years, problems over issues of human rights, trade deficits, and arms proliferation threatened to provoke a new downturn. Controversy over the possible development of an atomic device by the North Koreans suggested a sustained period of tension analogous to that of the *Pueblo* era, involving both more friction and more contact than at any time in between. Weapons questions also continued to bedevil relations with Pakistan, as did Islamabad's reputed support for terrorist activities, yielding threats to cut off aid and plunge American relations on the subcontinent of south Asia into angry exchanges reminiscent of the Johnson era.

5. Reed Kramer, "U.S. to Focus on Africa, Lake Says," *Washington Post,* May 4, 1993, p. A15.
6. John M. Goshko, "Clinton to Stress Democracy, Human Rights in Latin America Policy, *Washington Post,* May 4, 1993, p. A15.

Finally there was Vietnam. Clinton inherited Johnson's most troubling legacy in the form of a decision about whether to establish diplomatic relations with Hanoi. That it took twenty-five years for the two nations to reach that point testified to the depth of the trauma each had experienced. By the 1990s what remained were unanswered, and perhaps unanswerable, questions about prisoners of war and Vietnam's need for the kind of economic development that Lyndon Johnson had hoped to offer in exchange for peace when he spoke at Johns Hopkins University in April 1965.

The biggest alteration, of course, came with the end of the Cold War and the collapse of the Soviet Union. Lyndon Johnson could not have imagined a world so transformed, but he would have welcomed the implications with much energy and enthusiasm. For him the new world order would have been a time of active engagement, not in foreign affairs traditionally conceived but in an effort to extend the benefits of democracy and capitalism across the globe. Johnson was never a man of small dreams or limited aspirations. He would have grasped the moment and used presidential power – whether wisely or not – to try to shape a more prosperous world community.

Suggestions for Further Reading

Lyndon B. Johnson: Change and Continuity

Admiring biographies of LBJ are scarce, but his undoubted strengths do emerge in most accounts. A balanced and extensively researched treatment through the congressional years is Robert Dallek, *Lone Star Rising: Lyndon Johnson and His Times, 1908–1960* (New York, 1991). Paul K. Conkin, *Big Daddy from the Pedernales: Lyndon Baines Johnson* (Boston, 1986), is short, incisive, and insightful. Doris Kearns Goodwin, *Lyndon Johnson and the American Dream* (New York, 1976), takes a psychoanalytical approach. Most critical of Johnson are Ronnie Dugger, *The Politician; The Life and Times of Lyndon Johnson: The Drive for Power, from the Frontier to Master of the Senate* (New York, 1982), and Robert A. Caro, *The Years of Lyndon Johnson: The Path to Power* (New York, 1983).

Of more special interest are: Rowland Evans and Robert Novak, *Lyndon B. Johnson: The Exercise of Power, a Political Biography* (London, 1967), a Washington insider view of Johnson's political rise; Richard N. Goodwin, *Remembering America: A Voice from the Sixties* (Boston, 1988), a poignant and powerful memoir by a Johnson aide; Philip Geyelin, *Lyndon B. Johnson and the World* (New York, 1966), still useful on LBJ's world view; and Larry Berman, *Planning a Tragedy: The Americanization of the War in Vietnam* (New York, 1982), excellent on the Vietnam mindset.

Johnson, Vietnam, and Tocqueville

For understanding the collapse of consensus during the 1964–8 years and the rise of the problems that Tocqueville prophesied, five books are especially useful. Oddly, historians and political scientists have done little empirical work on the relationships among policymakers, foreign policy, and creating and maintaining a domestic consensus, but of particular importance is Theodore J. Lowi, *The Personal President: Power Invested, Promise Unfulfilled* (Ithaca, N.Y., 1985). For the overall collapse of the consensus, key studies are Allen J. Matusow, *The Unraveling of America: A History of Liberalism in the 1960s* (New York, 1984); Charles DeBenedetti, *An American Ordeal: The Antiwar Movement of the Vietnam Era,* Charles Chatfield, assisting author (Syracuse, N.Y., 1990); and Melvin Small, *Johnson, Nixon, and the Doves* (New Brunswick, N.J., 1988). A pioneering, highly significant account of how the media did – or, more notably, did not – affect public support of the war is William M. Hammond, *The United States Army in Vietnam. Public Affairs: The Military and the Media, 1962–1968* (Washington, 1988).

Some of the concerns of the essay are examined in the splendid comparative study by Ariel Levite, Bruce W. Jentleson, and Larry Berman, *Foreign Military Intervention: The Dynamics of Protracted Conflict* (New York, 1992). Important on the media are Kathleen J. Turner, *Lyndon Johnson's Dual War: Vietnam and the Press* (Chicago, 1985), which plays down the threat from the left and plays up the threat from the right; and Daniel C. Hallin, *The "Uncensored War": The Media and Vietnam* (New York, 1986). How central policymakers viewed (and sometime even changed their view of) the necessary consensus to wage the war can be examined in Dean Rusk, *As I Saw It,* as told to Richard Rusk (New York, 1990); Warren I. Cohen, *Dean Rusk* (Totowa, N.J., 1980), the best biography and the story of a troubled liberalism; Clark M. Clifford with Richard Holbrooke, *Counsel to the President: A Memoir* (New York, 1991), especially for its several references to the business community; William C. Berman, *Fulbright and the Vietnam War: The Dissent of a Political Realist* (Kent, Ohio, 1988), for the Senate's leading antiwar voice; and Deborah Shapley, *Prom-*

ise and Power: The Life and Times of Robert McNamara (Boston, 1993), on the secretary of defense's growing disillusionment. For the purposes of this essay, the most useful books on Johnson include Eric Goldman, *The Tragedy of Lyndon Johnson* (New York, 1969); Doris Kearns, *Lyndon Johnson and the American Dream* (New York, 1976); and the essays on Vietnam and the media in Robert A. Divine, ed., *Exploring the Johnson Years* (Austin, 1981).

A Time in the Tide of Men's Affairs: Lyndon Johnson and Vietnam

U.S. policy toward Vietnam during the Johnson presidency must not be divorced from the broader contours of America's thirty-year involvement in the former French colony. The scholarly literature is immense, but recommended surveys include George C. Herring, *America's Longest War: The United States and Vietnam, 1950–1975*, 2d ed. (New York, 1986); George McT. Kahin, *Intervention: How America Became Involved in Vietnam* (New York, 1986); David Levy, *The Debate Over Vietnam* (Baltimore, 1991); Marilyn Young, *The Vietnam Wars: 1945–1990* (New York, 1991); and David L. Anderson, ed., *Shadow on the White House: Presidents and the Vietnam War, 1945–1975* (Lawrence, Kansas, 1993). William Conrad Gibbons has published the first three parts of his exceptionally detailed multivolume study *The U.S. Government and the Vietnam War: Executive and Legislative Roles and Relationships* (Princeton, 1986–   ), and such journalistic accounts as Michael Maclear, *The Ten Thousand Day War, Vietnam: 1945–1975* (New York, 1981), and Stanley Karnow, *Vietnam: A History* (New York, 1983), remain valuable.

Those interested primarily in Johnson's policies should begin with, in addition to the foregoing, Larry Berman, *Planning a Tragedy: The Americanization of the War in Vietnam* (New York, 1982); John P. Burke and Fred Greenstein in collaboration with Larry Berman and Richard H. Immerman, *How Presidents Test Reality: Decisions on Vietnam, 1954 and 1965* (New York, 1989); and Brian Vandemark, *Into the Quagmire: Lyndon Johnson and the Escalation of the Vietnam War* (New York, 1990). Don Oberdorfer, *Tet!* (Garden City, 1971), is still the most comprehensive examination of the communist offensive, but it should be read in conjunction with Herbert Y. Schandler, *Lyndon Johnson and Vietnam: The Unmaking of a President* (Princeton, 1983), and Larry Berman, *Lyndon Johnson's War: The Road to Stalemate in Vietnam* (New York, 1989). On the military dimensions see Harry G. Summers Jr., *On Strategy: The Vietnam War in Context* (Carlisle Barracks, 1981); Bruce Palmer Jr., *The 25-Year War: America's Military Role in Vietnam* (Lexington, 1984); Andrew Krepinevich, *The Army and Vietnam* (Baltimore, 1986); and Ronald H. Spector, *After Tet: The Bloodiest Year in Vietnam* (New York, 1993). Several memoirs are essential: Lyndon Baines Johnson, *The Vantage Point: Perspectives of the Presidency, 1963–1969* (New York, 1971); Maxwell D. Taylor, *Swords and Ploughshares,* (New York, 1972); William C. Westmoreland, *A Soldier Reports* (Garden City, 1976); Dean Rusk, *As I Saw It* (New York, 1990); and Clark Clifford, *Counsel to the President: A Memoir* (New York, 1991).

Threats, Opportunities, and Frustrations in East Asia

The literature on American–East Asian relations during the Johnson years, with the notable exception of the Vietnam War, remains exceedingly thin. The richest area covers China, particularly Chinese policy and attitudes. John Wilson Lewis and Xue Litai, *China Builds the Bomb* (Stanford, Calif., 1988), perceptively explore the development that frightened the Johnson administration. Allen S. Whiting, in his usually thorough and thoughtful way, examines Chinese deterrence policies regarding India and Indochina and the impact on relations with the United States in *The Chinese Calculus of Deterrence* (Ann Arbor, Mich., 1975). On the American side Gordon Chang's provocative *Friends and Enemies: The United States, China and the Soviet Union, 1948–1972* (Stanford, Calif., 1990) virtually commands the field at present, with the exception of the pieces by James C. Thomson Jr., "On the Making of U.S. China Policy, 1961–1969," *China Quarterly* 50 (April–June 1972), and Wang Jisi, "From Kennedy to Nixon: America's East Asia and China Policy," *Beijing Review* (1988). Leonard A.

Kuznitz views policy from a more specialized but exceedingly useful perspective in *Public Opinion and Foreign Policy: America's China Policy, 1949–1979* (Westport, Conn., 1984).

The relationship with "the other China" has been most closely scrutinized by Nancy Bernkopf Tucker in *Taiwan, Hong Kong and the United States, 1945–1992: Uncertain Friendships* (New York, 1994). See also the older but still useful Ralph Clough, *Island China* (Cambridge, Mass., 1978). On the central if specialized economic relationship see Walter Galenson, ed., *Economic Growth and Structural Change in Taiwan* (Ithaca, N.Y., 1979) and Stephan Haggard, "The Politics of Industrialization in the Republic of Korea and Taiwan," in Helen Hughes, ed., *Achieving Industrialization in East Asia* (New York, 1988).

Relations with Japan are best explored in the firsthand accounts by Edwin O. Reischauer, *My Life Between Japan and America* (New York, 1986), and U. Alexis Johnson, *The Right Hand of Power* (Englewood Cliffs, N.J., 1984).

The problems of Korean–American relations receive attention in Frank Baldwin, ed., *Without Parallel* (New York, 1974); Koo Youngnok and Suh Dae-sook, eds., *Korea and the United States* (Honolulu, 1984), and Lee Yur-bok and Wayne Patterson, eds., *One Hundred Years of Korean–American Relations* (Tuscaloosa, 1986). Economic issues are again explained by Stephan Haggard in "The Transition to Export-led Growth in South Korea, 1954–1966," *Journal of Asian Studies* (1991) 50:850–73.

Toward Disillusionment and Disengagement in South Asia

The Johnson administration's policy toward south Asia is partially covered in several broad studies of U.S. relations with India and Pakistan, including most notably William J. Barnds, *India, Pakistan, and the Great Powers* (New York, 1972); G. W. Choudhury, *India, Pakistan, Bangladesh, and the Major Powers; Politics of a Divided Subcontinent* (New York, 1975); Shivaji Ganguly, *U.S. Policy Toward South Asia* (Boulder, Colo., 1990); and Robert J. McMahon, *The Cold War on the Periphery: The United States, India, and Pakistan* (New York, 1994). For more specialized studies, see Lloyd I. Rudolph and Susanne Hoeber Rudolph, eds., *The Regional Imperative: The Administration of U.S. Foreign Policy Towards South Asian States under Presidents Johnson and Nixon* (Atlantic Highlands, N.J., 1980); Carolyn Castore, "The United States and India: The Use of Food to Apply Economic Pressure, 1965–67," in Sidney Weintraub, ed., *Economic Coercion and U.S. Foreign Policy: Implications of Studies from the Johnson Administration* (Boulder, Colo., 1982), pp. 129–53; and Howard B. Schaffer, *New Dealer in the Cold War:The Role of Chester Bowles in U.S. Foreign Policy* (Cambridge, Mass., 1994).

Numerous bilateral studies of Indo–American and Pakistani–American relations exist, but few treat the Johnson years in more than a cursory fashion. Among the more useful are H. W. Brands, *India and the United States: The Cold Peace* (Boston, 1990); S. C. Tewari, *Indo–US Relations, 1947–1976* (New Delhi, 1977); Harold A. Gould and Sumit Ganguly, eds., *The Hope and the Reality: U.S.–Indian Relations from Roosevelt to Reagan* (Boulder, Colo., 1992); Dennis Kux, *India and the United States: Estranged Democracies* (Washington, 1993); Shirin Tahir-Kheli, *The United States and Pakistan: The Evolution of an Influence Relationship* (New York, 1982); and Leo and Noora Husain, eds., *United States–Pakistan Relations* (Berkeley, Calif., 1985). Useful memoirs that touch on U.S.–south Asian relations during the Johnson presidency are Lyndon B. Johnson, *The Vantage Point: Perspectives of the Presidency 1963–1969* (New York, 1971); Mohammed Ayub Khan, *Friends Not Masters: A Political Autobiography* (New York, 1967); George W. Ball, *The Past Has Another Pattern: Memoirs* (New York, 1982); Zulfikar Ali Bhutto, *The Myth of Independence* (London, 1969); and Chester Bowles, *Promises to Keep: My Years in Public Life, 1941–1969* (New York, 1971).

Lyndon B. Johnson, Germany, and "the End of the Cold War"

There have not been many historical studies of Lyndon Johnson's relations with western Europe. Granted extensive interviews by Johnson administration officials, Philip Geyelin wrote the best contemporary account, *Lyndon B. Johnson and the World* (New York, 1966). Along with Geyelin's book, John D. Steinbruner, *The Cybernetic Theory of Decision* (Princeton, N.J., 1974), is particularly helpful on the 1964 phase of the Multilateral Force story. See also McGeorge Bundy, *Danger and Survival: Choices about the Bomb in the First Fifty Years* (New York, 1988). An insider's account of U.S.–European relations is Harlan Cleveland's *NATO: The Transatlantic Bargain* (New York, 1970). For the role of a key outsider, see Douglas Brinkley, *Dean Acheson: The Cold War Years, 1953–71* (New Haven, 1992). George Ball, *The Past Has Another Pattern* (New York, 1982), offers an important memoir. Henry A. Kissinger, *The Troubled Partnership* (New York, 1965), and Harold van B. Cleveland, *The Atlantic Idea and Its European Rivals* (New York, 1966), are the works of two mild critics, both of whom enjoyed close contacts with government officials in Washington and in European capitals. Former Ambassador George McGhee's *At the Creation of a New Germany* (New Haven, Conn., 1989) offers documentary evidence and commentary.

Important scholarly analyses of NATO include Lawrence S. Kaplan, *NATO and the United States* (Boston, 1988) and "The United States and NATO in the Johnson Years" in Robert A. Divine, ed., *The Johnson Years: LBJ at Home and Abroad* (Lawrence, Kansas, 1994). See also Jane E. Stromseth, *The Origins of Flexible Response* (New York, 1988), and David N. Schwartz, *NATO's Nuclear Dilemmas* (Washington, 1983). For relations with specific countries, see Robert M. Hathaway, *Great Britain and the United States: Special Relations since World War II* (Boston, 1990), Frank Ninkovich, *Germany and the United States* (Boston, 1988), Wolfram F. Hanrieder's magisterial *Germany, America, Europe* (New Haven, Conn., 1989), Gregory F. Treverton, *The Dollar Drain and American Forces in Germany* (Athens, Ohio, 1978), Thomas Alan Schwartz, "Victories and Defeats in the Long Twilight Struggle: The United States and Western Europe in the 1960s" in Diane Kunz, ed., *The Diplomacy of the Crucial Decade: American Foreign Relations During the 1960s* (New York, 1994). Gustav Schmidt, "Die sicherheitspolitischen und wirtschaftlichen Dimensionen der britisch-amerikanischen Beziehungen 1955–1967," *Militärgeschichtliche Mitteilungen* (February 1991): 107–38, and

Frank Costigliola, *France and the United States: The Cold Alliance* (New York, 1992). For bridge building, see Bennett Kovrig, *Of Walls and Bridges* (New York, 1991).

The Promise of Progress: U.S. Relations with Latin America During the Administration of Lyndon B. Johnson

As indicated in the course of the chapter, the secondary literature on Johnson's Latin American policy is not rich. With some exceptions, the studies of his foreign policy generally say little or nothing about Latin America. On the other hand, histories of inter-American relations provide very little information about the Johnson years. Students of the period must content themselves with books on various episodes or subjects that are contemporaneous or very nearly contemporaneous with the events they discuss. A good example is the intervention in the Dominican Republic. The closest thing to a scholarly monograph is Abraham Lowenthal, *The Dominican Intervention* (Cambridge, 1972), or Jerome Slater, *Intervention and Negotiation* (New York, 1970). Both are based largely on documents in the public record and on extensive interviews with the participants. Lowenthal's point of view owes more to his interest in Graham Allison's models of decision making than it does to distance from the events or documents made public in the period following the intervention. Other studies of the episode are unapologetically those of participant observers, such as John Bartlow Martin, *Overtaken by Events* (New York, 1966); or critics, such as Theodore Draper, *The Dominican Revolt* (New York, 1968).

The same is true for the Alliance for Progress. No one has taken the trouble to dig through the mountain of documents to write the history of a complex, fascinating, though flawed effort at social engineering. Except for apologists for U.S. policy, most of the early appraisals of the Alliance reflected the disillusionment of those who expected more than they felt was delivered. Some examples are Simon G. Hanson, *Five Years of the Alliance for Progress* (Washington, 1967); Harvey S. Perloff, *Alliance for Progress* (Baltimore, 1967); and Jerome Levinson and Juan de Onís, *The Alliance That Lost Its Way* (Chicago, 1970). A more optimistic appraisal is George C. Lodge, *Engines of Change* (New York,

1970). A more recent, balanced appraisal is L. Ronald Scheman, ed., *The Alliance for Progress: A Retrospective* (New York, 1988).

One of the most significant developments of the Johnson years was the growing number of angry published statements by Latin Americans over what they saw as the combination of neglect and imperious domination. Although these books are not commentaries on Johnson's foreign policies in the academic sense of the term, they are themselves documents of the period and important points of inflection in relations between the United States and Latin America, opening the period of writing on dependency. Two useful compilations of such statements are Julio Cotler and Richard R. Fagen, eds., *Latin America and the United States* (Stanford, 1974), and Cole Blasier, ed., *Constructive Change in Latin America* (Pittsburgh, 1968).

Keeping Africa Off the Agenda

General analyses of the policy challenges for the United States posed by Africa written during the 1960s include Rupert Emerson's *Africa and United States Policy* (Englewood Cliffs, N.J., 1967) and Waldemar A. Nielsen's *The Great Powers and Africa* (New York, 1969). The most detailed account of Johnson's policies by a diplomatic historian can be found in the relevant chapters in Thomas J. Noer's *Cold War and Black Liberation: The United States and White Rule in Africa, 1948–1968* (Columbia, Mo., 1985). Russell Warren Howe's *Along the Afric Shore: An Historic Review of Two Centuries of U.S.–African Relations* (New York, 1975) includes several lively case studies.

Other relevant case studies include Anthony Lake's *The "Tar Baby" Option: American Policy Toward Southern Rhodesia* (New York, 1976) and Stephen R. Weissman's *American Foreign Policy in the Congo, 1960–1964* (Ithaca, N.Y., 1974). On Nigeria consult the relevant sections of Robert B. Shepard, *Nigeria, Africa, and the United States: From Kennedy to Reagan* (Bloomington, Ind., 1991). Two good memoirs written by Johnson's ambassadors in Africa are William Attwood, *The Reds and the Blacks: A Personal Adventure* (New York, 1967) and Charles Darlington and Alice Darlington, *African Betrayal* (New York, 1968).

In the LBJ Library, Roger Morris's studies for the National Security Council provide the context and road map through the documents on several important issues. *Africa Report,* a monthly journal published by the African-American Institute, provides in-depth coverage and analysis of events and U.S. policy.

Balancing American Interests in the Middle East: Lyndon Baines Johnson vs. Gamal Abdul Nasser

George Lenczowski's books *The Middle East in World Affairs* (Ithaca, N.Y., 1980) and *American Presidents and the Middle East* (Durham, N.C., 1990), although quintessentially Arabist in viewpoint, provide useful background and context. Ethan Nadelmann, "Setting the Stage: American Policy toward the Middle East, 1961–1966," *International Journal of Middle East Studies* 14 (1982): 435–57, is excellent, especially on the transition between the Kennedy and Johnson administrations. The relevant portions of Warren I. Cohen, *Dean Rusk* (Totowa, N.J., 1980), and Lyndon Baines Johnson, *The Vantage Point* (New York, 1971), provide the perspectives of American leaders.

The Cold War in the Middle East is surveyed neatly by the essays in J. C. Hurewitz, ed., *Soviet–American Rivalry in the Middle East* (New York, 1969), and Paul Y. Hammond and Sidney S. Alexander, eds., *Political Dynamics in the Middle East* (New York, 1972). Relations with Iran are covered by James A. Bill, *The Eagle and the Lion* (New Haven, Conn., 1988), and Mark J. Gasiorowski, *U.S. Foreign Policy and the Shah* (Ithaca, N.Y., 1991).

The best writing on the United States and the Arab–Israeli conflict, especially the Six Day War, is by William B. Quandt. See his *Decade of Decisions: American Policy Toward the Arab–Israeli Conflict, 1967–1976* (Berkeley, Calif. 1977), and "Lyndon Johnson and the June 1967 War: What Color Was the Light?" *Middle East Journal* 46 (1992): 177–97. See also Robert B. Parker, "The June 1967 War: Some Mysteries Explored," *Middle East Journal* 46 (1992):177–97, and Abba Eban, *An Autobiography* (New York, 1977).

Index

Abrams, Creighton, 69, 79, 90
Acheson, Dean: adviser to Johnson, 24; and Africa, 269; and Cold War, 188, 193, 194–5, 196, 198; and Cyprus, 284; and Germany, 175, 182; and Israel, 282n2; on Vietnam disengagement, 77–8
Adenauer, Konrad, 25, 185
Adoula, Cyrille, 256
Africa, 245–50, 260–6, 274, 276–8, 315, 318, 319
Africa Report, 330
Agency for International Development (AID), 114, 157, 168, 216, 219, 242, 264
Agricultural Trade Development and Assistance Act of 1954. *See* Public Law 480
Agriculture Department, 168
Ahmed, Bashir, 137
Ahmed, Ghulam, 148, 149
Akihito, Emperor, 121n82
Alexander, Sidney S., 330
Alliance for Progress, 211–20, 223, 225, 227, 230, 234, 237–8, 240, 242, 313
American Committee on Africa (ACOA), 272
American Friends of Vietnam, 38, 39n40
American Military Assistance Advisory Group, 114
American Negro Leadership Conference on Africa (ANLCA), 272
American–Southern African Council, 271
Americans for Democratic Action, 44
Anderson, David L., 323
Angola, 266
anti-ballistic missile system, 4–5, 109, 207–8, 209
Apple, R. W., Jr., 48
Aqaba, Gulf of, 298, 299, 300, 404
Arab–Israeli conflict, 296–306

Argentina, 212, 232
arms control, 3, 4, 108–9, 174n6, 308
Arms Control and Disarmament Agency (ACDA), 182
arms sales, 286, 292–3, 294
Army of the Republic of Vietnam (ARVN), 63, 65, 69, 72
Arnett, Peter, 43, 45
Asian and Pacific Council, 115, 128
Asian Development Bank, 115, 125
Atlantic Nuclear Force (ANF), 189–91, 196, 199–202
Attwood, William, 258, 329
Ayub Khan, Mohammed: and China, 144–5, 162–3; and India, 156; Johnson letter to, 139–40; memoirs, 326; proposed Washington visit, 148–54; relations with Johnson, 136, 142, 158–60, 165, 169; terminates Peshawar lease, 171
Azores, 267

Badeau, John, 287–8, 289
Baghdad Pact, 280
Balaguer, Joaquin, 233
Baldwin, Frank, 325
Ball, George: and Africa, 267; on Bhutto, 138; and Cyprus, 284; and Egypt, 290–1; and France, 189, 195; and Germany, 176–7, 185; Johnson's relations with, 24; memoirs, 326, 327; and Multilateral Force, 181, 183, 185–8, 191, 192; on sanctions, 268; on South Asia policy, 164–5; and Vietnam, 41–2, 51, 62, 101n6
Ball Mission, 128
Baltimore Sun, 44
Barnds, William J., 325

Lightning Source UK Ltd.
Milton Keynes UK
UKOW052129280312

189786UK00001B/58/P